Land Reform Revisited

Afrika-Studiecentrum Series

VOLUME 36

The titles published in this series are listed at *brill.com/asc*

Land Reform Revisited

Democracy, State Making and Agrarian Transformation in Post-Apartheid South Africa

Edited by

Femke Brandt
Grasian Mkodzongi

BRILL

LEIDEN | BOSTON

Cover illustration: Photo 'Land Claims' by Grasian Mkodzongi, Photo 'Karoo Landscape' by Femke Brandt.

Library of Congress Cataloging-in-Publication Data

Names: Reflections on South Africa's land and agrarian questions after 20 years democracy (Conference) (2014 : Cape Town, South Africa) | Brandt, Femke, editor. | Mkodzongi, Grasian, editor.
Title: Land reform revisited : democracy, state making and agrarian transformation in post-apartheid South Africa / edited by Femke Brandt, Grasian Mkodzongi.
Description: Boston : Brill, 2018. | Series: Afrika-Studiecentrum series ; volume 36 | "This edited volume is the result of an international conference titled 'Reflections on South Africa's land and agrarian questions after 20 years democracy'. It took place on 14 and 15 August 2014 at the Centre for African Studies (CAS) at the University of Cape Town (UCT)." | Includes bibliographical references and index.
Identifiers: LCCN 2018001095 (print) | LCCN 2018001740 (ebook) | ISBN 9789004362550 (E-book) | ISBN 9789004362109 (pbk. : alk. paper)
Subjects: LCSH: Land reform--South Africa. | Land use--Government policy--South Africa. | Land tenure--South Africa. | Agriculture and state--South Africa. | South Africa--Economic conditions.
Classification: LCC HD1333.S6 (ebook) | LCC HD1333.S6 R43 2014 (print) | DDC 333.3168--dc23
LC record available at https://lccn.loc.gov/2018001095

Typeface for the Latin, Greek, and Cyrillic scripts: "Brill". See and download: brill.com/brill-typeface.

ISSN 1570-9310
ISBN 978-90-04-36210-9 (paperback)
ISBN 978-90-04-36255-0 (e-book)

This book is printed on acid-free paper and produced in a sustainable manner.

Contents

Acknowledgements

This edited volume is the result of an international conference titled 'Reflections on South Africa's land and agrarian questions after 20 years democracy'. It took place on 14 and 15 August 2014 at the Centre for African Studies (CAS) at the University of Cape Town (UCT). The editors of this volume were postdoctoral fellows at the time in the NRF Chair in Land Reform and Democracy in South Africa; and the A.C. Jordan Chair in African Studies.

The main funder of the conference was the Heinrich Boll Foundation (Heinrich Böll Stiftung) and we thank them for their generous financial contribution and the collaboration, especially Kulthoum Omari, Paula Assubuji and Layla Al-Zubaidi.

We thank all the participants in the conference, – consisting of scholars, civil society members, activists and friends –, for their engagement and the inspiration they provided for pursuing this book project.

We acknowledge the financial contribution from CAS and would like to thank prof. Lungisile Ntsebeza, Noma-Afrika Maseti and colleagues at the centre for their involvement and support. We also thank the UCT Research Office and post-graduate Office for making funds available for the conference. Many people at UCT assisted and we thank Stacey Moses, Mica la Vita, Tinashe Matonga, Rutendo Hadebe, Lilian Jacobs, and Selina Mudavanhu.

We owe gratitude to all the scholars who reviewed book chapters and took the time to provide all the authors with feed-back on their work. This undoubtedly improved the quality of the volume. The positive and constructive comments of two reviewers who commented on the volume as a whole were very encouraging and appreciated. We hope we managed to engage meaningfully with all of your questions and suggestions.

Lastly, we are grateful to the people at Brill Publishers ASC/Savusa series who enthusiastically agreed to support this project. Special thanks to Brill and the Afrika Studie Centrum (ASC) in Leiden for the financial contribution to enable the reprinting Chapter 2, which was published in the Journal of Contemporary African Studies in 2016. We thank Frans Kamsteeg, Harry Wels and in particular our main contact prof. dr. Marja Spierenburg for assisting in the process of preparing and publishing the outcome presented here.

Harare and Johannesburg 2017
Grasian and Femke

Notes on Contributors

Kezia Batisai
is a senior lecturer in the Department of Sociology at the University of Johannesburg who holds a PhD in Gender Studies from the University of Cape Town (UCT). Her research gaze is on gender, sexuality, political change, questions of being different and politics of nation-building in Africa. Beyond the academy, Kezia has more than ten years working experience as a senior researcher/consultant for local and international organisations such as USAID, SIDA, Dorcas Aid International, IOM, Institute of Women and Gender Studies (University of Pretoria) and the African Gender Institute (UCT). Her work with these organisations mainly focused on gender, sexuality, HIV/AIDS, health, migration and development; human rights and the judicial system. She is an active member of the International Sociological Association (Language and Society; and Women and Society working groups); the South African Association for Gender Studies; and the South African Sociological Association (Gender Studies Coordinator: 2015-present).

Femke Brandt
is a Global Excellence Stature Fellowship (GES) postdoctoral fellow at the Department of Anthropology and Development Studies at the University of Johannesburg where she has also worked as anthropology lecturer. Until 2016 she was a postdoctoral fellow in the NRF Chair on Land reform and democracy in South Africa at the University of Cape Town. Her research interests are re-configurations of power, forms of resistance, land reform, state formation, autonomy and questions of belonging.

Sarah Bruchhausen
is a PhD fellow with the History Workshop at Wits University, Johannesburg. Her research interests include the history and politics of rural resistance in South Africa and questions of land, ethnicity, citizenship and belonging in contemporary Africa. Her work engages with these and other issues specifically in relation to the history of the Mpondo revolts and interrogates the significance of this historical moment in influencing present day forms and praxes of popular and potentially emancipatory politics in South Africa.

Elene Cloete
holds a PhD in socio-cultural anthropology from the University of Kansas, USA. Her research interests include youth development, rural political landscapes,

reproductive health care, and the genderisation of state-sponsored social assistance.

Nerhene Cindy Davis
holds a PhD from the Institute for Land and Agrarian studies (UWC) and is a lecturer affiliated at the University of Pretoria. Her research concentrates on issues related to land reform and livelihoods; with a specific focus on configurations of power, gender and access to resources in relation to land reform outcomes.

Tariro Kamuti
is a postdoctoral research fellow at the Centre for Africa Studies at the University of the Free State, Bloemfontein, South Africa. He holds a joint PhD in Geography from the VU University Amsterdam and the University of the Free State. His research interests are land and environmental policy, governance issues surrounding sustainable utilisation of natural resources and the social dimensions of biodiversity conservation.

Tarminder Kaur
is a postdoctoral research fellow at the Institute for Reconciliation and Social Justice at the University of the Free State in Bloemfontein in South Africa. She graduated in April 2016 with a PhD from the University of the Western Cape, South Africa. Her doctoral thesis is entitled: Sporting Lives and 'Development' Agendas: a critical analysis of sport and 'development' nexus in the context of farm workers of the Western Cape. Her ethnographic work focuses on the everyday sporting lives and experiences of those in spaces and collectives identified as in need of 'development', specifically in the Western Cape.

Grasian Mkodzongi
is an Executive Director at the newly formed Tropical Africa- Land and Natural Resources Research Institute (Tropical Africa LNRRI) based in Harare Zimbabwe. Until 2015, he was a Lecturer in Anthropology at the University of Western Cape and A.C. Jordan Post-Doctoral Research Fellow at the University of Cape Town. He obtained his PhD from the University of Edinburgh (United Kingdom). His current research focusses on the interface of agrarian change, mineral resource extraction and rural livelihoods in Zimbabwe and the southern African region.

Camalita Naicker
is a lecturer in the Department of Historical Studies at the University of Cape Town. Her research interests include histories of land, labour and migration

in South Africa. She has written on the trade union movement, the Marikana Massacre and land occupations in South Africa. She is interested in how people use different forms of political practice, some historically rooted some pure invention, that are often outside of the state and institutional structures to organise and to resist domination.

Fani Ncapayi

holds a PhD (2013) in sociology from the University of Cape Town (UCT), and is currently an Honorary Research Associate of the Centre for African Studies (CAS), in UCT. His passion for poor rural people has linked him to the land-based non-governmental organisation (NGO), called Cala University Students Association (CALUSA), based in Cala, Eastern Cape. He is its current director and combines research with action, including supporting rural residents in their struggles for socio-economic justice.

Mnqobi Ngubane

is a PhD student at the Institute for Poverty, Land & Agrarian Studies (PLAAS). His main research and activist interests include rural struggles for democracy and accountability, as well as politics of land reform in the context of state support, farm production, and contested theories of success in land reform. He also works as a volunteer at Zibambeleni Community Development Organisation in KwaZulu-Natal, where he is currently having an advisory role in various projects including water infrastructure, and other state services on land reform farms, as well as decentralizing tertiary education to small rural towns.

Chizuko Sato

is a research fellow at the Institute of Developing Economies in Chiba, Japan. She researches a wide-range of topics related to the South African politics and history, including land reform, small-scale farming and international migration.

PART 1

Introduction

CHAPTER 1

Revisiting South Africa's Land and Agrarian Questions

Grasian Mkodzongi and Femke Brandt

This book reflects on South Africa's land and agrarian questions after the 20-year milestone, post-apartheid. The book results from a conference held at the University of Cape Town in August 2014. The main motivation of the conference and the book was that after 20 years of democracy, as well as over 100 years after the implementation of the notorious Natives Land Act of 1913, the land question in South Africa remains largely unresolved. The legacy of the uneven distribution of land, with blacks being allocated only 13% of the land under communal tenure in the so called native reserves, is that landownership patterns remain highly uneven and the agricultural sector is increasingly dominated by agribusiness and large-scale farming operations. South Africa's three-pronged land reform approach (land reform, land restitution, and tenure reform) has not transformed the bi-modal agrarian structure inherited from apartheid. Since 1994, very little land has been transferred from white landowners to black people, and there has been a significant shift in directing policy-making away from supporting poor people to creating a class of capitalist small holders (Hall, 2004; Lahiff, 2007; Ntsebeza & Hall, 2007). Meanwhile, rural poverty has increased steadily. The end of apartheid was expected to deepen the process of social and economic transformation in favour of South Africa's black citizens, however, very little in terms of transformation of social relations has taken place.

Land and agrarian questions in South Africa are intertwined with broader questions of nation building and state-making. For the conference, we specifically invited emerging scholars working on agrarian issues across South Africa to present their research findings in order to broaden debates on South Africa's agrarian questions beyond the theoretical generalisations that have dominated scholarship. The chapters included in this book highlight, inter alia, people's experiences and engagements with land and land reform, and the socio-economic and political dynamics that have underpinned the land-reform processes.

South Africa's land-reform programme provides a lens for viewing the process of post-apartheid state-making. The process resembles what James Scott

 | DOI 10.1163/9789004362550_002

has called 'state high modernism' (1998). Successive South African governments have adopted a paternalistic approach to land reform based on a centralised technocratic process, with very little input from potential land beneficiaries. The ideology of state high modernism assumes that the main engineers of the transformation processes are bureaucrats, technicians, and planners rather than directly affected people in rural and urban areas. Moreover, one of the paradoxes in modern state-making according to Scott (1998, p. 93) is that the engineers of social transformation have been inherently authoritarian and willing to use the state's monopoly on violence to achieve the implementation of a fixed social order. In South Africa's postcolonial state-making process there is little space for competing ideas brought forward by ordinary citizens. The African National Congress (ANC) has privileged a narrow interpretation of land reform, which largely favours agribusinesses, whereas this book illustrates that there are certainly competing interpretations of what land reform should be about and how to measure success in land reform projects. In the process of balancing economic reform with historical redress, South Africa's postcolonial governments have designed land policies mainly focused on a narrow technical indicator, namely productivity. This is despite the fact that beneficiaries of land reform view land as a multipurpose resource that can be used for diverse activities beyond farming.

As noted above, South Africa's land reform is driven by a technocratic and narrow interpretation of land reform by the state (Hall, 2004; Lahiff, 2007; Mkodzongi & Rusenga, 2015). Moreover, a minority of landed elites and agribusiness have exercised undue influence over government policy; for example, they have been able to utilise productivity discourses as a form of scare-mongering tactic to delay the transfer of land rights to the historically marginalised black population. According to Moyo those involved in '...debates on land reform tend to be hostile to large-scale land redistribution because of specific settler-colonial and racial influences on the land discourses' (Moyo 2000, p. 7). A result of the above is that some white landowners have utilised their privileged status as 'agricultural experts' to access state resources set aside for land reform after being hired as consultants on land-reform projects (Bernstein, 2003; Somerville, 2014).

Unlike white farmers, many black people aspiring to access land through the land-reform programmes have exercised limited influence over land-reform policy. They have not been able to decide how they access land and how they utilise it. The shifts in policy direction (Hall, 2004) make it yet more unlikely that land redistribution will be designed to meet the needs and wishes of poor people. Under the initial Settlement/Land Acquisition Grant (SLAG), land redistribution was supposed to address poverty, whereas the later Redistribution for Agricultural Development (LRAD) programme sought to create a cohort of emerging black capitalist farmers. Since 2006, there has been the Proactive Land Acquisition and Recapitalisation Strategy (PLAS), in combination with recapitalisation that is supposed to 'ensure that we rekindle the class of black commercial farmers that was disrupted by the 1913 Natives Land Act', said the Minister of the Department of Rural Development and Land Reform (DRDLR) in a press statement of July 2015.[1] The department allocated R204 million funding for emerging farmers to upgrade the infrastructure on the land. Under PLAS, the state leases out land to beneficiaries and facilitates 'strategic partners – who tend to be experienced commercial farmers'. In the role as strategic partners and mentors of land beneficiaries, white commercial farmers have retained control over the land-reform process and have thus influenced dominant narratives about how land-reform projects are conceptualised and implemented.

The policy shift was largely influenced by productivity discourses popularised by the white farmers lobby that presents land reform as a threat to food security. The focus on productivity is heavily influenced by those who view the big farm model as more productive than smallholder agriculture, which is viewed as a potential threat to food security and agricultural productivity. The framing of the issue of 'food security' is however based on specific ideas of the problems with the global food system and a set of ideological commitments that emphasize economic growth and further liberalization of the global food system as a solution (Tomlinson, 2011). Opposing this neoliberal framing of the problems of food security are 'agro-ecology' and 'food sovereignty' discourses that focus on the inherent contradictions of a food system relying on industrial agriculture. McMichael and Schneider (2011) have argued that 'while the market-centric perspective focuses on the opportunity to reinvest in agriculture and develop agricultural value chains, the food sovereignty perspective views this moment as an opportunity to refocus agriculture around questions of social and ecological sustainability' (2011, p. 120).

The productivity lobby has gained support in some sections of South African academia. For example, Ben Cousins (2015, p. 66), who has been a critic of the slow pace of land reform, has recently argued that the top 20% of agricultural food producers should be 'left alone' by the state for the coming 20 years in order to secure South Africa's most productive part of the rural economy. Such proposals show how landed elites and agribusiness are influencing academic debates on South Africa's land reform. While landed elites have influenced

1 Source: http://www.gov.za/speeches/rural-development-and-land-reform-approves-r206-million-rands-funding-emerging-farmers-8 (accessed 10 October 2015).

government policies, the voices of people directly affected by land reform or the lack of land reform are largely ignored by the government.[2] As a result, the government's top-down approach to land reform has failed to restructure agrarian relations in favour of the poor. Instead, it has focused on creating a black commercial farming elite rather than addressing historical injustices in the landownership structure.

Throughout the book, and in the concluding chapter, different sets of questions are posed that have been given limited attention in the literature on land and agrarian questions in South Africa. For example, how have land-reform projects unfolded across the South African countryside? How can one conceptualise success in land-reform projects, given competing notions of success between the state and land-reform beneficiaries? How are discourses of land restitution, identity, and belonging influencing the way ordinary people perceive land reform? How can we utilise gender lenses to conceptualise/theorise South Africa's agrarian questions? What kinds of subaltern struggles against high state modernism are taking place in the countryside? And, finally, how do experiences in South Africa compare to countries such as Zimbabwe, where a controversial 'fast-track' land-reform programme was recently implemented? Addressing these kinds of questions is critical in broadening our reflections on South Africa's land and agrarian questions after 20 years of democracy.

Land and Agrarian Reform Scholarship

The book contributes to ongoing debates focusing on the political economy of land and agrarian reform in post-apartheid South Africa. It seeks to go beyond these classical political economy debates by utilising empirical and ethnographic data to highlight the diverse meanings of land and competing interpretations of success in land-reform projects that have received limited attention in the literature. While the classical conceptualisation of South Africa's agrarian questions has been central to our understanding of the historical trajectory of the land question in South Africa, it has proven to be largely inadequate in addressing the many aspects of land beyond its utility in agricultural productivity. As a result, a revisionist debate heavily influenced

2 Sithandiwe Yeni who is the national co-ordinator of Tshintsha Amakhaya, a civil society alliance for land and food justice in South Africa, called for government to listen to ideas and needs of rural people: https://www.dailymaverick.co.za/article/2017-04-13-putting-land-at-the-heart-of-radical-economic-transformation-a-perspective-from-the-ground/#.WQ7JdNyZHIU (Accessed on 7/05/2017).

by the classic agrarian question has dominated the literature at the expense of other perspectives (Bernstein, 1996, 2003, 2009). A problematic assumption of this literature is that it has sought to downplay the need for land among residents of former Bantustans and farm workers in favour of a 'labour question' based on the assumption that there is no longer a need for land among South Africa's (poor) citizens (Bernstein, 2009; Hendricks, 2013). In their study based in the Eastern Cape Province, Chitonge and Ntsebeza (2012) highlighted how land reform has enhanced livelihoods among the inhabitants of former Bantustans, who benefited from the land reform. Published research on land and livelihoods has shown that access to land as a means for livelihood matters to people and that there is certainly a demand for land among residents of former Bantustans. Furthermore, the broader meanings of land to indigenous Africans who were dispossessed of their ancestral lands have largely been ignored in mainstream debates. Few studies (James, 2007; Connor, 2014; Mabandla, 2013; Mkhize, 2014) discuss land and agrarian questions through life histories and narratives of people in rural society. Such studies emphasize that land and commercial farms are sites of belonging, identity, and kinship (Connor, 2014, in Mkhize 2014, p. 37; Brandt, 2016).

In this book we aim to go beyond the narrow interpretation of South Africa's land and agrarian questions by broadening the debate about land reform and socio-economic transformation. We highlight what people are actually doing with land reform, or lack thereof, and how success in land-reform projects is relative, and open to diverse and competing interpretations. We approach land reform as a dynamic process through which transformation processes unfold in messy, contradictory, and complex ways.

As mentioned before, we suggest analysing change through seeing land reform as a state-making process in which people engage the state in different ways: to challenge and resist, or to carve out a space for their own needs. We believe Scott's concept of 'state (authoritarian) high modernism' is useful in conceptualising the trajectory of land-reform policymaking which has marginalised the voices of ordinary citizens in favour of a centralised technocratic process driven by experts and specialists. This has denied the majority of South Africans a say over how land-reform policies are formulated and implemented. Nevertheless, we acknowledge agency and resistance strategies of people fighting against state high modernism. As Scott (1998, p. 191) has argued, 'state plans rarely go as anticipated!' Studies undertaken in other regions of the Global South show how the landless resist state high modernism in land-reform projects. In Brazil, Rosa (2012), as well as Schneider and Niederle (2010) recognize 'family farming' as a resistance strategy against the hegemony of agribusinesses in food production. In these studies, land is not just seen as an economic asset or a commodity but also as a means to struggle for autonomy or a way to build a legitimate relationship with the state (through social movements). Similarly, in this book we show how landless residents of former Bantustans and farm workers respond to shifting power relations and politics of land in their environment; how they utilise 'weapons of the weak' (Scott, 1984) to organise, assert agency, resist, arrange livelihood strategies, and engage with the state in their quest to access land and other livelihood opportunities. Furthermore, we highlight how current struggles of the landless poor have had limited influence in the politics of land (Mkodzongi and Rusenga, 2015; Mkodzongi, in this volume), as they fail to utilise popular resistance from below to influence the trajectory of land reform. At the same time, we want to reflect on 'the role of more profane and less absolute kinds of social change led from below' (Ballard 2014, p. 219). The role of land-based social movements in articulating demands for land from below is another important theme often missing in classical agrarian questions debates. This needs to be addressed, especially if we recognise the 'ability of ordinary people to influence their own lives and the path of history itself' (Ballard 2014, p. 215).

The book is thus an addition to a growing list of literature focusing on the legacies of land dispossession and the outcomes of South Africa's land reforms (Ntsebeza and Hall, 2007; O'Laughlin et al., 2013; Cousins and Hebinck, 2013; Hendricks et al., 2013; Cousins and Walker, 2015; Wisborg et al., 2013; Van der Waal, 2014). These contributions have alarmingly confirmed the implications of the slow pace of land reform, the increasing financialization of agriculture, and the elite capture of public resources through land-reform subsidies. In short, the state's land-reform programme has not achieved its own goals. Given the above, there is now growing discontent among the poor and marginalised in both rural areas and the urban periphery. This requires new ways of conceptualising the land question and new approaches to land reform transcending the current neoliberal orthodoxy that has largely failed. Lastly, the book adds to a growing voice from the 'South' (Moyo et al., 2013), which has challenged the Eurocentric nature of the classical agrarian question that is unable to articulate complex agrarian questions faced by many African countries in the post-colonial era. By utilizing empirical data gathered across South Africa to highlight ordinary people's experiences with land reform, we believe this book brings new epistemological approaches rooted in fresh empirical material, which broadens debates about land reform in post-apartheid South Africa and the wider southern African sub-region.

The chapters in this volume offer insights into what is actually happening on the ground, beyond the state's technocratic conceptualisation of land reform. It offers an understanding of relations between the state, land beneficiaries, white landowners, farm workers, and indigenous people. As part of their field-work, researchers whose chapters are presented in this book spent considerable amounts of time building relationships with people to make sense of their realities. Their analysis and reflections on these realities and research processes ultimately inform and challenge dominant narratives and theories about land and land reform, which have so far dominated scholarship on South Africa's land reform. All the chapters provide viewpoints that help us to re-visit South Africa's land and agrarian questions 20 years post-apartheid.

Introducing the Chapters

The work presented in the following chapters is based on new empirical data gathered from across the South African provinces by emerging scholars. The data has been generated through the application of qualitative or ethnographic methods. We have encouraged researchers to reflect on the research process and relationships that shaped their interpretations in the field. This engagement with positionality provides insights into the various places and peoples under study as well as the – often contentious – process of knowledge generation. The book chapters have been divided roughly into three thematic sections: (1) the meanings of democracy; (2) land reform and state-making processes; and (3) agency, identity, and belonging. However the thematic sections are by no means absolute as most of the chapters engage with cross cutting themes, which tend to be interconnected.

The first four chapters engage with the meanings of democracy in the context of South Africa's neoliberal land reforms. The chapters highlight the historical trajectory of the land question in South Africa and dynamics that continue to shape discourses of land reform, democracy, and citizenship in post-apartheid South Africa. Bruchhausen and Naicker's chapter focuses on the subaltern politics of migrant workers by exploring alternative conceptions of land, citizenship, and democracy stemming from pre-colonial society. Cloete's chapter provides a conceptual and theoretical discussion by tracing historical debates on the Eastern Cape's agrarian past. Her chapter shows how such historical debates have been shaped by different ideological assumptions about the emergence of capitalist colonial relations in the province. This, she argues, requires new analytical approaches to the study of poverty and inequality in democratic South Africa. The following chapter by Brandt illustrates how, in the Eastern Cape, Karoo farm conversions to trophy-hunting enterprises directly affect the lives of black workers whose experiences indicate that the rural transformation as rhetorically promised by subsequent post-apartheid governments has been compromised. In Chapter 5, Batisai unpacks the relationship between gender and nationhood by capturing the experiences of elderly women living in a peri-urban area in Johannesburg. These women's notions of democracy and freedom manifest themselves through their ongoing struggles over access to affordable housing; this illustrates the need for land reform beyond agrarian reform.

The next three chapters highlight the dynamics of land reform and state-making processes in post-apartheid South Africa. The chapters demonstrate that land reform as a state-making process is highly contested and influenced by competing interests, which have undermined the successful transfer of land from landowners to the landless poor. Kaur's chapter elucidates the way farm workers are incorporated in 'development' discourses and sports programmes in the Western Cape. Farm workers are seen by the state as development subjects in need of skills training, facilitated by various government departments. In this way the state obscures the political contestations of agrarian relations and inequalities in the region. Central to Kamuti's chapter is the way land-reform policies have been largely influenced by landowners, while beneficiaries of land reform have limited influence over how land-reform policies are formulated and implemented. So-called experts who are involved in implementing land-reform projects tend to view land-reform beneficiaries as traditionalists who are unlikely to succeed in their agricultural enterprises. Beneficiaries of land-reform projects are thus trapped in complex processes involving different levels of government that delay and confuse the process of restitution. Again, we see in this chapter government's bias towards wildlife farming projects rather than supporting smallholder-farming projects. In the following chapter, it becomes apparent how the state employs a strategic partnership model of land reform that enables the state to exert control over land use and access without necessarily owning it. Davis exposes how this shapes land claimant's expectations and experiences. Finally in this section, Mkodzongi's chapter departs from Zimbabwe's recent experience with 'fast-track' land reform so as to contrast it with experiences in South Africa. Mkodzongi argues that both the South African state as well as civil society could learn important lessons from its neighbour to restructure agrarian relations in favour of rural transformation. He argues for state-led land reform in which the state more actively disrupts the agrarian structure inherited from settler colonialism.

The last set of three chapters focuses on the dynamics of agency, identity, and belonging in terms of the way the landless have utilised claims of identity and belonging to make claims over land that was lost under apartheid. A key theme highlighted in these chapters is that beneficiaries of land reform have a broader view of land beyond its utility for agricultural production.

Sato's chapter explores the dynamics of Khoisan revivalist groups and traces how groups engage in land-reform policy debates with the state. She argues that this is a new politics of ethnicity that both facilitates and complicates the politics of land in South Africa. In Chapter 11, Ncapayi presents a detailed story of how a land redistribution project in the Eastern Cape has improved beneficiaries' livelihoods and transformed wider agrarian relations. An important factor underpinning the success of the land-reform project has been the continuous support of an NGO working with land beneficiaries. More importantly, the role of women in leadership positions further enhanced the success of the land-reform project. Similarly revealing is the empirical work presented by Ngubane in Chapter 12. These counter narratives from land beneficiaries who dismantled community game farms in Kwa-Zulu Natal generate questions about the criteria for successful land reform. By their 'disruptive' practices, land beneficiaries stake their claims of belonging in a context that protects private conservation areas at the cost of rural transformation.

Conclusion

A key contribution of the book is that most of the chapters provide a wealth of recently generated empirical material that enables a fresh reflection on South Africa's land and agrarian questions, which then enable critical engagement with the theoretical generalisations and entrenched positions that have so far dominated scholarship. The empirical material presented in the chapters provides new conceptual insights that challenge some of the dominant narratives that have so far informed policymaking. By questioning and exploring further the role of the state and agrarian capital in land-reform processes, the book highlights the intersectionality of race, class, ethno-regionalism, and gender in land-reform processes. Although the empirical material utilised in this book does not cover all of South Africa's provinces, it does provide a nuanced analysis of ordinary people's experiences with land reform. In this way the book provides grassroots perspectives gathered across diverse locations in South Africa in terms of geography, history, and perspective.

The concluding chapter highlights the key findings of this book and the complexities underpinning South Africa's land and agrarian questions. We discuss the insights provided in the chapters about how South Africans experience land reform and democracy, and what contestations take place in cities and in the countryside. There is no agreement over the conceptualisation of South Africa's agrarian questions: some scholars have claimed that South Africa's agrarian question was resolved under apartheid (Bernstein, 1996); others have claimed that the landless do not need land but jobs in cities (Hendricks et al., 2013); and there is the position that historically marginalised people in former Bantustans are in need of land and that land reform has the potential to address rural poverty (Chitonge & Ntsebeza, 2012). The wealth of new empirical evidence demonstrates that South Africa's land and agrarian questions are far from being resolved. The chapters presented in this book highlight the dynamics of state-making, grassroots agency, and the politics of land after twenty years of democracy in South Africa. Lastly, the book demonstrates that land reform remains a contested process in terms of interpretation, expectations, and outcomes across race, ethnicity, class, and gender.

References

Ballard, R. (2014). Geographies of development III: Militancy, insurgency, encroachment and development *by* the poor. *Progress in Human Geography*, *39*(2), 214–224.

Bernstein, H. (1996). South Africa's Agrarian Question: Extreme and Exceptional? *Journal of Peasant Studies*, *23*(2–3), 1–52.

Bernstein, H. (2003). Farewells to the Peasantry. *Transformation: Critical Perspectives on Southern Africa*, *52*, 1–19.

Bernstein, H. (2009). VI Lenin and AV Chayanov: looking back, looking forward. *The journal of peasant studies*, *36*(1), 55–81.

Brandt, F. (2016). Power battles on South African trophy-hunting farms: farm workers, resistance and mobility in the Karoo. *Journal of Contemporary African Studies*, *34*(1), 161–185.

Chitonge, H., & Ntsebeza, L. (2012). Land Reform and Rural Livelihood in South Africa: Does Access to Land Matter? *Review of Agrarian Studies*, *2*(1).

Connor, T. (2014). *Conserved Spaces, Ancestral Places: conservation, history and identity among farm labourers in the Sundays River Valley, South Africa.* Pietermaritzburg: UKZN Press.

Cousins, B. (2015). "Through a glass darkly": Towards agrarian reform in South Africa. In Cousins, B., & Walker, C. (Eds.). *Land Divided Land Restored, land Reform in South Africa for the 21st Century* (p. 250–269). Johannesburg: Jacana.

Cousins, B., & Hebinck, M. (Eds.) (2013). *In the Shadow of Policy: Everyday Practices in South Africa's Land and Agrarian reform:* Johannesburg: Wits University Press.

Cousins, B., & Walker, C. (Eds.) (2015). *Land Divided Land Restored, land Reform in South Africa for the 21st Century*, Johannesburg: Jacana.

Hall, R. (2004). A political economy of land reform in South Africa. *Review of African Political Economy*, *31*(100), 213–227.

Hendricks, F. (2013). Rhetoric and Reality in Restitution and Redistribution: Ongoing Land and Agrarian Questions in South Arica. In F. Hendricks, L. Ntsebeza & K. Helliker (Eds.), *The promise of land: Undoing a Century of Dispossession in South Africa* (p. 27–53). Johannesburg, Jacana.

Hendricks, F., Ntsebeza, L., & Helliker, K. (Eds.) (2013). *The Promise of Land: Undoing a Century of Dispossession in South Africa*: Johannesburg, Jacana.

James, D. (2007). *Gaining Ground?: 'Rights' and 'Property' in South African Land Reform.* Johannesburg: WITS University Press.

Lahiff, E. (2007). 'Willing buyer, willing seller': South Africa's failed experiment in market-led agrarian reform. *Third World Quarterly*, *28*(8), 1577–1597.

Mabandla, N. (2013). *Lahla Ngubo: the continuities and discontinuities of a South African Black middle Class.* African Studies Centre: Leiden.

McMichael, P., & Schneider, M. (2011). Food Security Politics and the Millennium Development Goals. *Third World Quarterly*, *32*(1), 119–139.

Mkhize, N. (2014). Game farm conversions and the land question: unpacking present contradictions and historical continuities in farm dwellers' tenure insecurity in Cradock. *Journal of Contemporary African Studies*, *32*(2), 207–219.

Mkodzongi, G., & Rusenga, C. (2015). *Land and Agrarian Reform: Towards an Inclusive Poverty Alleviation Agenda.* Cape Town: Institute of Justice and Reconciliation.

Moyo, S. (2000). *Land reform under structural adjustment in Zimbabwe: land use change in the Mashonaland provinces.* Uppsala: Nordic Africa Institute.

Moyo, S., Jha, P., & Yeros, P. (2013). The Classical Agrarian Question: Myth, reality and relevance today. *Agrarian South: Journal of Political Economy*, *2*(1), 93–119.

Ntsebeza, L., & R. Hall (Eds.) (2007). *The land question in South Africa: the challenge of transformation and redistribution.* Cape Town: HSRC.

O'Laughlin, B., Bernstein, H., Cousins, B., & Peters, P.E. (2013). Introduction: Agrarian change, rural poverty and land reform in South Africa since 1994. *Journal of Agrarian Change*, *13*(1), 1–15.

Rosa, M. (2012). Landless: Meanings and Transformations of a Collective Action Category in Brazil. *Agrarian South: Journal of Political Economy*, 1–2, 205–231.

Schneider, S., & Niederle, P.A. (2010). Resistance strategies and diversification of rural livelihoods: the construction of autonomy among Brazilian family farmers. *The Journal of Peasant Studies*, 37–2, 379–405.

Scott, J.C. (1984). *Weapons of the Weak: Everyday Forms of Peasant Resistance.* New Haven: Yale University Press.

Scott, J.C. (1998). *Seeing like a state: How certain schemes to improve the human condition have failed.* New Haven: Yale University Press.

Somerville, M. (2014). Financial investments in agriculture and their implications for land reform processes and agrarian transition in South Africa: Paper presented at the first conference on Land Grabs in Africa, Midrand, South Africa, 20–21 October.

Tomlinson, I. (2011). Doubling food production to feed the 9 billion: A critical perspective on a key discourse of food security in the UK. *Journal of Rural Studies*, 1–10.

Van der Waal, C.S. (Ed.) (2014). *Winelands, Wealth and Work: Transformations in the Dwars River Valley, Stellenbosch.* Pietermaritzburg: University of KwaZulu-Natal Press.

Wisborg, P., Hall, R., Shirinda, S., & Zamchiya, P. (2013). *Farm workers and farm dwellers in Limpopo, South Africa: struggles over tenure, livelihoods and justice.* Cape Town: PLAAS, University of the Western Cape.

PART 2

Meanings of Democracy

CHAPTER 2

Broadening Conceptions of Democracy and Citizenship: The Subaltern Histories of Rural Resistance in Mpondoland and Marikana

Sarah Bruchhausen and Camalita Naicker

Introduction

The purpose of this chapter is to attempt to broaden perspectives on citizenship, democracy, and land struggles in post-apartheid South Africa with reference to current and historical examples of subaltern politics in the former Bantustans. The chapter follows, what Henri Lefebvre (1991, p. 65–7) called a 'regressive-progressive-method', which as Gill Hart (2013, p. 19) expressed so succinctly in her book, 'entails starting with a description of the present and its contradictions; then moving to an explanation of the historical production of the present, and from there to a moment of opening to the future – and to the possibilities present in current contradictions',

The chapter focuses on two spaces within South Africa, which have specific significance for both land and labour questions in South Africa and where we have focused our research: Mpondoland in the Eastern Cape and *Nkaneng* Shack Settlement in Marikana, North West Province. Both of these places are situated in the former colonial-apartheid Bantustans and are still governed under the Council of Traditional Leaders Act, No 10 of 1997, and the Traditional Leadership and Governance Framework Amendment Act, No 41 of 2003. This connection is not an arbitrary one either. Of the 45 people who lost their lives at Marikana, during the strikes of August 2012, 31 were from the Eastern Cape Province in South Africa. Of them, the majority were from Mpondoland in the Transkei (Alexander et al., 2012, p. 196).

The Eastern Cape, and Mpondoland specifically, has a special significance in the history of mineworkers in South Africa as the primary source of cheap labour ever since the discovery of Gold on the Witwatersrand in the late 1800s.

---

* This chapter is a reprint of Naicker, C. and S. Bruchhausen. (2016) Broadening conceptions of democracy and citizenship: the subaltern histories of rural resistance in Mpondoland and Marikana. *Journal of Contemporary African Studies*, 34, 388–403.

 | DOI 10.1163/9789004362550_003

Rock-drilling, the most dangerous and labour intensive part of mining minerals like gold (and now platinum) has been a category of work historically occupied by men coming from Mpondoland in the Eastern Cape. Dunbar Moodie (1994) has explored this relationship and the kinship ties between migrant labourers who came to the mines from Mpondoland in his book, *Going for Gold* (Moodie, 1994). Today, however, the mining economy has moved from the urban centre of the former Witwatersrand, now Gauteng Province, into the land of the former Bantustans, namely the North West Province and Limpopo province. The discovery of new minerals in these provinces has meant that mining companies have had to enter into negotiations with traditional leaders for mining rights on what is still considered traditional land under the new South African constitution. In Marikana, the Bapo ba Mogale Traditional Community, also now known as Bapo ba Mogale Investments, is a multimillion rand trust, which used to receive approximately R20 Million ($1,423,594) a year from Lonmin Platinum (Lonplats) in direct cash transfers (Grieve, 2014). In 2014, an agreement was reached stating that the Bapo ba Mogale Traditional Authority would cease to receive these royalties in 2019 and would instead be paid a large lump sum by Lonplats in order to buy shares in the mining company, thereby fulfilling their Black Economic Empowerment (BEE) requirements (Grieve, 2014). While the Bapo ba Mogale Trust is committed to enriching the members of its traditional community, it continues to endorse the migrant labour system linking Mpondoland to Lonmin mines in Marikana.

As the example of migrant workers and other people of the *Nkaneng* Shack Settlement at Marikana will illuminate, the institution of Traditional Authorities, as well as the narrowly conceived ethnic and racialized basis upon which it still functions, remain central to the politics of land and citizenship in South Africa. More importantly, we argue that the ways in which the men on the mountain, who refused trade union representation, mobilised around and, in many instances, rejected this form of elite politics during the Marikana Strikes, is reminiscent of historically older modes of political organisation and can be linked to popular forms of resistance used during the Mpondo Revolts in the 1960s. When taken seriously, both these moments of resistance reveal a political sphere in which, when ordinary people reject forms of top-down representation and engage in praxes of participatory democracy, it deepens the meaning of citizenship and belonging in post-apartheid South Africa. It is this living subaltern history, and its related forms of politics, which have been almost completely excluded within the many contemporary attempts at thinking about South Africa's land and citizenship questions over the last twenty years, particularly those relating to the politics of land and governance in the former Bantustans. Analysing the politics of land in the former Bantustans necessarily requires a critical interrogation of the system of Traditional Authorities, which, twenty years since the collapse of apartheid, continues to be a central element in geographically fixing black people in rural areas under forms of land tenure, which are secured solely by customary law (Myers 2008, p. 99).

In his book entitled *Indirect Rule in South Africa: Tradition, Modernity, and the Costuming of Political Power,* J.C. Myers (2008) provides an analysis of the institution of Traditional Authorities and the role of chiefs in the post-apartheid era. What is most interesting about the text is that it reveals the dominant tendency in South African scholarship and policymaking circles to think about the question of Traditional Authorities from within the narrow conceptual framework of nationalist and state histories – a tendency within the text, which Myers (2008) himself is not entirely free of.

In its failure to take seriously the living history of subaltern politics in South Africa, such an elite perspective is incapable of thinking beyond the silences of the constitution in relation to this blatantly autocratic system of governance in the former Bantustans, and thus is equally unable to see the potential value of alternative conceptions and practices concerning the politics of land, citizenship, democracy, and belonging, which have and continue to be practiced by ordinary people outside of the sphere of state subjectivities. This chapter will argue that, when thinking through land related questions in South Africa, it becomes increasingly obvious that state policies, like land restitution and redistribution programmes, and traditional authorities are inadequate as a means of redistributing land in South Africa, as they are currently conceived and practiced on the basis of narrow conceptions of citizenship and civil society. From this perspective, it is clear that how, when, and where people gain access to land cannot be divorced from the politics and political organisation that play out in particular contexts, what we have called, following the Indian Subalternist School of thought, a 'subaltern sphere of politics'; and these alternate forms of politics and decision-making practices must be included in any conception of a 'new' and truly 'post-colonial' nation.

A Note on Theoretical Conceptions

In using subaltern studies, we follow historian Ranajit Guha, whose focus was peasant insurgency in colonial India in the mid to late 1800s. For Guha, there was a distinct split in the domain of politics, in which the elite politics of the official domain made invisible the 'unofficial' subaltern domain of politics, where 'central to subaltern mobilizations was 'a notion of resistance to elite domination'. The experience of exploitation and labour endowed this politics with many idioms, norms, and values that put it in a category apart from elite politics' (Chakrabarty 2000, p. 8). This formulation is very useful for the South African experience, as Guha's focus on rural peasant insurgency allows us to think about the elements of the rural, in both the present and the past, as outside of the domain of national government institutions – and yet still political. By illuminating this sphere of peasant activity, he opens up the debate about what counts as political post-European thought. By rejecting what both liberal and Marxist historians have often regarded as pre-political or backward forms of consciousness, Guha, as Chakrabarty (2000, p. 9) discusses, 'was prepared to suggest that the nature of collective action against exploitation in colonial India was such that it effectively stretched the imaginary boundaries of the category "political" far beyond the territories assigned to it in European political thought'.

We argue, as a point of departure, that understanding the history of traditional authorities, its inseparable relationship to the politics of land and citizenship, as well as popular responses to it by rural dwellers and migrant workers (both during and since the period of colonial cum apartheid rule) is of critical importance for recognising how this system of governance has and continues to work to disadvantage and exclude some based on their 'ethnicity' and how this, in turn, functions to circumscribe citizenship and geographically fix people. Mamdani's emphasis on space and origin as the key terms of colonial classification is also useful in understanding how 'the (colonial) state portrayed the native as the product of geography rather than history' (Mamdani 2013, p. 47). This spatial differentiation is central to understanding how the 'native reserves' and later Bantustans functioned as 'zones of exclusion' (Pithouse 2012, p. 7), outside of 'civil society', and how rural African people were subject to traditional authority enshrined in customary law. This 'tribalisation' serves to crystallise tradition and culture, in a way that 'tribesmen' are still seen and regarded as outside the 'modern'.

Land Questions and Ethnicity in *Nkaneng*, Marikana

An illustration of how Traditional Authorities and their associated system of land tenure function still create barriers to land, citizenship, and access to the nation can be found in the *Nkaneng* Shack Settlement in Marikana. '*Nkaneng*' named by people who live there, is a Sesotho word, whose equivalent in isiXhosa is '*Inkanini*' described by people who live there as, 'by force' or 'forceful determination'. *Nkaneng* symbolises the on-going struggle for land and services and the fact that people live on the land through their own 'forceful determination'.

Chingono (2013, p. 12) notes that it represents the intersection between ethnicity and settlement patterns. *Nkaneng* is home to mostly isiXhosa speaking people from the Eastern Cape, and a few other provinces in South Africa as well as a few other migrant labourers from Lesotho and Mozambique. This has created tension between people who live in the shack settlement, and those who are able to live in RDP houses and receive services based on their ethnicity because the land here is owned and governed by the Tswana Chief Bob Edward Bapo ba Mogale of the Batswana Traditional Authority.

Before 1994, most mineworkers lived in single-sex hostels; there were no women and children at the mines, and the mining companies did not offer a living-out allowance. In the 1980s, when mining companies knew that apartheid was ending, they began to restructure the ethnically segregated hostels and to offer money to workers to 'live-out'. However, they did not provide any alternative housing and, as a result, there was a major growth of shack settlements around the platinum belt (Hartford, 2012). In 2010, Lonmin estimated that '50% of the population who lived within a 15km radius from its mining operations lived in informal (sic) dwellings and lacked access to basic services' (Chingono 2013, p. 9). Today, *Nkaneng* is home to a variety of people, directly and indirectly linked to the mining economy.

Most people in *Nkaneng* live in shacks without access to water or electricity; many of them have to buy water from those with access to taps. There are no roads, which makes access to transportation extremely difficult. This became a painful issue during the 2012 strikes as well as after the massacre, when wounded and injured members of the community could not be transported easily to hospital. Furthermore, during periods of high rainfall people are not able to leave their homes because of mud and flooding. They attribute their current living conditions to three sources: Lonmin, traditional authorities, and the government. Even though for many living in *Nkaneng* their hope is to one day return to their rural homes in the Eastern Cape, others have begun to make their homes at the mines. Many women and children have joined male family members in the mines, or to find work there for themselves. Like any people who migrate to different places for work, they expect Lonmin to provide housing, and, as citizens, they expect to be provided with basic services when they arrive. However, in Marikana, this is not the case, and people from the Eastern Cape are met with a differentiated system of access based on their ethnicity. For this reason, ethnicity is still a major source of tension at the mines, as has historically been the case (see Moodie, 1994).

The land that the residents of *Nkaneng* occupy is supposed to be Tswana traditional farming land; they want the government to buy the land for them because currently the municipality will not provide them with any basic services, since they are not 'from there'. In addition, there are no schools or crèches on the mine. It becomes increasingly clear that mine companies still function according to Wolpe's (1972) 'cheap labour and reserve subsidy' thesis by paying the mineworker only enough money to reproduce himself, ignoring the growing poverty in rural areas as well as the very obvious new households at the mines. As such, it becomes clear that it is due to past land arrangements, which have been carried over into the present, that the lives of those in *Nkaneng* continue to be cast in an ethnic mould.

Tswana Chief Kgosi Bob Edward Mogale of the Bapo ba Mogale Royal Family controls the land on which the platinum mine is situated, including *Nkaneng*, barring his permission, they cannot build formal housing. The formal housing (brick structures) that does exist belongs to Tswana people, who receive RDP housing in the area because of their ethnicity. Furthermore, since the massacre, the families of the slain mineworkers have requested that a memorial be erected at the mountain where the workers were shot down by police. Again, the Traditional Authority told people that the land is not for amaXhosa, and that they should build a memorial in the Eastern Cape. The Bapo ba Mogale family was not happy with the shack settlement on their land and began demanding more money from Lonmin. Lonmin, however, has ignored the entire community there and refuses to help or to pay any money to the Bapo ba Mogale family, who, according to women in *Sikhala Sonke,* demand that their children and relatives receive jobs over isiXhosa speaking people. The only time the women remember seeing the traditional leader was during the strikes, when he was accompanied by other royal leaders and kings from the Eastern Cape who came to address the workers. In fact, the relationship between traditional leaders and the mining company has been on going since the massacre and they are frequently called in to settle disputes between the workers and the mine. Traditional leaders are flown in from the Eastern Cape or mining bosses fly to the Eastern Cape to meet with them there, amongst them, notably, the amaMpondo Kings (see News24, 2012; Feni, 2014).

Ethnicity, then, takes on a particular character in *Nkaneng*, which must be read through the complex structure of people's lives in that area. What should be the right of access to land and services for all citizens moving freely from one place to another in their own country, now becomes a contestation of who is originally from the area, and reflects the socio-economic and political dynamics in the community. What is interesting to note is that, while the women of Sikhala Sonke complained about differentiated access based on ethnicity, all their community organising and initiatives during the strikes were based on broader conceptions of citizenship and democracy. For them, their activities were open to everyone regardless of where people were from, or what language they spoke, because they were all there 'working in the same place and trying to live well'. An alternative form of political community, however, will only be inclusive if it is informed by the political practice of people that falls outside of the ambit of, and is excluded from elite civil society and state politics. Traditional authorities are an illustration of the continuation of colonial geographical fixing, in which origin is used as a justification for control and where freedom has not meant freedom for all, particularly freedom of movement and fluidity.

Mamdani notes that during colonialism native access to land, administration, representation, and dispute settlement was organised through traditional authorities established for differentiated groups of 'natives' based on 'tribal ethnicity', even if there were more similarities amongst different groups of native people than there were between different races (Mamdani 2013, p. 51). This not only led to a different political trajectory, which was not meant to evolve or change, but it also led to 'monoethnic governance of multi-ethnic societies, specifically when it came to "immigrants to tribal land"' (Mamdani 2013, p. 52).

This spatial differentiation is central to understanding how the 'native reserves' were conceptualised as outside of 'civil society' and how rural African people were subject to traditional authority enshrined in customary law (itself a misnomer). Today, the incorporation of Traditional Authorities into the South African governmental system has meant the perpetuation of a colonial system of customary law, where some people are, on the basis of their space, subject to a different system of law, which still functions to exclude them from civil society as 'natives' or 'tribal'. As Mamdani, (2013, p. 51) explains, 'Unlike race, which claimed to mark a civilizational hierarchy, tribe was said to be a marker of cultural diversity',

Land then, has not just been something expropriated through colonialism, it has also been the tool with which to 'fix' and 'anthropologise' people; keeping black people within reserves was not merely to ensure a cheap supply of labour to the mines and farms for white settlers, it was also a mechanism of control under tribalisation. Returning land to people may in fact become a messy process when people are required to prove their location or relationship to the land, if the colonial questions are not resolved and if citizenship and democracy are not deepened through a re-scripting of the political in South Africa, especially with regard to traditional authorities. The way in which the state currently conceptualises traditional authorities, 'ethnicity', and citizenship is not inclusive to the way these institutions are actualised in everyday lived experience. If 'native' still functions as a 'political identity', as Mamdani (2013) has noted, then speaking about land questions in South Africa and re-distribution without speaking about how to create a more inclusive political community will only serve to reify colonial geography.

If then we are to attempt to better understand the politics of land and belonging in South Africa's former Bantustans, based on the notion of subaltern politics, we must, in line with Mamdani's warnings, begin from an acknowledgement of people, in terms of ontology, as historical agents, and not as geographically or socially fixed beings. In relation to rural dwellers and migrant workers in the former Bantustans, this leads us to the recognition of a marginalised history of rural resistance. Thembela Kepe and Lungisile Ntsebeza (2012, p. 5) have argued that the rural sphere in South Africa's countryside has been marginalised in the history of resistance against colonialism and apartheid in South Africa. For them, 'The question that faces South Africans, as well as those who have an interest in South African issues, is how history features in post-Apartheid South Africa. Critical questions include, what is remembered, recorded, and by whom, and crucially the manner in which different histories contribute or do not contribute to current understanding of nationhood' (Kepe & Ntsebeza 2012, p. 3).

The Mpondo Revolts, which lasted in the form of widespread open revolt for nine months and, in many regards, endured well into the 1960s, were sustained for a longer period than most urban struggles in South Africa. As such, Kepe and Ntsebeza (2012, p. 21) make the important point that urban struggles culminating in the Sharpeville Massacre of 1960 still do not over-shadow the popularity and significance of the events in Mpondoland occurring roughly around the same time. Yet this event, which presented an organic, organised, militant peasant rebellion, has been silenced in most nationalist historiography, and the rural sphere has been portrayed as quiescent and backward. The Mpondo revolts, which were a sustained resistance to colonial and apartheid policies and an affirmation of people's defence of democracy in Mpondoland, in many ways shatter modernist conceptions of the political and the way struggle should be organised, which has always been seen as an almost exclusively urban, 'progressive', project. The ways in which idioms and symbols associated with this form of militant rural resistance, which were present in the Marikana Strikes of 2012, such as traditional dress, weapons and medicine, and song, were endowed by journalists and political analysts with the characteristics of backwardness, traditionalism, and violence, and demonstrates the way in which the official political domain is conceptualised in South African society through the media and the academy. However, if we are able to extend our analysis beyond these narrow forms of representation to the ways in which people actually practice politics in the everyday, we are able to grasp alternative ways of imagining democracy and citizenship beyond liberal constitutionalism and state subjectivities.

Rethinking Land, Citizenship, and Belonging through the Mpondo Revolts

In Mpondoland by the late 1800s, traditional authority was a loose association of district chiefs, usually recognising a paramount chief according to lineage. People chose their allegiance on the basis of the area that they occupied, and people could also chose to change their allegiance by moving to another area (Myers 2008, p. 4; Landau, 2010).[1] The mutual relationship between the chief and his people was measured by the generosity of the chief. Similarly, in Mpondoland before and during the late 1800s, any taxes which were collected by the chief would be used for the benefit of his people in times of dearth; and, furthermore, the process of tax collection would have to be open to negotiation and the spending of any funds would have to be transparent to the community (Lodge, 1983). The significance of this is that it provides a brief sketch of the many limitations placed on the power of the chiefs in the pre-colonial political landscape of Mpondoland as well as the way in which the institution of chieftaincy was, to an extent, controlled and conditioned by the will of the people within a given community. Furthermore, this suggests that under certain forms of pre-colonial traditional governance people in the community had a very different understanding, and much more meaningful experience, of belonging in society than that afforded to black rural-dwellers under the system of Traditional Authorities during the colonial/apartheid as well as during the current post-apartheid era.

Emerging from within a widespread context of rurally based resistance to the implementation of the apartheid state's Betterment and Rehabilitation schemes in the 1940s and 1950s, as well as the introduction of the institution of Bantu Authorities in 1951, the Mpondo revolts can be understood as the most important event within a historical sequence of political resistance in the rural areas of South Africa. However, in order to understand what it is that sets the Mpondo revolts apart from other instances of resistance against the newly imposed authoritarian system of governance and land tenure during the 1940s and 1950s, it is important to understand (at least broadly) the nature of this wider context of state power and popular resistance against it in the former Bantustans.

It was Proclamation 31 of 1939, which was gazetted under a provision of the 1936 Land Act, which stipulated that any area of land could be declared a 'Betterment area' by the government (Hirson 1977, p. 118). The essential aim

1 For a detailed discussion on popular politics in South Africa before the 1800s see: Landau, P.S., 2010, *Popular Politics in the History of South Africa, 1400–1948*. Cambridge: Cambridge University Press.

of the Betterment scheme was to conserve the land in the reserves by limiting livestock and replacing 'unscientific' African land-use practices with 'modern' 'scientific' methods developed in the West. When the proposal for Betterment was finally introduced in the mid-1940s in practice it was called Rehabilitation and entailed, in addition to stock-culling: the re-division of African land into residential, grazing, and cultivating areas; an acute increase in the limitations placed on rural dwellers' access to natural resources (such as fire wood); as well as the forced demarcation of fallow lands resulting in a significant limitation on access to communal grazing land (Chaskalson 1986, p. 47). Collectively, these stipulations of Rehabilitation embodied a top-down process of 'villagization', which forced rural dwellers who were dependent upon wages to live in rural townships – at times becoming completely alienated from the land. However, it is crucial to note that at this stage Rehabilitation did more than just threaten the majority of rural dwellers; it also undermined the position of chiefs (Chaskalson 1986, p. 48).

At first, the introduction of Betterment and then Rehabilitation undermined the power of the chiefs in the reserves by taking away their control over the allocation of land. While some chiefs accepted and promoted amongst their constituencies the Rehabilitation scheme and its new system of land use and allocation, many chiefs felt that their legitimacy and popular support would be undermined by their acceptance and thus they joined the popular resistance against it. Chaskalson (1986, p. 49) argues that it was the need to 'consolidate the support of this [former] collaborationist class against the resistance which rehabilitation provoked that the state introduced the 1951 Bantu (Tribal) Authorities Act'. At the time of its implementation the Bantu Authorities Act functioned so as to increase the powers of the chiefs, which had been undermined by the policy of Rehabilitation. However, this increase in power was based on the condition that chiefs accept their new role as bureaucrats upwardly accountable to the Native Affairs Department as opposed to their constituencies.

In *The Peasant's Revolt,* Govan Mbeki rigorously describes the 'bastardisation' of the traditional system by the South African colonial government, and the attempt to draw the chiefs and headmen into the machinery of the state. In many ways Mbeki's discussion of the bastardised system of Traditional Authorities in the former Transkei was a precursor to the theoretical insights implicit within Mahmood Mamdani's *Citizen and Subject: Contemporary Africa and the Legacy of Late Colonialism.* Of particular significance for thinking the agrarian question in South Africa is Mamdani's historical analysis of the Traditional Authorities system, in which chiefs were at once autonomous but dependant agents operating as the extended arm of the apartheid state. However, almost twenty years since the publishing of *Citizen and Subject,* it is necessary to attempt to think beyond some of the limitations of Mamdani's thesis in order to take cognisance of the contemporary realities of the South African political landscape. Perhaps the most significant critique of Mamdani's text is that it lacks a critique of bourgeois conceptions of civil society so prevalent in post-apartheid South Africa and neglects a subaltern sphere of politics and resistance history, which, when acknowledged and taken seriously, poses a significant challenge to the predominance of state subjectivities and elite forms of politics in articulating the politics of land, agriculture, citizenship, and democracy in South Africa.

This chapter argues that, even though Mamdani's analytical task is to illuminate the link between politics in the Native Authority and that of civil society, as well as resistance against them, under the conditions of decentralised despotism (1996, p. 218), without providing a critique of civil society, the insights he provides remain to a large extent embedded within dominant elitist accounts of politics and liberal democracy. Even though Mamdani does make reference to the contrived heritage of liberal thought and its anchoring in Western history, he fails to problematize the epistemological and material foundations of liberal notions of citizenship, and still clearly privileges bourgeois civil society as the ideal institution for democratization in contemporary African states.

Subaltern studies scholar Partha Chatterjee (2004, p. 38) has claimed that in most of the world 'civil society as an ideal continues to energize an interventionist political project, but as an actually existing form it is demographically limited', Chatterjee (2004, p. 38) argues that the practical functioning of civil society in 'most of the world' (problematically termed the 'developing' or 'third' world) is such that it is an exclusively bourgeois sphere whose membership has been almost entirely reduced to NGOs, bourgeois technocrats, and bureaucrats. In this narrow space that is the reality of civil society, all members ultimately share in the same antidemocratic and elitist ontology that believes ordinary people are fundamentally irrational and apolitical, are incapable of collective decision-making, and therefore need to be managed as if they were subjects requiring guidance from enlightened political experts. The consequences of this has been the reduction of the majority of *citizens* (political agents participating in the sovereignty of the state) to mere *populations* (apolitical subjects represented by numerical proportions) in most of the world; this, in turn, has given rise to the ironic situation in which the NGOs and agents of civil society – who claim to be the 'trustees' of the people – actually propagate the inequalities and injustices in society that they claim to be working against, and systematically silence the genuine voice of the people – deemed as illegitimate and even criminal (Neocosmos 2011, p. 2). This understanding of the distinction between the inclusive *ideal* of civil society and the exclusive *reality* of civil society is a fundamental insight, which seems to have been downplayed in Mamdani's work.

In a self-created zone of political autonomy, which is situated *outside* of bourgeois civil society – a domain which Michael Neocosmos (2011, p. 13) terms *un-civil society* and Chatterjee (2004, p. 50) calls *political society* – one can witness an 'emancipatory and inclusive process of collective self-determination' (Hallward, quoted in Pithouse, 2011, p. 227), as well as the operation of the 'will of the people', which has been met with hostility and violent repression by the state and NGO-based civil society at large. Chatterjee (2004, p. 41) warns that theoretical practice must recognise the politics of the people or risk 'governmental techniques that will continue to proliferate and serve, much as they did in the colonial era… as instruments of class rule in a global capitalist order'.

By applying Chatterjee's (2004) nuanced problematic of civil society to *Citizen and Subject*, it is clear that an understanding of the politics of land and experiences of democracy in contemporary South Africa, which is anchored solely on nationalist, state, NGO, or other elitist perspectives, is incapable of thinking beyond state subjectivities, and making sense of subaltern forms of popular politics and democratic praxes both past and present. However, in his most recent work, *Define and Rule: Native as Political Identity*, Mamdani (2013, p. 106) highlights the need for alternative historiography and broadening conceptions of citizenship and democracy, in which he outlines, that 'the formulation of an alternative historiography would not be enough to overcome the colonial political legacy; it also required an alternative political practice, one that would create a form of citizenship adequate to building an inclusive political community'.

In the book, Mamdani (2013) goes on to describe how British colonial indirect-rule created two differentiated systems of law: 'civil' law and 'customary' law, which he referred to in *Citizen and Subject* (1996) as the *bi-furcated* state. In the colonial occupation of Africa, it was not merely that people were divided and ruled, but rather that the project became to 'define and rule' – a process whereby the colonised were divided into two different categories, which would have two different trajectories of growth (Mamdani 2013, p. 49). This categorisation saw the colonised split between, 'races', and 'tribes', in which 'non-natives' (i.e. migrants or those not indigenous to sub-Saharan Africa, like Asians, Europeans, Arabs, etc.) were defined as separate races and the 'native' populations (indigenous to Africa) were separated into tribes (Mamdani 2013, p. 47). This separation meant two different legal systems. All *races* were governed under a single law: civil law, and thus formed part of civil society. However, tribes, which were far more differentiated by colonial authority, were governed by different sets of customary law. Mamdani, (2013, p. 48) describes this technology of the colonial state as having very specific ends:

> With *races*, the cultural difference was not translated into separate legal systems. Instead, it was contained, even negotiated, within a single legal system and was enforced by a single administrative authority. But with *tribes*, the case was the opposite: cultural difference was reinforced, exaggerated, and built up into different legal systems, each enforced by a separate administrative and political authority. In a nutshell, different races were meant to have a common future; different tribes were not. The colonial legal project – civil and customary – were an integral part of the colonial political project (author's emphasis).

Similarly, applying the insights of the subaltern studies scholars to theorisations of citizenship in postcolonial African states requires us not only to provide a critique of the institution of Traditional Authorities in the rural areas but also of the certain kinds of liberal institutions and elite forms of politics, such as civil society and modern nationalism, which claim to represent the full extent of democratic practices and possibilities in South Africa.

What made the Bantu Authorities system so unpopular with rural dwellers at the time of its introduction was firstly the fact that they now had to pay a host of additional taxes in order to finance the – at times lavish – lifestyles of the Tribal Authorities, and, secondly, they directly bore the burden of the rising institutionalised corruption amongst chiefs who were compliant with the state. Therefore, Chaskalson (1986, p. 50) explains, 'the total drain on the reserve population increased substantially at the same time as the rehabilitation measures (which were now enforced by the Tribal Authorities) undermined their material position', In addition to these, Tribal Authorities became closely associated during the 1950s with the increased policies and practices of 'influx control', which included the extension of the pass system to women as well as the forced removal of 'illegals' from urban areas to the reserves. All of these processes were carried out and enforced by the Tribal Authorities in the reserves during the 1950s and 1960s, resembling Mamdani's description of chiefs embodying a great fusion of powers.

A comparative analysis of the various instances of resistance documented in the literature reveals, despite the opposition of some historians, that the popular politics in the reserves during the 1940s and 1950s cannot be simply dismissed as 'reactionary', 'parochial', or evidence of some 'innate peasant conservatism' (Chaskalson 1986, p. 50). However, it must be noted that of all the instances of popular political organisation, which comprised this broad moment of rural resistance, it is the Mpondo revolts that stand out as the most politically important event within the sequence. It was in eastern Mpondoland during the nine months of sustained open resistance in 1959–1961, where tens of thousands of rural dwellers and migrant workers gathered on mountains, in forests, and in villages to organise a campaign of resistance in which they rejected the institution of Tribal Authorities as well as the idea of chieftaincy *entirely*.

The significance of this point cannot be overstated. In many of the other instances of resistance during this period, people in the rural areas fought against what was understood as a bastardised version of the chieftaincy, usually against one particular chief seen as 'illegitimately' placed in power by the apartheid state, and called for a reinstatement of a system of 'legitimate' traditional governance under a chief who was horizontally accountable to his constituency. As Govan Mbeki argued, 'when a people have developed to a stage that discards chieftainship, when their social development contradicts the need for such an institution, then to force it on them is not liberation but enslavement' (Mbeki 1964, p. 47). In the case of the Mpondo revolts, no such collective call for a return to some idea of a benevolent or legitimate chieftaincy took place. The call made by the members of the *Intaba* movement in eastern Mpondoland was instead a call for self-governance, equality, and democracy, which amounted to a complete rejection of their allotted social location as subjects and not citizens under the system of Bantu Authorities.

Tom Lodge (1983, p. 282) argues that, unlike in the previously discussed examples, in eastern Mpondoland 'the traditional political structure was completely discredited and consequently dissatisfaction was unlikely to cohere around any representative of the old order', As a consequence of this rejection of the traditional political structure, Lodge (1983, p. 282) claims that the people in eastern Mpondoland 'were compelled to create *new* leadership structures' (emphasis added). This insight highlights that the Mpondo revolts represented a moment in which people were creating something new, an alternative form of politics and political community which was not based on either the traditional political structure or modern nationalism and party politics. It is this element of 'the new', as discussed above, which makes the Mpondo revolts such a significant historical moment for scholars to draw on in their attempts to think afresh about the politics of land, citizenship, and governance in the former Bantustans twenty years since the fall of apartheid.

A defining feature of the Mpondo revolts was the use of mountains as sites of subaltern politics and spaces for the organisation of resistance by ordinary male rural dwellers and migrant workers (Bruchhausen 2014, p. 7). It is important to note that women's politics, although rarely acknowledged by historians, was taking place and being organised in the villages and in the fields (see Naicker 2013, p. 56–60). While women were not expected to attend mountain meetings directly, they played a fundamental role in facilitating the men on the mountain's gatherings by providing them with food, water, and intelligence reports throughout the duration of the revolts. An important aspect of the mountain meetings involved the issue of egalitarianism, the distribution of power, and specifically the issue of power being overly concentrated in the hands of chiefs who were widely considered illegitimate, autocratic, and incapable of acting on behalf of the will of the people (Bruchhausen 2014, p. 12). The commitment to egalitarianism held by the actors of the Mpondo revolts is evidenced by the fact that during mountain meetings all decision-making was done collectively and according to a praxis of democracy by consensus – as opposed to democratic practices in which participation for the majority is reduced to the act of voting. Such a form of subaltern political praxis required extremely high levels of discipline and patience from members as meetings were necessarily long in duration and comprised of many contributing voices. We argue that a very similar democratic political praxis could be seen on the mountain of Marikana during the days preceding the massacre of 16th August 2012.

Another important feature of the mountain movement during the nine-month period of 1960 is in relation to the question of land. By May of 1960 the *Intaba* had a constituency of over 180,000 members and was 'establishing itself as an alternative political authority to the prevalent order, assuming, for instance, the functions of the chief's courts in settling land allocation matters…' (Lodge 1983, p. 279). What is significant about the way in which the mountain movement dealt with the issue of access to land is that it represented a new type of politics that did not inaugurate private ownership of land, which is seen as the most progressive and modern form of land tenure by liberal scholars, nor did they simply replicate the so-called traditional politics of land by choosing for themselves a new chief to establish a court and take up the responsibility of land allocation. Instead, the men on the mountain adopted aspects of the communal land tenure system and reinvented it to fit with a process of collective decision-making, in the context of a participatory democratic movement. By taking the authority to allocate land out of the hands of the autocratic traditional authorities and placing the responsibility upon themselves, the members of the Mpondo revolts engendered a moment in South African history, which we today can draw insights from in order to consider the possibility of alternative and new means of land allocation.

The practice of meeting on mountains, which characterised the Mpondo revolts, can be traced back to the earliest years of the 1900s in the former

Transkei and was taken up by migrant workers all over the country, but, most significantly, at the mines on the East Rand throughout the twentieth and twenty first centuries. In the space of the mountain, poor and working class people, who are usually considered and treated as lesser beings (both materially and intellectually) by dominant social groups in society, demand that their full humanity and political agency be recognized and that they be treated with equality, dignity, and respect. Dunbar Moodie (1994) has demonstrated in his work that during the period between 1946 and 1982 on the gold mines in South Africa amaMpondo migrant workers often organized themselves and other workers on the mines in ways very similar to those seen during the Mpondo revolts. In these instances of resistance on the mines, just as in the case of the Mpondo revolts, emphasis was placed on meeting attendance and on democratic forms of participation in decision-making processes, which used consensus as the means by which to elect spokespeople as well as collectively decide upon which forms of action were to be taken. These instances of organized resistance on the mines presented organic forms of democracy, which amaMpondo miners were already accustomed to from their experiences and histories at home in the Transkei. This more organic and horizontal praxis of democracy occurs in a subaltern sphere of politics, which takes place in different forms and spaces compared to what Guha (1997, p. xvi) describes as the 'official domain' of politics.

Recalling our earlier discussion of the politics of land and belonging in the *Nkaneng* shack-settlement, it is important to note that the parallels that can be drawn between the Marikana/Lonmin strike of August 2012 and the political praxes of the Mpondo revolts are in many cases stark. In both instances, people chose to occupy a mountain and, via means of democratic consensus, elected a mountain committee to act as spokespersons and maintain peace and order. In his book, *Murder at Small* Koppie, Greg Marinovich (2016, p. 83) describes the workers move to the mountain, 'They book base themselves at the oval-shaped reddish hill off the South-Western edge of Nkaneng; this koppie was known simply as thaba, 'the mountain' despite its underwhelming height', This should not be understated, a few pages later Marinovich (2016, p. 89) notes that '"the koppie" was transformed into a ritual place in more than just a religious sense. The mountain was to become imbued with power – the site where the all-powerful and wealthy Lonmin boss would be forced to come to his workers', In both instances, at Marikana and during the Mpondo Revolts people demanded to be treated as equals in the space of the mountain and, furthermore, insisted that they were not represented by anyone and instead spoke directly for themselves. In both instances, the praxis of a subaltern form of politics consists of a much deeper conception and practice of democracy and notion of citizenship than that offered to us by political parties, NGOs, or other elite forms of politics in the 'official domain', which tend to categorise the majority of black South African citizens (particularly those with direct ties to the rural areas) as 'the unthinking masses' in need of guidance by some kind of 'enlightened' vanguard. It is also important to recall that no less than 31 of the 45 people who died on and since the 16th of August 2012 held their regular homesteads in the Eastern Cape Province.

Keith Breckenridge (2012) as well as Gavin Hardford (2012) were the only scholars who wrote early accounts of the massacre at Marikana, which identified the importance of the fact that the initial driving force behind the strike was not just RDOs, but mainly they were migrant workers from Mpondoland. Gavin Hartford (2012, p. 3) also identified the fact that the RDOs, who held their rural bases in Mpondoland and were a significant force in the Marikana strike, were generally between the ages of 45 and 55 years old. This means that they would possibly have already been born at the time of the Mpondo revolts, or at the very least and even for those who had not yet been born, it is extremely likely that many of the people would have grown up hearing stories of their parents involvement in the rural resistance politics of the late 1950s and early 1960s in the former Transkei. This can be seen in the many songs that were sung by mineworkers as well as other cultural features of the Marikana strikes, which made reference to rural struggles like the Mpondo Revolts. It is also important to note that, in both the Mpondo revolts and the Marikana strikes, actors displayed a strong commitment to the avoidance of random terror and focused on fostering collective solidarity in the context of increasing threats of violence from the state. Furthermore, just as the Ngquza Hill massacre of 6th June 1960 led to a strengthening and broadening of resistance throughout Mpondoland, so too did the massacre at Marikana lead to an intensification of resistance that spread throughout the mining sector and into other South African industries (Bruchhausen 2014, p. 9).

Although, this is not the space to go into elaborate detail about these parallels between the Mpondo revolts and the Marikana/Lonmin strike, what is most significant for the purpose of this chapter is to highlight that the connections between the two events represent a *living* subaltern history of politics in South Africa, which, when taken seriously, offers us insights into existing practices and conceptions of democracy and citizenship, which challenge the limitations of representative democracy and the sustained existence of the system of Traditional Authorities twenty years after the fall of apartheid. While some have viewed 'ethnic politics' as 'backward' or 'pre-modern', there must be an attempt to understand how ethnicity functions in South African society, and how people who are the subject of traditional and customary law themselves feel discriminated against and are struggling for a kind of citizenship that is more inclusive and a democracy that embraces their political desires and organisation. Furthermore, by taking seriously the forms of politics employed by ordinary black South Africans during the Mpondo revolts, we are presented with a stunning challenge to many dominant assumptions underpinning mainstream understandings of South African resistance history. In many ways both the Mpondo revolts and the Marikana/Lonmin strike create the conditions for – to borrow a phrase from Michel-Rolph Trouillot – 'thinking the hitherto unthinkable', that ordinary rural Africans are political, rational, and complex agents who are not tied to a static notion of 'tradition' in the sense that they are ontologically fixed within the realm of the pre-modern and apolitical.

Some Conclusions

The political insight that can be gained by considering South Africa's history of subaltern politics is of fundamental importance for our attempts to rethink South Africa's land, governance, and citizenship questions in relation to the former Bantustans today. This re-thinking has allowed us to understand how colonial governance mechanisms are being reified in the post-apartheid state, and how land has been used to geographically fix and control people. The chapter aims to broaden conceptions of democracy and the political, and to stress that we cannot afford to ignore the way ordinary people practice politics in the everyday. The usefulness of this insight is that it encourages us to begin our deliberations by starting from the simple assertion that 'people can think' and equips us with the understanding that the politics, which has and continues to take place outside of the 'official domain', and which are conceived outside of the sphere of state subjectivities and forms of elite politics, (Guha 1997, p. xvi), in certain instances, presents examples of practices of democracy, citizenship, dignity, and belonging within a subaltern sphere.

It also serves to illustrate that, when we think about South Africa's land questions, it cannot be narrowly defined through land restitution claims or farming co-operatives alone, rather it must of necessity be linked to broader struggles for justice, dignity, and humanity that require structural socio-economic and political change, in line with how people practice politics. In *Disabling Gobalisation* (2002), Gill Hart stresses that 're-articulating the land question could potentially link together diverse demands and thus help to unite a broader opposition to the brutal neoliberal economic policies that were ravaging livelihoods... (and) how framing demands in terms of a social wage might contribute to forging alliances between at least some elements of organised labour and the newly emerging movements'.

What the examples of the Mpondo revolts and the Marikana/Lonmin strikes reveal to us is the fact that, once again, at certain moments, ordinary people organise themselves collectively and engage in political acts of resistance, which defy their social location. In the case of the Mpondo revolts, rural dwellers, who in line with the state's narrow ethnic and racial conception of 'identity politics' were collectively perceived as ontologically beholden to obeying a hereditary system of chieftainship, defied their allotted social location as subjects and created new forms of political leadership. This was based on popular participation in democratic decision-making processes and notions of egalitarianism, which stood in opposition to the institution of chieftaincy and the apartheid state. In the case of the Marikana/Lonmin strike, migrant workers totally confounded the basic assumptions held by traditional labour historians by rejecting trade union representation and bringing to the fore the politics of human dignity, access to land and resources, as well as the meaning of democracy in post-apartheid South Africa, in conjunction with the call for a living wage of R12,500.

References

Alexander, P. Lekgowa, T. Mmope, B. Sinwell, L., & Xezwi, B. (2012). *Marikana: A View from the Mountain and a Case to Answer*. Auckland Park: Jacana Media.

Breckenridge, K. (2012). 'Revenge of the Commons: The Crisis in the South African Mining Industry', in *Histories of the Present*, available online at http://www.historyworkshop.org.uk/revenge-of-the-commons-the-crisis-in-the-south-african-mining-industry/ (Accessed on 22 February 2013).

Bruchhausen, S. (2014). Understanding Marikana Through the Mpondo Revolts. *Journal of Asian and African Studies*. doi: 10.1177/0021909614531892.

Chakrabarty, D. (2000) Subaltern Studies and Postcolonial Historiography. *Nepantla: Views from the South*, *1*(1), 9–32.

Chaskalson, M. (1986) Rural resistance in the 1940s and 1950s. *Africa Perspective*, *1*(5–6), 47–59.

Chatterjee, P. (2004). *The Politics of the Governed.* Delhi: Permanent Black.

Chingono, C. (2013). Marikana and the Post-Apartheid Workplace Order. *Working Paper 1: Society, Work and Development Institute.*

Feni, L. (2014). Mines ask kings to end strike, *Dispatch Live.* Available online at: http://www.dispatchlive.co.za/news/mines-ask-kings-to-end-strike/.

Grieve, N. (2014). Lonmin inks landmark BEE deals with traditional community. *Mining Weekly* (Creamer Medias). Available online at: http://www.miningweekly.com/article/lonmin-inks-landmark-bee-deals-with-traditional-community-2014-07-30.

Guha, R. (1997). Introduction. In R. Guha (Ed.) *A Subaltern Studies Reader.* New York: Oxford University Press.

Hart, G. (2013). *Rethinking the South African Crisis: Nationalism, Populism, Hegemony.* University of KwaZulu-Natal Press: Durban.

Hart, G. (2002). *Disabling Globalisation: Places of Power in Post-Apartheid South Africa.* University of California Press: California.

Hartford, G. (2012). 'The Mining Industry Strike Wave: What are the causes and what are the solutions?' in *Ground Up*, available online at http://groundup.org.za/content/mining-industry-strike-wave-what-are-causes-and-what-are-solutions. Accessed 22 February 2013.

Hirson, B. (1977). Rural revolt in South Africa, 1937–1951. In *Collected Seminar Papers* (115–132), *Institute of Commonwealth Studies, 21.*

Kepe, T., & Ntsebeza, L. (2012). Rural Resistance in South Africa: The Mpondo Revolts after Fifty Years. Cape Town: UCT Press.

Landau, P.S. (2010). *Popular Politics in the History of South Africa.* New York: Cambridge Press.

Lodge, T. (1983). *Black Politics in South Africa since 1945.* Johannesburg: Ravan Press.

Mamdani, M. (1996). *Citizen and Subject: contemporary Africa and the legacy of late colonialism.* New Jersey: Princeton University Press.

Mamdani, M. (2013). *Define and Rule: Native as Political Identity.* Johannesburg: Wits University Press.

Marinovich, G. (2016). *Murder at Small Koppie: the Real Story of the Marikana Massacre.* Cape Town: Penguin Books.

Mbeki, G. (1964). *South Africa: The Peasants' Revolt.* Middlesex: Penguin.

Moodie, D.T., with Ndashe, V. (1994). *Going for Gold.* London: University of California Press.

Myers, J.C. (2008). *Indirect Rule in South Africa: Tradition, Modernity, and the Costuming of Political Power.* New York: University of Rochester Press.

Naicker, C. (2013). Marikana: Taking a Subaltern Sphere of Politics Seriously. *MA Thesis.* Rhodes University.

Neocosmos, M. (2011). Transition, Human Rights & Violence: Rethinking a liberal political relationship in the African neo-colony. (Unpublished Manuscript).

News24 (2012). Traditional Leaders Head to Marikana. *News24.* Available online at: http://www.news24.com/SouthAfrica/News/Traditional-leaders-head-to-Marikana-20120820.

Pithouse, R. (2011). Fidelity to Fanon. In N.C. Gibson (Ed.), *Living Fanon: Global Perspectives* (225–235).

Pithouse, R. (2012). *Thought Amidst Waste, Conjunctural Notes on the Democratic Project in South Africa.* Paper presented at the Wits Interdisciplinary Seminar in the Humanities, WISER, University of the Witwatersrand, 28 May 2012.

Wolpe, H. (1972) Capitalism and cheap labour-power in South Africa: From segregation to apartheid. *Economy and Society, 1*(4), 425–456.

CHAPTER 3

From Material to Cultural: Historiographic Approaches to the Eastern Cape's Agrarian Past

Elene Cloete

Introduction

An understanding of a region's history sheds light on its current socio-economic predicament. In his recent work on South Africa's Eastern Cape Province, the historian Clifton Crais (2011) supports this claim, drawing a direct link between the region's systemic poverty and intrusive colonial history. He argues that the region's current state of poverty is not only rooted in the violent nature of colonial conquest but equally so in the forced changes in agricultural production ensuing the colonial intrusion. Current realities, Crais (2011) maintains, are therefore rooted in historic instances. Following this argument, we cannot understand South Africa's agrarian questions, 20 years after democracy, without considering historic events and trajectories.

Over the last two decades historians have, however, shown a limited interest in the roots of socio-economic issues, in particular poverty (Bundy, 2006; Du Toit, 2010; Westerway, 2008). This means that the radical and neo-Marxian inspired historiographies of the 1970s and 1980s that articulated the intrusive nature of capitalism on local livelihoods, made way for studies focused on identity, heritage, and ethnic particularities. Westerway (2008) attributes this change to the post-apartheid government's desire to establish a new unified image and national identity. Additionally, as Cobley (2001) argues, this altered interest also coincides with the international post-structuralism and post-modern trends of the 1990s. As a result, research focused on the roots of poverty and social inequality succumbed to theoretical shifts in historiographic inquiry. What is involved in these epistemological shifts? Furthermore how, if at all the case, do these historiographic changes align with agrarian questions 20 years after democracy?

This chapter traces some of the prominent theoretical approaches to South Africa's agrarian past, using the rural Eastern Cape Province's colonial history as reference point. My aim is not to construct a chronological narrative of the Eastern Cape's colonial period. Monica Hunter (1961), Jeff Peires (1983, 1989) and Noel Mostert (1992), among others, have done this in an impeccable manner.

 | DOI 10.1163/9789004362550_004

Instead, my goal is to highlight some of the primary objectives and focal points articulated by these different approaches, and subsequently reflect on how these objectives relate to current agrarian questions. In this regard, I value the contributions radical historiography can make to current social debates, in particular its focus on the socio-economic and political instigators of poverty and wealth inequality. Even though cultural readings do articulate different facets of colonial domination, including colonial perceptions and manipulation of certain cultural ideologies, which in turn provide for a broader understanding of the region's past, I argue that the focal points and research objectives of radical historiographies might carry a stronger correlation with current agrarian issues. This includes the persistent construction and reconstruction of social classes, the continuous struggle of people with and against the capitalist market, and women's marginal position with regards to production and landownership.

I delimit my review to historiographies produced during the last forty years and focused on the rural Eastern Cape under British colonial control (circa 1810–1910).[1] Agrarian focal points range from the region's settler communities and corresponding wool production (Switzer, 1993) to the African population's relationship to cash crop production (Bundy, 1979; Crais, 2011). This review therefore includes a selection of scholars, all focused on the same region and time-period, but drawing from different theoretical foundations. In the first part of the chapter, I review the radical and political economy of the 1970s, focusing specifically on the work of Colin Bundy, William Beinart, and their contemporaries. Using these scholars' work as a reference point, I discuss some of the primary focal points and objectives of this particular approach to the Eastern Cape's colonial past. In the second part of the chapter, I follow the cultural-specific approaches of the 1990s and 2000s, with the work of Clifton Crais (1992a, 2002, 2011) as departure point. Similar to the preceding discussion on radical historiography, this section highlights the primary themes and objectives articulated by this approach to historic inquiry.

From Critical Liberalism to Radical Marxism

Historiographies of the early 20th century, concerned with rural South Africa, differentiate along two lines: Those written against a nationalistic Afrikaner backdrop versus those critiquing such scholarship, regarding it as a mere

1 Even though the Cape Colony's first period of Dutch rule (1652–1806) might be the longest, the British administration had the most dominant effect on the country's politics.

perpetuation of nineteenth century evolutionary thought (Thompson, 2001). Prominent in this regard was the work of W.M. MacMillan and his student, C.W. DeKiewiet, who set out to expose the racial biases of their nationalist Afrikaner contemporaries, and to report on the rising socio-economic hardships accompanying 1920s industrialization and urbanization (Macmillan and Marks, 1989). Both these authors addressed the historic roots of poverty, showing a 'great concern for black welfare' (Visser, 2004), subsequently setting the stage for a liberal branch of South African historiography.

The early 1960s was particularly fruitful for the liberal movement. This started with a group of English-speaking South African scholars, advocating for the inclusion of all African groups in South African history. Scholars such as Leonard Thompson, John Omer-Cooper, and Monica Wilson,[2] emphasized the experiences, dynamics, and uniqueness of South Africa's African peoples (Stolten, 2006). This liberal movement reached its pinnacle with Wilson and Thompson's (1969, 1971) *Oxford History of South Africa* (Crais, 1992a). The liberal approach was, however, not without its critics, the strongest being a wave of new radical history, which, drawing from neo-Marxian theory, interpreted South Africa's past in terms of capitalist expansion, class division, and means of production. Also labeled as political economy or materialism, this radical historiography started to recognize and evaluate dichotomies of peasant/farmer and production/consumption, as well as to analyze processes of capitalist expansion and class formation. A prominent front-runner of this new wave of historic writing was Shula Marks and Anthony Atmore's (1980) edited volume *Economy and Society in Pre-Industrial South Africa*.

Radical historiography questioned, among other things, the liberal movement's historic narrative, particularly this movement's use of modernity as measuring stick (Crais, 2002). This includes depicting the country's African population as non-modern, static, and apolitical, whilst disregarding the intrusiveness of capitalism on South Africans' livelihood strategies (Crais, 1992a). This disregard, radical historians argued, ignores a fundamental facet of colonial and apartheid domination.

The radical historiographies of the 1970s and 1980s also became active manifestations of social critique (Du Toit, 2010). With a growing social and political relevance that coincided with the narratives of the anti-apartheid struggle, these historiographies acted as intellectual resistance to the apartheid struggle, and a subsequent influence on popular discourse (Bundy, 2006). As the

2 It was also during this time that a second edition of Wilson's (1961) *Reaction to Conquest: Effects of Contact with Europeans on the Pondo of South Africa depiction of the past and then current realities of the Mpondo people* saw the light of day.

1970s and 1980s progressed, radical historiography constructed a critique reflecting on the destructive socio-economic impact of the country's colonial and apartheid past.

Radical Readings of the Eastern Cape's Colonial Past

The historiographies of Jeff Peires (1982, 1989) and Noel Mostert's (1992) serve as indispensable points of reference for the Eastern Cape's colonial and pre-colonial pasts. Additionally, these authors worked hard at debunking misconceived Afrikaner-nationalist and settler inspired interpretations of the frontier. This includes depictions of the African population as disorganized, apolitical, aggressive, and violent. Peires and Mostert's work therefore pays close attention to the pre-colonial and colonial social structures of the Eastern Cape's amaXhosa people, ranging from intricate political systems to complex religious and social organizations. But even though both these authors refer to the changes in agrarian production and articulate the intrusiveness of the colony's capitalist expansion on African communities, a Marxian analysis was not the primary premise of their historic inquiry.

Colin Bundy's (1979) *The Rise and Fall of the South African Peasantry*, on the other hand, took a more materialistic approach to the Eastern Cape's colonial past. Regarded as 'probably the most influential account of rural history produced in the 1970s' (Beinart et al. 1986, p. 12), Bundy analyzes the Eastern Cape's rural economic landscape through an explicit neo-Marxian lens. This includes an emphasis on agricultural productivity, the change from a quasi-feudal system under traditional authorities to individually driven market production, and the effect of altered agricultural production on the region's socio-political landscapes. With this in mind, Bundy consciously rejects depictions of the Eastern Cape's African population as unresponsive to the dominating demands of the emerging nineteenth century's market economy. Instead he illustrates, by means of agrarian archival record,[3] some Africans' positive response to the growing agricultural market accompanying South Africa's nineteenth-century mineral boom (Cooper, 1981). Subsequently, this demand for agricultural goods prompted the rise of a productive peasantry, fully adaptive to the colonialists' growing agricultural market economy. Such adaptability was especially prominent in the district of Herschel, a North Eastern Cape African reserve established during the mid-nineteenth century under colonial rule. Because of its close proximity to the Kimberly diamond mines and the

3 Among others, Bundy draws heavily on data collected by Macmillan during the early 1920s.

Free State gold fields, this district saw record levels of grain exports toward the end of the 1800s. The financial possibility accompanying cash crop production encouraged many former subsistence farmers to switch to cash crop production rather than wage labour (Bundy 1979, p. 13). Subsequently Herschel became a primary site of late nineteenth-century agricultural developments and the rise of an African peasantry.

A primary objective of Bundy's work was to identify a rising African peasantry, who moved beyond pre-colonial forms of subsistence living and adopted a 'more complex social structure with novel economic and political obligations' (Bundy 1979, p. 11). This adaptation altered the region's pre-colonial egalitarian socio-political structures and established a clearly differentiated class structure, comprising of a clearly defined group of peasant farmers and a corresponding proletariat. Local people's varied levels of economic involvement also led to the emergence of a clearly defined class structure *within* the rising peasantry. This was linked to the individual peasant's level of economic involvement and affluence, which ranged from illiterate peasants who occasionally used wage labour to purchase a metal plow to missionary-educated individuals who hired outside labour at harvest time and became more affluent.

Hershel's rising peasantry was, however, short lived. Whereas varied rainfall and ensuing draughts continuously hampered peasants' yearly production, the colonial government's bureaucratic changes during the late 1800s and early 1900s restricted the individual peasant's economic conditions. Firstly, the colonial government's landownership restrictions damaged the peasants' economic development. Secondly, the colonial government's implemented system of indirect rule resulted in quasi-traditional leaders overseeing and managing communal activities (Delius, 2008). These leaders often imposed communal ownership on production, derailing the market-oriented and individual approach of peasant farmers. The combination of both natural and colonial forces eventually led to the peasantry's eventual 'fall' in the early 1920s. But, however short lived this affluent peasantry was, Bundy's emphases contradict conservative histories of the rural Eastern Cape's African population, depicting them as stagnant, backwards, and uninterested in the nineteenth century's booming market economy. Instead, Bundy's reading reveals agency, adaptability, and maneuverability.

In a true scholarly fashion Bundy's (1979) 'rise and fall' thesis attracted its fair share of critics. True to the radical movement, such critique does not necessarily question Bundy's neo-Marxian reading of the Eastern Cape's agrarian past but instead highlights his omission or limited interpretation of the active capitalist and social machinery. One such omission, as Lewis (1984) pointed out, was a consideration of pre-existing class structures, embedded in the region's pre-colonial socio-political structures. Lewis argues that the Eastern Cape's pre-colonial society was not as egalitarian as Bundy wants us to believe, but consisted of clearly defined working poor, who made significant labour contributions to the means of production in pre-colonial societies, and those wealthier classes, who benefited from such production through wealth accumulation. This demarcation of pre-colonial classes, Lewis claims, survived the colonial conquest and merely resurfaced in the colonial period. The rising peasantry was therefore not Africans' adaptive response to the market economy but rather a prolongation of existing pre-colonial structures.

In addition to existing pre-colonial class structures, ethnic groups' political maneuvering further contributed to clearly defined colonial class structures. This maneuvering is another aspect Lewis (1984) finds missing in Bundy's reading. Lewis argues that the migration of African groups such as the Mfengu into the colony, and their subsequent alliances with the colonial government, allowed them to obtain more arable land and more prosperous labour positions. The Mfengu's political disposition vis-à-vis the colonial government also gave them access to the emerging market economy that accompanied the South African mineral boom. Not surprisingly, Mfengu farmers were amongst the more affluent Herschel peasant farmers, constituting a great percentage of the 'rising' peasantry. Arguably, the Eastern Cape's short period of peasant prosperity was therefore less about Africans' adaptability to capital markets and more about the demographic and political circumstances of the pre-colonial and colonial periods. Furthermore, the poverty experienced with the 'fall' of the peasantry at the beginning of the twentieth century, refers only to a small percentage of Africans. The majority of the region's African population was already subject to extreme poverty. As Lewis (1984, p. 24) states: 'impoverishment has been a very long term phenomenon traceable almost from the moment that effective conquest was achieved'.

More recent analyses of Bundy's 'Rise and Fall' thesis include Helen Bradford's (2000) valuable feminist reading of the Herschel district's colonial past. Bradford (2000) raises a pertinent concern regarding existing histories: Where are the women? Bundy's reading of the Herschel district pays little attention to women's contributions, focusing instead on the 'rise' of the peasant man and Victorian masculinity enabled by participating in progressive capitalist activities. Speaking to this void, Bradford (2000) stresses the active role women played on both household and socio-political fronts. She maintains that women were active participants in the socio-economic sphere, by working in the fields, contributing to household capital through wage labour, and, additionally, resisting the colonial government's administrative changes by withholding produce from the market. Not considering the role of women therefore provides a partial view of the district's colonial past, in particular its so-called rising peasantry. Similar to Lewis, Bradford's critique is not aimed at Bundy's neo-Marxian reading of the Eastern Cape's agrarian past per say. But like other feminists, she builds her argument around historians' frequent omission of women from economic activities.

Even when considering these shortcomings, Bundy's work remains seminal when interpreting the Eastern Cape's colonial past. Crais (2011, p. 16) argues that the 'rise and fall' model 'offer[s] a particular powerful way of understanding rural change in large areas of Africa', Most importantly, Bundy's (1979) study 'strip[ped] away the mythologies of the backward African cultivators and raise[d] basic questions about the structures and dynamics of African agricultural history' (Cooper 1981, p. 314).

William Beinart's (1982) *The Political Economy of Pondoland* represents another important reading of the rural Eastern Cape's economic activities. Here Beinart (1982) aims 'to analyze the connection between the prosperous capitalist economy of South Africa and the poverty of African agriculture' (Cooper 1981, p. 297). Whereas Bundy's (1979) study incorporates different case studies from both homogeneous and heterogeneous regions, Beinart (1982) focuses solely on the Mpondo. Building on Wilson's (1961) ethnographic work of the 1930s, Beinart analyses the Mpondo's economic transformation against the backdrop of South Africa's late nineteenth-century industrial revolution. Since Pondoland was the last of the Eastern Cape's traditionally African regions to become part of the Cape Colony, the region's exposure to colonial rule was somewhat delayed. The Mpondo people therefore enjoyed a fair degree of independence and exclusion from colonial rule. A great number of traders nevertheless infiltrated the region from as early as 1860 (Bundy, 1979), but their success was subject to the goodwill of the local Pondo chiefs who not only controlled but also monitored their people's access to the market economy. In turn, such political control regulated the Mpondo's interaction with the colony's growing capitalist markets. Changes to the social and political structures of the Mpondo peoples, in particular as far as the capitalist market was concerned, were therefore controlled and steered from *inside* their own society. Like Bundy, Beinart's work therefore questions interpretations of local populations as passive bystanders, and 'backward' participants in capital development and change. Based upon their own immediate needs, Africans more than often resisted, alternated, or adjusted their position vis-à-vis the market economy.

In their co-authored *Hidden Struggles in Rural South Africa* (1987), William Beinart and Colin Bundy broaden their radical inquiry to other parts of the Eastern Cape. Similar to their respective earlier works, Beinart and Bundy

(1987) are adamant in debunking any understandings that perpetuate the nineteenth and early twentieth century rural Eastern Cape as passively accepting colonial rule. The authors therefore work toward articulating local people's resilience and protest against colonial domination and, in this case, the district of Herschel surfaced again. Here Beinart (1987) reports on Herschel's 'die-hard' women's protestation against the government's regulations of agricultural production and land occupancy. The Die-hards also rebelled against fluctuating agricultural markets, particularly the often below market prices traders offered for their cash crops. Keeping Bradford's critique of the male-centred 'rise and fall peasantry' in mind, Beinart's (1987) reference to Hershel's women's movements is particularly powerful.

Like Bundy rise and fall analysis, Beinart and Bundy (1987) also elaborate on the economic processes that accompanied colonial rule and eventually culminated in clearly defined social classes. But in *Hidden Struggles in Rural South Africa,* Beinart and Bundy (1987) also associate social stratification with people's attitudes to pre-colonial customs and traditions. Whereas some African groups treasured pre-colonial ways, others accepted and subsequently adapted to colonial changes. Communities therefore differentiated between the progressive liberals with missionary education, and the traditionalists remaining loyal to traditional forms of authority and communal economies, actively resisting the way of the white man. The ramifications of such stratification affected the political landscape of heterogeneous districts where both traditionalists and populists fended for the same resources.

While Beinart and Bundy's (1987) focus on the politics of the Transkei, Les Switzer's (1993) *Power and Resistance in an African Society* investigates the impact of colonial expansion on the neighboring Ciskei. Whether consciously or not, Switzer's work adheres to Lewis' (1984) critique of Bundy (1979) by incorporating an analysis of the region's pre-colonial past into his understanding of the subaltern's resistance to colonial rule. Additionally, Switzer's interpretation also accentuates the affect of different manifestations of power: material and symbolic power. Material power, he argues, manifests itself through economic systems such as capitalism. In short, capital economies severely altered, if not destroyed, the pre-colonial reproductive capacity of the African population. Capitalism therefore 'expand[ed] in articulation with and at the expense of the indigenous African population', creating in the process the 'super exploited excluded classes' of people restricted to the region's African reserves (Switzer 1993, p. 5).

But this is not where Switzer's analysis ends. Instead, he considers other non-economic factors that contributed to the region's historic trajectory, in particular the power of symbolism. Whereas material power siphons through economic systems, symbolic power resides in cultural mechanisms such as the state, church, and school. This largely entails processes of cultural hegemony, and, in this regard, Switzer (1993) quite fittingly draws on Gramsci's hegemonic state thesis to substantiate his argument. By means of an administrative bureaucracy, missionary education, and alliances with peripheral African groups and chiefdoms, the colonial government steadily worked at changing the societal and cultural structure of the African population. These changes unknowingly changed people's internal perceptions regarding their culture and its relation to the colonial government – an eventual 'colonization of consciousness' (Comaroff and Comaroff, 1991). Symbolic power therefore produced a passive and altered population, eager to build and sustain the colonial empire.

But symbolic power expands further than merely externally imposed ideologies. In response to the abrupt cultural changes colonial domination imposed on the Eastern Cape's African population, some African groups 'continually contested [by means of] ideologies of resistance' (Switzer, 1993). Exemplary, as Switzer demonstrates, was the cleavage between red and school folk. Whereas the school folk identified with a literate Christian community, the red folk bluntly resisted any form of modernization or contact with missionaries. This latter group viewed the school folk as weaklings, succumbing to white domination, whereas they still preserved the identity and purity of pre-colonial societies. The red folk therefore resisted and ultimately contested hegemonic ideologies through the perpetuation and subsequently strengthening of their own cultural ideals.

Do Radical Interpretations Provide the Full Story?

The radical historiographies of Bundy, Beinart, and to some extent Switzer, consciously contradict perceptions of the rural Eastern Cape as static, ahistorical, and merely organized along ethnic and tribal lines (Crais, 2011). On the contrary, changes in the region's agricultural and economic activities saw rising crop production, a progressive black elite, and a politically active rural landscape. But, as critics of the radical movement would argue, these materialistic interpretations happened at 'the expense of intellectual, philosophical, religious, literary, and cultural developments' (Hamilton et al., 2010, p. 5). Furthermore, social relations comprise 'more intricate intermeshing of race, gender, ethnicity, religions, language, and locality than those that a class-based analysis alone can supply' (Lester 2001, p. 3). Therefore, not bringing additional social and cultural dynamics into consideration one might end up with a one-sided view of the Eastern Cape's colonial past. Driven by such criticisms in mind, radical historiographies of the 1970s and 1980s were overshadowed in the 1990s by a holistic and culturally sensitive form of history writing.[4] Corresponding with post-modern trends and the historical anthropologies of, among others, Stoler and the Comaroffs (Lester, 1997; Crais, 2002, 2011), the new wave of historiography focused on identity, memory, and the production of history (Crais 2011, p. 7). Similarly, rather than a focus on market forces, capital penetration, and class formation, these studies lean toward the deconstruction of discourses, representation, and power relations (Crais, 1992a, 2011). The intention of the post-radical approach is not only to deconstruct ideological inventions and myths of the colonial period but also to unravel the forces constructing such myths in the first place, that is, the conscious and unconscious processes involved in creating mythical narratives (Hamilton et al., 2011). This then became the objective of a post-radical 'cultural turn' that slowly replaced the neo-Marxian analyses of the preceding decades.

The *Cultural Turn* and the Eastern Cape's Colonial Past

Historic inquiry written from a cultural perspective does not necessarily disregard economic processes but instead incorporates such processes into a broader cultural context, or what Crais (1992a) refers to as the 'messiness' of culture. For example, Lester (2001) incorporates settler capitalism as a set of practices *into* his analysis of the rural Eastern Cape. He interprets these practices through a cultural lens, considering them as 1) 'culturally conditioned and regulated through discourse', 2) related to broader networks across all British colonies, and 3) subject to the acceptance of the local populations. Keeping these points in mind, capitalism and its accompanying agricultural activities appear subordinate to non-economic factors. Therefore, in the work of, among others, Alan Lester (1997, 2001) and Clifton Crais (1992a, 2002, 2011) agricultural activities are considered cultural, and not necessarily an independent and autonomous economic category.

Understanding the 'Colonial Mind'

In *White Supremacy and Black Resistance,* Clifton Crais' (1992a) interpretation starts with the latter part of the eighteenth century, allowing him to incorporate the Eastern Cape's pre-colonial period as well as the region's early years

4 This include Hamilton's (1998) focus on historical depictions of the Zulu kingdom, Eldredge's (2007) Foucaultian analysis of Basotho politics, and Landau's (2010) recent emphasis on political structures in the Free State highlands before and during colonial rule.

of missionary expansion into this historiography.[5] Subsequently, Crais' (1992a) historic approach avoids the narrow temporal view of Bundy's (1979) *Rise and Fall* analysis. Crais' work also moves beyond a purely materialistic interpretation of the Eastern Cape's colonial past, emphasizing instead the socio-cultural dynamics of the frontier zone. These dynamics pertain to, among other things, the power relations between the Cape Colony's settler communities and the region's African population. In a true post-structural approach, Crais closely probes the creation, execution, and reception of power in the colonial Eastern Cape. He holds that the continuously changing approaches of, first, the Dutch and then the British governments with regards to the Eastern Frontier, influenced the ensuing power relations that developed between European settlers and the region's African population. These approaches ranged from the early nineteenth century's 'governing from a distance' to the mid-century British government's eventual 'full-scale centralized governance'. The strongest factor influencing power relations on the Eastern Frontier was, however, the different 'structures of thought' prominent during the nineteenth century (Crais 1992a, p. 3). This refers to how people continuously constructed specific information systems with which to interpret the 'other', whether that be the colonizers' perceptions of the region's African communities or the African population's view of the colonial government and growing settler population. More often than not, the government authorities and administrators used such knowledge structures to strengthen their power over the frontier populations.

Like Crais (1992a), Lester's (1997) interpretation of the Eastern Cape's colonial past concerns the colonizers' 'formulations of otherness' (Lester 1997, p. 636). He argues that these formulations followed either missionary discourses of civilization and Christianity,[6] or reflected the land and labour desires of frontier settlers (Lester 1997, p. 638).[7] The power of these formulations lies in the manner they dictated, in an ideological sense, the colonial government's stance vis-à-vis the frontier region and its African population. This especially

5 To further articulate the social dynamics on the Eastern frontier, Crais (1992) pays close attention to the occurrences accompanying slave emancipation at the Cape in 1834, and the changes in interaction between the European settlers and the African population.

6 Discourses of civilization and Christianity articulated the urgency of saving the African people from their savage existence through the introduction of Christianity, the subsequent route to civilization.

7 During the nineteenth century, newly settled farmers in the frontier area were in desperate need of labourers. Needless to say, the African population were not interested in swopping their pre-colonial subsistence living for wage labour on settler farms. The colonial government therefore had to find alternative solutions to the labour shortage. Limiting Africans' access to land and introducing tax systems were amongst such options.

influenced the colonial government's decision whether or not to include the African population in its projects of colonial expansion. Formulations of the 'other' also impacted any relations between the colonial government and the Eastern Cape region.

Ideological formulations changed as the nineteenth century progressed. Lester (1997, 2001) identifies three different periods, each with a specific ideological mindset. During the first period (1806–1816), the colonial government followed a strict separatist approach in its relation to the Eastern frontier zone. Misinformed narratives of the savage and dangerous African population, and underlying ideas of racial purity, greatly informed this separatist mentality. The second period of colonial involvement (1816–1846) was humanistic in nature, thanks to an influx of missionaries into the region. Whilst still maintaining some degree of separatism, colonial officials started to consider the prospects of assimilating the African population into the colonial order.[8] Assimilation entailed the neutralization of amaXhosa 'otherness', by first converting the Eastern Cape's African population into British subjects and, secondly, transforming them into docile neighbors (Lester 1997, p. 642). To realize these objectives, colonial officials turned to missionaries who were to convert Africans to Christianity, promote English culture through education, and replace traditional subsistence farming with modern cash crop agriculture.

This planned assimilation was not as successful as the colonial government envisioned. Toward the end of the 1830s, both the colonial administration and the missionaries recognized an unexpected degree of resilience amongst the African population toward these assimilation plans. Apart from the orphaned and homeless Africans seeking shelter from missionaries, the general African population had no interest in Christianity or missionary education. Similarly Africans showed limited interest in wage labour. This was especially problematic, keeping the white settlers' newly established wool-based economies in mind. For the first time in the Cape Colony's history, the frontier gained economic importance. But without a sufficient labour force such importance was destined to be short lived. Additionally this economic growth resulted in a greater demand for land, in particular land of neighboring African communities. The Eastern Cape's settler communities became increasingly impatient and resilient toward the colonial government. To adhere to the settlers' demands as well as stimulate the region's economic activities, the colonial government's humanistic disposition regarding the Eastern Cape no longer

8 This movement consolidated ideas about the 'savage' and the non-civilized 'other' to subsequently cemented ideas of racial domination and inferiority in the minds of both colonizers and colonized (Crais 1992).

proved functional. Instead it opted for an active and more direct involvement in the socio-political landscape of the Eastern Cape and its peoples.

The last of Lester's (1997) nineteenth century epochs concerned a period of direct involvement (1846-c. 1880s) that represented the economic ideals of the region's settler community. This includes an increased access to land, labour, and markets. More often than not, the African population came into play as bringing about settlers', and by implication the colonial government's, economic development. In contrast to preceding periods, the government was now 'willing to expend the recourses necessary to exert more effective controls over the frontier Xhosa' (Lester 1997, p. 652). In tandem with the devastating 5th and 6th frontier wars, the colonial government and their power-hungry governors turned the Eastern Cape into clearly demarcated magistrate regions, each with an accompanying colonial administration. The latter was not only implemented to oversee law and order but also to enact the thorough taxation of local populations.

The Politics of Evil, Crais' (2002) second major work is a further representation of the 'cultural turn', Similar to the radical historiographies of Bundy and Beinart, this work stresses the region's close relation to agriculture, especially during its pre-colonial period. But Crais (2002) is less concerned with a materialistic and class analysis. Instead, *The Politics of Evil* stays within the realm of the colonial mind, depicting how the colonial conquest played into the African population's existing pre-colonial political imagination. Before colonial domination, the Eastern Cape's African population saw a strong correlation between political authority and agriculture, in particular, a chief's access to magic and rainmaking. For example, if a region saw good rainfall and subsequent prosperous crop production, the region's people attributed such prosperity to a chief's magical abilities and good relations to the rain-bringing ancestors. Additionally, the local population attached particular cultural meanings to droughts, famine, or the loss of cattle to disease or illness. According to Crais (2002, p. 28) this pre-existing 'theater of politics', or the close relation between authority and magic, subsequently played into Africans' perceptions of colonial conquest and colonial authority.

The subaltern's pre-colonial political consciousness did, however, become an indirect target of colonial domination, not only during the conquest period but also thereafter. Crais (2002) argues that this infiltration and ultimate domination of the local population's political imagination, helped bring about the authoritarian systems of the twentieth century's traditional authorities. This entailed the colonial government's implementation of chiefs and headmen, a supposedly pre-colonial form of traditional authority (Ntsebeza, 2005); newly created colonial bureaucracies; administrative boundaries; and colonially crafted tribalism, affected people's political consciousness and ultimately cemented the racially defined oppressions of twentieth century South Africa. (Crais 2002, p. 28–29). Ultimately, the processes that infiltrated the subaltern's political imagination were what Crais (2002) considers evil 'writ large'.

The Recognition of Structural Violence

Crais' (2011) recent *Poverty, War and Violence in South Africa,* shows alternative interest in the Eastern Cape's colonial past, moving slightly away from a cultural analysis to incorporate questions that align with a neo-Marxian analysis. In contrast to his earlier interest in the colonial mind and political consciousness, he now turns to the region's socio-economic history, particular the economic implications of systemic violence. In doing so, he not only addresses post-structural and post-modern historians' limited attention to the historical roots of poverty but also reflects on neo-Marxian and radical historiography approach to poverty. According to Crais, this latter group uses a particular 'arc of historic change' to explain rural economics and by implication poverty, and its accompanying socio-economic hardship (Crais 2011, p. 123). This arc describes a progression from subsistence to colonial peasants and then to wage labour. The end point of such change is a capitalist or post-capitalist modernity. But for Crais this approach to the Eastern Cape's past inadequately explains poverty's root causes, especially since it fails to incorporate the detrimental effects of violence and conflict. Crais further argues that neo-Marxian and materialistic readings merely use violence and conflict as a prequel before diving into the mechanisms of capitalist expansion. In the process, we are left with an incomplete understanding of socio-economic hardship's historic trajectory.

As a proponent of political economy during the 1980s, Mamdami (2005) recognizes materialism's limited attention to political violence. Similarly Beinart (1994, p. 3) asserts that South Africa's nineteenth century history cannot be written without 'constant reference to violence and military engagement', In comparison to the civil strivings of the twentieth century, the nineteenth century was by far the most violent period in South Africa's past (Peires, 1989; Price, 2008). The Eastern Cape, in particular, saw unknown levels of violence during the nineteenth century, setting in motion unknown levels of poverty, psychological hardship, and subsequent famine.[9]

9 On the part of the colonial government, conquest and violence, especially evident during the frontier wars, was not necessarily aimed toward obtaining economic prosperity, but rather the pacification and thus control over the African population (Crais 2011, p. 63).

Crais (2011) identifies the 8th Frontier War (1851–1853), as exemplary in its degree of violence. War, on the side of the colonial forces was not only concerned with fighting the enemy soldier, but more so, destructing local African communities by means of the 'starving-out system', Following the brutality of the 8th Frontier War was the equally devastating yet well documented cattle-killings of 1856–1867.[10] In the aftermath of this 'twin disaster', devastating hardship set in among the region's African population, leading to unknown levels of poverty, displacement, and increased migration. The Eastern Cape's pre-colonial social structure, mostly linked to agrarian and kinship ties, succumbed to the destructive nature of violence.

People's post-war survival depended on gaining access to capitalist monetary economies of which wage labour was often the only option. In other cases, people had to adhere to market demands, forcing them consider crops that can easily be converted into money (Crais 2011, p. 146). Instead of tending to their immediate nutritional needs, people grew corn for the market, and in this case an established network of traders. In many cases, people sold their eagre corn harvests to gain access to money, only to purchase their own corn back at a later stage at a much higher price. Engaging with the market in this manner subsequently entrenched people into deeper financial and social hardships. Bringing them to this particular point, however, was the violence associated with colonial conquest.

When industrialism overwhelmed the country toward the end of the nineteenth century, as Crais argues, the Eastern Cape was already deeply entrenched in systemic poverty and inequality. Capitalism merely exacerbated such poverty by limiting people's access to the means of production and forcing them further into a system of wage labour. Violence and conquest therefore had significant economic consequences, but, as Crais argues (2011, p. 64), one cannot reduce such violence to the logic of capitalist development: 'to do so is to read history backwards'.

Not surprisingly, Crais (2011) revisits Bundy's (1979) *Rise and Fall* thesis to identify a contradictory relation between the origins of the Eastern Cape's systematic poverty and Bundy's rise in prosperous peasants during the nineteenth century. By scrutinizing both archival documents and Bundy's analysis of a rising peasantry, Crais (2011) argues that Bundy's supposed groups of prosperous peasants of the nineteenth century were insignificantly small compared to the large amount of people suffering from systemic poverty. The rising peasantry manifested the growing cleavage of economic inequality, with a small percentage of black elite, predominantly Mfengu, participating in the market

10 For a seminal depiction and discussion of the Cattle Killings, see Jeffrey Peires' (1989).

economy. Contrarily, the rise in poverty inserted itself into the daily existence of the region's majority, forcing people to engage in the market with whatever means available to them. Yes, the African population did enter the market economy on their own accord, but such participation was not by their own choosing.

Conclusion

Twenty years after South Africa's first democratic elections, the rural Eastern Cape Province, in particular the former Transkei and Ciskei, still sees some of the country's highest levels of social inequality, unemployment, and poverty (Westerway, 2008; Crais, 2011). To a degree these realities reflect the apartheid regime's programme of segregation and separate development (King and Mccusker 2007, p. 6). But Mamdami (1996) also reminds us that much of Africa's contemporary problems are rooted in the continent's colonial heritage, in particular colonial rule's intrusion on pre-colonial political structures and social institutions. As far as the Eastern Cape is concerned, Crais (2002, 2011) draws a direct link between this region's systematic poverty and nineteenth-century colonial domination. It was especially the violent nature of this intrusion that took shape in the destruction of people's pre-colonial livelihood practices and people's increased denial of land and agricultural activities that laid the foundation for the region's ensuing poverty and social hardships. The current conditions of socio-economic hardship are reflections both of the region's period of colonial and apartheid rule. As social scientists and commentaries engaged in current agrarian questions, we can therefore not overlook the contributions of historic analyses.

But as I have illustrated in this chapter, the historic inquiries of the last four decades differ significantly in their theoretical approaches, essentially reflecting different facets of the region's colonial past. The radical neo-Marxian readings of Bundy, Beinart, Lewis, and Bradford interpret the region's history in terms of people's reactions to and involvement in the colonial capitalist market. In addition to articulating the African population's engagements with these markets via agricultural activities, the historiographic approach focuses on the consequences of capitalist expansion on local people's livelihoods, either by minimizing their access to land or marginalizing their participation in agrarian markets. In contrast to these neo-Marxian readings, the cultural interpretations that emerged during the 1990s turn our attention to social processes that look beyond a pure economic reading. This includes the ideologies that drove and justified colonial expansion, local people's interpretation of and reactions to colonial forces, and prominent discourses and cultural representations of social events. The radical neo-Marxian-inspired historiography of the 1970s and 1980s therefore made space for a more culturally inspired epoch that in many cases still remains the leading modus operandi (Crais, 2011). But how effectively does this approach relate to or reflect current agrarian questions?

Discussions at the 2014 conference *Reflections on South Africa's Agrarian Questions after 20 years of Democracy* were more geared toward agrarian issues that either exacerbate or address the country's persistent state of wealth inequality and poverty. Driving these discussions was the place of agriculture in addressing such inequality, people's limited access to land, women's marginal position with regard to agricultural activities, the debate between small-scale and commercial farming practices, and farmworkers' relationship to the means of production. Arguably these conversations share the same objectives as the radical historiographers of the 1970s and 1980s, and recent feminist interpretations. For example, there seems to be a rather striking resemblance between the struggles of rural women during the late 1920s, as articulated by Bradford and Beinart, and those of rural women, twenty years post-apartheid. This is especially in light of rural women's marginal position with regard to traditional authority and land access (Walker, 2013). But as Crais's (2011) research on the detrimental affects of systemic violence suggests, aspects that stand outside the realm of political economy should also be incorporated into our discussions. This is especially relevant when considering the violent ways people have lost access to land or been forced into the labour market. Even though historical inquiry into colonial discourse, representations, and the colonial mind might shed a more informed light on the region's colonial past, there is also a close relationship between a historical analysis of the region's economic activities, and current socio-economic and political predicaments.

References

Beinart, W. (1982). Political Economy in Pondoland, 1860–1930. Cambridge, New York: Cambridge University Press.

Beinart, W., & Bundy, C. (1987). *Hidden struggles in Rural South Africa: Politics and Popular Movements in the Transkei and Eastern Cape*. Berkeley: University of California Press.

Beinart, W. & Delius, P. (1986). Introduction. In W. Beinart, P. Delius, & S. Trapido (Eds.), *Putting a Plough to the Ground: Accumulation and Dispossession in Rural South Africa, 1850-1930* (p. 1–55). Johannesburg: Raven Press.

Bradford, H. (2000). Peasants, Historians, and Gender: A South African Case Study Revisited, 1850–1886. *History and Theory*, *39*(4), 86–110.

Bundy, C. (1979). *The Rise and Fall of the South African Peasantry*. London: Heinemann.

Bundy, C. (2006). New Nation, New History? Constructing the Past in Post-Apartheid South Africa. In Hans Erik Stolten (Ed.), *History Making and Present Day Politics: The Meaning of Collective Memory in South Africa* (p. 73–97). Uppsala, Norway: Nordiska Afrikainstitutet.

Cobley, A. (2001). Does Social History have a Future? The Ending of Apartheid and Recent Trends in South African Historiography. *Journal of Southern African Studies*, 27(3), 613–625.

Comaroff, J., & Comaroff J. (1991). *Christianity, Colonialism and Consciousness in South Africa, Volume 2: The Dialectics of Modernity on a South African Frontier*. Chicago: University of Chicago Press.

Cooper, F. (1981). Peasants, Capitalists, and Historians: A Review Article. *Journal of Southern African Studies*, 7(2), 284–314.

Crais, C.C. (1992a). *White Supremacy and Black resistance in pre-industrial South Africa: The making of the colonial order in the Eastern Cape, 1770–1865*. New York: Cambridge University Press.

Crais, C.C. (1992b). *White Supremacy and Black Resistance in Pre-Industrial South Africa: The making of the colonial order in the Eastern Cape, 1770–1865*. In Richard Price (2008), *Making Empire: Colonial Encounters and the Creation of Imperial Rule in Nineteenth-Century Africa*. New York: Cambridge University Press.

Crais, C.C. (2002). The Politics of Evil: Magic, State Power and the Political Imagination in South Africa. Cambridge: Cambridge University Press.

Crais, C.C. (2011). *Poverty, War, Violence in South Africa*. Cambridge, New York: Cambridge University Press.

Delius, P. (2008). Contested Terrain: Land Rights and Chiefly Power in Historic Perspective. In Aninka Claassens & Ben Cousins (Eds.), *Land Power and Custom: Controversies generated by South Africa's Communal Land Rights Act* (p. 211–237). Athens, Ohio: Ohio University Press.

Du Toit, A. (2010). The Owl of Minerva and the Ironic Fate of the Progressive Praxis of Radical Historiography in Post Apartheid South Africa. *History and Theory*, *49*, 266–280.

Eldredge, E.A. (2007). *Power in Colonial Africa. Conflict and Discourse in Lesotho, 1870–1960*. Madison: The University of Wisconsin Press.

Hamilton, C., Mbenga, B.K. & Ross, R. (2010). The Production of Preindustrial South African History. In C. Hamilton, B. K. Mbenga & R. Ross (Eds.), *The Cambridge History of South Africa*: Volume 1: From Early Times to 1885. (p. 1–62). Cambridge: Cambridge University Press.

Hopkins, A.G. (2009). The New Economic History of Africa. *Journal of African History, 50*, 155–177.

King, B.H., & Mccusker, B. (2007). Environment and Development in the Former South African Bantustans. *The Geographical Journal, 173*(1), 6–12.

Landau, P. (2010). *Popular Politics in the History of South Africa, 1400–1948*. New York: Cambridge University Press.

Legassick, M. (1980). The Frontier Tradition in South African Historiography. In Shula Marks & Anthony Atmore (Eds.), *Economy and Society in Pre-industrial South Africa* (p. 44–79). London: Longman Press.

Lester, A. (1997). The Margins of Order: Strategies of Segregation on the Eastern Cape Frontier. *Journal of Southern African Studies, 23*(4), 635–653.

Lester, A. (2001). *Imperial Networks: Creating Identities in Nineteenth Century South Africa and Britain*. London, New York: Routledge Press.

Lewis, J. (1984). The Rise and Fall of the South African Peasantry: A Critique and Reassessment. *Journal of Southern African Studies, 11*(1), 1–24.

Macmillan, H., & Marks, S. (Eds.). 1989. *Africa and Empire: W.M. Macmillan, Historian and Social Critic*. Aldershot: Institute of Commonwealth Studies.

Mamdami, M. (1996). *Citizen and Subject: Contemporary Africa and the Legacy of Late Colonialism*. Princeton: Princeton University Press.

Mamdami, M. (2005). Political Identity, Citizenship and Ethnicity in Post-Colonial Africa. Keynote Address at the Arusha Conference, New Frontiers of Social Policy, December 12–15. http://thinkingafrica.blogspot.com/2013/05/political-identity-citizenship-and.html. Accessed 15 March 2014.

Marks, S., & Atmore, A. (Eds.) (1980). *Economy and Society in Pre-Industrial South Africa*. London: Longman Press.

Mostert, N. (1992). *Frontiers: The Epic of South Africa's Creation and the Tragedy of the Xhosa People*. New York: Knopf, Random House.

Peires, J. (1982). *The House of Phalo: A History of the Xhosa People in the Days of Their Independence*. Berkeley: University of California Press.

Peires, J. (1989). *The Dead Will Arise. Nongqawuse and the Great Xhosa Cattle-Killing Movement of 1856–7*. Johannesburg: Raven Press.

Price, R. (2008). *Making Empire: Colonial Encounters and the Creation of Imperial Rule in Nineteenth-Century Africa*. Cambridge: Cambridge University Press.

Stolten, Hans Erik (Ed.) (2006). *History Making and Present Day Politics: The Meaning of Collective Memory in South Africa*. Uppsala, Norway: Nordiska Afrikainstitutet.

Switzer, L. (1993). *Power and Resistance in an African Society: The Ciskei Xhosa and making of South Africa*. Madison: University of Wisconsin Press.

Thompson, L.M. (2001). *History of South Africa*. New Haven: Yale University Press.

Visser, W. (2004). Trends in South African Historiography and the Present State of Historical Research. Paper presented at the Nordic African Institute, Uppsala, Sweden. 23 September.

Walker, C. (2013). *Uneasy Relations: Women, Gender Equality and Tradition*. Thesis Eleven, 115, 77–94.

Westerway, L. (2008). *Bare Life in the Bantustans of the Eastern Cape: Re-membering the Centennial South African Nation-State*. (Unpublished PhD Dissertation). East London: The University of Fort Hare.

Wilson, M. (1961[1936]). *Reaction to Conquest. Effects of Contact with Europeans on the Pondo of South Africa*. London: H. Milford Publishing.

Wilson, Monica, & Thompson, Leonard (Eds.) (1971[1969]). *The Oxford History of South Africa*, Volume 1. Oxford: Oxford University Press.

CHAPTER 4

South Africa's Dangerous Game: Re-configuring Power and Belonging on Karoo Trophy-hunting Farms

Femke Brandt

Introduction

This chapter contributes to debates about land reform and nature conservation in South Africa (Beinart, 1989; Connor, 2014; Nustad, 2011; Spierenburg & Brooks, 2014) by providing ethnographic insights on social relations on trophy-hunting farms in the Eastern Cape Karoo Midlands. In this region, the land question is extreme, meaning white farmers still own and farm the majority of the land. The majority of these farmers are converting their farms partly or completely to private game farming. Overt land struggles and land claims procedures are relatively non-existent due to the early and near-total land dispossession and the formation of a rural servile class in semi-arid areas (Mkhize 2012, p. 30). Land and wildlife owners in the Karoo claim a legitimate place and a sense of belonging for themselves under post-apartheid conditions through game farming and commercial hunting. The focus of this chapter is the experiences of farm workers and dwellers on these farms and their relations to the farmers. What do those relational dynamics mean for South Africa's democracy?

The answers to this question led me to interpret the increasing farm conversions to game farming as a metaphorically dangerous game. Farmers have anxieties about imposed transformation and potential land redistribution. Despite the introduction of land and labour reform, farm workers have very few options to negotiate and challenge the extremely imbalanced power relations on the farms. I analyse farm conversions to trophy-hunting as a configuration process driven by ongoing power battles between those who aim to regain power and those who constantly challenge it, overtly or disguised in institutional arrangements shaped over time (Elias, 1976). Sigaud (2006) provides a good example of how such a reconfiguration process could be described and understood. She studied the use of farm worker rights in Brazil in the context of changing social relations between farm workers, sugar cane plantation owners, unions, and the state in the 1960s. She studied people and

 | DOI 10.1163/9789004362550_005

their behaviours in relation to the history of their relations, and wider social contexts and conditions. Sigaud shows how domination and authority are part of personalized relations. This way she was able to understand why a plantation boss presents his compliance with workers' rights as a proof of kindness instead of submission to imposed legal frameworks and why workers likewise interpret the respect for their rights as the owner being a 'good man' instead of only driven by external coercion (2006). Likewise, Scott (1985) sees power relations as configured and resisted through everyday contestations over justice, morality, and manners. This chapter focuses on such everyday contestations through a detailed description of the relations between workers, farmers, and wildlife on Karoo trophy-hunting farms.

Firstly, the chapter sets out the context in which farm conversions take place generally and situates the ethnographic research specifically. It provides a background of farm relations in South Africa and several processes that reconfigure these relations under democratic government: privatization of wildlife ownership and land reform. The following section provides a detailed description of the ways in which power relations are experienced on the trophy-hunting farm by workers. Besides looking at workers' relations with the farmer, I consider how their interactions with wildlife and with me expose power dynamics on the farm. Section two focuses specifically on how workers' reflect on their experiences with wildlife on the farm. Their stories and experiences challenge farmers' self-proclaimed position as custodians of nature and wildlife. The section also reveals how risks are distributed very unevenly on the farm, which adds more substance to understanding the power configuration and notions of belonging on the farm. The third section illustrates how dominant hunting discourses have been presented historically and in the present. The experiences of two professional hunters in the hunting business illustrate how differences in access to land and wildlife shape players' position in this dangerous game. The final section is a discussion about the state of transformation in the context of game farming and state-led land reform.

The Setting: Farm Conversions to Wildlife in the Eastern Cape

Farm conversions have been enabled by privatized ownership of wildlife. The post-apartheid legal framework and constitution is closely aligned with the interests of landowners. This in itself seems a stark contradiction to South Africa's land-reform objectives as landownership patterns inherited from apartheid, where whites owned most agricultural land, are supposed to change in favour of black people. Just before the advent of South Africa's democracy in 1994, the Game Theft Act of 1991 effectively transferred property rights over wildlife from the state to private landowners (Snijders, 2014; Spierenburg & Brooks, 2014). The act consolidated a long process of privatizing ownership of, and access to, land and wildlife in the country. Wels' ethnography on the emergence of private wildlife conservation in Kwa-Zulu Natal (2015b) describes how wilderness landscapes have become places of normalised violence, excluding black people from access to land and natural resources, and how white men collaborating with state power justified the militaristic control of space. The economic position of landowners, mostly white as a legacy of colonial and apartheid state engineering, has been improved through adding financial value to animals and land, and means to maintain control over both as well (Snijders, 2015). Private property curtails and restricts access to wildlife and land, for people who do not own land like farm workers and dwellers who have been living and working on commercial farms under highly insecure tenure arrangements and harsh working conditions. Processes of farm consolidation and land concentration further dispossess black farm dwellers, who are gradually displaced from the farms and move to townships of the rural towns (Mkhize, 2012, 2014; Brandt, 2016; Brandt & Spierenburg, 2014). Mkhize (2014) articulates this as a slow erosion of farm workers' histories and presence as displacement continues gradually and silently. In light of this deepening of dispossession, there has been ongoing criticism towards the ANC's neoliberal policies that have worsened the situation for farm workers, especially tenure security, job security, housing, and livelihoods (Wesso, 2013).

In South Africa, the world of white commercial farmers and the relations with workers has been shaped by authoritarian paternalism (Du Toit, 1993). This means that white men on commercial farms are used to govern what they consider their turf according to their notions of wrong and right. These 'farm laws' have always been challenged by farm workers and dwellers (Connor 2014, p. 177) and since the 1990s the power balance is challenged in the law as well. Land-reform policies and labour regulations are therefore political and personal challenges in the world of the white commercial farmer who is anxious about maintaining his authority on the land. In response to these challenges, farmers have to find ways to re-assert their authority and legitimacy on the farm. By way of avoiding land claims, farmers have evicted farm workers and dwellers, and re-arranged their businesses as to place black people off the land. Helliker (2013, p. 92) suggests that conversions to private game farming could be read as an attempt by landowners to 'minimize the prospects of land redistribution'. Game farms have been hiking up land prices and require less labour than agricultural farms. Furthermore, their attraction for white and foreign buyers is that the game lodge has been recognised as a specific place of belonging where 'those who have lost power regain their sense of its possession' (Ndebele 1997, p. 99–101). Game farms are spaces with a 'colonial present' (Josefsson, 2014) where colonial relations and forms of belonging are cultivated in order to satisfy its producers and consumers.

The shift to game farming by private landowners is presented as necessary and beneficial for the rural economy where commercial farmers suffer from the decline of agricultural profits due to global competition (Van Zyl et al., 2001). Under neoliberalism, nature is increasingly commodified and 'protected' through its economic viability. Wildlife industry funded research (Langholz & Kerley, 2006) reports that conversions to game farms provide jobs and skills development and contribute to the upliftment of the rural poor. Game farming is perceived in the media as a viable economic option where 'big bucks'[1] are earned. The land use is associated with skyrocketing land prices per hectare, foreign investment, tourism, and (in hunting sector specifically) access to foreign capital, as wealthy hunting clients partner up with South African landowners in expanding farms or conservancies. Limited state regulation of the wildlife sector has enabled farmers to determine and influence wildlife policymaking, and build a multibillion rand wildlife industry (see Snijders, 2014; Kamuti, 2014) through which they continue to control natural resources in the country.

In the Eastern Cape Province, which is the focus area of this study, the trend to combine crop or livestock farming with wildlife is widespread among white commercial farmers. Statistics from 2007 indicated that about 90 per cent of the commercial farmers started to include wildlife in their farming businesses. About 7 per cent shifted completely to game farming (Snijders, 2014). Introducing wildlife species often happens gradually and includes the consolidation of farming units, the erection of high fences around the property, and the partial destruction of agricultural infrastructure such as low fences, sheds, houses, and roads. Depending on the kind of wildlife use – hunting, eco-tourism, breeding, or meat production – owners build tourist lodges, hiking trails, landing strips, and other facilities on the land to accommodate (international) clients. High fences are visibly enclosing more and more land for wildlife species attracting trophy hunters. The process of negotiating access to these farms and establishing relations with farmers, hunters, and workers generated many insights into the relations in these places.

This chapter builds on the research I did for my PHD thesis in 2009. The research was part of a bigger project comparing research in the Eastern Cape and

1 Source: http://mg.co.za/article/2012-01-06-big-bucks-for-game-ranchers.

KwaZulu-Natal[2] (see special issue Spierenburg & Brooks, 2014). During 2009, I lived one year in a Karoo town to do ethnographic fieldwork on trophy-hunting farms in the area. This part of the semi-arid Karoo Midlands is characterised by sheep, goat, and cattle farms where settler farmers have been living with few workers and their families on vast tracks of land. Along the Fish River, where water is available for irrigation, farmers produce lucern and maize. The dry and rocky landscape looks different from the greener and wetter parts of the Eastern Cape towards the coast where eco-tourism farms are more prominent. During my research, I initially negotiated access to the farms through the owners, who were mostly white men. Several farmers enabled me to participate in trophy hunts and regular farm activities, and one farmer allowed me to stay on the farm for ten days. I interviewed them and professional hunters about the histories of the farm, the farm conversions, and game management. We also talked about labour relations and land reform. Building relations with workers took a long time and required some distancing from the farmers, as these antagonistic worlds are difficult to navigate at the same time. With farm workers I participated in their farm work, went to church services, practiced isiXhosa, and paid visits to their families in the township. The research process and my position in the field were charged with suspicion, and the explicit and implicit question on whose side I was on, as a young white woman from the Netherlands (Brandt & Josefsson, 2017). During my position as post-doc at the Centre for African Studies, I have returned regularly to the region and continued doing research with farm workers.

Power Relations on Karoo Trophy-hunting Farms

This section focuses on the power relations between workers and farmers. Moreover, it includes workers' interaction with wildlife and understanding the power configuration on the farm. While I stayed on one of the trophy-hunting farms, my whereabouts during the day was mostly determined by the farmers' routines and schedule. Here, I call the farmer John and the farm Smith's Safaris. I promised all the respondents anonymity and so I use fictional names for the people and farms mentioned here. John is a descendant of the British 1820 settlers and came to farm in the Karoo Midlands area during the mid-1960s. He arrived as a young bachelor farmer with a flock of sheep and a group of workers. During the 1970s, John started diversifying his farming and introduced the first

2 NWO-WOTRO Research Programme 'Farm Dwellers the Forgotten People? Consequences of Conversions to Wildlife Production in the Provinces of KwaZulu-Natal and the Eastern Cape'.

game animals. Over a period of 20 years, John bought up neighbouring properties and fenced off more than 10,000 hectares of land for game farming. In the early 1990s, John sold the last sheep and goats and focused on trophy-hunting business only. In the process of conversion and extending the game farm, one of the properties has been sold to a foreigner.

During my stay on Smith Safaris I wandered around on my own at times, went out with workers, or stayed in John's office by the house. One day two women workers on the farm Nomsa and Nandi approached me with a question. Could I go with them to the temporary stone enclosure close to the farmers' house to have a look at the rhino that was kept there? The young animal was kept in a small enclosure, because it tried to escape the farm several times by trying to break through the fence. It was being disciplined. The previous morning I had observed him standing in a shady corner with bloodstains on his face from hitting the wall repeatedly with his head. The bounces had echoed through the night and woken me up. According to John the animal had to be 'broken' before being released again. Nomsa and Nandi wanted to see the rhino, but did not dare to go look on their own. Their movements were confined and defined by invisible boundaries that I could only see when I became part of crossing them. When I looked with the two women at the enclosed rhino, I wondered how they felt about the situation. Nomsa commented the animal looked so young still, and Nandi was too scared to look at it. Another worker approached me to go and see the rhino. Bulelwa said she felt she could not just do that without the farmers' approval. 'I am afraid of Sir',[3] she said, although she anticipated that, if she went with me, it would be ok. Being white and accommodated by the farmer made me an extension of his authority, and these privileges became leverage for the workers to navigate the farm space.

There were more instances where farm workers used my presence as a way to negotiate boundaries on the farm. They would ask me for small favours through which I was able to learn about their lives and strategies to negotiate the conditions on the farms. When I gave workers a lift somewhere, they would remark how they never got to sit in the passenger seat of white people's cars, because they are always expected to sit at the back. Or when I approached workers speaking the local African language isiXhosa, they would introduce themselves with their Xhosa names instead of the English names they were known by the farmer. Through such instances I learned how both the movements of workers and animals on the farm were tightly controlled by John and his rules. Those who challenge or cross boundaries are disciplined. The stories

3 Field notes, 14 August 2009.

I was told about the punishments ranged from losing favour with John to being dismissed or denied bonuses or other rewards.

Farm workers have a vested interest in maintaining their relationship to John as there is much at stake for them. This causes a lot of tension and 'jealousy' among the workers who were treated differently by farmer John and by white farm managers. Du Toit identified that 'paternalism creates a culture of back-biting and jealousy, pitting worker against worker in rivalry for the farmers' approval' (1993, p. 324). On Smith's Safaris workers occupy different sizes of workers' houses in the workers' compound, which resembles their personal relationship with the farmer. Maintaining the relationship with the farmer could result in arranging casual jobs on the farm for relatives. Workers like Nomsa approaching retirement not only lose their work but also their accommodation on the farm, and they face an insecure future in townships where they rely on relatives and the state for meeting basic needs and services. The seemingly inevitability of the move to town for farm workers was both associated with anxiety as well as the desire to establish a home away from the farms.

Joseph's story is an example of how his personal relationship with the farmer is important, yet rife with distrust. He was born as a son of farm workers during the 1960s and had moved around quite a bit during his life, including taking up jobs in the construction sector. When he started working at Smith's Safaris in 2001, he earned 450 rand a month. Almost ten years later he was earning 1800 rand a month, of which 75 rand was deducted for accommodation, water, and electricity. Despite the fact that it was higher than the minimum wage at the time, Joseph regarded it as a meagre salary. And the annual hunting tips distributed in December 2009 caused tension and stories of witchcraft amongst the workers, as John gave each worker different amounts based on his judgement as to how well they performed. Joseph expressed a lot of resentment about the fact that the young white manager earned more and had more privileges than him, just because he was white. In terms of knowledge and skills, he thought of himself as more advanced. Moreover, Joseph complained about the poor state of his accommodation on the farm. He said the farm accommodation was not a home, and he aspired to buying a house in the township, where he could live with his wife and kids.

More insights on the relationships between people on the farm can be generated by looking at relationships to the wildlife. Including non-human species into the analysis of social configurations reveals understandings on how humans see themselves and how they see other humans (Brooks, 2006; Swart, 2014; Wels, 2015a). In colonial society, for example, Europeans justified great power differences through the claim that they treated animals better.

A counter argument that has been given to this claim is that colonialism firstly caused animal suffering ranging from shooting wildlife to the point of extinction (Beinart, 1989) to the suffering of animals living with Africans who were forcibly removed and dispossessed of land (Swart 2014, p. 699). British legislation in the Colony banned animal cruelty in 1856, paradoxically the very same year as the notorious cattle killings, which was a call to destroy Xhosa society as a whole through a call to kill animals (Crais 1992, p. 100; Peires, 1981). The moral imperative of the British rulers behind disciplining those accused of animal cruelty, both in Britain and Africa, was to civilise subordinate classes who could potentially challenge the rulers. The aristocracy and landed elites, however, were not condemned for practicing blood sports. In the Eastern Cape, British settlers managed to reserve exclusive hunting privileges, mediated by the state, which issued permits exclusively for sports purposes. Hunting traditions of Africans (and Afrikaners) were categorized as primitive and unsporting (Gess, 2014). These nineteenth-century hunters shaped ideas and discourses around game preservation (Beinart 1989, p. 149). Moreover, landowners ever since have made instrumental use of the emergence of commercialised hunting to claim the right to own land.

The Risky Business of Working with Wildlife

Although white landowners have claimed custodianship and the moral high ground regarding preserving, and this includes utilizing, Africa's wildlife, it is black workers on game farms who mostly interact with them. On Smiths' Safaris, it is especially male farm workers like Joseph who interact directly with wildlife, and dangerous animals like buffalo and rhino, every day. The men feed the animals, track their movements and whereabouts, catch those who are sold and move them to the new owners' property, or capture sick animals that need treatment. Workers have to chase game if they encroach on the compound and interfere with activities such as gardening or fetching wood. On another trophy-hunting farm, workers' children share roads to school with the lions offered to trophy hunters. Trackers and skinners handle dead animals when they skin, slaughter, cut, drag, transport, or prepare animals for taxidermy. They take photos of clients with their trophies, and sometimes their pictures are taken and returned framed as appreciative gesture from hunting clients. Farm workers feed and monitor the game, which requires contact at a close distance, whereas the farmer observes and manages wildlife from a greater distance and usually from the safe surrounding of a big 4X4 vehicle.

On several occasions I went out with farm workers to feed the wildlife in the morning.[4] One morning I helped distribute the pallets and bales for the animals at one of the feeding places. We were in an open field that allowed a clear view of the wildlife. Once, I asked Joseph about the three rhinos that were curiously watching us offloading the bales. Wasn't he afraid of them? I certainly felt a slight discomfort being so exposed to these gigantic creatures at such close proximity. He responded that he knew how to behave in their presence: he keeps his distance, stays near the vehicle, and closely observes the animals' behaviour to see if they intent to charge. He parked the car in a way that the wind would not blow the feed and dust in our faces, and he prepared the bales. It turned out that it is crucial to remove the ropes holding the bales together. 'I have to remove them otherwise the animal dies and it is my fault', he mentioned. Then Joseph climbed into the back of the small white bakkie and asked me to slowly manoeuvre the vehicle alongside all the tractor tyres used as feeding bowls, which he then filled with pallets. The animals waited while observing us. When I asked Joseph about our safety he responded:

> *Joseph*: They know me and this vehicle. If they see a white face they know it means danger. For example if they see John they run, they won't get as close as with us now.
> *Femke*: But I have a white face as well.
> *Joseph*: But they smell you now and you came in this vehicle.

Joseph experiences that the animals know him and associate him with caring for them, as opposed to potentially killing them. He assumes animals have the ability to know humans' intentions and assess, through their sense of smell and vision, which humans are a threat. They decide to come close or flee if they feel they are in danger. Whether the animals distinguish their judgement of humans on the basis of racial categories ('if they see a white face') is questionable, but surely Joseph thinks so. And when I mentioned my own whiteness, he easily adjusted his explanation by stating I came in his vehicle, which is not perceived as threatening by the animals. In doing so, he makes a clear distinction between John and us; and he subverts the moral superiority based on the British colonial idea of civility and sportsmanship in hunting. The power disparity between himself and John was also clear in the example of Joseph's responsibility for the well-being of valuable game. Being held accountable for causing damage to animals or animal products like skins and horns is a big

4 Field notes, 12 & 17 August 2009.

risk, as farm worker wages are so much lower than the values of these wildlife 'products'.

The presence of wildlife makes farm workers on game farms potentially scared and vulnerable. Marvellous, a young Zimbabwean migrant worker[5] on another trophy-hunting farm in the area, said that as soon as he leaves the enclosed lodge where guests are received he feels unsafe: 'Once you are out of the gate, you are out in the wild'. He referred to his daily walk from the guest lodge to the staff residences outside the enclosed area, especially at night in the dark. The relations with the local South African resident farm workers were rife with tension and suspicion, and Marvellous mentioned they were fighting all the time. He left the farm after a month, as he was 'fed up' with the social and working conditions on the farm. Although the farmer had promised him and his friend and colleague Tendai proper accommodation and promised benefits, the experience was a big disappointment. They experienced an extremely violent incident on the farm among workers, and Tendai left knowing the farmer would never take responsibility for the incident. According to the workers, the risks of subjecting oneself to the violence and dangers on farm were not worth staying there.

For farmers, the coming and going of workers is a great source of stress and frustration. Leaving or staying away from farms remains a profound widespread resistance strategy (Scott, 1985) shaping black people's lives in the Karoo profoundly (Brandt, 2016; Mkhize, 2012). John would often mention he does not understand why the workers do not follow the rules or his instructions, not show up for work, or show up drunk after weekends, or simply do not return to the farm at all again. In his mind workers have no reason to be dissatisfied as he treats them well, by which he means he pays them salaries and does them favours. That is the way it has always been done. Besides having to deal with the unruly people on the farm, John also has to manage the unruly wildlife. Animals constantly escape the game farm and defy the spatial boundaries imposed on them. When that happens, farm workers are send out to capture the animal and bring it back. For farmers this is a costly undertaking, as fences have to be repaired and transport arranged; sometimes helicopters are used to trace and capture animals on neighbouring properties, where the animals could potentially damage crops or harm other animals or people. The language and the equipment employed in (re)capturing wildlife on farms is reminiscent of a militarised space or even a war zone, where daily activities involve tracking, escapes, capture, chase, death, killing, attacking, and defending. With

5 Interview, 24 July 2009.

farmers and hunters, I constantly drove around in 4X4 vehicles carrying rifles and binoculars, and adrenaline levels were up due to the potential dangers lurking around the corner.

For farm workers, tracking wildlife is a risky business. All the tracking I observed during trophy hunts and work in the field was done by black workers who were not carrying rifles. A casual labourer on Smiths' Safaris, Simon,[6] spoke with great resentment of farmer John who sat safely in his bakkie, while he and Joseph were chased by a buffalo.

> *F*: Can you remember an incident or do you have an example of a moment where you felt this was actually dangerous?
> *S*: Yeah, at the time when other buffalos, eh, went off the fence, you see, to the next farm, then they didn't use a chopper; they were using us to just chase these things away. But when I was working, I was with Joseph that day, you see; we started to chase this buffalo, but it turned to us and…
> *F*: stormed you?
> *S*: Yes, and we were very lucky because we were going to the old river, it is like an old river, you see, and you go there and it went. The bakkie that we use was standing there (far)! With John, you see, you can see how safe is he, sitting in the bakkie. We have to chase this buffalo, and this buffalo chase us. That day I felt that I can lose this job; I don't go (back to the farm). We were so lucky because the buffalo having four feet and we got two feet so we can't do anything; we were safe because of that river. If there was no river, we should maybe be dead.

The presence of dangerous game like buffalo in the environment brings the power relations on the farm into sharper focus. The animal is not accused of being aggressive by Simon, because it is defending its life. That behaviour is acceptable and justified. It is the behaviour of the farmer that is perceived as unjust. In Simon's account of the incident, it is clear that he knows John could have gotten out of the bakkie and done something as soon as the buffalo started chasing the workers. But he did not. And the fact that he did nothing and watched the workers being chased from the vehicle parked at a safe distance from the scene demonstrates how tense the relationships are.

In its extremist interpretation, the hierarchy on the farm determines who is in control of survival and death. In this situation, the risks for John were significantly less than the risks workers' faced in doing their work. Farmers' bodies

6 Interview, 10 January 2010.

and lives are protected through arms, vehicles, and insurance. Farmers, contrary to workers, have access to healthcare and comfortable homes to return to after having been out tracking and hunting wildlife. Workers and wild animals are at the mercy of farmers. Clearly, Simon felt that his life and his body were unnecessarily in danger due to the abusive relationship with the farmer. He left the farm and did not return.

Wildlife attacks on humans are not publicised often and rarely spoken about by farmers. I have witnessed wildlife charging humans and an attack when they felt trapped. I heard workers' stories like Simon's of tricky wildlife encounters with dangerous game. For farmers, bad publicity is to be avoided at all costs. The well-organized animal activists' lobby fighting for the rights of animals are a big concern for game farmers. Farmers and hunters would check with me whether I was not a 'greeny' or 'bunny hugger' secretly infiltrating in their circles and exposing their practices. Given the constant critique from this powerful lobby and uncertainties in the ANC's policy directions regarding the regulation of endangered species and hunting, game farmers are anxious about the future. During the research process I was phoned by a representative of Wildlife Ranching South Africa (WRSA)[7] who demanded to know who I was talking to and what I publish. For game farmers, there seems to be something at stake and so they attempted to control me, and the research process.

In 2015, I visited Joseph in his rdp house in the township. In the cupboard I observed prominently displayed mugs with images of the Big Five printed on them. He said they were a present from another worker on Smith's Safaris. Behind the mugs there was a print of trophy-hunting pictures showing Joseph with foreign clients and their trophies. He enthusiastically talked about the time the photos were taken. And then he got angry, stating that he had never received the rewards he deserves for selling his knowledge and labour. On the contrary, Joseph and his wife were dismissed together with another couple earlier in the year. Joseph was accused together with other workers of being drunk and not doing their work properly. Joseph holds it is not true. On the day of the accusation, the private labour consultant (see also Brandt & Ncapayi, 2016) operating for most employers in the area was called in and told the workers that, if they would not sign a settlement agreement, they would get no money upon their departure that evening. Joseph and his colleagues signed, received 9 days' worth of wages, and left Smith's Safaris.

7 Monday, 8 June 2009.

Game Farming in the Eastern Cape: Who Participates in the Wildlife Business?

Historically and presently game farming and hunting are presented in the dominant public discourses according to the perceptions and positions of the land and wildlife owners. During the nineteenth-century settlers started fencing property and enclosed land in the name of 'civilising' the landscape (Van Sittert, 2002). The fences assisted in controlling livestock and labour, which in a pastoralist system proved a big challenge to settlers. The Karoo, and Karoo black people, were 'tamed' and 'ordered' through commercial farming practices. Meanwhile, white farmers contributed to environmental degradation of the Karoo with their commercial farming activities (Hoffman, 2014). Game farmers are now undoing this history and its civilising discourse by pulling fences down, destroying infrastructure, and creating 'wilderness landscapes' (Brandt & Spierenburg, 2014). In doing so, Karoo game farmers perpetuate the idea and belief system that they know better than black people, and animals for that matter, how to use the land. In the world of the white commercial farmer, the Karoo environment would be lost without an authoritarian patriarch to control and manage it.

Since the nineteenth century, British sport hunters' ideas of preservation were dominant in the politics of colonial conservation and, from the start of the twentieth century, scientific and aesthetic motives became dominant in preservation discourses (Beinart 1989, p. 149–150). These ideas are still prevalent today as evidenced in the way this Karoo farmer talks about the 'correct' management of the Karoo.

> Yes, the landscape has improved. It does under correct management, when there is a well-educated landowner. It can also go the opposite way with game; they can be even more destructive than livestock, if you have some business guy from Jo'Burg who doesn't have the skills to manage the land. But game improves insect and bird life as well. I noticed that with sheep here, for example, you give them internal pesticides, which are then coming out through sheep dung, and when we had livestock here we had no dung beetles! When we re-introduced the game the dung beetles came back! So obviously there was something in the sheep dung.[8]

Historically there has always been great contestation between colonial rulers and African farmers as to how land should be settled and used (Beinart 1989,

8 Interview, 26 November 2009.

p. 158). Such discourses are still ongoing. John once pondered while we were sitting on a hilltop overlooking the farm: 'This land will never do for a subsistence farmer, he won't do it'.[9] Subsistence farming is associated with black farmers and their land uses. Game farmers present themselves as custodians of the Karoo environment, which defines their land use as superior and legitimate. Such a self-appropriated identity as nature conservationists has deep colonial roots (Carruthers, 2003; McDermott Hughes, 2010). In the post-apartheid era, game farmers easily adjusted their justification for game farming to current neoliberal discourses on poverty reduction, rural development, and economic growth. They do so with the firm conviction that white farmers (and not business men from Johannesburg) are the right men to take care and exploit of South Africa's natural resources.

Within the Eastern Cape's growing wildlife sector, hunting generates most of the income[10] through revenues from permits and lodging fees (Lindsey et al., 2006). The wildlife industry is visibly present in the landscape and its developments are regularly reported in local media. The newspapers and agrarian magazines like *Farmer's Weekly* and *Landbou Weekblad* continuously mention the growth of the wildlife industry in the country and the province. In July 2014, Arthur Rudman, previous chairperson of Wildlife Ranching South Africa,[11] was quoted in Landbou Weekblad saying that hunters have become the single crucial actors in nature conservation 'through the barrels of their rifles'.[12] A local newspaper announces at the start of the 2014 hunting season, on the front page,[13] in Afrikaans, that game farms in the region are again receiving record numbers of hunting visitors attracted by the wildlife. The wildlife industry is reported to grow 30% per year, developing the Karoo into a tourist paradise. Experts claim that hunters are especially attracted by the hunting packages and the hospitality offered by the Karoo farmers that are turning the region into a 'mecca' for tourism and hunting.

Here is an example of how local media regularly reports, in Afrikaans and English, on the profitability of the wildlife industry.

---

9 19 August 2009.

10 The game meat industry seems to be the currently important growth sector within the wildlife industry.

11 WRSA was established in 2005, merging existing provincial bodies representing game farmers. It represents 1500 members of 9000 registered game ranches. Source: wrsa.co.za.

12 Translated from Afrikaans by author: '*deur die loop van hulle gewere het jagters onregstreeks die belangrikste enkele factor tot bewaring geword*'.

13 Midland Nuus, 27 June 2014.

> *Game on at Wildsfees as records fall*
> NEW national and provincial record prices for game were set at the annual Absa Kirkwood Wildsfees auction which kicked off the festival in the town yesterday.
> …A provincial record of R975.000 was paid for a two to four-year old buffalo cow from the Addo Elephant National Park. This was shortly after a record of R650.000 was set for a cow aged between eight and 10 years. The 30 disease-free Addo buffalo on auction raised close to R9-million.
> *John Adendorff*, acting manager of the Addo Elephant National Park, said park officials were pleased with the prices realised at the auction. The funds raised will be invested back into conservation.
> A National record of R7.8-million was set for a rare ram called 'Top Deck', which was sold to Gamevest, based in the Northern Province town of Thamabazimbi. The ram's brother, Mnumzane, sold for R4.2-million at an auction in Limpopo in May.
> Another record was R400.000 for a yellow blesbok ram. The auction of 140 lots of prime game realised R26.5-million, by far the biggest total ever for the 13-year old auction according to convener Johan Swart.
> In 2013 the auction raised R9.5-million (Weekend Post, 28 June 2014).

The market for game is presented as thriving, as private landowners and the state (National Parks) trade wildlife species for thousands and sometimes millions of rands per animal. It has been argued, in line with Harvey's work on accumulation by dispossession, that private game farms have created a new landscape for capital accumulation (Mkhize, 2012).

Participating in this landscape depends on access to land and wildlife. The following life and career trajectories of two professional hunters illustrate how their differences shaped their experiences and participation in the sector. Land and wildlife prices have become so high that it is hard to enter the industry without capital. The career trajectories of Johan and Luvuyo illustrate how access to capital and importantly social networks define boundaries and ways in which participation is possible. For Johan, born in the 1980s,[14] as a son of a local sheep farmer, the wildlife industry presents a strategy to secure wealth without owning land. His older brothers inherit family farms, and he will inherit livestock and money. His plan is to invest this in his career as a professional hunter and invest in wildlife. In 2014[15] he bought, with help from his employer, his first dangerous game animal, a pregnant buffalo cow.

14 Interview, 6 January 2010.

15 Field notes, 24 April 2014.

Such an investment is hard to pursue for black farm workers in the Karoo who did not have generations of privilege to acquire wealth through landownership. Luvuyo[16] is a black professional hunter I met in the Karoo. He was born on a farm and worked there until one day the farmer asked him if he wanted to pursue a career as a professional hunter, working for him. Although Luvuyo was quite aware that he would be an exceptional figure in the scene dominated by white South African men, he eagerly took the opportunity and he has been working as a PH ever since. Contrary to Johan he does not have similar access to land or capital to invest in wildlife and become an independent farmer or hunting outfitter (guiding hunting clients as independent business) in the long run. His employer, Steward, said in an interview:[17]

> They are now starting a PH school for illiterate people. It is X who does that with government funding. But you don't need to be literate to be a PH; it is the outfitter anyway who does the forms and the permits.

It was clear the farmer does not envision Luvuyo, who is not illiterate, as having his own outfitter business one day. He assumes Luvuyo will always work for him, maintaining the lifelong imbalanced interdependency between them. Luvuyo suggested that it would be hard to build his own network in the white-dominated hunting scene, as already other PHs and game farmers react surprised when they meet him. When he appeared at the gun collection point at the airport, other PHs looked at him suspiciously. One man once asked him what he was doing there. When he said he was fetching a client because he was his PH, the men could not believe it. They probed who he was working for.[18] In the men's minds Luvuyo's position only became legitimate when tied to a white farmer who is his boss.

But Luvuyo imagines himself on his own farm one day, and he is teaching his children about farming; he wants to farm with boerebok, dorper sheep, and Nguni cattle. He also mentioned that he would like to have some game animals on his farm. The species of domesticated animals he prefers are typically not the species associated white farmers, namely angora goats and merino sheep, which he calls 'sickly'. I think he meant they do not belong in the area, not with Xhosa men. He tried to access land through the land-reform programme, and so far has not been successful. Initially, he went to the Land Bank where they told him that he needed to apply for a farm with a group, which he refused

16 Interview, 4 January 2010, in Afrikaans.

17 26 November 2009.

18 Field notes, 5 February 2011.

because he wants his own farm. The second time he applied within a specific reform project, with an endorsement letter from Steward; he never received a reply.

Discussion: Game Farms and Transformation?

Conversions to game farming reconfigure social relations between workers, farmers, and the state. Farm workers' realities in the Karoo expose often harsh and violent outcomes of 20 years into post-apartheid society. Land and natural resources are increasingly concentrated in fewer hands, and wildlife encounters bring existing power disparities and mobility (or displacement) patterns on the farms into sharper focus. Although white farmers continue to present themselves as custodians of wildlife, farm workers subvert this claim by questioning farmers' authority and moral conduct in relation to wildlife as well as workers. The world of the white farmer is made of a deeply held conviction that the Karoo cannot do without a white patriarch ruling the land. Black workers in the Karoo navigate the personalized relations with farmers that allow them to generate income and negotiate privileges. However, the relations and interdependencies negotiated on farms are rife with tension, distrust, suspicion, and resentment. The trophy-hunting farm arranges space and movements of people and animals in alarming ways; the distribution of risks is uneven and undemocratic. The imbalanced power relations, and the constant challenges to them, continue to result in farm workers leaving farms (protest by walking out), farm workers being dismissed by private labour consultants and a severe lack of access to justice (see also Brandt & Ncapayi, 2016).

The relations between game farmers and the state are ambivalent. Land-reform discourses generate anxieties and resistance from landowners who are better positioned to protect their interests. Game farmers minimize the presence of black farm workers on farms and break down interdependencies to the bare minimum. On the other hand, the ANC government accepts the claim that game farming contributes to rural development and nature conservation, which enables the game farming lobby to ensure that game farms are unlikely candidates for land-reform purposes. Furthermore, the ethnographic evidence reveals how participation in the trophy-hunting industry depends on access to capital and social networks dominated by white landowners, who are the drivers and main beneficiaries of this industry. Race matters a great deal in the Karoo, which reveals the deep ideological consistencies in ideas of land tenure and property rights carried over from the past (Ramutsindela, 2012). If someone as experienced and knowledgeable as Luvuyo, who is actively seeking land, has not managed to access land or benefit from the state's land reform policies, how will state-led land reform make it work for the majority of South Africans in need of access to land and natural resources? What kind of state could enforce the kind of disruptive reform that would be necessary to topple the balance of power in the Karoo? The reconfiguration of personalized relations on farms and the injustices articulated by workers, sometimes through their relations with wildlife, constitute the dangerous game played in the context of land reform and nature conservation in South Africa.

References

Beinart, W. (1989). Introduction: The Politics of Colonial Conservation. *Journal of Southern African Studies, 15*(2).

Brandt, F. (2016). Power battles on South African trophy-hunting farms: farm workers, resistance and mobility in the Karoo. *Journal of Contemporary African Studies, 34*(1), 161–185.

Brandt, F, & Josefsson, J. (2017). Sexuality and power on South-African game farms; reflections on positionality and emotions in ethnographic research. *Emotion, space and society, 23*, 26–32.

Brandt, F., & Ncapayi, F. (2016). The meaning of compliance with land and labour legislation: understanding justice through farm workers' experiences in the Eastern Cape. *Anthropology Southern Africa, 39*(3), 215–231.

Brandt, F., & Spierenburg, M. (2014). Game fences in the Karoo: reconfiguring spatial and social relations. *Journal of Contemporary African Studies, 32*(2), 220–237.

Brooks, S. (2006). Human Discourses, Animal Geographies: Imagining Umfolozi's White Rhinos. *Current Writing, 18*(1), 6–27.

Carruthers, J. (2003). Past & Future Landscape Ideology: The Kalahari Gemsbok National Park. In W. Beinart & J. McGregor (Eds.), *Social History & African Environments* (255–266). Oxford: James Curry.

Connor, T. (2014). *Conserved Spaces, Ancestral Places: conservation, history and identity among farm labourers in the Sundays River Valley, South Africa.* Pietermaritzburg: UKZN Press.

Crais, C. (1992). *White Supremacy and Black Resistance in Pre-Industrial South Africa: The Making of the Colonial Order in the Eastern Cape, 1770–1865*. Cambridge: Cambridge University Press.

Du Toit, A. (1993). The Micro-Politics of Paternalism: The Discourse of Management and resistance on South African Fruit and Wine Farms. *Journal of Southern African Studies* 19(2), 314–336.

Elias, N. (1976). Towards a Theory of Established-Outsider Relations. In *The Established and the Outsiders: The Collected Works of Norbert Elias* Vol. 4. (p. 1–38) by C. Wouters (Ed.). Dublin: University College Dublin Press.

Helliker, K. (2013). Reproducing White Commercial Agriculture. In *The Promise of Land: Undoing a century of dispossession in South Africa.* (p. 76–102) by F. Hendricks, L. Ntsebeza, and K. Helliker. (Eds.) Johannesburg: Jacana.

Gess, D. (2014). *Hunting and Power: Class, Race and Privilege in the Eastern Cape and Transvaal Lowveld, c. 1880–1905.* ma Thesis Stellenbosch University.

Hoffman, M.T. (2014). Changing patterns of rural land use and land cover in South Africa and their implications for land reform. *Journal of Southern African Studies, 40*(4), 707–725.

Josefsson, J. (2014). Safe-guarding the Colonial Present: Game Farms on the Frontier in KwaZulu-Natal's 'Battlefields' Route. *Journal of Contemporary African Studies, 32*(2), 258–274. doi: 10.1080/02589001.2014.925302.

Kamuti, T. (2014). The fractured state in the governance of private game farming: the case of Kwa-Zulu Natal Province, South Africa. *Journal of Contemporary African Studies, 32*(2), 190–206.

Langholz, J.A., & Kerley, G.I.H. (2006). *Combining conservation and development on private lands: an assessment of ecotourism-based private game reserves in the Eastern Cape* (56). Port Elizabeth: Centre for African Conservation Ecology Nelson Mandela Metropolitan University and Wilderness Foundation South Africa.

Lindsey, P.A., Alexander, R., Frank, L.G., Mathieson, A., & Romanach, S. (2006). Potential of trophy hunting to create incentives for wildlife conservation in Africa where alternative wildlife-based land uses may not be viable. *Animal Conservation, 9*, 283–291.

McDermott Hughes, D. (2010). *Whiteness in Zimbabwe: Race, Landscape and the Problem of Belonging.* New York: Palgrave Macmillan.

Mkhize, N. (2012). *Private game farms and the tenure security of farm workers and dwellers in Cradock: implications for tenure reform in South Africa.* PhD Thesis, University of Cape Town.

Mkhize, N. (2014). Game farm conversions and the land question: unpacking present contradictions and historical continuities in farm dwellers' tenure insecurity in Cradock. *Journal of Contemporary African Studies, 32*(2).

Ndebele, N. (1997). Game Lodges and leisure Colonialists. In H. Judin & I. Vladislavic (Eds.), *Blank: Architecture, apartheid and after.* Rotterdam: NAi Publishers.

Nustad, K.G. (2011). Performing Natures and Land in the iSimangaliso Wetland Park, South Africa. *Ethnos, 76*(1), 88–108.

Peires, J. (1981). *The House of Phalo: A History of the Xhosa in the Days of their Independence.* Berkeley: University of California Press.

Ramutsindela, M. (2012). Property rights, land tenure and the racial discourses. *GeoJournal, 77*, 753–763.

Scott, J.C. (1985). *Weapons of the Weak: Everyday forms of Resistance.* New Haven: Yale University Press.

Sigaud, L. (2006). Traps of honour and forgiveness: the social uses of law in the Pernambuco forest region. *Mana, 1*.

Snijders, D. (2014). Wildlife policy matters: inclusion and exclusion by means of organizational and discursive boundaries. *Journal of Contemporary African Studies, 32*(2), 173–189.

Snijders, D. (2015). *Shifting Species in South Africa: Wildlife policy, Rural Consequences*. (Unpublished PhD Thesis). VU University Amsterdam.

Spierenburg, M., & Brooks, S. (2014). Private game farming and its social consequences in post-apartheid South Africa: contestations over wildlife, property and agrarian futures. *Journal of Contemporary African Studies, 32*(2), 151–172.

Swart, S. (2014). 'It is as bad to be a black man's animal as it is to be a black man': The politics of species in Sol Plaatje's Native Life in South Africa. *Journal of Southern African Studies, 40*(4), 689–705.

Van Sittert, L. (2002). Holding the Line: The Rural Enclosure Movement in the Cape Colony, c. 1865–1910. *Journal of African History, 43*, 95–118.

Van Zyl, J., Vink, N., Kirsten, J., & Poonyth, D. (2001). South African Agriculture in Transition: the 1990s. *Journal of International Development, 13*, 725–739.

Wels, H. (2015a). 'Animals like us': revisiting organizational ethnography and research. *Journal of Organizational Ethnography, 4*(3).

Wels, H. (2015b). *Securing Wilderness Landscapes in South Africa: Nick Steele, Private wildlife Conservancies and Saving Rhinos*. Leiden: Brill.

Wesso, R. (2013). *The farm workers strike and the politics of neo-liberalism*. Surplus People Project Report.

CHAPTER 5

Gendered Nationhood and the Land Question in South Africa 20 Years after Democracy

Kezia Batisai

The Gender/Land Battle in South Africa

Several scholars who profile the discourse of land reform in South Africa (Cousins, Du Toit, et al., 2013; Greenberg, 2013; Hall, 2010; Kahn, 2007; Ntsebeza, 2006; Rugege, 2004; Walker, 2003, 2002) take into account the racial tensions that have dominated the politics of settled/unsettled land in the epoch-making colonial and apartheid eras. It is against this backdrop that the land battle has been and continues to be fought in post-apartheid South Africa such that when answering the land question in the country today, one cannot afford to ignore these racial injustices. Although land-reform efforts often place emphasis on these racial divisions, and the subsequent need to redress past racial injustices, longstanding scholarship suggests that questions about gender have equally been central to colonial and post-colonial contestation over land, and to the process of building flag-democracies[1] in Africa. Such scholarship includes the works of Foucault (1978, 1990), Yuval-Davis and Anthias (1989), McClintock (1995), Alexander (1994), Yuval-Davis (1997), and Stoler (2002). Drawing on McClintock (1991) and Peterson (2000, p. 64) reveals how white women in apartheid South Africa, for instance, 'were exhorted to bear babies for Botha'. In order to fulfil their patriotic duty of giving birth to future inhabitants (Yuval-Davis 2006, p. 209), South African [white] women had to embrace their procreative role to ensure the future of the white nation. As a result, nationhood in apartheid South Africa was gendered simply because women negotiated their connection to land and/or the nation through liaisons with men (McClintock 1991, p. 112).

Approximately a year on the road to democracy, McClintock (1995, p. 386) predicted that gender issues would serve as a discursive weapon for reconfiguring post-apartheid South Africa. In the process of building post-apartheid South Africa, the state – through legislations and policy reforms – undeniably

1 A phrase that marks the era of decolonisation and nation building after the struggle for liberation in Africa.

 | DOI 10.1163/9789004362550_006

locates women in a hierarchal power structure, which often undermines their sense of ownership and belonging (Batisai, 2015, 2016). On that note, it is worth mentioning that South Africa in this chapter is framed as a nation, not in its capacity as a policy formulating unit (Ranchod-Nilsson & Tétreault 2000, p. 11) but as a piece of land on which fights for ownership and belonging to the nation are engaged. Similar to Beall, Geld, and Hassim (2005, p. 681) who adopt 'a "state-in-society" approach' as they unpack the interplay between the state and social groups in the context of transition to democracy in South Africa, this chapter also explores the politics of gender, land, and the process of nation building after 1994 – the year that marked the end of apartheid and the beginning of democracy. Thus, questions of gender and land are not only theoretical lenses through which one exposes the relationship between citizens and the state but they are intrinsic to understanding the idea of the 'nation' and the process of building a post-apartheid South Africa.

Emerging out of the intersectional observation that 'the land question in South Africa [...] does not only concern race, but also gender disparities' (Madletyana 2011, p. 14) is a gender gap in scholarship on land reform which is central to this chapter. It is however imperative to highlight to the reader that, although work has been done to try and address the gender gap, the silences observed in scholarship create a platform for scholars, who take seriously the politics of gender and land in South Africa, to illuminate how gender discourses often fall through the cracks. Thus, the intersection of race and gender, alluded to above, leads this chapter to gender and land questions that have been engaged and analysed by different scholars in South Africa post-1994. Such scholarship includes the work of Agarwal (2003, p. 185) who, for instance, points to the 'resurgence of interest in land reform and the agrarian question among both academics and policymakers' but acknowledges that 'the question of land rights for women' has been peripheral in scholarship on land and agrarian questions. In incidents where scholars engage the gender/land debate in South Africa, they further illuminate the gender gap in land-reform policy and discourse.

In her review of the land-reform process in South Africa, Walker (2002) reveals the shortcomings of the land-reform programmes that took place when the country became a democracy. She notes that the land-reform programmes of 1993/1994 and 2000 had not benefited poor women located in rural South Africa. She further reveals the bias of the 1999 policy reform towards a black commercial farming class (Walker 2002, p. iii; see also Moyo, 2008). The place of women in the land discourse is somewhat worrisome given that land is framed as 'a major avenue through which patriarchal power is exercised and maintained…' (Walker 2002, p. 5). The patriarchal nature of society often makes women access land through their fathers or husbands, as daughters and wives respectively, regardless of the fact that women are the ones who work on the land (Agarwal 2003, p. 190; Walker 2002, p. 28).

The analysis above points to the need for land policy reform aimed at reversing the patriarchal customary law, which somewhat restricts landownership rights to men (Rugege 2004, p. 17). Several scholars (Moyo, 2013; Tsikata, 2009; Claassens & Mnisi, 2009; Mbilinyi & Sechambo, 2009) reiterate that policy reform should endeavour to make the rights and realities of women visible vis-à-vis land and agrarian debates in Africa. If these gender disparities are taken seriously, then reform programmes will go beyond the black/white binary to ensure that South Africa adopts a comprehensive approach to questions of land, race, and gender. Such an approach in this chapter shifts focus from predominantly racialized agrarian and land discourses towards debates that encompass intersecting factors core to the land realities of South African women.

It is therefore imperative for one to further probe the place of women in the gender/land debate in South Africa 20 years after democracy, as well as the politics of belonging to the 20-year-old democracy. The question then is 'what shape should land reform in South Africa take in order to adequately address the needs of rural and urban-based women of this democracy?' In view of the question above and the argument that 'the land question was one of the driving forces of the liberation struggle' (Walker 2003, p. 1), I pose a seemingly simple question: 'What is the meaning of democracy in South Africa if women who also fought for this democracy are somewhat invisible from debates on the land question?' Before turning to empirical findings from South Africa's East Rand that respond to the preceding question, it is important to first present the methodological standpoints core to analyses and conclusions arrived at in this chapter.

Methodological Underpinnings

Building on my PhD work that explored elderly women's narratives of gender, nationhood, and the politics of belonging to colonial and post-colonial African countries (Batisai, 2013), I have been engaging in research aimed at gathering data on how citizens often negotiate 'the right to belong' to their motherland in very gendered, classed, raced, and political ways (Batisai, 2014, 2015, 2016). It is within this framework that I located a paper that I developed and presented at an international workshop hosted by the University of Cape Town's Centre for African Studies in 2014,[2] which reflected on agrarian questions 20 years after the advent of democracy in South Africa. The workshop created a platform for young career scholars to grapple with the ongoing debates on the meanings of land debates, which for me became a tool for unpacking questions of nationhood and the politics of belonging to the post-apartheid nation. Subsequent to the international workshop, I felt the need to gather more empirical data to broaden my initial discussion on the gender/land battle, but this time explicitly linking it to the process of building post-apartheid South Africa.

Consequently, I embarked on a fieldwork journey from mid-August 2014 to early October of the same year in Ekurhuleni, a local metropolitan municipality of the Greater Johannesburg Metropolitan Area, South Africa. Over and above easy access in terms of distance, both from home and work, I purposively selected Ekurhuleni as a research site because of the fights for settled and unsettled land, which often manifest as housing and service delivery protests in spaces like Daveyton and Benoni.[3] The urban housing protests, and the fact that it is women who are protesting, are often overlooked in agrarian scholarship such that there is enough reason to study these elderly women when reflecting on South Africa's land and agrarian questions. Overall, these housing protests illuminate how the need to redress historical raced, gendered, and classed injustices – mainly those around the notion of dispossession and forced removals – has been and continues to be at the core of contestations over land in South Africa (see Walker, 2003, 2004). The urban land protests in Ekurhuleni somewhat demonstrate the politics of land beyond agrarian questions and simultaneously suggest the shape land reform in South Africa should take. In other words, the biggest contribution of analysing urban land questions is the observation that land issues are not only rural and about livelihoods. Rather, they also encompass notions of nationhood and the politics of belonging evident in elderly women's narratives on the need for residential or housing land in urbanised spaces.

Data was collected through one-on-one in-depth interviews with ten South African women aged between 65 and 70 years of age, old enough to have witnessed the shifting socio-political and economic landscapes of South Africa. Given my positionalities (a foreign national who cannot speak any of the eleven

---

2 From the 14th to the 15th of August 2014.

3 See: http://www.sabc.co.za/news/a/d3850e00452886d9b38eb3a5ad025b24/Ekurhuleni-municipality-concerned-by-Daveyton-service-delivery-protest; http://www.news24.com/SouthAfrica/News/Ekurhuleni-to-tackle-service-delivery-20121017; http://benonicitytimes.co.za/187311/gungubele-asks-for-calm-as-daveyton-residents-rage-on-with-their-demands-for-land/.

official South African languages), in-depth interviews were conducted in isiZulu and Sepedi, transcribed and translated into English with the help of Mpho and Naledi – university students who live in Ekurhuleni Metropolitan. Inability to speak isiZulu and Sepedi exposed my foreign nationality because the elderly women wanted to know why a researcher, who was interested in their lived realities and the land question in South Africa, spoke to them through translators. It is imperative to note that I did not intent to hide my foreign nationality, but I thought that my identity as a researcher from a local university would suffice, rendering my Zimbabwean identity irrelevant. However, my pre-fieldwork assumption was wrong. Upon realising that I was Zimbabwean, the elderly women made remarks and posed questions that initiated and allowed conversations with them. Although I did not have immediate answers to some of their questions (captured below), my national identity emerged as a powerful tool for negotiating entrée and gaining trust throughout fieldwork in Ekurhuleni.

> Oh you are from Mugabeland… you are welcome to talk to me my daughter… Who knows… maybe you have solutions that South Africa does not have for us… yes lessons from Zimbabwe… Are you going to help us get land here in South Africa?

Beyond the introductions, Mpho and Naledi negotiated issues of entrée through their personal contacts, with whom they established rapport and generated a relatively small sample to allow one-on-one fieldwork engagement and subsequent in-depth data analysis. The ten elderly women were selected through snowballing – a sampling procedure where a few members of the target group are identified and interviewed and thereafter refer the researcher to potential interviewees from their sphere of influence. When fieldwork commenced, we met at Mpho's house, from where we set-off as a research team throughout the entire journey. Capturing the elderly women's lived realities meant that in-depth interviews had to be conducted at interviewees' homes where Mpho and Naledi had to cope with different disruptive sounds from family members as well as noises from the neighbourhood. Mpho and Naledi also set up appointment schedules with each woman ahead of the fieldwork visit to try and minimise disrupting their daily errands. In the same light, each interview lasted for about an hour, and we also made several follow-up interviews to clarify issues that emerged during our 'research team briefing sessions' and those that also surfaced after transcribing and translating the narratives. Although these sessions somewhat helped me to check the quality of the data as the principal researcher, I felt the impact of working across languages and the risk of losing data inherent in the translation process. These insecurities largely stemmed from the reality that I had to rely on translations (from isiZulu and Sepedi to English) because verbatim data was in languages foreign to me.

However, my inability to speak isiZulu and Sepedi did not deter me from being part of the research process. Though I could not make sense of isiZulu and Sepedi narratives, I sat and followed the interview processes taking note of non-verbal cues, which on several occasions conveyed frustration and despair. I inferred that these emotions stemmed from the politics of land in South Africa – observations which I confirmed with Mpho and Naledi after each interview session. Taking the language issue as an opportunity to navigate the research contours in between interviews, I managed to subtly engage with the community through personal observation. Observing the research site – the shacks people live in and the water and sanitation challenges they confront on a daily basis – revealed to me the complexities of everyday life for these women and ordinary citizens. Drawing from these observations, this chapter argues that the elderly women's immediate non-agrarian land needs and demands, particularly aimed at addressing the housing problem, should be equally central to the gender and agrarian issues in post-apartheid South Africa.

At this stage, it is important to note that, although elderly women's narratives reveal how complex their everyday realities are, I am particularly interested in their responses to specific questions. These questions include: 'What comes to mind when women are asked about the land question in South Africa? How do women identify with the land – South Africa – as a democratic space? What is women's relationship to the 20-year-old democracy, and how is this negotiated?' Consequently, interview excerpts presented and analysed in subsequent pages of this chapter are profound because of the way they use intersecting subjective experiences to construct meaning around the land question, notions of belonging and democracy in South Africa. Central to Daveyton and Benoni women's narratives below is the way they read the new democracy in relation to historical and contemporary (residential) land needs in the city.

Irrespective of the fact that empirical findings presented in this chapter were only drawn from Ekurhuleni, far reaching conclusions can still be drawn, because some of the questions on gender, land and the state raised here are shared across the Greater Johannesburg Metropolitan Area and South Africa at large. Protests across the country (from Du Noon, Diepsloot, Dinokana, Khayelitsha, KwaZakhele, Masiphumelele, Lindelani, Piet Retief to Samora Machel) not only bear testimony to the preceding claim but they also confirm the volatile relationship between citizens and the state.

Having discussed the methodological underpinnings, focus now shifts towards the stories of the ten elderly women from Ekurhuleni. The narratives in the following pages capture the lived realities of these elderly South African women and how they use such realities to assign meaning to the land question. The narratives also profile how these elderly women simultaneously make sense of the 20 years of democracy vis-à-vis the ongoing land debates in the country. Broadly, the discussion reveals that the elderly women read the land question and identify with the land – South Africa – in very politicised, gendered, raced, and classed ways. It is these intertwined complexities of gender, race, and class that make the case for an intersectional analysis of the urban land narratives of elderly women who live on the East Rand.

Reading the Land Question and 20 Years of Democracy

Writing from a feminist perspective, I adopt an intersectional approach in my analysis of the elderly women's narratives. The intersectional approach allows me to concurrently engage with issues of race and gender previously constructed in scholarship that addresses the land question as separate entities (see Madletyana 2011, p. 40). Thus, through the intersectional approach, I take note of the historical, socio-economic, and political contexts that are predominantly racial without undermining the gender debate (see Walker, 2009) and class issues central to the land question in South Africa. The approach, as demonstrated below, allows the analytic sections of this chapter to adequately engage with multiple intersecting factors (gender, class, race, and temporal and geographical landscape, for instance) believed by the interviewees to have impeded equitable access to land and simultaneously undermined their sense of belonging to South Africa 20 years after democracy.

Narratives that emerged out of the in-depth interviews conducted in Daveyton and Benoni, Ekurhuleni Metropolitan, reveal that all the ten elderly women migrated to Johannesburg at the dawn of democracy from different urban parts of the country, predominantly rural provinces like the Eastern Cape, KwaZulu Natal, and Mpumalanga. The underlying factor that attracted these women to Johannesburg confirms constructions of the city as an economic hub that offers solutions to everyday challenges for many South Africans, and increasingly the rest of Africa (Batisai 2016, p. 121). However, rural-urban migrants' lived experiences in the city prove otherwise. The ten elderly women share similar socio-economic backgrounds characterised by serious housing challenges and heavy reliance on government support through social grants. As heads of households, most of the elderly women are domestic workers who take care of grandchildren whose parents are either deceased or cannot support their children. Despite the persisting challenges, elderly women's narratives illuminate how they often exercise agency capitalising on 'opportunities' subtly presented by very complex socio-political and economic terrains, and make a living out of such structures.

Corresponding to women's stories of urban survival and agency in apartheid (Slater, 2000) and post-apartheid South Africa (Sisulu, 2006), one of the ten respondents, Landi, arrived in Johannesburg in 1994 at the age of 49 from Cape Town where she had lived and served as a domestic worker for the greater part of her life. Her story is that of endurance as evidenced by how she negotiated and survived restrictive boundaries of the apartheid system with no decent income and place to call home in the city of Cape Town. She then moved to Johannesburg in 1994 with her family with the hope of changing her situation in the new democracy, but upon arriving, reality kicked in. She realised that with no education she was bound to continue earning a meagre salary with very limited accommodation options. Landi, against this backdrop, reiterates that she has lived in a shack all her urban life, a narrative that heavily informs her response to the land question:

> I have lived a life of struggle… a battle, my dear. No home… no education… and no proper income… my story has not changed, from Cape Town to Johannesburg. I continue to live in a shack with a huge family here in Benoni. Look, all these are my grandchildren, and their parents are also struggling to survive. So what comes to mind when I hear questions about land are what I consider immediate needs… yes, everyday survival challenges pop up. What is the point of giving me land for farming when I do not have anywhere to live; where will I till the land from? Give us houses first before you talk about farming. With food, there is always an alternative… if one has the money of course. One can go to Shoprite, Pick n Pay, or Checkers and get some carrots, cabbages, spinach, among other vegetables, but there is no alternative for housing. You are either permanently on the street… a homeless person or a shack dweller. That's not good… at all… there is more to the land question than farming.
>
> LANDI, 70-year-old woman from Daveyton

It is clearly discernible that the land question for Landi means addressing the housing problematic along with other everyday complexities that South African women have to constantly deal with. Drawing on Landi's narrative, one has to acknowledge that access to land and the process of rethinking land reform in post-apartheid South Africa is indeed gendered because of the reproductive and productive functions women have to fulfil within and beyond the household. Similar to Landi, Lesego grew up in Limpopo and migrated to Johannesburg with her family around 1994. Lesego has lived in different townships and informal settlements across the city, and currently she lives in the East Rand where she shares a shack with her two daughters and five grandchildren. In response to the land question, Lesego challenges how projects in post-apartheid South Africa often fail to benefit the target population, especially the poor – a group comprising women and children:

> To be honest, I do not think the land-reform programme will benefit an ordinary person like me. They [elites] will make sure that they have enough land among other resources before they consider our needs... too much corruption... eish ...have you seen their houses... their cars... assets on national television? The rich continue to feed themselves while the poor... us women and children struggle to survive. Shame, I am not interested in this debate... yes, let us talk about other things because the elites make me sick... they want us to die poor without even a piece of land.
>
> LESEGO, 68-year-old woman from Daveyton

Out of Lesego's narrative above emerges complex ways in which gender intersects with race and class to produce inequalities and hierarchised access to urban land that women in Ekurhuleni have to confront on a daily basis. Beyond expressing little hope (if any) of benefiting from the land question, Lesego's narrative points at how a post-1994 black elite (mainly politicians) stands to enjoy the fruits of democracy. The black elite does so by building an economic muscle needed for acquiring residential land among other resources at the expense of the ordinary South African. When discussed in the light of the gap between the rich and the poor, the land question compels Ekurhuleni elderly women to rethink the meaning of freedom and democracy in post-apartheid South Africa as Zandi's narrative below suggests:

> My father came to work in the mines in Johannesburg long before 1994 leaving us and our mother living and relying on a small piece of land in a village in KwaZulu Natal. When my mother died, I had to take care of my five siblings so I moved to town and worked as a domestic... yes, in Natal. When Mandela was released from prison, I decided to come to Johannesburg with very high hopes... I thought life was going to be better in a post-apartheid country... I thought I was going to get a chance to do a course and get a job... but all this has remained a wish. My question is: what is freedom when I do not have access to land... not only for

> agrarian purposes but land for housing and other day to day activities? Maybe freedom is for the educated and the upper class. We are free but not free... what can I say.
>
> ZANDI, 65-year-old woman from Benoni

The land question further raises questions of nationhood and belonging to the post-apartheid state. Mary relays how her parents who were farm labourers in Mpumalanga died and were both buried on a white-owned farm simply because they had no place to call home. She continued to work on the same farm, and eventually quit around 1993 and relocated to Johannesburg's East Rand where she worked for an Indian couple as a domestic servant. Though Mary has changed employers over the years, her living and working conditions have not changed at all. These circumstances have forced her to infer that being foreign in South Africa is better than being a citizen:

> The land question for me raises questions around my identity as a South African. My parents died back then without any asset or place to call home. Home for us was the accommodation the white farmer provided. Here... I have lived in a shack since 1994 a situation which leaves me wondering... asking myself... who really I am. I see foreigners from Nigeria, Zimbabwe... when they come here, they buy houses, so in a way they own a piece of land. I then ask myself, am I only South African because I have an ID book [National Identity Document]? Clearly, an ID book is not enough, and I get the impression that a foreigner has a better relationship and connection to this new South Africa.
>
> MARY, a 67-year-old woman from Daveyton

The narrative above concurs with the work of Walker (2003, 2004) that hints at the link between land, citizenship, identity, nationhood, and belonging to the democracy. Failure to redistribute land especially among the black majority is perceived to be a huge let down, given the history of dispossession and forced removals captured by Walker (2002, p. 8) as central to the construction of 'the social and political identity' of this population group (Walker 2003, p. 5). To confirm this let down, Anele reminds us how central women were to the fight for democracy:

> Born in 1946, I was only 10 years old in August 1956 but I remember hearing that women including my mother had marched to the Union Buildings in Pretoria protesting against gendered and restrictive apartheid laws. We [women] fought hard for this democracy. Yes we appreciate that

> we no longer move around with passes but I am forced to conclude that this freedom is problematic if I, like my mother, do not have access to land. It is sad... we cannot rely on this government... the government has let us down.
>
> ANELE, a 69-year-old woman from Benoni

Anele's narrative speaks to the question I posed earlier: 'What is the meaning of democracy in South Africa if women who also fought for this democracy are somewhat invisible from debates on the land question?' Beyond illuminating the role women played in the struggle for democracy in South Africa, the question demonstrates how symbolic the 9th of August 1956 is. On this day, 20,000 women from across South Africa marched to the Union Buildings 'protesting the apartheid regime's imposition of hated laws requiring black women to carry passes in urban areas' (Sisulu 2006, p. 73). This inference – partly located in the realisation that the historic event as noted by Sisulu is celebrated today – legitimises my argument that women deserve equal access to land ensuring that their needs and rights are not submerged in the generic human rights discourse as well as the broad land-reform structure. Otherwise, 'failure to conceptualise tenure reform in terms of the very different needs of men and women' as observed by Walker (2002, p. 2) exposes the gender gap in land-reform policy and discourse. Elderly women's narratives for the same reason define/redefine the shape that South Africa's land reform should take if it is to benefit women. Having lived in different townships from childhood right into adulthood, Lusanda witnessed over decades the housing realities that women and children in urban South Africa grapple with on a daily basis. She relays:

> I grew up in the Eastern Cape... moved to Cape Town where my mother worked for a white couple. When my mother died, I went back to Eastern Cape and eventually travelled with a friend to Johannesburg... I think around 1994... yes... I lived first in Tembisa then moved to Benoni for strategic reasons... I wanted to be close to my employer. So I have seen it all... and I am in a position to suggest that land redistribution in South Africa has to address the land needs of those in townships and informal settlements. Otherwise, a focus on agrarian reform is only beneficial in the long run. Our concern right now as urban citizens who clean the streets of Gauteng... as domestic workers... as women... as mothers... who sustain the household and future generations... inhabitants of this country... as shack dwellers... is land for housing purposes... and other facilities... key to running the household.
>
> LUSANDA, a 70-year-old woman from Daveyton

Emerging out of Lusanda's narrative above is a profound interpretation of land that draws on the nature of work women do in public and private spaces. Lusanda specifically capitalises on women's diverse gendered roles and positions to probe their access to resources such as land for housing, clean water, and electricity essential to urban livelihoods. Her narrative brings to life Walker's (2003) conceptualisation that the value of land surpasses agrarian questions to encompass 'the non-commoditized resources it offers people, such as housing [...]' (see Razavi 2003, p. 19). Women's demand for residential or housing land becomes central to reading the land question and democracy in South Africa. Although women located in South Africa's East Rand have not identified land reform for agrarian purposes as a priority, the key question as posed by Agarwal (2003, p. 189) in India is 'does the absence of a widespread demand [in this case] indicate the absence of a need?' The answer to this fundamental question as Zanele suggests below is no:

> Let me tell you one thing... you only got to know about my needs when you spoke to me... I have been quiet all these years my grandchild but when you gave me a platform to talk... I was quick to make my request known... yes. But my silence over the years should not be misconstrued for lack of interest... or no need for land. My point is... I will farm when I have somewhere to live... a decent home... period! For now, my focus is on my family, making sure there is food on the table and that my grandchildren are educated... so that they will in future have a stable income... decent accommodation... a decent life... not this one. How can I put this without being rude? Oh ok... I know that if I have... eh... if I own a farm and I am productive... my needs and those of my family will be fulfilled but... allow me to own a piece of residential land first.
>
> ZANELE, a 70-year-old woman from Daveyton

Similar to Lusanda, Zanele reiterates the significance of land for housing among other urban daily needs, but, in addition, she speaks firmly against the notion that people do not want (agrarian) land because they do not demand it. It all depends on how we perceive people and what they consider to be their immediate needs or priorities. Elderly women's narratives concur with the 1997 White Paper on South African Land Policy, which noted the need to 'redistribute [land], to provide the disadvantaged and the poor with access to land for residential and productive purposes' as one of the main programmes for land reform (see Walker 2002, p. 39). However, as noted earlier, elderly women's narratives suggest a disconnection between policy and lived realities. The disconnection has provided scholars with a platform for further exploring 'the disjuncture between policy and practice' (see Walker 2001, p. 4), especially in the context of land reform. This mismatch is argued to be a manifestation of 'unreformed institutional structures which have remained intrinsically gendered' (Madletyana 2011, p. 45). If the narratives of Ekurhuleni women are anything to go by, the objective set in the 1997 White Paper has not been achieved almost two decades later. This compels one to acknowledge that indeed South Africa has a long way to go regarding land-reform programmes that are meaningful to its citizens occupying less privileged spaces.

Beyond their residential land needs, elderly women further discuss the land question in view of empowerment and they encourage the government to embark on land-reform programmes aimed at improving the lives of women. That notwithstanding, Madletyana (2011, p. 45) argues that, in instances where women become part of the land debate, they are merely accommodated in a way that does not resolve the gendered disparities. Instead, women are further marginalised, as they often occupy the lower level of the gendered hierarchy relative to men. Subsequent to reinforcement of these gendered identities by the state, women constantly navigate intersecting ideological and physical barriers to opportunities and key resources such as land. Joyce, in that vein, relays what failure to own land means for women like her:

> I have never owned a piece of land… not even in my village in Mpumalanga, but men did. I know that landownership is very important because I have had challenges when I tried to open a bank… a clothing account… and getting a contract phone… often they want proof of residence and if it is not in your name… eish… you go to the police with the landowner and you sign a form… just to confirm that you live there. Don't you think life would better if women were to own this precious asset? I am also told if you own a piece of land, you can use it as security when you want to apply for loans… I do not know if that is true but I am certain that a shack does not count. This is the challenge we have… I hope the government will include us in land programmes because I believe land is a useful tool that they can use to empower women.
>
> JOYCE, a 66-year-old woman from Benoni

The gendered land barriers outlined above are a hierarchical part of everyday social practices, and the disparities that men and women experience virtually in every sphere of life (including lack of access to education and employment opportunities) illuminate this power imbalance (Mathur & Gupta 2004, p. 2). Gendered access to land in post-apartheid South Africa, along with other politics of survival, propagate an image of a complex socio-political landscape for women. These factors also reinforce the hegemonic and masculinised process of building the flag-democracy. Contrary to the discourse of despair evident in the narratives of Lesego and Anele presented earlier, and those that hint at the diverse land-related challenges women have to deal with, Tumi and Qama illuminate ways in which agency is not constrained by contextual realities. The two, who often exercise individual and collective agency by participating in service delivery protests in different parts of the East Rand, are clear about what they expect the government to do for all women they represent. For Tumi and Qama, government failure to deliver the promises of democracy is a bone of contention:

> They promised us houses after apartheid… so we want them now… we want decent accommodation. We are tired of these RDP houses[4] that crumble a few years down the line. They are very small… we do not even have backyard gardens. We need proper houses so that we do not target and invade unoccupied… undeveloped municipal spaces and construct shacks for ourselves.
>
> TUMI, a 65-year-old woman from Daveyton

> We want houses here… nothing else! We will toyi toyi [protest] until we have access to land… yes… access to our motherland… Ekurhuleni is marching on!.
>
> QAMA, a 66-year-old from Benoni

The promise to *toyi toyi* alluded to above suggests that the service delivery protests in South Africa, which can be traced back to the brutal displacements of blacks in the eighteenth and nineteenth centuries (Razavi 2003, p. 6), continue to impact people as they have limited access to land and other resources. The situation translates to lack of basic services in this 20-year-old democracy, whose ironic birth is partly rooted in the African National Congress's need to transform society post-1994 through addressing land and housing needs, among other things (see Walker 2002, p. 8). Beyond revealing that women's gendered relationship to the post-apartheid state is negotiated through the question of residential/housing land and the right to better services that women fought hard for prior to democracy, their narratives hint at the complex process of building this democracy.

4 Reconstruction and Development Programme houses are low cost houses built with government subsidies.

Stitched together, the excerpts tell an interesting story about the meaning of land, gendered citizenship and the politics of surviving in South Africa – which concurs with ongoing debates on land, gender, nationhood, and belonging in the 20-plus-year-old democracy. Thus, the central argument here goes beyond the challenge of gender and land rights, which in the context of Southern Africa has been documented by Razavi (2003), Whitehead and Tsikata (2003), FAO (2002), and Gaidzanwa (1994), to question the issue of gender and land from the perspective of nationhood, citizenship, democracy, and nation building in South Africa.

Land, Democracy, and Gendered Nationhood in South Africa

The elderly women's land narratives above take this analysis to what Barchiesi (2010, p. 67) terms social citizenship, which, in the context of a democratic South Africa, refers to 'decent living conditions, protected jobs, and social provisions'. Their everyday realities – deeply embedded in a space where empirical evidence suggests 'a far greater concern with jobs, housing and the provision of basic services as immediate priorities in people's day-to-day lives' (Walker 2003, p. 1) – have pushed me to reconceptualise land reform in South Africa. Located outside the mainstream of land and agrarian scholarship, such re-conceptualisation probes the land question beyond agrarian reform and encompasses questions of residential land and provision of decent accommodation. The new conceptualisation is specifically relevant to the East Rand research setting – a context where, as observed during fieldwork, the elderly women reside in poorly serviced townships and informal settlements. Such conceptualisation is also evident in the need to address gender disparities in land discourses 'if land objectives, such as […] providing affordable housing […] are to be met' – a need that was endorsed by FAO (2002, p. 9) shortly after the turn of the twenty-first century.

From the foregoing, this chapter frames serious integration of the gendered, raced, and classed politics of land for housing into the broad land-reform programme in South Africa as fundamental, because these are battles of survival intrinsically linked to questions of nationhood and belonging to settled and unsettled land. If adopted by interested stakeholders, who include but are not limited to scholars, policymakers, and politicians, this approach will ensure that ordinary South Africans have access to land from where they can set-off as they battle for 'non-commoditized resources' (see Razavi 2003, p. 19; Walker, 2003) central to everyday life. Women in particular will regain their sense of belonging to the democracy, and they will start to grapple with land in agrarian terms once their immediate everyday needs are addressed. Razavi (2003, p. 29) equally concludes that 'land reform needs to be understood as a means to create conditions in which people can construct livelihoods from a variety of sources, both agricultural and non-agricultural, in more effective and productive ways'. If access to land from a non-agricultural perspective is a priority for women in this 20-year-old democracy, then understanding national and local land needs, along with the politics of survival (especially the housing problematic), is key to land reform and gender equity in South Africa. Land reform on that note becomes 'a possible means to several ends' (Walker 2004, p. 2) rather than a programme whose prospects are distant.

Conclusion

Engagement with longstanding scholarship in this chapter brought together various academic pieces that explore what has happened predominantly in the past two decades in South Africa. This scholarship placed an emphasis on the intersections of gender and race in the land debate framed as intrinsic to the process of nation building on the continent at large. Such scholarship formed the very foundation on which empirically based urban land debates from Ekurhuleni have exposed the intersections and dialogues between gender, race, class, and nationhood in the context of post-apartheid history. As such, the elderly women's narratives have demonstrated that the agrarian issues in present-day South Africa can be revisioned through a focus on debates concerning gender, race, class, and urban land questions. Ekurhuleni women's narratives are of great significance to those interested in the question around what shape land reform in South Africa should take. Combined, the narratives suggest that land reform that takes the politics of housing seriously grants urban women among other citizens a sense of ownership and belonging to the land, that is South Africa – the democracy.

Thus, this chapter infers that land policy reform programmes that acknowledge the need for land for housing are equally pivotal to the overall land question in South Africa, which, at the moment, is predominantly agrarian in nature. An engagement with the land question based on the lived realities of elderly women who live on the East Rand exposes the debates stemming from the process of 'being gendered, raced, and classed' in a nation. These are debates that enhance our understanding of nationhood and the land question in post-apartheid South Africa. Overall, the gender/land battle serves to examine the meaning of living in 'a land' where nation building is highly gendered, raced, and classed such that questions of land emerge as intrinsic to understanding the idea of the 'nation' in post-apartheid South Africa.

References

Agarwal, B. (2003). Gender and Land Rights Revisited: Exploring New Prospects via the State, Family and Market. *Journal of Agrarian Change*, *3*(1&2), 184–224.

Alexander, M.J. (1994). Not Just (Any) Body Can Be a Citizen: The Politics of Law, Sexuality and Postcoloniality in Trinidad and Tobago and the Bahamas. *Feminist Review, The New Politics of Sex and the State*, *48*, 5–23.

Barchiesi, F. (2010). Informality and Casualization as Challenges to South Africa's Industrial Unionism: Manufacturing Workers in the East Rand/Ekurhuleni Region in the 1990s. *African Studies Quarterly*, *11*(2 & 3), 67–85.

Batisai, K. (2016). Interrogating Questions of National Belonging, Difference and Xenophobia in South Africa. *Agenda*, *30*(2), 119–130.

Batisai, K. (2015a). Being Gendered in Africa's Flag-democracies: Narratives of Sexual Minorities Living in the Diaspora. *Gender Questions*, *3*(1), 25–44.

Batisai, K. (2015b). The Politics of Control and Ownership over Women's Bodies: Discourses that Shape Reproductive and Sexual Rights in Zimbabwe. Bodies, Morals and Politics. Reflections on Sexual and Reproductive Rights in Africa. *Perspectives Africa (Heinrich Böll Stiftung)*, 2, 6–11.

Batisai, K. (2014). Policies on Abortion: Women's Experiences of Living through a Gendered Body in Zimbabwe. *AG AboutGender, International Journal of Gender Studies*, *3*(5), 174–192.

Batisai, K. (2013). *Body politics: an Illumination of the Landscape of Sexuality and Nationhood? Re-seeing Zimbabwe through Elderly Women's Representations of their Sexual and Gendered Lives.* (Unpublished PhD Thesis) Cape Town: University of Cape Town.

Beall, J., Geld, S., & Hassim, S. (2005). Fragile Democracy: State and Society in Democratic South Africa. *Journal of Southern African Studies*, *31*(4), 681–700.

Claassens, A., & Msini, S. (2009). Rural Women Redefining Land Rights in the Context of Living Customary Law. *SAJHR*, *25*, 491–516.

Cousins, B., Du Toit, A.; Hall, R.; Neves, D., & Aliber, M. (2013). Introduction: Agrarian Change, Rural Poverty and Land Reform in South Africa since 1994. *Journal of Agrarian Change*, *13*(1), 1–15.

FAO (2002). *Land Tenure Studies 4. Gender and Access to land.* Rome: FAO.

Foucault, M. (1978 [1990]). *The History of Sexuality: An Introduction, Vol. 1.* (R. Hurley, Trans.) New York: Vintage Books.

Gaidzanwa, R. (1994). Women's Land Rights in Zimbabwe. *Issue: A Journal of Opinion, 22*(2), 12–16.

Greenberg, S. (2013). *The Disjunctures of Land and Agricultural Reform in South Africa: Implications for the Agri-food System, Working Paper 26.* Bellville: PLAAS, UWC.

Hall, R. (2010). *The Politics of Land Reform in Post-Apartheid South Africa, 1990 to 2004: A Shifting Terrain of Power, Actors and Discourses.* (Unpublished PhD Thesis.) St Antony's College, University of Oxford.

Kahn, N. (2007). Land and Agrarian Reform in South Africa. *Policy: issues and actors. 20*(12), 1–38.

Madletyana, P. (2011). *Race, Gender, Class and Land Reform: A case study approach on the Land Reform for Agricultural Development* (LRAD) *Sub-Programme.* (Masters research report). Johannesburg: University of the Witwatersrand.

Mathur, S., & Gupta, G.R. (2004). Addressing Young Women and Girls' Unique Vulnerability to HIV/AIDS. *Sexual Health Exchange,* 2004–3/4. (Royal Tropical Institute (kit) in the Netherlands, in collaboration with SAfAIDS (Southern Africa HIV and AIDS Information Dissemination Service), Zimbabwe).

Mbilinyi, M., & Sechambo, G. (2009). Struggles over Land Reform in Tanzania: Experiences of Tanzania Gender Networking Programme and Feminist Activist Coalition. *Feminist Africa. Land, Labour and Gendered Livelihoods, 12,* 95–104.

McClintock, A. (1995). *Imperial Leather: Race, Gender and Sexuality in the Colonial Contest.* New York: Routledge.

McClintock, A. (1991). 'No Longer in a Future Heaven': Women and Nationalism in South Africa. *Transition, 51,* 104–123.

Moyo, C.S. (2013). Rural Women and Land, the Inseparable Twins. *Gender and Behaviour, 11*(2), 5393–5401.

Moyo, S. (2008). *African Land Questions, Agrarian Transitions and the State: Contradictions of Neo-liberal Land Reforms, Working paper series.* Senegal: CODESRIA.

Ntsebeza, L. (2006). The Land and Agrarian Questions: What do they mean in South Africa Today? (Key Note Address Presented on the Occasion of the 20th Anniversary of the Surplus People Project (SPP), Pinelands Bowling club, Pinelands, Cape Town, on 24 February 2006).

Peterson, V.S. (2000). Sexing Political Identities/Nationalism as Heterosexism. In S. Ranchod-Nilsson & M.A. Tétreault (Eds.), *Women, States and Nationalism At Home in the Nation?* (54–80). London: Routledge Taylor & Francis.

Ranchod-Nilsson, S. & Tétreault M.A. (Eds.) (2000). *Women, States and Nation At Home in the Nation?* London: Routledge Taylor & Francis Group.

Razavi, S. (2003). Introduction: Agrarian Change, Gender and Land Rights. *Journal of Agrarian Change, 3*(1, 2), 2–32.

Rugege, S. (2004). Land Reform in South Africa: An Overview. *Int'l J. Legal Info., 32*(283), 1–28.

Sisulu, E. (2006). The 50th Anniversary of the 1956 Women's March: a Personal Recollection. *Feminist Africa Subaltern Sexualities, 6*, 73–76.

Slater, R. (2000). Using Life Histories to Explore Change: Women's Urban Struggles in Cape Town, South Africa. *Gender and Development, 8*(2), 38–46.

Stoler, A.L. (2002). *Carnal Knowledge and Imperial Power Race and the Intimate in Colonial Rule.* Berkeley and Los Angeles: University Press of California.

Tsikata, D. (2009). Gender, Land and Labour Relations and Livelihoods in Sub-Saharan Africa in the era of Economic Liberalisation: Towards a Research Agenda. *Feminist Africa. Land, Labour and Gendered Livelihoods, 12*, 11–30.

Walker, C. (2009). 'Elusive Equality: Women, Property Rights and Land Reform in South Africa', *South African Journal on Human Rights. 25*(3), 467–490.

Walker, C. (2004). The Land Question in South Africa: The Challenges of Transformation and Redistribution. *Human Sciences Research Council, Harold Wolpe Memorial Trust*, Conference Cape Town, 25–27 March 2004.

Walker, C. (2003). The Limits to Land Reform: Reviewing 'The Land Question'. Paper presented on 19 November 2003: *African Studies/History Seminar*. Durban: University of Natal.

Walker, C. (2002). Agrarian Change, Gender and Land Reform: A South African Case Study. *Social Policy and Development Programme*, Paper Number 10. United Nations Research Institute for Social Development.

Walker, C. (2001). Piety in the Sky? Gender Policy and Land Reform in South Africa. Paper presented: *UNRISD Conference on Agrarian Change, Gender and Land Rights.* Geneva: United Nations Research Institute for Social Development.

Whitehead, A., & Tsikata, D. (2003). Policy Discourses on Women's Land Rights in Sub-Saharan Africa: The Implications of the Return to the Customary. *Journal of Agrarian Change, 3*(1, 2), 67–112.

Yuval-Davis, N. (2006). Belonging and the Politics of Belonging. *Patterns of Prejudice, 40*(3), 197–214.

Yuval-Davis, N. (1997). *Gender and Nation.* London: Sage Publications.

Yuval-Davis, N. & Anthias, F. (Eds.) (1989). *Women-Nation-State.* London: The Macmillan Press.

PART 3

State-Making

CHAPTER 6

Farm Worker "Development" Agendas: What Does Sports Have to Do with It?

Tarminder Kaur

Introduction

> Manual labourers and farm workers cannot achieve goodness, because their lives lack leisure, and leisure is necessary for virtue.
>
> NUSSBAUM, 1988, p. 156

Interrogating Aristotelian philosophies on place of menial labour in societal hierarchies, Nussbaum draws attention to a line of argument that connects goodness or virtue with leisure. A response to above statement might be to probe: if leisure was found to be a part of form workers' lives, would their lives be virtuous? This connection between virtue and leisure, which I discuss here in terms of "development"[1] and sports, is what I explore in my study with the farm workers of the Western Cape.

In this chapter, I take sports as the main subject of my analysis and "development" as the analytical framework around which arguments are organised. I draw from James Ferguson's (1990) approach to "development" as an 'anti-politics machine', where he positions the examination of "development" beyond the narrow confines of its self-defined problems and programmes. Instead of asking if "development" really works or how it can be done better, Ferguson examines the broader processes of "development", from its conceptualisation, its theoretical logics, diverse set of political and economic interests that shape such projects and discourses, to its intended and unintended consequences. In so doing, he demonstrates how the structures within which "development" interventions are conducted are 'multi-layered, polyvalent, and often contradictory' (1990, p. 17), arguing that "development" discourses tend to obscure such complexities and engage with "development" problems as if

1 I place "development" in double quotation marks, following Ferguson, where he demonstrates that "development" has remained a problematic concept. The double quotation marks also make it possible to distinguish between when the term *development* is used in a normative manner (without quotation marks) and where it is problematized.

 | DOI 10.1163/9789004362550_007

these were self-evident and outside the realms of politics. In the process, often distorted, ill-informed and oversimplified solutions are conceptualised that bear little or no resemblance to the social and economic realities they intend to change.

In a similar register, Gavin Williams (2005, 2003), Andries du Toit (1994), Du Toit and colleagues (2008), among others, argue in the context of South African agriculture and wine industry that "development" has served as a 'linguistic bridge', absorbing multiple meanings, and starkly different and conflicting political interests. Despite the post-development critique[2] and reported failure of lauded programmes, "development" continues to serve as a language for desired change in the socio-economic realms and geo-political relations. Similarly, an idea that farm workers need "development" has retained a place in the policy and political debates on land reform and agrarian transformation in South Africa, even after 20 years of democracy. The emergence and proliferation of a whole new sector, Sports for Development and Peace (SDP), known as such for about 17 years, is another example of the continued faith in the ambitions and objectives of "development".

As a concept, SDP is understood as a 'strategy of social intervention in disadvantaged communities throughout the world', where sports are used to achieve a broad range of "development" objectives (Kidd 2011, p. 603; 2008). As a sector, SDP finds its significance in the proclamations and endorsements by some influential international organisations, such as the United Nations, the International Olympic Committee, and other major international sports federations, national governments, international and national multi-sports bodies, along with multiple and growing number of non-governmental organisations (NGOs) that conduct SDP projects (Kidd, 2008; Levermore, 2008). As a research topic, SDP examines the practical and theoretical usefulness of sports as a tool for education, diplomacy, inclusion, and awareness on a diverse set of social, health, and economic issues. While SDP is not always a self-asserted designation, the discourses and practices I examine here are those that engage in various combinations and forms of sports and "development" activities in the specific context of farm workers of the Western Cape.

For example, in May 2004, the provincial government Department of Agriculture announced the Farmworker Development programme, arguing "development" of farm workers as one of their priority areas.[3] This instigated the

2 See among others: Escobar, 2011; Gunder Frank, 1966; Sachs, 2010.

3 See: http://www.elsenburg.com/ruraldev/ruraldev.html (Accessed on 27 November 2014).

Department of Cultural Affairs and Sport (DCAS) to launch their Western Cape Farmworker Sport and Recreation Development initiative in 2008. Apart from these relatively recent government initiatives, I recorded a number of non-government and private sector programmes, some dating back to the late 1970s, which would fit a general description of SDP (Kaur, 2016). While not a major component, sports were generally accepted as beneficial, either as an indicator of, or a tool for, farm workers' "development" (see for example The Wine Transformation Charter (SA Wine Council, 2007). Within the limited scope of this chapter, I examine farm worker "development" discourses and selected practices to discuss the question: What does sports have to do with it?

This chapter proceeds in six sections. The first section elaborates on the concept of and debates on SDP, ascertaining the questions I engage with in this chapter. In the second section, I reflect on my ethnographic fieldwork, elaborating on the processes of garnering information and the manner in which the arguments are presented here. The third section offers a broad-brushed discussion of the history of farm worker "development" in the Western Cape. The fourth section presents a historically informed analysis of the contemporary "farm worker development" discourses and practices. The fifth and sixth sections draw on my ethnographic work to discuss the ways in which sports and "development" discourses, programmes, and practices intersect among the farm workers. Attending to counter narratives and contradictions in the projections of farm workers' sports and "development" needs, I conclude the chapter with some reflections, questioning how SDP discourses and practices relate to the occupation of farm labour. What kinds of farm worker concerns do SDP addresses, and what remains unaddressed, unacknowledged, and unaffected?

SDP

A subset of physical culture, sport has been increasingly acknowledged and debated for its role in "development". To this end, SDP is a reference to sports programmes conducted in 'low- and middle-income countries (LMICs) and the disadvantaged communities of the First World' (Kidd 2008, p. 370). Coalter defines SDP as a continuum between two broad approaches: sport plus (sport programmes with a didactic add-on) and plus sport (social, educational, and health programmes that use sport as an add-on to attract young people) (2008, p. 71). The up-to-date literature on SDP composes a long list of "developmental" uses of sports as: a health imperative; an avenue to lobby against political injustices; a space to empower and include marginalised sections of the society;

a crime preventative, diversion, and rehabilitation measure; a child and youth development process; an arena to acquire social capital and network; and an economic opportunity (SDP IWG, 2007). There is a plethora of SDP interventions promoting such agendas, which mostly rely on didactic means, where sports participants are facilitated with educational or awareness programmes or life-skills training. It is in this context that Guest argued: 'The idea that sport directly socializes particular characteristics, historically discussed as "building character" and currently discussed as "developing life-skills", is both very popular and very difficult to support empirically' (2005). His ethnographic fieldwork at an Angolan refugee camp illustrates how SDP projects operate with distinct understandings and misinterpretations of needs, values and purposes of sports and "development". For example, Guest argues:

> Olympic Aid [a SDP intervention] implicitly understood sport as a tool for intentional development and socialization; in this understanding Pena residents [targeted beneficiaries] should be grateful for the opportunity to play and develop 'life-skills'. Pena residents, in contrast, generally considered sport and play as a worthwhile amusement for children with little relevance to adult life unless it provided professional opportunities; in this understanding Olympic Aid should compensate participants for their services (2009, p. 1345–1346).

Guest's research draws out the contradiction between the ideals and objectives of the "developers" and 'to be developed', raising important questions about the knowledge and understandings of "development" conditions, intentionality and relations of power in SDP practices. While applied sciences models for research, which collate evidence, design interventions, and evaluate impact dominate knowledge production on SDP, it is critical and ethnographic modes of inquiry that has challenged some of the basic assumptions on which SDP discourses and practices are based and promoted.

Drawing on Ferguson's deconstructionist approach, my aim is to present a critical analysis of SDP discourses and practices directed at farm workers of the Western Cape. For such an inquiry, the empirical research questions had to be historically grounded, politically tactical, and locally specific, as the following illustration demonstrates:

> As long as the question is 'Why is Qwa-Qwa (as a national economy) poor?' then one must point to lack of resources, overpopulation, and 'dependence'. If one asks instead why the people who live in Qwa-qwa are poor (and why they live in Qwa-Qwa!), one generates a rather different

> sort of answer, of course: a long sad tale of conquest, land loss, forced removals, influx control, repression, denial of political rights, depressed wages, and enforced 'redundancy'.
>
> FERGUSON, 1990, p. 64

Ferguson goes on to show why 'there is little room for these kinds of questions and answers in "development" discourse' (ibid). My analysis of the literature on SDP suggests that applied models to study SDP are similarly limited by the kinds of questions posed. To this end, instead of asking how sports might cause "development", I asked why is it that the farm workers of the Western Cape need "development" and what does sports have to do with it? More specifically, I probe: what historical and political events and conditions have shaped farm worker "development" discourses; and to what understandings was sports advocated and put to use for their "development"?

Ethnographic Reflections

This chapter draws from the fieldwork I conducted at the farmlands in and around Rawsonville, a small rural town in Cape Winelands, from April 2012 to May 2013. In the process, I attended multiple SDP practices directed at farm workers, recorded the ways in which government and non-government organisations projected "development" problems and needs, and immersed myself in the everyday sporting practices of farm workers that existed outside of the programmes of "development". The overarching empirical question guiding my observations was: how do SDP discourses and solutions correspond with the social and political realities?

While locating and attending SDP projects for farm workers was relatively easy, as it was in the interest of organisers to publicise their programmes, there were fewer and mostly discouraging clues to the everyday practices of sports. For example, during the early explorations, an executive from the wine industry shared:

> ...there are very little sport and wellness activities generated along those farms. Farming, rural life does not lend itself to that. If you look at the farms, just behind that, where the heck do you build the soccer field! You can, but farming is not oriented towards that.[4]

4 Extract from an interview conducted during the preparatory stage in June 2011.

I had to move beyond the discourses of 'lack' of sports to understand the meanings and reasons for this lack among the farm workers. Thus, the fieldwork started with attending sports events organised under the "development" banner, asking official sports bodies for their farm worker membership, and attending the official league games at the central sports facility in Rawsonville. Exploring the sporting geography and history of this rural town, I discovered, and was able to access, a rather active sporting life of farm workers, which operated outside the official sports structures and programmes of SDP.

Methods employed to gather information included: participant observations, digitally recorded semi-structure and unstructured interviews, formal and informal conversations, and active participation in different sports activities, and at differing levels of engagement. Along with recording extensive descriptions and personal reflections on daily research events in the form of field notes, I archived newspaper articles, official documents, and information available on the Internet, along with artefacts shared by research participants.

The apolitical impression of, and enthusiasm for, sports often made the field easy to access, still the extent to which I could ask questions on the politics of "development" had its limitations, often resulting in the closing of doors. It is important to point out that the majority of my research participants were first-language Afrikaans speaking, but my proficiency in the language remained limited throughout the fieldwork. Despite this being among the main research limitations, unable to fully understand the spoken-words allowed undistracted observations on how different roles in the society were performed, and how the knowledge of my limited grasp of the language was used to include or exclude me.

The credibility of ethnographic analysis is in the way a written account continues to examine the competing interpretations and maintains a reflexive approach. To this end, the chapter continues with the analytical and interpretive process by engaging in a dialogue between my primary findings and critical self-reflections, accentuating how I accessed the specific cases discussed here. I contextualise my analysis by discussing the history and politics of farm worker "development" in the Western Cape, in what follows.

History of Farm Worker "Development"

Historians André du Toit and Hermann Giliomee (1983) have argued that over 170 years of Cape slavery had set the tone for labour and social order of South Africa for the years to come (also see Watson, 2012, 1990; Worden & Crais, 1994).

The racial hierarchies and 'authoritarian paternalism inherited and adapted from early Cape slave society' persisted and maintained the basic character of labour arrangements on the vinyards of the Cape into the late twentieth century (Ewert & Du Toit 2005, p. 318–319; also see Watson, 2012). The ideas of social change and improvements in the life conditions of the people who laboured in the Cape's agricultural farms can be traced in humanitarian contestations over the abolition of slavery since the early nineteenth century, still, the concept of farm worker "development" did not emerge until the late 1970s, and that too with a shift towards modernisation of agricultural production (Ewert & Du Toit, 2005; Mayson, 1990; Worden & Crais, 1994).

With changes in legislation in the agriculture and wine industry, mounting international pressures against apartheid and trade boycotts, which manifested in the 1980s economic and political crises, farm worker "development" approaches began to dominate the farming scene. In 1982, the Rural Foundation (or *Landelike Stigting* in Afrikaans) 'embarked on an extensive programme of "community development" to improve farm workers' conditions' (Du Toit 1993, p. 317). Indeed, the Rural Foundation (RF) was one among many other efforts facilitating up-gradation of the agricultural workforce in the Western Cape in the early 1980s: still, the RF offers a useful example of the early farm worker "development" discourse.

The managerial 'reform from above' efforts of the RF did bring some important changes to the living conditions of the permanent workforce and their dependants, without necessarily challenging the absolute authority of the farmers over the operations (and workers) at their farms. Nor did they questioned the unequal and 'racialised power relations of white mastery'; instead they 'tried to regularise and modernise' these relations as a pragmatic business approach (Ewert & Du Toit 2005, p. 319; Du Toit, 1994). Farm-owners were able to control every aspect of "development" to be delivered on their farm (Mayson, 1990).

Despite the traditional image of the farmer as 'the sovereign patriarchal master of all who dwell and work on his farm' (Du Toit 1995, p. 4), the conditions and treatment of farm workers were not all that uniform; significant discrepancies have been reported across the farming institutions and over different historical times (Scully, 1990; Du Toit, 1993). While some farmers chose coercive ways, others opted to provide higher wages, better housing and living standards, subsidised food, sports, recreation, crèches, clinics, and other facilities to 'keep workers on the farms' (Wilson et al. 1977, p. 11) and to improve worker productivity (Mayson, 1990). In this sense, "development" activities of the RF were not all that radically different from benevolent projections of paternalist order. Indeed, the aim of the RF was to build a committed and productive labour force, and to improve 'the poor image of the industry in the face of looming sanctions' (Ewert & Du Toit 2005, p. 319; Mayson, 1990).

Nevertheless, these reform efforts of the 1980s did not last for too long. By the early 1990s, a large number of farmers had already unsubscribed from the RF. With changing political environment, transition from apartheid to democracy, and gradual cuts in government funding, the RF came to an end in 1998 (Ewert & Du Toit, 2005; Williams, 2010). These changes did 'broaden the scope of rural reform' and were to 'set the scene for burgeoning and complex policy debate', which, however, as Du Toit argues:

> ...proceeded on very different terms from preceding discussions about change in South Africa. Most importantly, it has tended to conceptualise basic social ills, not in political terms, but as *development problems*. This meant that a new conceptual space opened up: a technocratic discourse that transcended old political divisions and made possible agreement on new policy initiatives across old ideological divides (1994, p. 376, my emphasis).

While the new government saw the RF 'as a product of apartheid reformism', farm workers' need for "development" was not questioned, nor was the post-apartheid "development" discourse to sound any different from its antecedents (Ewert & Du Toit 2005, p. 319). Indeed, the 'identification of "development" with black people outlasted the late apartheid regime' (Williams 2003, p. 39, double quotes in original). "Development" provided 'a linguistic bridge', as Williams puts it, which not only absorbed conflicting political interests, but 'discursively reconcil[ed] the claims of growth and redistribution and displac[ed] issues of class inequalities and class politics' (2003, p. 40). Despite this historical baggage, the contemporary discourses and programmes for farm worker "development" tend to focus on awareness campaigns around substance and alcohol abuse, health promotion, as well as work-related and life-skills training. The next section discusses the contemporary farm worker "development" discourses and programmes, highlighting the continuities and divergences from its paternalistic and disempowering roots.

Contemporary Farm Worker "Development"

In the context of sports and "development" among farm workers of the Western Cape, the RF had clearly left a mark. Many of the sports clubs, sports fields, and other physical infrastructure for the use of farm workers in my study region were attributed to the RF.[5] Also, RF's "development" philosophy, the conceptions of 'attitude' training to improve farm workers' 'self-image', and the role of sports (Mayson 1990, Ch. 5), all seemed to have found continuities in the contemporary discourses of farm worker "development". This was particularly instructive in the way the Western Cape's Government Department of Agriculture (DoA) advertises its sub-programme, the Farmworker Development. In May 2004, the Department announced development of farm workers as one of their priority areas. Until 2011, this sub-programme was under the Farmer Support and Development programme, but recent restructuring has placed it under the programme for Rural Development Coordination.

This shift of the sub-programme from the Farmer Support and Development to the Rural Development Coordination took place in the context of changing political environment and labour management practices in the Western Cape. Until 1993, farm workers were 'almost entirely without legal protection' (Du Toit 1995, p. 4). Despite the reform in agriculture labour laws, which included the extension of basic rights and conditions of employment, minimum wage, collective bargaining, etc., the government has not been too successful at enforcing these. This is partly due to weaknesses within the state institutions and inadequate measures to access justice by those in resource-constrained and structurally insecure circumstances. This is a point that Susan Levine (2013) demonstrates in her recent book through the stories of the brutal treatment of child labour, highlighting the limitations within the justice system to address injustices inflicted upon the poor, while protecting the wealthier sections of the society. The unrelenting and distinctive character of 'Western Cape paternalism' has also created a situation where the 'labour relationships are simultaneously governed both by the formal codes of legislation and by the personal relationships and implicit contracts of paternalist practices' (Ewert & Du Toit 2005, p. 325). It is in this context that Du Toit and Ally record:

> Even progressive farmers who accepted the modernisation of labour law were at pains to point out that workers were better off in the 'wise' care of the farmer, and would not be much helped by the meddling of lawyers, trade unionists or other outsiders (Du Toit, 1993). Labour relations continued to involve much more than the exchange of cash for labour. Above

5 References to the RF often came up during the interviews and conversations with farmers and farm workers, particularly in the context of sports. Reminisces of the activities of the RF seemed to shape an understanding of "development" even today.

> all, the institution of tied housing persisted on Western Cape wine and fruit farms, and farmers continued to rely on on-farm permanent labour. To work on a farm as a permanent employee remained linked to *dwelling* on the farm as part of a broader community whose well-being was the responsibility of farm management (2004, p. 4).

The fact that the provincial DoA channelled 'Farmworker Development' through 'Farmer Support and Development' until 2011 suggests how normalised, entrenched, and accepted farm paternalism had been. However, the introduction of labour laws did 'disrupt the institutional order of paternalist labour management' and the material conditions for a shrinking core of permanent on-farm labour did improve (Ewert & Du Toit 2005, p. 325). At the same time, increase in externalisation and casualization of farm labour had made the situation only more complex, creating new conditions for exploitation, poverty and vulnerability, more so for the off-farm seasonal, casual, and contract labour (Du Toit, 1995, 1994; Du Toit & Ally, 2004; Ewert & Du Toit, 2005).

Explaining the reasons for the Farmworker Development being administered under the Rural Development Coordination, an official from the DoA shared in an interview that:

> ...what we do is, we fund non-profit organisations that want to do social development amongst [farm workers]. In the past, I now must state this, we only used to focus on farm workers, but since we are rural development now and also part of the integration of communities, a lot of the farm workers don't necessarily stay on the farms. Because farmers also have enormous problems from extended family members, they don't necessarily work on the farm and they come and squat on the farm, and you know that type of thing, do illegal stuff like drug smuggling, alcohol abuse and such. And as you know, lately farmers tend to not house their workers on the farm but in local communities. And then it is municipality's responsibility to supply those people with RDP houses as well. So, now what I am saying is that we now fund communities as well, not only farm workers. So, we've a criterion for funding.[6]

Clearly, the communities targeted for "development" were not strictly farm workers but included the unemployed, landless, working-class people, who live in rural townships and informal settlements in close vicinity to commercial

6 Interview recorded in July 2012.

farms. While referring to the programme as Farmworker Development is misleading, this conflation of farm workers with lower socio-economic sections of the broader rural community was quite normalised in the public discourse. The above explanation also reflects the changing conditions of farm labour management practices and on-farm politics. Therefore, unpacking this programme allows for an analysis of mixed and multiple meanings, that farm worker "development" discourses and practices take on across the province.

> The Sub-programme: Farmworker Development is to *enhance the image* and *socio-economic conditions* of farm workers and their family members through facilitation of *training and development initiatives* to improve their quality of life.
>
> The Western Cape has approximately 175 000 farm workers and is home to almost 24% of the farm workers in the country. This is an indication that farming in the Province is relatively more labour intensive than is the case in the rest of the country. Geographically the Western Cape Province *farm activities are very large and diverse* and *therefore* it is *important to uplift and assist our farm workers on all levels.*
>
> In general farm workers and their family members are *isolated from the main stream social interaction* and *do not have regular access to life skills training*. Furthermore, in most cases they *lack the awareness of the dangers of substance abuse* and the effects it may have on the breakdown of the social fabric in their communities. It is *therefore* essential to *build pride* amongst farm workers and their family members *as they contribute towards the success of the sector.*
>
> …
>
> *Following the farm worker strikes in 2012/2013* this project was *prioritised as a provincial wide survey* with the Overberg and Cape Winelands as focus areas to start with. The aim of this initiative is *to collate reliable information* on farm workers and their needs to inform appropriate government response interventions.[7]

The assumptions and objectives of the sub-programme (see above) accommodates for the changing patterns of farm employment and living arrangements for the farm workers, without necessarily changing the generic kinds and

7 This block quotation is taken from the Western Cape Government Department of Agriculture's website, where they describe the sub-programme: Farmworker Development, See: http://www.elsenburg.com/ruraldev/ruraldev.html (accessed on 27 November 2014).

methods of needed "development". The content of the Farmworker Development focuses directly on the 'farm workers and their family members', pointing out the problems, processes, and reasons for "developing" the farm workers (which, according to the explanation of the official interviewed from the DoA, now also includes broader rural lower socio-economic classes).

For instance, the objective to 'enhance the image and socio-economic conditions of farm workers' was to be achieved, not necessarily by negotiating a better salary package or developing policies that enhance job security or balance the inherited unequal relations of power in farm labour practices, but through the 'training and development initiatives' that target poor working class. Such an articulation sets up "development" experts and NGOs to apply for funds to conduct programmes that may or may not be relevant to the occupation of farm labour. Furthermore, the geographical largeness and diversity of farm activities is deduced to indicate the need to 'uplift and assist our farm workers', and their isolation 'from the mainstream social interaction' as lack of 'access to life skills training'. Is it even possible that the problematic framed in geographical terms would almost exclusively affect the farm workers, but not the farm-owners or other inhabitants of the same physical spaces? What has remained implicit in such objectives is the class and material marginality and 'adverse incorporation' of landless rural working class in the way the social, political, and economic geography of commercial farming in the Western Cape is organised (du Toit, 2004).

Since 2004, when the department first announced this sub-programme, only very slight modifications to its objectives have been made, despite some significant changes in the labour laws and labour management practices over this period. It was in reference to the farm worker uprising of 2012–13 that the sub-programme was (re)prioritised, with an additional strategic goal 'to collate reliable information on farm workers and their needs to inform appropriate government response interventions'. Apart from this objective, the Farmworker Development seems to be consistent with the objectives and activities of the RF. For example, at least for the past four decades, the need for image enhancement, skills training, social awareness campaigns on 'dangers of substance abuse' to 'improve the quality of life' and 'build pride', have remained essential to the "development" of farm workers, that too because 'they contribute towards the success of the sector'. This sort of explicit focus on "development" aimed at changing (via education or training) the person of the farm worker (who may or may not be working on a farm) tends to purge this discourse of broader politics and problems within the labour regimes. By placing the most immediate and apparent problems at the forefront of farm worker "development" discourse, it not only obscures the structural, material, and political conditions that underpin "development" problems (for example, the issues of poor cash wages), but such depoliticised and dehistoricised renderings also reproduce, influence, and are influenced by, "development" discourses and its fragmented practices.

It is useful to return to the points that the DoA's official clarified about the programme in the interview.[8] As he explained, the Department relies on the proposals submitted to them by NGOs or "development" specialists, which were considered according to a formal application process and predetermined criteria. The change in the scope of the programme from on-farm resident workers to the broader rural communities, new responsibilities of the municipalities to supply housing for off-farm labour, and the 'enormous problems of farmers', sheds some light on the complexity of the social and political spaces within which "development" solutions are sought. These changes are among the ramifications of introduction of stricter farm labour laws. Although these laws did disrupt the 'institutional order of paternalist labour management' (Ewert & Du Toit 2005, p. 325), they also led to externalisation and casualization of farm labour (as pointed out earlier, also see Du Toit & Ally, 2004). The farming institutions have been moving towards employing a small core of skilled permanent workers and a larger number of contract labour for cash wages. Therefore, a large number of workers now live off the farm premises. The "development" services once facilitated by the RF on the farms are now provided by isolated and piecemeal efforts of individuals, not-for-profits, or other forms of social welfare organisations, as and when they are able to secure funds. Although the various "farmworker development" programmes no longer exclusively focus on those who labour on the commercial farms, the reference 'farm worker' continues to have political relevance in that it implicates organisations like the DoA and others within the government, as well as private agriculture sectors, in the allocation of funds for "farmworker development". I elaborate on this point by discussing how the provincial Department of Cultural Affairs and Sport (DCAS) engages with the farm worker sports "development".

Farm Worker SDP

Among the strategic goals of the Department of Agriculture's Farmworker Development programme was to 'coordinate the involvement of different

8 Interview Recorded with a DoA official in July 2012.

government departments'.[9] In response, the DCAS honoured their objective by launching the Western Cape Farmworker Sport and Recreation Development (WCFSRD) initiative in 2008,[10] with following set of objectives:

- To bring farm workers into the mainstream of sport and recreation
- To stage farm-based events
- To capacitate farm workers, enabling them to take control of their own sport and recreation programmes
- To form club structures at farms
- To create opportunities for girls and women in sport and recreation
- To develop positive role models at farms.[11]

In an unpublished policy draft (2007) on farm worker sports, DCAS acknowledges that only sporadic sports and recreation programmes had been organised in the rural areas, which include farms as part of the broader rural community but do not focus on the farm workers as 'a separate group', consequently, causing 'systematic marginalisation of them'.[12] In order to focus on farm workers as 'a separate group', the Western Cape Provincial Farmworkers Sport Committee (the Committee, hereafter) was established in 2008. The primary mandate of the Committee, according to their constitution, was to promote, administer and organise sports opportunities for farm workers of the Western Cape, in the form of competitions, training, and coaching. While DCAS aimed to help set up the sport 'club structures at the farms' and 'capacitate farm workers' to manage their own sport, the objectives of the Committee were to 'encourage and develop high standards of administration, discipline, playing, coaching and umpiring' and to select 'players and official[s] to … various levels of participation' (as stated in the Committee's constitution). This discrepancy in the DCAS's and the Committee's objectives for the same initiative suggests differences in their knowledge and understandings of sports practiced among farm workers. Yet, it was the DCAS sponsored annual *Farm Worker Sports Day* that served as the flagship event for both.

The Committee consisted of representatives from eight regions, into which the DCAS, with the help of the DoA, had divided the Western Cape (see Map 6.1). These representatives, as well as executive members of the Committee, were all rooted in their respective rural farming regions in different ways and roles,

9 See: http://www.elsenburg.com/ruraldev/ruraldev.html (accessed on 27 November 2014).
10 I draw from the DCAS's official documentation on this initiative, as shared by a DACS official for the purpose of this research.
11 Ibid.
12 Ibid.

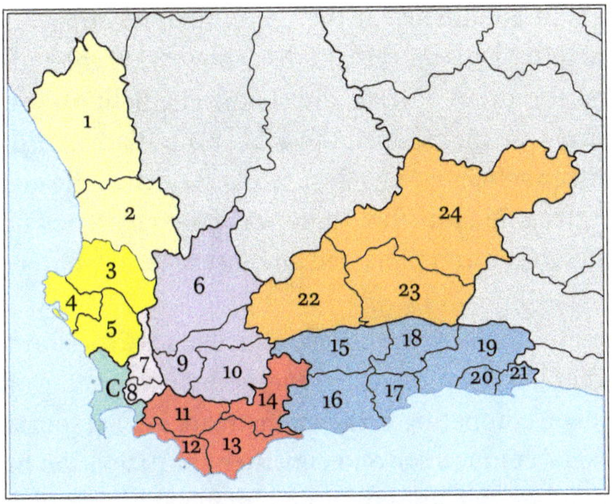

Map key	WCFSRD Regions	Representation on the Committee from:
6, 9, 10	Cape Winelands 2	Robertson/Ashton (10)
7–8	Cape Winelands 1	Stellenbosch (8)
22–24	Central Karoo	Beaufort West (24)
C	Metropolis	Durbanville (C)
15–21	Eden	Oudtshoorn (18)
11–14	Overberg	Swellendam (14)
1–2	Upper West Coast	Citrusdal (2)
3–4	Lower West Coast	Piketberg (3)

MAP 6.1 *Map of the Western Cape with colour-coded demarcations of the DCAS's WCFSRD regions, and numbered local municipalities (Adapted from online[13] source).*

and were responsible for bringing together the sports teams to the annual Sports Day. They were a small number of people who represented very large and sparsely populated farmlands stretched across the province. As noble as the idea of bringing farm workers from across the province to *mainstream*[14] sports seemed, the participation at the annual Sports Day was localised and limited to the individual representatives' personal networks of farm workers. While none of the executive members were themselves workers at a farm,

13 Adapted from: http://en.wikipedia.org/wiki/List_of_municipalities_in_the_Western_Cape (Accessed on 14 August 2014).

14 Conventionally, *mainstream sports* is understood as sports organised by the official competitive sports structures, such as regional, national, and international sport governing bodies.

there were a few farm workers in attendance at the Committee meetings in the lead up to the Sports Day to be held on the 18th May 2013.[15] My interactions with the Committee and the DCAS officials did shed some light on the organisational and political structure that shaped the WCFSRD initiative; still, these told me little about sports practices among farm workers outside the annual Sports Day. Over time it became clear that there was no consistency in the ways in which sport was organised and practiced among the farm workers from across the province.

The objectives of the Committee to select the players and officials to perform at higher standards of sports suggests the presence of sports clubs consisting of farm workers who must have been competing in the mainstream official sports structures. Still, the farm workers' competitive and consistent participation in sports had remained constrained by transportation and financial limitations, as most of the Committee members unequivocally shared. My fieldwork with farm workers of Rawsonville also confirms that official and unofficial sports have been practiced in organised competitive forms by workers for at least last half a century, if not longer. Such practices were usually a result of efforts of individuals, including farm workers and other members of rural community from disparate backgrounds, who were at least partially successful in accessing resources to run their sports clubs. Among the Committee members were such individuals who had been involved in organising sports for farm workers in their respective region long before the Committee was formally established.

Particularly those who had close ties with a specific farm worker community and associated sports club spoke proudly about their sports teams and personal investment in the success of their athletes. To them, the purpose of being part of the Committee was to seek recognition and resources for their respective sports teams. For instance, over a suggestion that the Sports Day should be oriented towards friendly participation, rather than competitiveness, a committee member argued that he would have to bring together the strongest team for the event or how else would he justify the selection of the athletes from his region. These kinds of contentions were bound to arise, given the obscurity and discrepancies in the objectives of the DCAS and the Committee. The Sports Day itself was promoted with vague and inconsistent messages. At times, it claimed to provide the farm workers with an opportunity to participate in mainstream sports, and at other times it was a non-competitive sports event to enjoy participation and meet people from other regions. At a discursive level, the emphasis seemed to be on projecting sports' positive "development" impact, and, thus, the level of vagueness probably helped absorb

15 I attended three committee meetings in Robertson and the Sports Day in Paarl.

very different and conflicting meanings of what might be considered 'positive' by different people.

Part of the problem in organising such an initiative was the understanding of 'farm worker' as a distinct category to be serviced. It was clear from my conversations with a DCAS official that they had not considered farm workers as a separate category, but assumed it as part of their rural sports programmes. It was only when some farm-based civil society projects and sports clubs started to approach DCAS for funding and lobbied for attention to farm sports as distinct from rural sports that the DCAS made some funds available for these selected projects and sports clubs. Still, it was not until the provincial Cabinet, led by DoA, resolved on 'the strategic plan for the Farm Worker Community' in 2005 that the DCAS considered launching a province-wide sports initiative for farm workers, which, as the DCAS official I interviewed explained, focused on:

> ...getting farm workers to do something, at least, on the 1st of May, Workers' Day ... that will be our Workers' Day programme, but only for farm workers.[16]

While this Sports Day was among my main leads going into the fieldwork, it was not too long before I discovered that Rawsonville (and the whole municipal region Rawsonville is situated in) had no representation on the Committee. None of the farm workers involved in soccer, rugby, or netball I engaged with during fieldwork in Rawsonville had ever heard of this initiative, or the Committee, or the provincial Farm Worker Sports Day, despite the fact that the annual Sports Day of 2010 was held in Worcester, roughly 15 kilometres from Rawsonville. This is no surprise, given the geographical representations at the Committee were not according to municipalities but by province, which was divided into eight regions, coordinated by one or two representatives (Map 6.1). The DCAS claimed in a public document entitled *Reach Your Full Potential with DCAS* that for the Farm Worker Sports Day:

> Regional teams are chosen after trials in the districts and the strong competition at the tournament demonstrates that sport plays a key role in bringing people together. DCAS is determined to ensure that farm workers have the same access to organised sport and recreation as everyone else (DCAS, n.d., p. 40; online).[17]

16 Interview conducted with a DCAS official (January 2013).

17 Source: http://www.westerncape.gov.za/assets/departments/cultural-affairs-sport/dcas_generic_brochure.pdf (Accessed on 3 August 2014).

Contrary to DCAS's claims, there were no regional or district level competitions, nor were all the municipal regions, let alone smaller farming towns, represented on the Committee or at the annual Sports Day. The 'trials in the districts' was probably a reference to the localised efforts of those Committee members who might have been able to garner resources from elsewhere and were managing a relatively well-established sports network. These networks did not cover the whole region they represented but the network of farm communities they were part of. This certainly shows the level of commitment of these individuals to the development of sports in their respective farm worker community, in spite of the limited resources and their geo-political marginality. Still, this was no achievement of the WCFSRD initiative; instead whatever success WCFSRD had was from the fact that farm workers were participating and organising sports on their own.

As such, sports practiced among the farm workers were informally organised. To draw these informal sports practices and networks into the mainstream (as one of the DCAS's objectives) would require the kind of time, commitment, coordination, and infrastructure, which, at the time, was absent in the provincial sports "development" efforts. Neither the DCAS, nor the Committee, had the capacity to conduct province-wide district level trials for farm workers, or expand this programme systematically to include all the farming areas. Furthermore, I am unsure what a mainstream sports structure specifically for farm workers would really mean. According to what understanding of 'farm worker' would it include or exclude participants? Or might such efforts further exclude farm workers from existing mainstream sports structures? As things were, the farm worker sports development culminated in an annual Western Cape Farm Workers Sports Day, and its "development" significance rested on its attention to a group identified as in need of "development".

Notwithstanding, beyond the sports-based "development" practices, a very many farm workers participated actively in organising and competing in various sports in their everyday lives, while often feeling limited by lack of resources to take their endeavours further (for examples, see Kaur, 2017). When considered against this backdrop, the "development" agendas theorised in terms of their lack or need for 'life skills' to compensate for their isolation seemed, at best, an irresponsible misrepresentation. On the other hand, engaging with complex and messy realities was unlikely to advance "development" agendas that take deficiencies in the person or the community of farm worker as their starting point. While the attention to ameliorating personal-level deficiencies may help justify farm worker "development" plans and programmes, the contradictions and counter narratives were available even at the sites where these practices unfold, which I illustrate next by focusing on an aspect of "development": the life-skills training.

Life-skills for Farm Worker "Development"

> There was also a dire need for life-skills training, including family financial management, time management, social skills, HIV and TB management. Many farmers were keen to build employees' skills but training colleges and training courses are few. Government-sponsored training services are bureaucratic and cumbersome.[18]

This extract from an opinion piece authored by Doreen Atkinson was published in *Business Day* on 8 August 2014, in response to a policy proposal put forward by the Minister of Rural Development and Land Reform, which suggested 50% ownership of privately owned farmland to be made available to the farm workers who have been working that land. Arguing against this proposal, Atkinson proposes prioritising the 'dire need for life skills' instead of opportunity for landownership by the farm workers. Despite such patronising undertones, life-skills training is rather normalised in the broader "development" discourses in South Africa. Sports also features as a method to impart life-skills to all sorts of groups in need of "development", from young school children to youth-at-risk, from women to criminals, and from the unemployed to farm workers in full-time employment.

While it is possible that the way DoA defines farm workers' need for 'life-skills training' might be among the reasons for a large number of seemingly fragmented and isolated projects, the ideas and programmes labelled life-skills also did not seem to share a coherent theory of practice. Over the course of my fieldwork, I met and engaged with a few life-skills facilitators, some of whom were self-employed, while most were associated with an organisation, an NGO, or even a University's community relations project. I was particularly interested in learning how the concerns of "development" among the farm workers were understood by these facilitators, and how they connected life-skills training to "development". In an exchange with a facilitator, who was looking for funding so that her organisation might deliver a sports and life-skills programme to rural/farm worker communities, I learned about the programme and the overall ambition of the NGO. She explained that their programme uses sports as a medium to teach life skills. The programme had been very effective with another underprivileged community, and given their experience and success with the programme, they wanted to expand their operations to other

18 See: http://www.bdlive.co.za/opinion/2014/08/08/ownership-no-longer-the-key-to-empowering-farm-workers (Accessed on 3 September 2014).

underprivileged communities in South Africa, and perhaps to the rest of Africa. Still, I could not get her to comment on any specific social concern that might be affecting farm workers beyond the rhetoric that they were identified as a group in desperate need of "upliftment".

At a conversational level, I was only learning vague and, at times, contradictory explanations of life-skills. Conceptually, the term life-skills could be found in fields like applied psychology and pedagogy focusing on children and youth. In South Africa, it is part of school curriculum to educate learners on aspects ranging from healthy living to career guidance. As for the "development" of farm workers, life-skills training included assorted didactic lessons, ranging from time management, debt and financial management, work ethic, conflict resolution, disease prevention, personal hygiene, awareness campaigns, motivational speeches to 'uplift themselves', or how they should be nice to each other. Specific to sports, one facilitator shared how they train soccer coaches to teach life-skills alongside soccer tactics. He shared a video, in which a coach was shown to employ coaching on defence tactics in the game of soccer, and then he draws an analogy to teach the importance of safe sex, explaining how soccer players need to defend themselves from potential diseases. At the end, players reiterated what they had learned, when one player summed up the lesson as: he should 'never have sex'. Accordingly, the facilitator claimed that this was 'the only programme that has been sustainable and successful in this area',[19] before asking me if I knew any farmers from my research field who would like to sponsor this programme on their farm. While I met this facilitator at a commercial farm, where he delivered a life-skills programme, the example of soccer related life-skills training he shared was generic and the video clip was not specifically targeted at farm workers. The life-skills training session, delivered directly to a group of farm workers and that I attended, was the one with a facilitator, who I shall call John.[20]

John introduced himself as a life coach, who worked independently with the farmers and the farm workers. His approach to "development" was influenced by his moral or religious convictions. As he explained, his calling was helping others, and he used sports and games to give a 'creative twist' to the

19 'Sustainable and successful' meant that the facilitator had managed to persuade enough farmers to buy into the project and fund different aspects of it, including an annual sports day. The racial and religious identity of the facilitator, that is, 'white' Afrikaner and Christian, might have had a part to play in the success of the programme (field notes, 20 June 2012).

20 I use a pseudonym here, as I do not have permission from the facilitator to use his actual name.

life-skills training sessions he conducted. He had been a keen rugby player in his youth, and was coaching both farmers and farm workers, albeit on different aspects of sports and life. His training with the local farmers included psychological preparation to help with their sports performance goals. For example, some of the farmers in the area had entered a major cycling competition, and he would work with them to help set realistic goals, keep up the motivation to train, and overcome any mental barriers in achieving their goals. His work with farm workers, however, involved life-skills training, that is, how they could be better workers, and learn to improve their everyday lives. He conducted this training with the workers once a week for thirty minutes, at the end of their day's work. While he was convinced about the importance of this training and the impact it had on the farm workers, he often expressed unhappiness with the amount he was paid by the farmers for training their workers.

One evening, he invited me to join one of his training sessions with about ten workers from the same farm. He introduced me to the workers and agreed to play the translator as all of the workers were Afrikaans speaking. Besides the language barrier, the workers were not too communicative. Even simple questions like, if they were interested in sports or were connected to any local soccer or rugby clubs, did not get me very far. Given the dynamic, it was best for me to play the role of a passive observer and record workshop contents and interactions between the workers and John.

The first session I attended was themed 'team work' and workers were to work in teams to solve a puzzle, which followed a moral lesson on usefulness of working together to solve problems. The second session, a week later, was themed 'hard work'. The key point John wanted to make was that through hard work and perseverance any level of success can be achieved. He did so by sharing a video clip on his phone from a British TV show called Pop Idols. Through the clip, he shared a story of a person from a modest background who had won the talent contest because of the hard work he had put into his singing. John went on to persuade the workers how this could be their reality, if only they were willing to commit to hard work. To add another testimony, John drew me in, asking me to attest that it was really possible to achieve anything with hard work. I was hardly prepared to contribute and felt that I needed more information, so I softly asked John: 'What kind of negotiation power do they have in relation to time and work at the farm? Can they negotiate to finish a certain amount of work within a certain time so they can work hard towards something they have talent for, or were passionate about, or had higher chances of achieving success?' Even before John could respond or translate my question, one of the workers responded: 'At the farm, work never ends, you finish one thing and there is another that needs to be done!'

Conclusion

The counter narratives, contradictions, and critiques that I draw out here are not to suggest irrelevance or insincerity on the part of "development" agents, but to exemplify and argue that these agendas, however well intended, serve many different ends and conflicting interests. The programmes of farm worker "development" operate with a broad definition of "farm worker", often loosely, if at all, connected to the concerns of farm labour regimes in the Western Cape. By focusing on life-skills, sports, and sporadic sports day events, "development" activity could be conducted and justified, without necessarily disturbing the *status quo*. Situating my analysis in the history and politics of labour relations and farm worker "development" in the Western Cape, I tried to tease out continuities and contradictions in the way SDP discourses and practices take shape in this context. The fact that a group is identified as in need of "development" according to their occupation suggests that the problems farm worker development programmes seek to solve might lie in the broader farm labour relations practices and conditions of employment.

Not only did farm worker "development" discourses tend to depoliticise the historical, political, and economic implications of the conditions to which such programmes were conceptualised, but the managerial ways in which these were conducted also released farmers from the responsibilities that came with the paternalist order. This dynamic was particularly evident in the manner in which post-apartheid political contestations over land and labour were resolved in the funding and administration of "development" programmes by different actors and sectors associated with agricultural production (see for example Du Toit, 1994; & Williams, 2005, 2003). To this end, "development" did work like an 'anti-politics machine', where deeply divided political interests could find accord (Ferguson, 1990). The attraction of "development" programmes was not merely in defusing political contestations: these activities were also celebrated and marketed for their benevolent contributions.

The "development" programmes of the kind discussed in the chapter not only served the sponsoring organisations in advertising their social and ethical responsibility, the government departments were also able to shift their responsibilities for providing basic welfare services for the rural poor by allocating funds towards sporadic short-term "development" projects. In the process, issues such as poor cash wages, social and political marginality, adverse incorporation, limited access to the justice system, and failures on the part of the state to enforce labour laws were absorbed in the claims of special programmes of "development". Moreover, rather than dealing with the complex structural and political issues, the "development" agendas seek solutions in changing the person of the farm worker either by developing their work-related skills, or by training them in life-skills, or providing them with opportunities to enjoy sports. Such understandings of "development" or farm workers' need for life-skills were presented as if their material conditions, and the history and politics of farm labour relations, commercial agriculture, and land-ownership in South Africa had no bearing on the lives farm workers live today. In framing the everyday life struggles in terms of "development" problems, the image of the farm worker that is put forward is that of an undifferentiated group without any agency or aspirations. It is only in the denial to engage with their everyday life conditions, and the history and the politics of continued poor cash wages, unequal power-relations, and exploitative terms of employment, that sports could be argued as an aspect of farm worker "development".

There is little doubt that the labouring classes in South Africa are calling out for change in their social, political, and economic status (as the introduction of this book argues), but in the use of "development" as a language for change, there remains a denial of farm workers' own agency and their own aspirations. The abolition of slavery in the early nineteenth century, the reform efforts of the RF, and introduction of farm labour laws in the late twentieth century, despite contradictory implications, did disrupt the on-farm power-relations. And while ideas of "development" may not immediately be equipped to challenge the racialized class inequalities, an on-going and critical interrogation of such discourses and practices does create possibilities for new understandings to be garnered and new debates to be had.

References

Coalter, F. (2008). *A Wider Social Role for Sport: Who's Keeping the Score?* London: Routledge.

Du Toit, A. (2004). Social exclusion' discourse and chronic poverty: a South African case study. *Development and Change, 35*, 987–1010.

Du Toit, A. (1995). *Paternalism and Modernity on South African Wine and Fruit Farms.* (Unpublished PhD Dissertation). University of Essex, England.

Du Toit, A. (1994). Farm Workers and the 'Agrarian Question'. *Review of African Political Economy, 21*, 375–388.

Du Toit, A. (1993). The micro-politics of paternalism: the discourses of management and resistance on South African fruit and wine farms. *Journal of Southern African Studies, 19*, 314–336.

Du Toit, A., & Ally, F. (2004). *The Externalization and Casualisation of Farm labour in the Western Cape.* Belville: PLAAS/CRLS.

Du Toit, André, & Giliomee, H. (1983). *Afrikaner Political Thought*. Berkeley: University of California Press.

Du Toit, A., Kruger, S., Ponte, S. (2008). Deracializing exploitation? 'Black economic empowerment' in the South African wine industry. *Journal of Agrarian Change, 8*, 6–32.

Escobar, A. (2011). *Encountering Development: The Making and Unmaking of the Third World*. Princeton: Princeton University Press.

Ewert, J., & Du Toit, A. (2005). A Deepening Divide in the Countryside: Restructuring and Rural Livelihoods in the South African Wine Industry. *Journal of Southern African Studies, 31*, 315–332.

Ferguson, J. (1990). *The anti-politics machine: 'development', depoliticization, and bureaucratic power in Lesotho*. Minneapolis: University of Minnesota Press.

Guest, A.M. (2009). The diffusion of development-through-sport: analysing the history and practice of the Olympic Movement's grassroots outreach to Africa. *Sport in society, 12*, 1336–1352.

Guest, A.M. (2005). *Thinking both critically and positively about development through sport*. (Retrieved July 13, 2007).

Gunder Frank, A. (1966). *The development of underdevelopment*. Boston: New England Free Press.

Kaur, T. (2016). *Sporting Lives and 'Development' Agendas: A Critical Analysis of Sport and 'Development' Nexus in the Context of Farm Workers of the Western Cape*. PhD diss., University of the Western Cape.

Kaur, T. (2017). (Un)becoming Mountain Tigers Football Club: an ethnography of sports among the Western Cape's farm workers, *Anthropology Southern Africa*, 40:4, 290–302.

Kidd, B. (2011). Cautions, questions and opportunities in sport for development and peace. *Third World Quarterly, 32*, 603–609.

Kidd, B. (2008). A new social movement: Sport for development and peace. *Sport in Society, 11*, 370–380.

Levermore, R. (2008). Sport: a new engine of development? *Progress in Development Studies, 8*, 183–190.

Levine, S. (2013). *Children of a bitter harvest: Child labour in the Cape Winelands*. Cape Town: Human Sciences Research Council.

Mayson, D. (1990). *The Rural Foundation, Management and Change* (Unpublished MA Dissertation). University of Cape Town, South Africa.

Nussbaum, M. (1988). *Nature, function and capability: Aristotle on political distribution*. Oxford Studies in Ancient Philosophy, 145–184.

SA Wine Council (2007). *The Wine Industry Transformation Charter*.

Sachs, W. (Ed.) (2010). *The development dictionary: A guide to knowledge as power*. London & New York: Zed Books.

Scully, P. (1990). *The Bouquet of Freedom: Social and Economic Relations in the Stellenbosch District, South Africa c. 1870–1900*. Cape Town: Centre for African Studies.

SDP IWG (2007). *Literature Reviews on sport for development and peace*. Toronto: University of Toronto.

Watson, R.L. (2012). *Slave Emancipation and Racial Attitudes in Nineteenth-century South Africa*. Cambridge: Cambridge University Press.

Watson, R.L. (1990). *The slave question: liberty and property in South Africa*. Hanover, NH: Wesleyan University Press; University Press of New England, (Middletown, CT).

Williams, G. (2010). Free and unfree labour in the Cape wine industry, 1838–1988. In B. Harris-White & J. Heyer (Eds.), *The Comparative Political Economy of Development Africa and South Asia* (p. 179–196).

Williams, G. (2005). Black Economic Empowerment in the South African Wine Industry. *Journal of Agrarian Change*, *5*, 476–504.

Williams, G. (2003). Studying Development and Explaining Policies. *Oxford Development Studies*, *31*, 37–58.

Wilson, F., Kooy, A., & Hendrie, D. (Eds.) (1977). *Farm Labour in South Africa*. Cape Town: David Philip; Southern African Labour & Development Research Unit (Saldru), University of Cape Town.

Worden, N., & Crais, C.C. (Eds.) (1994). *Breaking the chains: slavery and its legacy in the nineteenth-century Cape Colony*. Johannesburg: Witwatersrand University Press.

CHAPTER 7

Intricacies of Game Farming and Outstanding Land Restitution Claims in the Gongolo Area of KwaZulu-Natal, South Africa

Tariro Kamuti

Introduction

This chapter looks at the intricacies of the relationship between land reform and wildlife ranching (game farming) in South Africa. These intricacies are manifested through challenges of unsettled land restitution claims in the Gongolo area of KwaZulu-Natal Province. In the study area there are land claims involving private properties that have been – or are in the process of being – converted to game farming. One particular and intriguing case used in this chapter relates to the complications associated with the proposed Gongolo Wildlife Reserve (GWR), which covers a sizeable part of the Umtshezi Municipality. Given the historical imbalance of land distribution (Department of Rural Development and Land Reform, 2013), the surge in wildlife ranching (Kamuti, 2014; Spierenburg and Brooks, 2014) has further complicated the land question due to conflicting interests of different actors. On the one hand, game farmers identify land reform as the greatest threat to game farming. On the other, landless communities support land reform and argue that the rise of game farming is denying them the opportunity to earn a livelihood through access to land. Meanwhile, government's ambivalent position and its delay in settling the land restitution complicate the case. The state is caught up in a dilemma of taking game farms as drivers of local economic development, while also needing to respond to the urgency of land reform (in the form of land restitution). In this particular case, some government departments (including district and local municipalities) buy into the arguments in favour of the proposed game reserve, while others are more ambivalent, so the whole process is stalled.

The chapter takes an institutional approach where institutions, defined as systems of rules (Fleetwood, 2008) governing the ownership of and access to land and wildlife resources, are critical. These institutions can be local governments, government agencies, and the majority of organisations that are described and explained by rules, norms, and shared strategies (Imperial, 1999). I take the intricacies of the relationship between land reform and wildlife

 | DOI 10.1163/9789004362550_008

ranching to be 'linked to institutional deficits in land-tenure and property rights systems, as well as to the values attached to land and natural resources by various actors' (Van der Duim et al. 2015, p. 2). As witnessed elsewhere in eastern and southern Africa, these intricacies are manifested through the push to change land use from conventional agriculture to wildlife-based developments under private hands without addressing concerns of landownership and access to wildlife resources (Van der Duim et al., 2015) by land claimants. Hence I adopted the 'Rock-in-Pond' analogy, which is a further consideration of Frances Cleaver's (2012) institutional bricolage. The state of affairs explained in this case study reflect the challenges that have been encountered in the land restitution programme (De Villiers, 2003; Walker, 2008), with implications for South Africa's agrarian reform for at least 20 years since democratic rule. I therefore explore the institutional implications of the interactions between game farmers, state authorities, other organisations, and communities at the local level through the example of the GWR. This is an attempt to unpack and explain the idea of competing needs over land through the intricacies posed by game farming on land restitution. As the case will show, there may be a need to restructure institutions or bring in new ones after carefully mapping a given situation, and paying attention to the ecological, economic, and social dimensions of the issues at stake, with use of transparent social dialogue (Slavíková et al., 2010; Van Wijk et al., 2015).

Method

The case study method was adopted as a pragmatic research project focused on a current issue happening *in situ* where there is no distinct demarcation between itself and its background (Yin, 1989). The study used different data-gathering methods (Yin, 1989) to maintain 'the multiple realities, the different and even contradictory views of what is happening' (Stake 1995, p. 12). This approach is line with the diverse actors involved in the wildlife ranching sector. It was important to collect the data in a manner that was flexible and sensitive to the context of the research environment (Remenyi, 2012). Due to background and contextual issues involved in the case study, findings were meant to answer specific research questions of the intricacies of the nexus between game farming and land reform. The findings therefore are treated as unique to the Gongolo case, which has its own contingent factors (Minichiello et al., 1990; Stake, 1995; Flyvbjerg, 2006). Drawing upon Stake (1978) this situation shows that case studies may be epistemologically in sync with personal experiences that improve a person's understanding. However, case studies are used outside the specific case study area to reflect on the broad context. The Gongolo area (see figure 7.2), at the local municipal level, was chosen as the geographical context of the study (Curtis et al., 2000).

The data were obtained through in-depth interviews of key informants from major stakeholder organisations and communities linked to the private wildlife sector in KwaZulu-Natal province. There were observations and conversations with respondents through visiting the study area in addition to analysis of documentary evidence. Stakeholders were regarded as 'groups or individual[s] who can affect or are affected by an issue' (Schiller et al. 2013, p. 1). The stakeholders' social identity (Crane and Ruebottom, 2011) or their involvement was crucial (Ozesmi and Ozesmi, 2003; Carsten et al., 2005) to identify their 'interests' (Orts and Strudler, 2009), which in a way guide their views and actions. Thus, when doing the research, I was aware that interviewees would project views directed toward portraying a particular meaning. Issues of land and its nexus to natural resources management for the benefit of marginalised people are of great interest to me.

In carrying out this study, I was also aware of my disposition as a citizen of Zimbabwe, a country characterised by fierce contestation over land (see Chapter 9). The experience of working in the fields and herding cattle for a great part of my upbringing as a son of peasants, all have a bearing on my views in this study. The study drew upon Henriques and Sardorsky's (1999) stakeholder types, which are regulatory stakeholders, organisational stakeholders, community stakeholders, and the media. The respondents mainly include the game farmers, officials from the provincial Department of Rural Development and Land Reform, Department of Agriculture and Environmental Affairs, Gongolo Wildlife Reserve (GWR), and the local municipality. Officials from the Association for Rural Advancement (AFRA), which is the main non-governmental organisation that has worked with the Gongolo community for over a decade, were also interviewed. There were interactions with the Gongolo Committee,[1] which represents the interests of the affected community of land claimants and labour tenants.

The Game Farming, Land Reform Nexus

This section emphasises the link between game farming and land reform to contextualise the case study in South Africa's agrarian reform. Game farming here refers to wildlife-based land use. The purpose of land reform in South Africa was 'to redress the imbalances of apartheid, foster national reconciliation and

1 This committee does not have a particular name, and for convenience purposes I will be referring to it as the Gongolo Committee. The committee represents the interests of the residents and claimants of the Gongolo region that is under claim but earmarked for the proposed Gongolo Wildlife Reserve.

stability, underpin economic growth and, lastly, improve household welfare and alleviate poverty' (Manji 2001, p. 330). The country's land-reform programme set a target of redistributing 30% of commercial agricultural land by 2014. However, the land-reform programme has been progressing at a snail's pace. Approximately 80% of South Africa's agricultural land is still privately owned, mainly by the white minority (Cousins et al., 2008; Bond et al., 2009; Department of Rural Development and Land Reform, 2013). The land-reform programme (encompassing restitution, redistribution, and tenure reform) cumulatively gave a total of 2.8 million hectares, or 3.4% of commercial farmland back to black beneficiaries between 1994 and mid-2005, well below the target (Walker, 2005). This is regarded as a 'blot' on the accomplishments of South Africa's democracy, since the critical question of the role of land (as a basic source of livelihood) in the fight against poverty is still facing policymakers (Cuthbertson 2008, p. 297). Given the historical imbalance of land distribution in South Africa, the increasing role of game farming (Brink et al., 2011; Snijders, 2012; Davies-Mostert, 2014) is complicating the land question. Game farming is on the rise through the trend of conversion of land use from conventional faming (Spierenburg and Brooks, 2014). In the study area, there are land claims involving private properties that have been – or are in the process of being – converted to game farming. Land that was successfully claimed has not been handed over to the claimants due to a proposal for wildlife ranching on the same land, hence the tension among the interested parties.

Theoretical Approach to the Intricacies of Game Farming and Outstanding Land Restitution Claims

The analytical research question was to contextualise the intricacies of the nexus between game farming and land reform in the Gongolo area of KwaZulu-Natal Province by using Jessica de Koning's (2011) 'Rock-in-Pond' analogy. Institutional bricolage is 'a process by which people consciously and unconsciously draw on existing social and cultural arrangements to shape institutions in response to changing situations' (Cleaver 2001, p. 26). Institutional bricolage says that formal institutions formulated through design principles do not provide the right mechanisms to intervene in the governance of natural resources (Cleaver, 2012). Instead people less deliberately start to use and modify already existing customs and practices to provide mechanisms through which new institutions serving a variety of functions are formed (Cleaver, 2012). The resultant institutions from the perspective of institutional bricolage are 'invariably uneven in functioning and impact, and are often fuzzy assemblages of meaningful practices, which overlap and serve multiple purposes' (Cleaver 2012, p. 45). Thus the

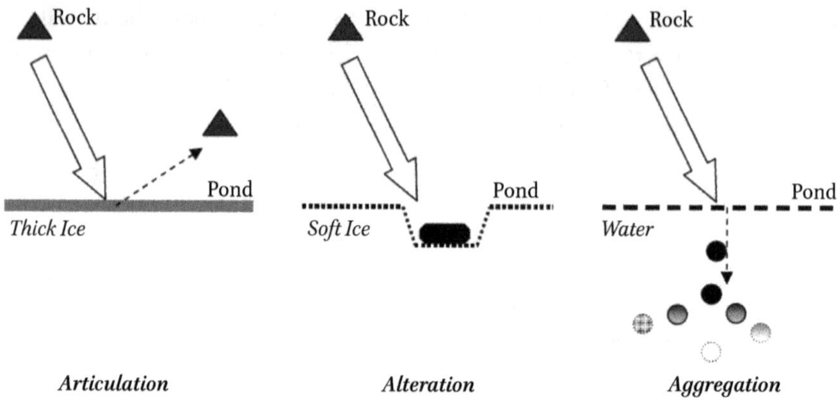

FIGURE 7.1 *A Diagram showing Three Ways of the Rock-in-Pond Analogy (de Koning, 2011: 215).*

'Rock-in-Pond' analogy point towards a plurality of institutional settings that emerges when institutions avoid design and are reconfigured by the different ways through which articulation, alteration and aggregation (figure 7.1) work together (De Koning, 2011). There is a gradual change in the institutions that govern the use of natural resources (Van Wijk et al., 2015).

The rock is here taken to represent the competing thrusts of formal land restitution and game farming processes, while the pond represents the people and their socially embedded institutions. Articulation can be seen as the rock hitting on ice where 'the bureaucratic institution bounces off the shield of socially embedded institutions' (De Koning 2011, p. 215), resulting 'in a situation resembling a clash, a friction or a discord between the different types of institutions' (De Koning 2011, p. 216). In the Gongolo case, this refers to the tension culminating in outright rejection of game farming by the community of land claimants as they fight to go ahead with their own land use plans according to their social and cultural values. Alteration is similar to when the rock hits 'half frozen water' (De Koning 2011, p. 215). In this instance, 'the bureaucratic institution leaves a mark on the local institutional framework but does not achieve its original objective' such that this 'results in a modification in the institutional framework' and the outcome is difficult to determine (De Koning 2011, p. 215). Outright implementation of game farming in accordance with the investors' initial plans, which disregard the inspiration of the land claimants, will not be possible. Maybe there would be a set up like that of community game farms (Ngubane & Brooks, 2013), where land beneficiaries become game farmers. With respect to aggregation, the rock sinks into the pond signifying that 'external regulations and norms are to a certain extent adopted and combined with the local institutions' (De Koning 2011, p. 215). The result of aggregation is when bureaucratic institutions are level with the socially embedded institutions (De Koning, 2011). Aspects of game farming are possibly incorporated into the local people's natural resource management plans as the rightful owners of the land. The theoretical argument suggested here is that institutional processes of trying to resolve the land restitution claim in Gongolo gradually resemble De Koning's (2011) 'Rock-in-Pond' analogical processes of articulation, alteration, and eventually aggregation.

The Enduring Gongolo Wrangle

In the Gongolo area, land restitution has slowed due to issues related to game farming. The major part of the land under dispute is found in Umtshezi Local Municipality, while the rest is found in neighbouring municipalities of Okhahlamba and Mpofana. The process of claiming land is complex as Walker's (2008) account attests, which Atuahene (2014) puts into five phases of lodgement, validation, verification, negotiation, and valuation. The people in Gongolo[2] lodged restitution and labour tenant claims before the 31 December 1998 deadline in terms of two pieces of legislation that is, Restitution of Land Rights Act (No. 22 of 1994) and Land Reform (Labour Tenants) Act (No. 3 of 1996). All land claims should have been finalised by 2008, but this was not the case (Boudreaux 2010) including the Gongolo claim. Almost 80,000 rural- and urban-based land claims were lodged by the 31 December 1998 deadline but 4296 claims were outstanding by 31 March 2009 especially from the rural areas, and the greatest number (1 652) of them from KwaZulu-Natal Province (Boudreaux, 2010). Thus the Restitution of Land Rights Amendment Act (No. 15 of 2014) was passed in order to extend the deadline[3] for lodging land claims from 31 December 1998 as was provided for in the Restitution of Land Rights Act (No. 22 of 1994) to 30 June 2019.

Gongolo (see figure 7.2 below) is an area that is between Estcourt, Mooi River, and Weenen, cumulatively covering approximately 40,000 hectares of farms previously owned by 16 individual landowners. The claimants lodged the claim as 7 *isigodi* (otherwise referred to as wards) under two traditional authorities

2 Gongolo, which is the name used to refer to this area, is derived from one of the rivers that runs through the area. This is according to AFRA's 'Community Status Report 2011'.

3 The South African President referred to the issue of the opening another window for citizens to launch fresh claims. See 'State of the Nation Address by His Excellency Jacob G Zuma on the occasion of the Joint Sitting of Parliament, Cape Town' 12 February 2015 (online) URL: http://www.thepresidency.gov.za/pebble.asp?relid=19024 (Accessed on 11 March 2015).

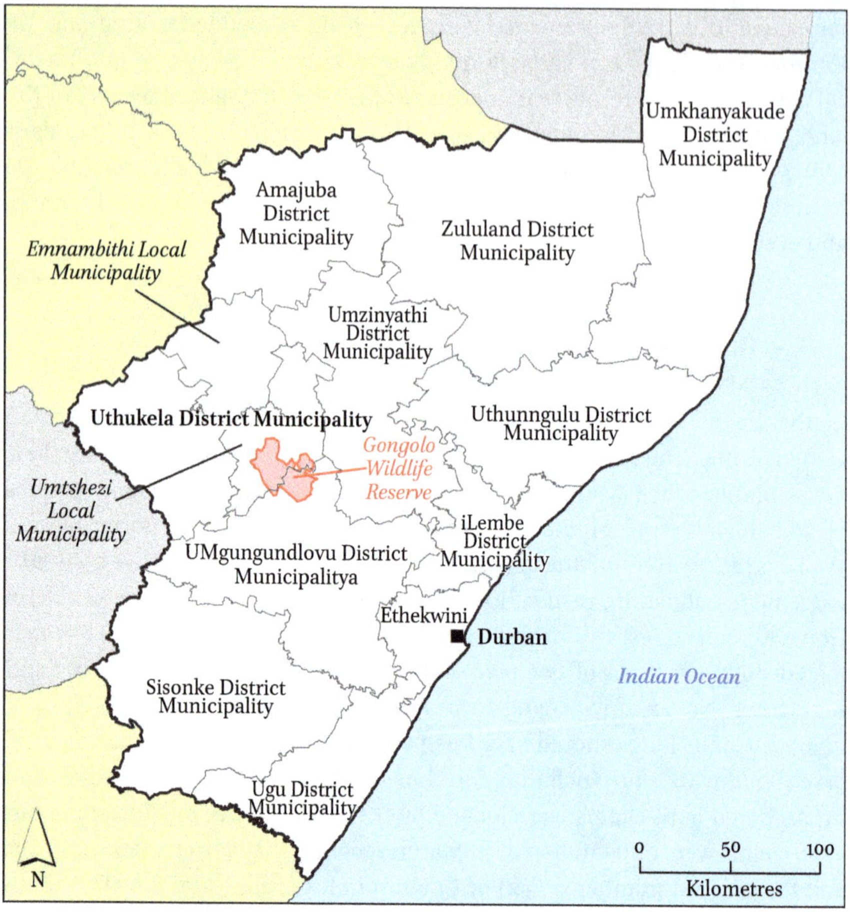

FIGURE 7.2 *A Map of KwaZulu-Natal Province showing Proposed Gongolo Wildlife Reserve (Kamuti, 2016: 17).*

that is, Mchunu with 3 *isigodi* and Mthembu with 4 *isigodi*. The amaChunu *isigodi* are Phofini, Nhlangwini, and Mhlumba, while the amaThembu *isigodi* are Matshesi, Mngwenya, Ntunda, and Nontethe.[4] There was a third community called Motane that lodged a restitution claim which took seven years (up to February 2006), as compared to the other two which took three years (up to February 2002) to be confirmed and gazetted.[5] An official from the RLCC

4 This is according to AFRA's 'Community Status Report 2011' and the same information was also corroborated by a chairperson of the committee representing the claimants.

5 See 'Gongolo Court Case Briefing', http://www.pambazuka.org/images/articles/522/Gongolo%20Court%20Case%20Brief%2023%20March%202011.pdf (Accessed on 5 December

explained that Zulu people are organised in *isigodi*, which crudely translates to a ward, though an *isigodi* is not a ward. An *isigodi* is a section of people that have a similar kinship and similar lineages to a particular chieftainship, and that group of people is spread in a particular area. That area is called an *isigodi*. People in each *isigodi* would then access land and use natural resources in accordance with local institutional processes determined through their social, economic, and cultural values and norms. Adherence to the *isigodi* in the context of the land restitution programme can be interpreted in the sense that it was convenient for the land claimants and government officials to validate and verify the land claims according to the phases described by Atuahene (2014). Walker (2008) gives intriguing accounts of people's stories of 'loss and hurt' to authenticate their identities, as this was crucial to a successful land claim. An *isigodi* therefore becomes a critical local institutional framework, which is part of the socially embedded institutions referred to by De Koning (2011). According to the official, an *isigodi* has been entrenched in people's everyday lives since time immemorial. So one challenge of land restitution in KwaZulu-Natal relates to differences between what individuals would have claimed against where their *isigodi* belonged to, as is the case in Gongolo.

Landowners who own farms that were part of the claimed land formed a company, Gongolo Wildlife Reserve (GWR), and made a draft proposal to establish a grand game reserve after government delayed buying the claimed land. The Gongolo people started a committee[6] of 15 representatives from the 7 *isigodi*. The Gongolo Committee, rooted in the *isigodi*, constitute part of the socially embedded institutions in the Gongolo area. The Gongolo Committee with the help of AFRA started to negotiate with the landowners and the government through the Department of Land Affairs (now Department of Rural Development and Land Reform: DRDLR) and the Regional Land Claims Commission (RLCC). This kind of negotiation between a committee (representing the claimants) and government is alike other restitution cases in the country (Atuahene, 2014).

According to the land restitution process, once land has been successfully claimed, government should take steps to purchase the land from the current owner (Boudreaux, 2010; Atuahene, 2011a). The land can then be restored to its rightful owners who were once disadvantaged or some form of compensation

2012); and 'Gongolo Heads of Argument', http://www.afra.co.za/upload/files/heads%20of%20argument%20gongolo.pdf (Accessed on 5 December 2012).

6 This committee does not have a particular name, so it will be referred to as the Gongolo Committee. The committee represents the interests of the residents and claimants of the Gongolo region that is under claim but earmarked for the proposed Gongolo Wildlife Reserve.

worked out in the form of money or with land elsewhere (Boudreaux, 2010; Atuahene, 2011a). Information from the Gongolo Committee and the RLCC substantiate that government was going to buy the land. This is understandable in the context that 'restitution claims are all claims against the South African state, not against individual landowners' (Boudreaux 2010, p. 15). The thrust was to implement land restitution following the successful land claim, for the beneficiaries to own, access, and utilise the land. The Gongolo Committee agreed with the RLCC that government was going to buy the land. However, the landowners went ahead to appoint a consultant to plan for the development of the GWR, which they intended to be KwaZulu-Natal's major attraction.

Research by Brooks et al. (2012) in this area shows that farm dwellers (mainly labour tenants) are perceived as a hindrance to the realisation of the creation of a wilderness impression. The wilderness impression is based on the idea of a 'third nature', which involves reworking landscapes to support a certain level of wildlife to 'pristine' levels that are in turn packaged to attract international tourists (Hughes, 2005; Brooks et al., 2011). The planned reserve was modelled on ideals similar to the framing of transfrontier conservation areas under neoliberal leanings (Ramutsindela, 2007). Tensions coupled with minimal benefits to the community caused by the neoliberalisation of conservation on the Makuleke land claim in Kruger National Park have been acknowledged (Tapela and Omara-Ojungu, 1999; Ramutsindela and Shabangu, 2013). However De Villiers and Van den Berg (2006) present the Makuleke case as one of the 'trailblazers' of the land restitution programme. Such a neoliberal approach to land rights on the part of the current owners does not cater for the need for transformation (Atuahene, 2011b) in order to restore the 'dignity' of the disadvantaged people (Atuahene, 2014). The Kameelkop Community Game Farm next to Greytown in KwaZulu-Natal Province is a case where wildlife ranching has continued as the major land use after successful land restitution (Ngubane & Brooks, 2013). However, Ngubane and Brooks (2013, p. 399) are critical of the new institutional set up of the community game farm concept 'which works to conflate or deny the distinct historical identities of the beneficiary groups'. This is contrary to the dismantled Ngome Community Game Reserve around Ladysmith, where there is now communal ownership of pastureland for the land restitution beneficiaries (see Chapter 12).

According to their officials, AFRA commissioned a study to assess the environment, soil types, and rainfall patterns, and to find out whether people can still use the land for agriculture. Some parts were identified as fertile and can still be used for cropping and grazing purposes, while other parts were found to be suitable for game farming. The Gongolo Committee and AFRA officials pointed out that some claimants were not completely opposed to game farming, especially if there is support from government and other stakeholders. In a study about resettlement of people to pave the way for the Limpopo National Park in Mozambique, Milgroom and Spierenburg (2008) noted that, while initially most residents refused to move, later due to different pressures, some residents changed their views as new alliances were forged. Therefore, the idea of restitution was attractive since government would buy the land and hand it over to them as the rightful owners. The landowners' perspective was that restitution through the same land was not a possibility. The GWR official indicated that once the restitution took place the claimants would be given land elsewhere on the periphery of the GWR land or the people would get financial compensation for their land. GWR was prepared to put up houses and talked about promises of jobs[7] and shares in the game reserve for the Gongolo community. Citing the plan to establish a 'Heritage Park' in the North West Province where conservation is propped up, Bologna and Spierenburg (2015, p. 119) argue that the 'rhetoric of economic opportunities and poverty alleviation ... further marginalizes local populations'.

Due to the popularity of game farming as a possibility of investment as well as an economic growth engine (Spierenburg and Brooks, 2014), the provincial authorities were impressed by the GWR plan. The provincial government through its Finance and Economic Development Department supported the idea.[8] The GWR project was perceived to boost the economy of the province. The affected District Municipalities of uThukela and uMgungundlovu also supported the idea. The Umtshezi Local Municipality, which has the bulk of the GWR land and which is a struggling local authority, saw the GWR as an opportunity for development. So in the eyes of the provincial and local authorities, the farmers' plans looked better, because the farm dwellers' plans for the area are mainly small scale or subsistence farming.

Government is seen to have countenanced land transfers that involve coopting post-settlement support, since the lack of such support was causing failure of land redistribution projects elsewhere in the country (Hall, 2009). In their land-use plan, people made huge demands from the government in terms of support, and this could have made government unsupportive of land transfer directly to the claimants. An AFRA official argues that since land reform started, government has not shown the political will to address this issue. Jara and Hall (2009) contend that the lack of political will has characterised the first decade of democracy in South Africa since 1994. The AFRA official noted that

7 See 'Bureaucracy stalls almost 2000 jobs' by Fiona Macleod in the Mail and Guardian of 29 July 2011, http://mg.co.za/article/2011-07-29-bureaucracy-stalls-almost-2nbsp000-jobs (Accessed on 21 October 2011).

8 This information is from a document entitled: 'Outcome of the Gongolo Dialogue on Future Land Use Options, Imperial Hotel, Pietermaritzburg, 24 June 2008' prepared by AFRA.

the lack of political will is especially clear in cases of claims that have some political connotations.[9] He regarded Gongolo as one of the cases, given the GWR proposal drafted by the landowners who form part of Agri SA, a powerful white dominated agricultural organisation. Jara and Hall (2009, p. 215) concur that 'Agri SA has invested heavily in its close relationship with the highest echelons of government' so there was a question of power at play here.

Meanwhile, even if trade-offs exist due to conservation (Hirsch et al., 2010) there is no practical comparison of the financial benefits from the farm dwellers' idea of subsistence farming and the game farmers' plans. One possible reason is that 'small-scale food production, processing and marketing are considered by some to be unproductive, inefficient and incapable of producing quality outputs reliably' (Adolph and Grieg-Gran 2013, p. 2). Hence there is 'an obvious preference for supporting black farmers who will become counterparts in a white-dominated commercial farming sector, rather than poor people whose interests in and use of land differ significantly from those of established farmers' (Hall 2009, p. 22). However, Aliber and Cousins (2013) argue that smallholder farming can be far reaching in terms of the large number of beneficiaries and improvement of their livelihoods, though there is need for contextual support (see also Aliber and Hart, 2009; Aliber and Hall 2012; Chapter 7). Small-scale food production, despite being sidelined (McMichael, 2009), may in fact have direct effects in alleviating poverty and malnutrition (Adolph and Grieg-Gran, 2013). Elsewhere, Li (2011) argues, that large-scale land acquisition has not resulted in poverty reduction. Integration of contemporary ecological systems with indigenous knowledge systems presents powerful approaches to the sustainability discourse (Lertzman, 2009) in a situation that would resemble De Koning's (2011) aggregation.

Community Concerns to the Idea of a Game Reserve

The chairperson of the Gongolo Committee pointed out that the landowners did not consult the community and that is why some community members were against the project. He said that the farmers came to tell them that they were going ahead with the project as he argued:

> The other thing that confuses which makes people angry is that the farmers introduced this thing as if they are going to employ people again to earn more than R1200 per month. The people said that this means that

9 Interview with an AFRA official, 9 November 2011.

> we are still going to be in a situation similar to that under apartheid government and we are still going to be slaves. It is not like this thing is going to be for everyone. There is no clear benefit for the people except jobs. They said they are going to lease the land from us for 99 years for money to come to the community. This is not clear as to how much and how will that money come and reach the community. Our biggest fear is that we do not have anything in our hands, so even if we agree today it seems we will only be workers and slaves again. There has always been a question that remains unanswered: What will be our role if this game reserve is established?[10]

The chairperson of the Gongolo Committee also expressed a sentiment of powerlessness on the part of the residents:

> If Gongolo Wildlife Reserve or government would make it clear the better. This is because we do not have money, they have money, we do not have the skills and they have the skills. We need to check these things. Who will be there? It is their wives and kids because they have skills.[11]

So according to him some people did not like the idea of the game reserve at all, while some were saying that they need the land transferred to them first to have a strong negotiating position. People who were against the game reserve needed to use the land for cropping and livestock grazing purposes, since dangerous animals would pose a threat to their lives and livestock.[12]

In my conversations with AFRA officials, their reasoning was that the affected people wanted to have their land rights addressed first and then the idea of the game farm would be discussed thereafter. So the position of AFRA was that farmers should recognise the status of the landless people. The situation is complex from the land reform point of view, because there are restitution claimants, labour tenants, and just farm dwellers who are farm workers or living on the farms without the status of labour tenants. This is in addition to the two tribal authorities and a couple of municipal boundaries that intercept in the contested area. The people's and AFRA's position were in contrast to the GWR proposal that the people should be relocated to give way to the game

---

10 Interview with Gongolo Committee Chairperson, August 2012.

11 Interview with Gongolo Committee Chairperson, March 2013.

12 Interview with Gongolo Committee member, March 2013, Estcourt; similar sentiments were also echoed by the Secretary of the KwaZulu-Natal Region of the Landless People's Movement on 5th August 2012, Pietermaritzburg.

reserve. It seems people did not like that idea of relocation. AFRA purports to prop up the farm dwellers' status (an attempt to give them agency) when they negotiate with landowners. These different status positions illustrate different power relations among the actors as well as a milieu of institutions, which are intertwined in a way that reflect a move towards a plurality of institutional settings of the 'Rock-in-Pond' analogy.

An official from the RLCC explained the concept of the *isigodi*, which might shed some light on the concerns of the community. He elaborated that:

> You are dealing with a community that does not understand a concept even if you try to explain it to them. It is not that they do not understand but it is just that the way you explain the concept to them is not to their level of comprehension because you do not understand them that way. If you have these dynamics, believe me in KwaZulu-Natal you will not do anything, it becomes seriously complicated. The complication is that you do not understand why there is serious resistance to what looks like a very rational business proposal. It is because the language you are talking, the translation to the people who are affected, they simply do not understand you. Until you come down to their level and make them understand what you are trying to do then they will say fine, since you put it that way let us think about it.[13]

The issues singled out by the RLCC official point to the clash of the game farmers' and the people's views, aspirations, meaning, and attachment to the value of their land. The resistance by the land claimants to game farming illustrates De Koning's (2011) articulation. According to his view, the GWR is an interesting project but the investors did not do enough research to understand the area and acknowledge that the affected people have a right to own and use the land according to their needs.

There is also the implication of traditional authorities in game farming, because, as a lucrative sector, the traditional authority benefits, his subjects benefit too but the extent of benefits is questionable. AFRA (2004) reports that divisions arose within the Gongolo Committee and were exacerbated by the RLCC's support of some committee members and the farmers. The RLCC was going to buy the land and make an *Inkosi* (chief), a trustee but the Gongolo Committee needed a judge and a lawyer to be added as trustees. The Regional Land Claims Commissioner proceeded to appoint the *Inkosi* as a sole trustee without the committee's approval. Subsequently the community took the

13 Interview with Regional Land Claims Commission Official, August 2012.

Regional Land Claims Commissioner to the Land Claims Court. The court action was an affront to the *Inkosi* and traditional authorities in Gongolo, which precipitated conflict between the *Amakhosi* (chiefs) and the Committee. The Land Claims Court made landmark decisions, which the chairperson of the Gongolo Committee confirmed in one of our conversations. The purchase of land would proceed, the power of the *Inkosi* as a sole trustee was rescinded, and the legitimacy of the Committee would be recognised by the RLCC according to the Order of the Court.

However, the AFRA official who was working with the Gongolo community indicated that traditional authorities (Mchunu and Thembu) have no specific role with regard to this project. It is the Gongolo Committee that is leading the process on behalf of the claimants. This Gongolo Committee has a relationship with the two traditional authorities, in so much as the committee regularly gives feedback to the traditional authorities for consultation purposes. The chairperson of the Gongolo Committee said that actually the committee was put in place with the blessing of the traditional authorities, from whom the committee carries its mandate to represent the communities. The RLCC official had this to say about the traditional authorities:

> You have a group of people who have well entrenched traditions, these guys have a very sound ear of what their people are saying because they are there on the ground, and they are not aloof. They say as long as it is good for our people this is not a problem, but talk to our people first. One of the things that I have learnt about the Zulus is that they listen to their inkosi, so when an inkosi makes an instruction he must be very careful because everybody will follow that instruction to the letter. So the Amakhosi are very careful about what is best for their people, because they listen to each other.[14]

The RLCC official views this as an important institutional set up of practices, rules, and norms that work well for the people. This may resemble De Koning's (2011) socially embedded institutions, though there is criticism about the role of traditional authorities in a modern day democracy (Ntsebeza, 2005). Observations and interactions made through visits to the area showed that some of the land is occupied by former labour tenants who are not doing much cropping, though they have livestock in numbers larger than what they used to keep during the time when the farmers were still around.

14 Interview with Regional Land Claims Commission Official, August 2012.

There are problems, which have arisen due to the government's choice of course of action. The two types of claims, which are overlapping, are being dealt with by two arms of the same department. The Department of Rural Development and Land Reform (at district level) is dealing with labour tenant claims, while the RLCC (at provincial level) is dealing with land restitution claims. There is confusion relating to the role of each of these two arms of government, as they are not integrated to resolve the claims. The biggest challenge, according to an AFRA official, is that the office of the RLCC has a reputation of high staff turnover as the RLCC official corroborated:

> That is the problem with this claim. Very few people have stayed with it for more than a year. I am the only individual now who has known this case for four full years. I was not part of the decisions that were made, I do not know why, but I am the project officer for this claim.[15]

There have been different Commissioners, and each Commissioner has his/her own strategy of how the Gongolo issue should be resolved. These dynamics reflect the ongoing development of institutions (which are defying design) in a less deliberate way by using and modifying already existing customs and practices. This situation points to a long drawn out process of providing mechanisms, through which new institutions serving a variety of functions are formed in people's use of natural resources as articulated by De Koning (2011). In this way, institutions avoid design and are reconfigured in different ways that are not predictable.

Land claims in Gongolo have been a staggering process characterised by accusations and counter-accusations amongst the stakeholders. A GWR official said that initially the government supported the project, but then everything came to a halt, and he said: 'Although we expected land claims we did not expect them to be corrupt. All of a sudden in 2002 we were told that there were all these restitution claims'.[16] So the GWR official disputed the land restitution claims on the basis that there were no Africans who had settled in the Gongolo area when the whites took over the land. The RLCC official explained to me that, in buying the land, GWR assumed rights over the properties, and they had to register those under the title of GWR. The transfer of landownership is an expensive exercise, which GWR undertook involving the previous landowners who were now shareholders as he explained:

15 Interview with Regional Land Claims Commission Official, March 2013.

16 Interview with Gongolo Wildlife Reserve Official, July 2012.

> However restitution is not part of that deal. With restitution, when they say property description, what they do is to go to the Deeds Office and find out who is the current owner of that property. So no property transfer will happen for that property. We come here Regional Land Claims Commission [RLCC] and do a letter to the farmer so that we can offer him a certain amount of money for that land. The problem is that the farmer and Gongolo Wildlife Reserve are fighting as to whom we should buy the land from. As Regional Land Claims Commission we say in the Deeds Office this is the owner therefore the farmer is the person we are legally bound to buy that land from. Gongolo Wildlife Reserve would not hear of that.[17]

Some of the properties were not transferred because they were under claim, but there was already an agreement between GWR and the original landowner. The landowners' initiative to establish a reserve was to some extent an effective strategy to block land restitution. The dispute dragged for nine years by going to court, as far as to the Parliamentary Portfolio Committee on Rural Development and Land Reform. This drove the then Minister of Land Affairs Lulama Xingwana to sign a notice of possible expropriation of the land on 31 October 2007, though it is a decision that was never implemented.[18] Subsequently, due to this long drawn dispute some of the landowners who had an agreement with GWR opted to withdraw from the GWR arrangement and started to consider offers from government to dispose of their land.[19]

The RLCC official denied the argument by the GWR official of false land restitution claims by arguing that:

> There was a talk that the claims were not valid but everybody forgot to do a little bit of digging when they pronounced that the claims were invalid. The Section 42D is a signed document that says yes this is a valid claim. The claims became valid when the minister signed that Section 42D approving that the land be disposed of to the claimants. Now the issue of the claims being invalid goes out the window completely unless of course

17 Interview with a Regional Land Claims Commission Official, July 2012.

18 This is according to a memorandum that was signed by the Minister on 31 October 2007 to approve a notice of possible expropriation of the disputed land after a deadlock was reached and therefore a dispute declared.

19 This is according to a settlement agreement between Gongolo Wildlife Reserve and Maint Farms CC and David Mervyn Green Will Trust as legal personalities linked to the individuals who have signalled their withdrawal from the Gongolo Wildlife Reserve venture.

> you write to the minister to reverse that or if you go to court and a decision is made that the minister was wrong.[20]

As a result, he attributes 90% of the delays and complications in the Gongolo land claim to the actions of the GWR. However, the government's position (through its Department of Finance and Economic Development Department) was thus complicit with the landowners, as there was a delay in settling land claims, given the history of land dispossession in the area.[21] The GWR official said that one of their mistakes was that of letting government officials bid on the behalf of the community:

> The mistake we made was that the Department insisted, absolutely insisted that [since] they supported the project it was their role to liaise with the community while actually what they did was that they poisoned the communities against Gongolo Wildlife Reserve in a nasty way.[22]

This shows that there was tension between GWR and the RLCC in relation to how the handling of the Gongolo land claim later unfolded (a situation of De Koning's 2011 articulation). For GWR to let government officials lobby the community on their behalf and the subsequent imposition by government on the people as to how the land should be used constitutes an oversight, which is symptomatic of the neglect by 'outside' organisations on the aspirations of indigenous communities (Chernela and Zanotti, 2014). The government has been drawn towards banking on the private sector to work with land-reform beneficiaries as a way to speed up the land reform programme (Jara and Hall, 2009; Hall, 2009). Therefore government has been criticised for forcing land restitution beneficiaries into partnerships with white-owned agribusinesses (Shaker, 2003).

In terms of the land restitution process, the GWR people were not convinced that the Commission would resolve this issue, so they resorted to the courts as of March 2011.[23] The landowners wanted the court to declare that, even though

---

20 Interview with Regional Land Claims Commission official, March 2013.

21 See 'Gongolo Heads of Argument', http://www.afra.co.za/upload/files/heads%20of%20argument%20gongolo.pdf (Accessed on 5 December 2012).

22 Interview with Gongolo Wildlife Reserve official, August 2012.

23 See 'Legal Move has Land Claimants Worried' The Witness, 31 March 2011; 'Gongolo Court Case Briefing', http://www.pambazuka.org/images/articles/522/Gongolo%20Court%20Case%20Brief%2023%20March%202011.pdf (Accessed on 5 December 2012); and 'Gongolo Heads of Argument', http://www.afra.co.za/upload/files/heads%20of%20argument%20gongolo.pdf (Accessed on 5 December 2012).

there was a legitimate claim, there should be no transfer of land to the people. At one time GWR wanted the restitution cases to be moved from the RLCC to the DRDLR's provincial office (because of the overlap of the claims to be dealt with one office). I contend that GWR's position was informed by their allegation that there were spurious land restitution claims, which they would not recognise. So by the same token the farmers would also have wanted the restitution claims to be dealt with the land reform office. They are completely using the loopholes in laws to further their interest; they have the means and power to navigate legal procedures and institutions and access knowledge on how to do this. This is quite coincidental, as Walker (2008, p. 28) describes a case study of Cremin 'a former "black spot" ... located some 20 km northeast of Ladysmith in the northwestern corner of KwaZulu-Natal. This was the first restitution claim to be settled in the province, by means of a court order'.

A Twist to the Gongolo Issue

One landowner sold his farm to an African businessman who is also an anti-apartheid struggle politician. This transaction happened when the Gongolo Committee were working to stop establishment of the GWR, because this farm was part of the land under claim. Unfortunately the new landowner did not take into account of the plight of the land claimants. The new landowner relocated one of the resident families and left others settling on a portion of the farm. He fenced off the area and brought in animals like zebras (*Equus quagga*), kudus (*Tragelaphus strepsiceros*), giraffes (*Giraffa camelopardalis*), and even rhinos (*Ceratotherium simum*). The Gongolo Committee made representations to the then Department of Land Affairs officials and farmers' representatives to sort out the problem, as the occupation was infringing on the rights of the people settled on the property.

The chairperson of the Gongolo Committee said that the businessman told them that they could not stop him because he was involved with politicians. The chairperson was also advised by one senior member of the DRDLR that there was no way they could stop the new landowner as a black person. The argument is that government is taking properties from the whites to the blacks, so it is difficult to take land from a black person to another black person. In addition, it was not easy to stop the business because it was happening on his private property. The RLCC official also supported the idea of the new black game farmer:

> The land is still under claim, there is no doubt about that, but we still need to go to him. He is a black person, what is the point of buying land

> from a black person? My theory was that if there is a black person who owns land in the claimed area, the beauty about it is that that piece of land can be taken out of the claim and he can do better business, the business will outflow to the claimed land which later will also be owned by other black people anyway.[24]

This sentiment shows that government was prepared to bend over backwards, as part of elite capturing of state resources, to suit the needs of an individual at the expense of disadvantaged people. In addition, the chairperson of the Gongolo Committee expressed his fear, which seemed real and eminent:

> But our own fear is that his neighbouring farmers are collaborating with him to consolidate this farm with their farms to make a big game farm and maybe it will make a big impact. Originally this farm was a cattle farm.[25]

The people who reside on the new game farmer's land are waiting for government to purchase that portion of land for them, since it is part of the land under claim. In this case, land restitution on the part of the land claimants has not succeeded, while the new landowner went on to establish a game farm on disputed land. This institutional set up resembles De Koning's (2011) alteration.

Conclusion

The intricate and complex Gongolo land claim is an example of the contestation for land resources informed by different imperatives and meanings emanating from different groups, that is, landowners on one side and the labour and restitution claimants on the other. The contestations at local level have thus far prevented a major corporate investment programme based on wildlife from going ahead in line with the De Koning's (2011) idea of articulation. State authorities using formal institutions or governance mechanisms have struggled to intervene to ease the situation. It is probable that the province supported the landowners rather than supporting the farm dwellers, because the latter's plans for the area focus mainly on small scale or subsistence farming.[26] The game farmers would need the buy-in of the local people to build

---

24 Interview with Regional Land Claims Commission Official, March 2013.

25 Interview with Chairperson of Gongolo Committee, March 2013.

26 Interview with AFRA Official, November 2011.

cooperation. Maybe the conflicting parties would come up with a desirable institutional outcome in this context, given the way the power relations played out eventually.

However, this situation is indicative of a trend where landowners, sometimes inadvertently in cahoots with the state, fight against 'communities' towards their path to social and economic transformation. For the more than 20 years now since majority rule, further delay in the land reform process in South Africa can cause land invasions (Tong, 2014) or instability (Atuahene, 2014), such as what happened in Zimbabwe from 2000 (Atuahene, 2007; see also Chapter 9). Nevertheless there are signs of co-operation between the Gongolo Committee and the Gongolo Wildlife Reserve Task Team, showing the reconfiguration of power relations amongst the actors resulting in some form of De Koning's (2011) alteration. The actors are shaping new institutional processes based on advancing their interests in a manner that is less confrontational so far. The role of non-state actors like AFRA and the Gongolo Committee shows the fugitive nature of power, which is no longer confined within formal institutional authorities (Farell, 2004). The establishment of a game reserve by a new landowner (who disregarded the wants of the claimants) is some form of aggregation, albeit not in the manner envisaged by the GWR and the land claimants, thus further complicating the land claims in Gongolo. The institutional framework in the Mala Mala Game Reserve[27] in Mpumalanga Province, one year after settling of that land restitution case, is already showing reconfiguration in light of the tension that has ensued over benefits. Mixed results from the Gongolo and other cases show that institutions on natural resource management are not necessarily path dependent in accordance with design principles but go through an enduring process of development, though the poor continue to be marginalised.

References

Adolph, B., & Grieg-Gran, M. (2013). Agriculture and Food Systems a Sustainable Future: An Integrated Approach. (Online) URL: http://pubs.iied.org/17157IIED Accessed 20 December 2013.

27 See 'Mala Mala Limbo' written by Sipho Masombuka in *The Times* of 4 May 2015, http://www.timeslive.co.za/thetimes/2015/05/04/mala-mala-limbo (Accessed on 4 May 2015). The Mala Mala Game Reserve is South Africa's most expensive land restitution case up to date after compensation of almost R1Billion to the previous landowner for the benefit of 950 households.

AFRA. (2004). Communities Conservation Eco-tourism and Tenure Security Workshop Report. (Online) URL: http://www.afra.co.za/upload/files/AP19.pdf. (Accessed on 01 July 2011).

Aliber, M., & Cousins, B. (2013). Livelihoods after Land Reform in South Africa. *Journal of Agrarian Change*, *13*(1), 140–165.

Aliber, M., & Hall, R. (2012). Support for Smallholder Farmers in South Africa: Challenges of Scale and Strategy. *Development Southern Africa*, *29*(4), 548–562.

Aliber, M., & Hart, T.G.B. (2009). Should Subsistence Agriculture be supported as a Strategy to Address Rural Food Insecurity? *Agrekon*, *48*(4), 434–458.

Atuahene, B. (2007). From Reparation to Restoration: Moving Beyond Restoring Property Rights to Restoring Political and Economic Visibility. Southern Methodist University Law Review, *60*(4), 1419–1470.

Atuahene, B. (2011a). Paying for the Past: Addressing Past Property Violations in South Africa. *Law and Society Review*, *45*(4), 955–989.

Atuahene, B. (2011b). Property Rights and the Demands of Transformation. *Researching Law* 22(1) (Online) URL: http://scholarship.kentlaw.iit.edu/facschol/824 (Accessed on 01 July 2015).

Atuahene, B. (2014). The Importance of Conversation in Transitional Justice: A Study of Land Restitution in South Africa. Law and Social Inquiry, *39*(4), 902–937.

Bologna, S.A., & Spierenburg, M. (2015). False Legitimacies: The Rhetoric of Economic Opportunities in the Expansion of Conservation Areas in Southern Africa. In R. Van der Duim, M. Lamers, & J. Van Wijk. (Eds.). *Institutional Arrangements for Conservation, Development and Tourism in Eastern and Southern Africa: A Dynamic Perspective* (119–137). Dordrecht: Springer.

Bond, I., Child, B., De la Harpe, D., Jones, B., Barnes, J., & Anderson, H. 2009. Private Land Contribution to Conservation in South Africa. In B. Child, (Ed.), *Parks in Transition: Biodiversity, Rural Development and the Bottom Line* (29–61). London: Earthscan.

Boudreaux, K. (2010). Land Reform as Social Justice: The Case of South Africa. *Economic Affairs*, *30*(1), 13–20.

Brink, M., Cameron, M., Coetzee, K., Currie, B., Fabricius, C., Hattingh, S., Schmidt, A., & Watson, L. 2011. Sustainable Management through Improved Governance in the Game Industry. *South African Journal of Wildlife Research*, *4*(11), 110–119.

Brooks, S., Spierenburg, M., Van Brakel, L., Kolk, A., & Lukhozi, K.B. (2011). Creating a Commodified Wilderness: Tourism, Private Game Farming, and 'Third Nature' Landscapes in KwaZulu-Natal. *Tijdschrift Voor Economische en Sociale Geografie* (*Journal of Economic and Social Geography*), *102*(3), 260–274.

Brooks, S., Spierenburg, M., & Wels, H. (2012). The Organisation of Hypocrisy? Juxtaposing Tourists and Farm Dwellers in Game Farming in South Africa. In W. Van Beek & A. Schmidt (Eds.), *African Hosts and their Guests* (201–224). Rochester: James Carey.

Carsten, N.H., Christensen, S.M., & Tarp, P. (2005). Rapid Stakeholder and Conflict Assessment for Natural Resource Management using Cognitive Mapping: The Case of Damdoi Forest Enterprise, Vietnam. *Agriculture and Human Values*, *22*, 149–167.

Chernela, J., & Zanotti, L. (2014). Limits to Knowledge: Indigenous Peoples, NGOs, and the Moral Economy in the Eastern Amazon of Brazil. *Conservation and Society*, *12*(3), 306–317.

Cleaver, F. (2001). Institutional Bricolage, Conflict and Cooperation in Usangu, Tanzania. *Institute of Development Studies Bulletin*, *32*(34), 26–35.

Cleaver, F. (2012). *Development through Bricolage: Rethinking Institutions for Natural Resources Management*. London: Routledge.

Cousins, J.A., Saddler J.P., & Evans, J. (2008). Exploring the Role of Private Wildlife Ranching as a Conservation Tool in South Africa: Stakeholders Perspectives. *Ecology and Society*, *13*(2) (Online) URL: http://www.ecologyandsociety.org/vol13/iss2/art43/ (Accessed on 9 March 2010).

Crane, A., & Ruebottom, T. (2011). Stakeholder Theory and Social Identity: Rethinking Stakeholder Identification. *Journal of Business Ethics*, *102*, 77–87.

Curtis, S., Gesler W., Smith G., & Washburn S. (2000). Approaches to Sampling and Case Selection in Qualitative Research: Examples in the Geography of Health. *Social Science and Medicine*, *50*, 1001–1014.

Cuthbertson, G. (2008). South Africa's Democracy: From Celebration to Crisis. *African Identities*, *6*(3), 293–304.

Davies-Mostert, H.T. 2014. Overcoming Barriers to Understanding the Biodiversity Contribution of Private Ranchlands. *Animal Conservation*, *17*, 399–400.

De Koning, J. (2011). Reshaping Institutions: Bricolage Processes in Smallholder Forestry in the Amazon. Wageningen: Wageningen University.

De Villiers, B. 2003. *Land Reform: Issues and Challenges – A Comparative Overview of Experiences in Zimbabwe, Namibia, South Africa and Australia.* Johannesburg: Konrad-Adenauer-Stiftung.

De Villiers, B., & Van den Berg, M. (2006). *Land Reform: Trailblazers – Seven Successful Case Studies*. Johannesburg: Konrad-Adenauer-Stiftung.

Department of Rural Development and Land Reform. 2013. Land Audit (Online) URL: http://www.dla.gov.za/phocadownload/CadastralSurveymanagement/Booklet/land%20audit%20booklet.pdf (Accessed on 21 October 2013).

Farrell, K.N. (2004). Recapturing Fugitive Power: Epistemology, Complexity and Democracy. *Local Environment*, *9*(5), 469–479.

Fleetwood, S. (2008). Structure, Institution, Agency, Habit, and Reflexive Deliberation. *Journal of Institutional Economics*, *4*(2), 183–203.

Flyvbjerg, B. (2006). Five Misunderstandings about Case-Study Research. *Qualitative Inquiry*, *12*(2), 219–245.

Hall, R. (2009). Land Reform in South Africa: Successes, Challenges and Concrete Proposals for the Way Forward. In Konrad-Adenauer-Stiftung (2009), *Land Reform in South Africa: Constructive Aims and Positive Outcomes – Reflecting on Experiences on the Way to 2014* (5–35). Seminar Report No. 20. Johannesburg: Konrad-Adenauer -Stiftung.

Henriques, I., & Sadorsky, P. (1999). The Relationship between Environmental Commitment and Managerial Perceptions of Stakeholder Importance. *The Academy of Management Journal, 42*(1), 87–99.

Hirsch, P.D., Adams, W.M., Brosius, J.P., Zia, A., Bariola, N., & Dammert, J.L. (2010). Acknowledging Conservation Trade-Offs and Embracing Complexity. *Conservation Biology, 25*(2), 259–264.

Hughes, D.M. (2005). Third Nature: Making Space and Time in the Great Limpopo Conservation Area. *Cultural Anthropology, 20*(2), 157–184.

Imperial, M.T. (1999). Institutional Analysis and Ecosystem-Based Management: The Institutional Analysis and Development Framework. *Environmental Management, 24*(4), 449–465.

Jara, M., & Hall, R. (2009). What are the Political Parameters? In R. Hall (Ed.), *Another Countryside? Policy Options for Land and Agrarian Reform in South Africa* (206–243). Cape Town: Institute for Poverty, Land and Agrarian Studies.

Kamuti, T. (2014). The Fractured State in the Governance of Private Game Farming: The Case of KwaZulu-Natal Province, South Africa. *Journal of Contemporary African Studies, 32*(2), 190–206.

Kamuti, T. (2016). *Private Wildlife Governance in a Context of Radical Uncertainty: Dynamics of Game Farming Policy and Practice in KwaZulu-Natal, South Africa.* Unpublished PhD thesis Amsterdam: VU University Amsterdam.

Lertzman, K. (2009). The Paradigm of Management, Management Systems, and Resource Stewardship. *Journal of Ethnobiology, 29*(2), 339–358.

Li, T.M. (2011). Centering Labour in the Land Grab Debate. *Journal of Peasant Studies, 38*(2), 281–298.

Manji, A. (2001). Land Reform in the Shadow of the State: The Implementation of New Land Laws in Sub-Saharan Africa. *Third World Quarterly, 22*(3), 327–342.

McMichael, P. 2009. A Food Regime Genealogy. *The Journal of Peasant Studies, 36*(1), 139–169.

Milgroom, J., & Spierenburg, M. (2008). Induced Volition: Resettlement from the Limpopo National Park, Mozambique. *Journal of Contemporary African Studies, 26*(4), 435–448.

Minichiello, V., Aroni, R., Timewell, E., & Alexander, L. (1990). *In-Depth Interviewing: Researching People.* Melbourne: Longman Cheshire.

Ngubane, M., & Brooks, S.J. (2013). Land Beneficiaries as Game Farmers: Conservation, Land Reform and the Invention of the 'Community Game Farm' in KwaZulu-Natal. *Journal of Contemporary African Studies, 31*(3), 399–420.

Ntsebeza, L. (2005). *Democracy Compromised: Chiefs and the Politics of the Land in South Africa.* Leiden: Koninklijke Brill BV.

Orts, E.W., & Strudler, A. (2009). Putting a Stake in Stakeholder Theory. *Journal of Business Ethics, 88*, 605–615.

Ozesmi, U., & Ozesmi, S. (2003). A Participatory Approach to Ecosystem Conservation: Fuzzy Cognitive Maps and Stakeholder Group Analysis in Uluabat Lake, Turkey. *Environmental Management, 31*(4), 518–531.

Ramutsindela, M. (2007). *Transfrontier Conservation in Africa: At the Confluence of Capital, Politics and Nature.* Oxfordshire: CABI.

Ramutsindela, M., & Shabangu, M. (2013). Conditioned by Neoliberalism: A Reassessment of Land Claim Resolutions in the Kruger National Park. *Journal of Contemporary African Studies, 31*(3), 441–456.

Remenyi, D. (2012). *Case Study Research: The Quick Guide Series.* Reading: Academic Publishing International.

Schiller, C., Winters, M., Hanson, H.M., & Ashe, M.C. (2013). A Framework for Stakeholder Identification in Concept Mapping and Health Research: A Novel Process and its Application to Older Adult Mobility and the Built Environment. *BMC Public Health* 13:428. doi:10.1186/1471-2458-13-428.

Shaker, M. (2003). Restructuring of State Assets in Limpopo. *Service Delivery Review, 2*, 73–77.

Slavíková, L., Kluvánková-Oravská, T., & Jílková, J. (2010). Bridging Theories on Environmental Governance Insights from Free-market Approaches and Institutional Ecological Economics Perspectives. *Ecological Economics, 69*, 1368–1372.

Snijders, D. (2012). Wild Property and its Boundaries – On Wildlife Policy and Rural Consequences in South Africa. *Journal of Peasant Studies, 39*(2), 503–520.

Spierenburg, M., & Brooks, S. (2014). Private Game Farming and its Social Consequences in Post-Apartheid South Africa: Contestations over Wildlife, Property and Agrarian Futures. *Journal of Contemporary African Studies, 32*(2), 151–172.

Stake, R.E. (1978). The Case Study Method in Social Inquiry. *Educational Researcher, 7*(2), 5–8.

Stake, R.E. (1995). *The Art of Case Study Research.* Thousand Oaks: Sage Publications.

Tapela, B.N., & Omara-Ojungu, P.H. (1999). Towards Bridging the Gap between Wildlife Conservation and Rural Development in Post-Apartheid South Africa: The Case of the Makuleke Community and the Kruger National Park. *South African Geographical Journal, 81*(3), 148–155.

Tong, M. (2014). Decolonisation and Comparative Land Reform with a Special Focus on Africa. *International Journal of African Renaissance Studies – Multi-, Inter- and Transdisciplinarity, 9*(1), 16–35.

Van der Duim, R., Lamers, M., & Van Wijk, J. (2015). Novel Institutional Arrangements for Tourism, Conservation and Development in Eastern and Southern Africa. In R. Van der Duim, M. Lamers, & J. Van Wijk (Eds), *Institutional Arrangements for*

Conservation, Development and Tourism in Eastern and Southern Africa: A Dynamic Perspective (1–16). Dordrecht: Springer.

Van Wijk, J., Lamers, M., & Van der Duim, R. (2015). A Dynamic Perspective on Institutional Arrangements for Tourism, Conservation and Development in Eastern and Southern Africa. In R. Van der Duim, M. Lamers, & J. Van Wijk (Eds), *Institutional Arrangements for Conservation, Development and Tourism in Eastern and Southern Africa: A Dynamic Perspective* (239–260). Dordrecht: Springer.

Walker, C. (2005). The Limits to Land Reform: Rethinking 'The Land Question'. *Journal of Southern African Studies*, *31*(4), 805–824.

Walker, C. (2008). *Landmarked: Land Claims and Land Restitution in South Africa*. Athens: Ohio University Press.

Yin, R.K. (1989). *Case Study Research Design and Methods*. Newbury Park: Sage.

CHAPTER 8

Inclusive Business Models in South African Land Restitution: Great Expectations and Ambiguous Outcomes Explored

Nerhene Davis

Introduction

Joint venture arrangements, also known as inclusive business models, are often promoted as viable avenues for the insertion of the rural poor into profitable global value chains. In the post-apartheid restitution scenario, strategic and community private partnerships (CPPs), are designed to ensure the transfer of ownership of the land back to restitution communities, whilst production regimes on the land acquired are retained. Ownership of the land is therefore transferred to the claimant community, but they are not allowed to move back onto the land. Instead, claimant communities enter into agreements with agri-business partners who commit themselves to manage the land on their behalf with the contractual understanding that benefits are shared between the partners (DLA, 2008). This approach has been particularly prominent in Limpopo where large areas of high-value agricultural land and infrastructure are being transferred to community groups. In theory, the model should respond to a demand from claimant communities for technical and financial assistance in managing large agricultural enterprises. More importantly, the establishment of these types of partnership arrangements in the South African land restitution programme signalled a decisive policy shift in emphasis from land *access* by claimants, towards the *maintenance of agricultural productivity* through retention of existing farming systems and enterprises (Derman, Lahiff, & Sjaastad, 2006).

Some observers warn that strategic partnerships negotiated in terms of the restitution programme can create opportunities for existing actors in the commercial agri-food sector to gain access to valuable land and water resources, better control of upstream and downstream processes, and to lucrative government grants (Lahiff, 2007; Spierenburg et al., 2012). In instances where these types of partnership arrangements have been negotiated, as in the cases

 | DOI 10.1163/9789004362550_009

of Zebedele, Levubu, and Moletele, production on the land has continued (Lahiff et al., 2012). In the case of the Moletele, there is in fact evidence of production and export activities expanding (Davis, 2014), thus demonstrating the potential of these business arrangements to maintain the agricultural integrity on newly transferred land. What is less apparent is the extent to which *real* benefits or *effective control* of the land and the production activities are being transferred to the nominal owners of the land – the restitution communities. I therefore set out to understand the structure and nature of agreements applicable to the partnership arrangements on Moletele land and deployed an ethnographic approach to consider outcomes of the partnerships in terms of the expectations of community members regarding what they wanted to do with the land, measured against the actual opportunities created through the claim/partnerships. In the final part of the chapter, I reflect on the implications of these business models and its outcomes in the context of broader agrarian reform imperatives aimed at transforming the existing dualism in the South African agrarian structure.

Methodological Approach

The discussion in this chapter is based on the findings of a detailed case study of the Moletele partnership initiatives in South Africa, Limpopo. Research methods included field observations since 2009 and an analysis of the Moletele Communal Property Association's (MCPA) financial statements, annual reports, and contractual agreements in place for the partnerships. A crude value-chain analysis exploring the implications of the theoretic insertion of the community into the citrus value chain was conducted and the research process involved interviews with a wide range of key informants, which included the relevant strategic partners (or with their designated representatives) and the representative from the Citrus Growers Association based in Hoedspruit (November 2011 & June 2013). A sequence of key informant interviews were also conducted with two local representatives from the Business Trust's Maruleng and Bushbuckridge Economic Development Initiative (MABEDI),[1] who were tasked with capacity building functions tailored towards the needs of the

1 At the end of 2011, MABEDI was merged with other stakeholders and re-introduced as the Vumelana Advisory Fund, which is once again an organization tasked with capacity building for newly established CPA institutions.

new landowning community. The research also involved interviews with state officials involved in the project from the:

(1) Provincial Department of Rural Development and Land Reform (several interviews conducted between 2011–2013),
(2) Limpopo Provincial Department of Agriculture (2011), and
(3) Limpopo Regional Land Claims Commissions office (2 interviews were conducted between 2010 and 2013).

Of particular importance for my discussion in this chapter, is the findings from eighty semi-structured and open-ended interviews I conducted with a purposively selected (based on demographic characteristics) range of Moletele community members at their homesteads. The open-ended questionnaires were designed to gain an understanding of respondents' expectations and awareness of the Moletele claim, and to gain insights into their level of awareness and understanding of the functions and purpose of the MCPA structure. I also used the opportunity to ask respondents what they knew about the partnership arrangements in place on their newly acquired land and interviewed them about the strategies/structures they would use to 'voice' their concerns or interests regarding the management of their land. During the interview process, I engaged with respondents about the types of benefits they anticipated with the settling of the claim (trying to gauge their expectations), compared to what they eventually received (their level of contentment, ambivalence, disillusionment, or disappointment). The idea with the questionnaire was also to gauge the level of respondents' willingness to move back to the land and their general aspirations about farming. The urgency from some of the respondents for me to record their recollections was quite striking, and for some households, where younger members sat in on the interviews, the process of recollection about their claimed land presented the interviewees with an opportunity to engage with younger members about issues (according to them) not generally discussed.

I also encountered two distinct groupings of people (representing between 120–150 Moletele members) who had bi-weekly meetings to discuss land matters. These two Moletele sub-groupings conducted separate meetings to articulate their visions and expectations about the settlement of the remainder of the land claim, and both groupings denied the legitimacy of the MCPA. I realised that these groupings formed a crucial part of this research process as they articulated a clear resentment towards the MCPA and selected their own leadership structure to negotiate on their behalf with the Department of Rural

Development and Land Reform. I conducted four focus-group interviews with members from both these groupings.

Conceptual Framework: A Political Economy Approach to Partnership Arrangements

Vorley and colleagues (2009, p. 187) define inclusive business models as models in which 'the voices and needs of those actors in rural areas in developing countries are recognised'. Franco and Borras (2010, p. 11) warn that these notions of partnerships are usually based on 'a depoliticised and unrealistic vision of engagement between various actors that strips them of possibly conflicting interests and attempts to place them on equal footing'. They caution 'imagining equal footing and complementary interests where none exist is more likely than not, to lead to the poor losing out' (Franco & Borras 2010, p. 11). In the agrarian political economy literature dealing with partnership or contractual arrangements, the very notion of partnership deals between two 'equal partners' is therefore often questioned (e.g. Lahiff, 2008; Vermeulen & Cotula, 2010; Franco & Borras, 2010). These scholars are concerned with underlying structural dynamics and focus on the limited autonomy and leverage available to the 'less powerful' contract partner, compared to the potentially higher levels of autonomy and control of the more dominant partner (e.g. Derman et al., 2006; Bolwig et al., 2010; Spierenburg et al., 2012). This literature also reveals a focus on the contrasting pressures and motivations of different partners as well as of sub-groupings *within* contracting partners (Oya, 2012; Lahiff et al., 2012; Spierenburg et al., 2012).

In addition to probing power dynamics between contracting partners, agrarian political economy literature is also concerned with the accumulative and structurally transformative implications of institutions impacting on land property relations. For example, for the Marxist perspective, the notion of '*primitive accumulation*' is a primary concern. Akram-Lodhi and Kay (2010, p. 180) define '*primitive accumulation*' as the historical process of divorcing the producer from the means of production to create a class of workers that are 'free' (through their release from ownership of the means of production) to sell their labour power. David Harvey (2003) re-conceptualised the notion of '*primitive accumulation*' as '*accumulation by dispossession*', and highlights the importance of understanding how historic structures and processes of accumulation inform present-day processes of agrarian change. Tania Li (2009, p. 59) contributes to this debate and observes the spatial and temporal unevenness of capital investment in the context of agrarian reform. She refers to the intensification of processes allowing capital to incorporate some places and peoples, and eject or reject others. Li (2009, p. 60) warns, as capital 'hops' along, there is another dynamic that is potentially more lethal: one in which places (or their resources) are in fact useful, but the people are not, so that accumulation is detached from any prospect of labour absorption. This could lead to what Li (2005) terms '*detached accumulation*', where 'the land is needed, but the people are not needed for the global capitalist system' (Li, 2009).

In this chapter, I suggest that partnership initiatives in the context of land restitution could promote a form of '*detached accumulation*' where agribusinesses do not need to own the means of production to control the direction and frequency of benefits or profits derived from the newly acquired land, and where they are allowed to deploy rigorous accumulation strategies that are completely 'detached' from community interests/aspirations. I postulate that confirming the restitution community as owners of the land does not automatically translate into the ability for them to benefit from their land. These inclusive business models are thus seemingly structured or brokered in a way that allows agri-business partners to accumulate without the need to *dispossess* the newly restituted community. The resolution of restitution cases by means of joint venture arrangements on parcels of prime commercial land could thus result in communities being given formal ownership status to the newly acquired land, while agribusiness is allowed to move in and produce and profit at maximum capacity. In theory, the partnership arrangements should generate clear benefit streams in terms of employment, skills development, and capacity building for the restitution community, while the risks of the investment should be carried by the agribusiness partner. In reality, however (as I am hoping to illustrate in the following discussion), large agribusiness partners could also be guilty of having no intention/or the willingness to absorb the restitution community, that is, the 'surplus labour' (Li 2009, p. 60). The partnership restitution model could thus promote a scenario where agribusiness requires the land but not the labour; a 'detached accumulation' where the restitution community, for the most part, are still left marginalised with unfulfilled expectations.

The Moletele Restitution Case

The Moletele community is a large group of mainly Sepedi (Northern Sotho) speaking people originating from the South African lowveld. The community has claimed a vast area of land, in the order of 78,791 hectares, from which they were removed between the 1920s and the 1970s. According to the validation report issued by the Land Claims Commission's office, the Moletele people were dispossessed of their rights in land in terms of the racially discriminatory law and practices of the Native Land Act of 1913 (Act 27 of 1913), which allowed white people the right to own the land on which the Moletele already had customary rights thus forcing many of the Moletele to become farm labourers or be removed from the land. In terms of the provisions of the Native Trust Land Act of 1936 (Act 18 of 1936) there is proof that the Moletele people were evicted from farms in the Hoedspruit areas, and some of the Moletele were also removed from farms in terms of Section 12 and 14 of the Group Areas Act of 1950. Their removal of Moletele from Portion 8 of the farm Antioch 240KT, Berlin 209KT, Welverdiend 243KT, and Happyland 241KT was the result of the establishment and extension of the peri-urban area in Hoedspruit. Finally, the construction of the Blyde River dam was also used to remove people from what is currently known as the Swadini/Mariepskop area.

Currently, the claimed land predominantly situated around the small town of Hoedspruit is the centre of a large subtropical fruit economy, supplied with irrigation water from the Blyde River (figure 8.1). Land that is not under cultivation is generally used for game farming, cattle ranching, hunting, and wildlife tourism.

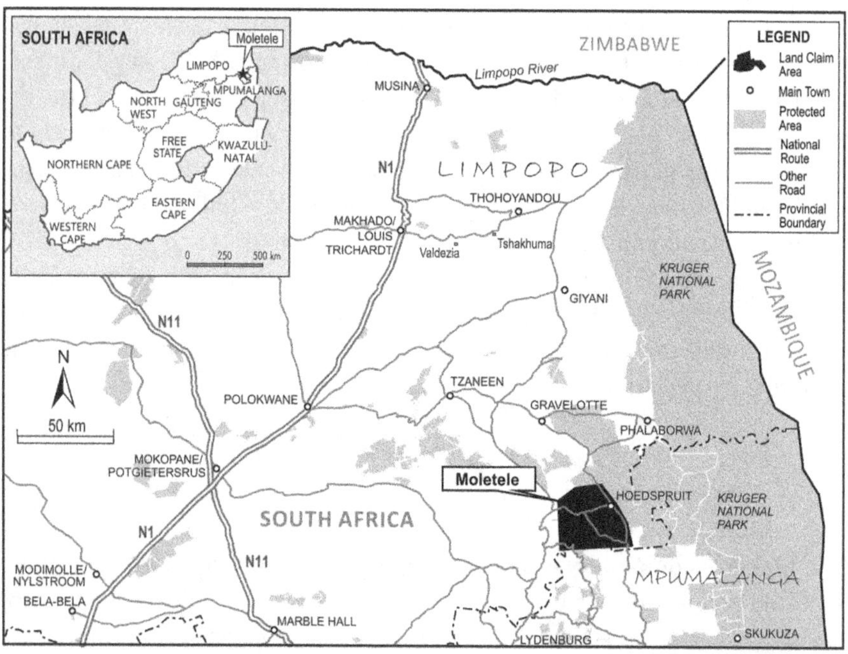

FIGURE 8.1 *Orientation map of the study area. Map produced by Ingrid Booysen University of Pretoria, Cartographic Unit, 2011.*

Leaders of the community made various efforts over the years to regain their land, culminating in the lodgement of numerous claims under the Restitution of Land Rights Act between 1995 and 1998. These claims were eventually merged into a single Moletele Community Land Claim in 2003. The Commission on Restitution of Land Rights accepted the validity of the claim in 2004, and from 2007 a total of 7,652 hectares of prime agricultural land was restored to 1,615 households organized under the Moletele Communal Property Association (MCPA). Claims were initially lodged on 28 farms, with 14 more added as part of the investigation process that followed (78,791 hectares in total). To date, merely 10% (a total of 7,652 hectares of the claimed land) has been returned to the community. The transferred land has been grouped into four blocks, comprising 42 distinct portions of the original farms claimed, and the total cost of land acquisition thus far is estimated at R194 million (Regional Land Claims Commission Annual Report, 2013). To enable the claimant communities to operate the newly acquired farms, the government has implemented a number of grants. In the case of Moletele land, the government committed to pay R35.2 million as a Development Assistance Grant, R4.8 million as the Restitution Development Grant and R2.3 million in the form of a Settlement Planning Grant (MCPA, Annual Report 2013).[2]

Apart from the challenging nature of the claim, due to competing claims from other tribal communities, the conflicting nature of the Moletele land claim was also evident in terms of the internal community dynamics that had surfaced during the land-claim process. The claim was initially headed by *Nduna* Enos Chiloane. A number of decisions made and agreements signed by *Nduna* Chiloane, during the interim phase of the claim, in his capacity as 'care taker' and legal custodian, were however deemed highly controversial. This resulted in the expulsion of *Nduna* Chiloane from the traditional council. He was denounced as 'the one who sold out the right of the community' because he signed an agreement for financial compensation in regards to some of the land under claim, currently owned by Swadini Aventura Forever Resort. As a consequence of his actions, the Moletele Traditional Council decided that his title and privileges as *nduna* of the Moletele should be revoked. Despite being stripped of his title, Chiloane established a rather vocal group of devoted followers, who decided to 'leave' with him. Chiloane and his group of followers asserted, that they were being ostracized from traditional council matters, and group members maintained that only Mr Chiloane could act on their behalf.

During the course of this research (2009–2014), the subgroup of the Moletele under the leadership of Mr Enos Chiloane still conducted bi-weekly meetings

2 At the time of writing this chapter, the Development Assistance grant (R35.2 million) has not been paid.

to talk about progress with the land claim (I conceptualised this sub-grouping as 'dissident group 1'.). They articulated their interests and expectations in terms of a desired outcome where they are all allowed to return to their land.

Overview of Partnership Initiatives on Moletele Land

The original vision to set up joint ventures on Moletele land came from the Department of Rural Development and Land Reform, which had concerns about the scale of the proposed land transfer and the ability of the community to cope with its new responsibilities. The potential impact that the 'inadequate' management of newly restored land would have on the local economy was a key motivator to consider private sector involvement. Shared equity with a partner with experience in commercial fruit farming was therefore considered as a pre-requisite for ensuring the successful operation of the newly acquired farms. It was assumed that a joint venture arrangement would allow the commercial partner to directly benefit from the income of the farm, whilst at the same time it would reduce the risk of the community, who were mostly unfamiliar with commercial farming activities and related decision-making. Stakeholders involved in the Moletele claim were aware of this new drive from the state, and, even before the claims were finalised, community leaders, landowners, and local public representatives were discussing possible collaboration through the local forum called the Moletele-Hoedspruit Land Initiative (Moletele Bulletin, 2008). It is thus interesting to note that negotiations with the former owners of Moletele land started in 2005, while transfer of the first land parcels only commenced in 2007.

After a tender and screening process in which the MCPA was assisted by MABEDI, three groups of local farm owners (or former owners) emerged as strategic partners for the Moletele CPA: Strategic Farm Management (SFM Pty) Ltd, Chestnet (Pty) Ltd, and the Boyes Group. A lengthy negotiation process ensued, supported by the Business Trust-MABEDI and the European Union-funded Limpopo Local Economic Development programme. At the end of the negotiation processes shareholding and lease agreements, as well as management contracts, were signed between the CPA and the respective strategic partners to form: New Dawn Farming Enterprise (Pty) Ltd, Dinaledi Farming Entreprise (Pty) Ltd and Batau Farming Enterprise (Pty) Ltd. The Batau partnership has subsequently collapsed, and, due to the community's unhappiness with the design of the strategic partnership model, the Moletele opted to introduce two community private partnerships on the Richmond and the previous 'Batau' farms.

The New Dawn, Dinaledi, and (the initial) Batau settlement agreement indicate that the claimants represented by the MCPA entered into a combined shareholding and lease agreement with selected strategic partners. In terms of these arrangements, suitable strategic partners with the capacity to attract operational capital and the entrepreneurial expertise to enter into the partnership arrangement with the MCPA were identified and selected. An operating company was established with the MCPA and the strategic partners as the shareholders. The operating company then entered into a lease agreement with the MCPA, which was determined at an agreed market-related rental cost. It is important to note that the settlement and lease agreements stipulated that land could only be leased by the operating company and could therefore not be used as collateral to obtain loans. The signed stipulations specified that the MCPA would act on behalf of the claimant community in forming part of the operating companies with the strategic partner. In terms of these arrangements, the allocation of shares varied, but the claimant community in all instances was the majority shareholder. As part of the strategic partnership contract agreement, skills were to be transferred to the MCPA and farm workers. It was also agreed that the shareholder proportions of the companies would depend on the equity contributions of each of the shareholders, thus what could be considered a "conventional" partnership' where risks, investment, and dividends would be allocated in terms of each partner's share in the company.

Stipulated in all of the Moletele shareholders' agreements is the fact that dividends that the operating company declares will be paid to the shareholders proportional to their shares. In the case of New Dawn, the MCPA currently holds 52% of the shares and the strategic partner holds 48% of the shares. In terms of the original Batau shareholders' agreement, once again, the strategic partner, Chester, held 48% of the shares and the MCPA held 52%, with no shares reserved for a workers' trust. The Dinaledi partnership agreement entails a 51% MCPA and a 49% Boyes Group shareholders' agreement. The absence of shares reserved for a workers' trust in all the updated shareholders' agreements is strikingly evident.

The shareholders' agreements also stipulate that, in addition to shares in the company, claimant communities should receive rental payments for the use of their land from the operating company. The shareholders' agreements that are still in place for the New Dawn and Dinaledi partnerships indicate that the rent for the land is set at 1.25% of the land purchase price (transfer value of the land) and is supposed to be paid on an annual, monthly, and even quarterly basis. The New Dawn and Dinaledi operating companies are thus owned jointly by the claimants and the strategic partners, but the day-to-day operations and management of the company are vested in the hands of the strategic partner, who has full control of financial and operational matters. Although the directors of the operating companies also include members selected from the MCPA, for now, the experience and knowledge of the market conditions of the strategic partners make them de facto decision-makers in the partnership. For this responsibility, the strategic partner then charges the operating company administrative fees. In terms of the New Dawn and Dinaledi shareholders' agreements, this fee, when combined with the salaries of key managers provided by the strategic partner, should not exceed 8% of the turnover of these operating companies. The strategic partners are also tasked with obtaining machinery and all the necessary equipment on behalf of the operating company.

In April 2009, the farm Richmond, as a full portion, was transferred to the Moletele community. At the time of transfer, the 2434-hectare farm was valued at R63 million. On 22 June 2010, a lease agreement was signed with Global Citrus Frontier (GFC), based on a business model negotiated along the line of what has been called a community private partnership. The chairperson of the MCPA explained that the MCPA, on behalf of the community, decided instead to sign community private partnership agreements due to the general unhappiness amongst community members about the lack of benefits transmitted back to them and the limited decision-making afforded to them in terms of strategic partnership arrangements. The signing of these community private partnership agreements has resulted in a high level of expectation among some of the members of the MCPA. The Moletele CPA chairperson explained that the new CPP model shifts the focus to signing an agreement with a private partner with the ability to farm profitably, provide for the development of the farms, and train prospective MCPA members in farming, while no additional funding is required from the restitution community (similar to a management contract).

Summary of the Outcomes of the Partnerships

Currently, there are two strategic partnership initiatives still operative on Moletele land: New Dawn (a partnership with Strategic Farm Management) and Dinaledi (with the Boyes Group). In addition to these two strategic partnerships, there are also two community-private partnerships (CPP) in effect on the Moletele land (on the Richmond farm and the former Batau farms). The design of the strategic partnerships was conceptualized as a 'conventional partnership', where joint ventures were established between the MCPA and different strategic partners in the form of operating companies. It was anticipated that 'the state', on behalf of the Moletele as the majority shareholder, would make the largest investment in the company, in the form of restitution discretionary grants. This payment was supposed to be matched by contributions from the respective strategic partners into the accounts of the operating companies. Problems emerged fairly soon when the envisaged grant payments from the state failed to materialize due to budgetary constraints, while contributions from the strategic partner to ensure production activities on the land continued. This implied that the majority shareholder (the MCPA) was unable to match the contributions of its business partner. This had devastating impacts on the envisaged benefit streams to the 'community'. Land rentals that were supposed to be paid by the operating company into the MCPA account have generally not been paid, and, where some payments have been made, they have been intermittent and partial. Income statements for the MCPA up until 2012 reflect no rental income for 2007 and 2008. The management fees that were supposed to be paid to strategic partners also failed to materialize. Additionally, by the end of 2014, dividends have not been declared and therefore nothing has been paid out to the community.

The envisaged benefits in terms of employment opportunities for Moletele people turned out to be grossly overestimated. As in the case of the broader citrus industry, an informalisation or casualization of labour (Barrientos & Visser, 2012) is also evident in the export-oriented citrus production activities taking place on Moletele land. The lack of extensive formal employment opportunities, in tandem with the long distances that community members would need to commute if they were employed on these farms, has invariably limited the number and types of employment opportunities available to Moletele members. Added to these constraints is the fact that the farms were transferred to the Moletele as 'going concerns', that is, the Moletele inherited non-Moletele workers already on the farms. According to the MCPA chairperson (Mr Mashile) and two of the strategic partners, these limitations on employment opportunities for Moletele members are exacerbated by their own 'fussiness', with members preferring employment in the pack houses as opposed to 'working on the land'. According to Mr Mashile, all these facts have translated into a scenario where less than 30% of the fairly unimpressive employment figures provided in Table 8.1 represent actual Moletele labourers.

Production on Moletele land is continuing, but there is increasing tension between the strategic partners and the MCPA regarding the flow of benefits and the long-term prospects of continuing the partnership. The flow of benefits from the strategic partnerships to claimants has been fairly limited to date (as summarised in table 8.2 on page161), causing a great deal of unhappiness amongst Moletele members. The 'limited' (and according to many respondents 'preferential') flow of benefits back to the community is a recurring issue in all of the MCPA AGM reports. The strategic partners also acknowledge that 'the

TABLE 8.1 *Summary of moletele partnerships. Source: Minutes of the Annual General Meeting of the* MCPA *(2011).*

Joint Venture Company	Total Ha managed	Current ha under production	Production	Employment created
New Dawn Farming Enterprise	1019 ha	405 ha	Citrus, mango, guava, and paw-paw	123 permanent and 390 seasonal
Dinaledi Farming Enterprise	686 ha	355 ha	Lemons, grapefruit, and Valencia oranges	150 permanent and 350 seasonal
Batau Farming Enterprise	855 ha	157 ha	Mango, citrus, litchi, and vegetables	72 (permanent and seasonal)
Richmond Estate	2434 ha	590 ha	Grapefruit, Valencia oranges, and mango	135 permanent and 440 seasonal

community might not have benefitted to the extent originally envisaged with these arrangements'.[3] Members of the MCPA executive committee insist that the Moletele are 'running out of patience' with the lack of benefits coming from the two remaining strategic partnership initiatives.

The strategic partners, on the other hand, warn that the 'profits' they are consistently being accused of capturing are in fact quite 'marginal'. In their view, benefits transmitted back to the community have been limited, because restitution communities are being inserted into agricultural value chains as producers, the most profit-constrained node within the value chain. The strategic partners also blame the model for imposing such a high level of dependence on state funding, while most of the risks of the farming activities on the land are being carried by them, the strategic partners. The New Dawn strategic partner, in particular, has been facing great difficulty in sourcing a loan from the Development Bank Southern Africa (DBSA). Based on my analysis of these models, findings to date thus suggests that the design of the strategic partnership model ultimately culminated into an overreliance on external (state) funding, which has created a degree of vulnerability for both the strategic

3 Interview conducted with Strategic Farm Management Director, July 2012.

TABLE 8.2 *Key outcomes of the partnership arrangements to date. Moletele CPA Annual General Meeting Report (2014).*

Key performance areas	Description of performance
Achievements	2007–2014
Land utilisation	• Restored farms currently produce high-value commodities for export, with a combined turnover of over R1 billion per annum (MCPA Property Portfolio Report, 2014). New land parcels currently under production and the partnerships are all exporting more than a million cartons per production cycle. • Two Community Private Partnership agreements in place. • Two strategic partnerships still in place: New Dawn and Dinaledi. • **Rental Income** from the deals are not consistent or at the agreed terms, because the grants from the state did not materialise. • **Dividends** have not been declared as these partnerships have been underperforming. • **Risk and Rewards:** The strategic partners all mentioned the risks these partnership deals have imposed on them. On the reward side, however, one can only speculate that they are staying afloat and that their export companies could be benefitting fairly well.
Residential	• A portion of Scotia farm has been cleared for residential settlement. • A total of 350 stands have been sold to members at an undisclosed amount. 'This will become an estate-like settlement to be admired and marvelled by many' Interview conducted with Mr. Thandos Mashile, Chairperson of the Moletele CPA, Hoedspruit, November 2011.
Stock farming	• There are +/– 600 community owned cattle on Scotia and Eden Farms with 32 cattle owners at Scotia and 12 owners at Eden farms occupied as of March 2011.
Disbursement	• The Department of Rural Development and Land Reform has provided a grant of R2,779,756 for disbursement to members. Only, 1505 households received payments of R1679.00.

TABLE 8.2 *Key outcomes of the partnership arrangements to date. Moletele CPA Annual General Meeting Report (2014)* (cont.).

Key performance areas	Description of performance
Challenges	
Landowners	• A large percentage of the claim is still being resisted by white commercial farmers in the area.
Existence of factions within the community	• Community unity is problematic as letters are sent to the DRDLR to complain about matters that should be handled by the MCPA.
Release of government grant	• Grant payments have not transpired to date.
Job creation & mentorship	• According to the MCPA, the Moletele people are seemingly not being mentored sufficiently to ensure effective takeover when partnerships come to an end. • **Job opportunities** created on Moletele land fairly limited.

partners and the 'community'. The design of the model also seemingly casts the strategic partners and communities into adversarial roles, where each entity apparently needs to compete for access to 'state' resources.

In response to the poor performance of strategic partnership arrangements, the community opted to sign two CPP agreements. The CPP arrangement is in effect a management contract between the community and an agri-business partner, who would be able to shoulder all the risks and investments required for production and export on the land, thus nullifying the reliance on funding from the state. In terms of these agreements, the chairperson of the MCPA in 2011 asserted:

> At least the pretence of community involvement is abolished, while the community is able to benefit more in terms of profit sharing and higher rental income.

The interest of 'the state' to break the reliance of strategic partnership initiatives' dependence on state funding by providing the restitution communities with the type of commercial partner that would be able to shoulder the risks and investment required to ensure continued production on the land, thus clearly converged with agri-business interests looking for opportunities to expand, consolidate, and integrate their production activities. The ability of agri-businesses to 'hop' in and benefit from the most productive parcels of land in the country without the remotest concern to re-invest in the capacities of the rural community that owns the land, thus allows some version of the dualism in the inherited agrarian structure to persist. The transformative potential of these models is therefore highly questionable, because communities are *not allowed to:* (1) move on to the land, (2) use or subdivide unused or 'open' land for other small-scale productive purposes, or (3) take full effective control of productive activities on their land. From the outcomes of the partnerships on Moletele land to date (summarised in table 8.2), the convergence between 'state-' and agribusiness interest in terms of these models is thus very noticeable, but it does raise questions about the extent to which the models are able to accommodate the land claimants' expectations and aspirations.

Expectations Articulated

The initial expectations regarding the restitution of Moletele land on the part of the state were articulated by the then Minister for Agriculture and Land Affairs, Ms Lulama Xingwana, at the land handover ceremony to the Moletele community.[4] The Minister framed a vision for the Moletele people asserting:

> This land that we are restoring today has some of the best oranges and mangos this country has ever produced. As from today, the people of Moletele are now exporters. You are going to be operating from the well-equipped pack houses that we have included in the purchase of this land. ...This deal will also accelerate value-adding in the produce coming from this land of milk and honey. This will ensure participation of the Moletele Community in the entire value-chain. ...These partnerships give credence to economic empowerment because the community will not only receive handouts in the form of lease rentals but will be participating in the day-to-day management of the farms.

4 Speech for the land handover celebration for the Moletele community claim delivered by the Minister for Agriculture and Land Affairs, Ms Lulama Xingwana, Limpopo, 1 July 2007.

In reality, the intention to turn the Moletele community into exporters did not materialise. The transfer of the land and pack houses did not automatically translate into the community becoming exporters of the fruit being produced on their land. Branding the community as a 'producer' in the value chain is, however, equally questionable, given their limited involvement in the day-to-day running and management of the farms.

Expectations Articulated by Moletele Sub-groupings

Focus group discussions with members of the dissident groupings and a content analysis of the 80 semi-structured interviews helped me to identify the following key trends in terms of expectations from the community's perspective.

The majority (n = 20, 80%) of older male (older than 60 and n = 25 interviewed) respondents indicated that they would have preferred the option of moving back on to their land. Two of these older male respondents felt that they needed to return back to the land in order to 'reconnect with their ancestors and their heritage'. They complained that the partnership model does not make provision for the issue of ancestral reconnection. Moletele members who aspired to move back onto the land for ancestral reconnection were therefore left fairly disillusioned in terms of their expectations.

All of the older male respondents interviewed maintained that there should be enough land for both commercial- and community-managed farming activities. For example, twenty of these respondents highlighted the need for more land to engage in cattle farming specifically. These respondents did not view commercial farming production and community-organised cattle farming activities as mutually exclusive and thought the initiative at Scotia was proof of this sentiment. They all insisted, however, that the procedure for members to gain access to the land for cattle farming should be 'opened up', because they complained that not all the Moletele knew about the procedures to gain access to grazing land. Respondents seemed inclined to believe that only Moletele members with close linkages to the *kgoshi* were the ones able to gain access to grazing land on the newly transferred land parcels. Simon, a 70-year-old Buffelshoek resident, stated:

> Cattle farming is a common practice in our community. Members can engage profitably in cattle farming without the help of a commercial partner. Why should all the Moletele land be used for commercial farming? We will always need a commercial partner… But, cattle farming we can do on our own and we can be profitable on our own. The MCPA only dance to the tune of the partners! It should not matter who you are, or who you know, if you are a Moletele and need land, there should be options available.

During an interview conducted in November 2011, Mr Enos Chiloane, one of the leaders of the dissident groups, shared a similar perspective:

> Right at the start of this process, we were very clear about what we wanted to see on the land. We told them, we want to move back on to the land. Even while production is happening! Now we just hear about some people who have been allowed to move their cattle on to Scotia Farm. We hear about some who have received payments. But us, the rightful beneficiaries of the land, are not receiving anything, while those so-called partners and community members with linkages and connections are benefitting.

During my interviews with these older male Moletele members (both those forming part of the dissident groupings and those not part of the groupings) my overriding impression was that these were the individuals mostly concerned with Moletele land matters. This subgrouping of individuals felt they had the most to gain from the restitution process, because they experienced the relocation first hand and they were involved in initiating the claim. Ultimately, most of these members feel disillusioned by the outcomes of the partnerships to date. They maintain that they do not mind commercial production happening on the land, but they do ask why additional (i.e. open) parcels of land cannot be made more available to everyone in the community, especially for cattle farming or other activities.

When I questioned older female respondents (n = 30) about their expectations regarding the claim, the possibility of returning to the land also surfaced. These older female respondents expressed grave reservations about the possibility of moving back onto Moletele land. Many of these older women (aged 60 and older) explained that their reservations about moving back onto the land stemmed from a range of factors, but some common themes emerged. They all mentioned: (1) they would not want to disrupt their church and broader community ties ('*stokvel*' and funeral societies amongst others are mentioned); (2) challenges in terms of their grandchildren, who might not be able to accompany them should they relocate; (3) their 'comfortable' houses, often wondering where they will stay should they decide to move; and (4) concerns about their age and their health should they opt to leave Buffelshoek. When I asked them what they expected from the actual claim, many of these women (60%, n = 18) said that they would be happy to remain where they were, if only some cash payments could reach them at some time. For many of these older women, their expectations have been left unfulfilled.

The responses from younger women (the 25–59 years age group, n = 15 interviewed) were somewhat mixed. Most of these women (n = 12) seemed less concerned about severing family, church, and community ties, and said that they would have welcomed the option of moving back to their land. The majority of the women in this category (n = 10) suggested that they would have liked to engage in food garden types of production, yet the model seemingly did not make provision for these activities. Two interviewees mentioned that the prospect of new houses closer to the town of Hoedspruit was mentioned. They said that new residences closer to Hoedspruit would have improved their (and people like them) job prospects significantly, but they were informed that the houses being planned at Scotia were going to be 'estate type houses'. Pina, a 40-year-old unmarried mother of two wanted to know, 'who made the decision to build expensive houses when so many Moletele could not even afford to live there?'

The adult men (aged 25–59, n = 10) on the other hand, all indicated that they expected to gain access to land for commercial agricultural purposes. This grouping of respondents were less inclined to get involved in small-scale farming production and actually acknowledged the importance of continued commercial farming on the land with the help of more established white farmers. All these respondents expressed the desire to eventually also engage in the management of these farms, but, in the meantime, they would be far happier with the activities on their land if they were kept more informed, saw more job opportunities, and received some cash payments.

From the interviews I realised that the expectations articulated by Moletele members ranged from highly charged and expansive sets of expectations infused with notions of material wealth and symbolic restoration, to more delimited and perhaps more realistically framed expectations. For the most part, however, expectations amongst the Moletele have been left unfulfilled. For the majority of the Moletele, very little has changed in their lives since the transfer of land back to them. This part of the research thus highlighted the disjuncture between the expectations regarding the land restitution process as opposed to what the partnership model has been able to deliver in terms of articulated land use, access, and benefits. Despite expectations to return to the land of 'milk and honey' (as mentioned to them by the then Minster of Land Affairs in her speech at the land-handover ceremony) the majority of the Moletele are still trapped on the dry and barren land of the former Gazankulu and Lebowa reserves where they eke out a rather desperate living, in stark contrast to conditions on the profitable and lavish fruit-bearing commercial land they now own. Also, the interviews revealed that these beneficiaries wanted different things from the restitution process depending on where they are situated, and the kinds of relations and networks they have managed to form a part of. A very revelatory finding from the interviews is also the fact that people did not necessarily want to be absorbed into the capitalist circuits! They wanted access to land for various purposes, not all of which included their absorption into commercial farming production or even farming purposes.

Partnerships and the 'Voice' of the Community?

The voice or the interest of the 'community' is supposed to be represented by members of the MCPA executive committee who attend monthly board meetings with strategic partners. Some crucial constraints should be noted in this regard. A significant number of Moletele admitted that they do not attend MCPA or tribal council meetings, so very often the range of diverse interests, needs, and expectations of community members are not even noted at the MCPA meetings. In the second instance, even those members attending meetings seem to feel marginalised. Older male (older than 60) respondents (n = 25 interviewed), who all said they attended both the traditional council meetings and the MCPA Annual General Meetings, confessed that they still only had a vague idea about these initiatives. Simon, a 70-year-old Buffelshoek resident in November 2012 explained '*only those members that can speak commercial farming are the ones that can talk at the AGM's … we remain quiet*'. From all the women interviewed, 93% said that they have no idea what is currently happening on their land, they do not know what the role of the CPA is, and they have only heard 'rumours' about some types of partnerships that have been established. The younger women were also seemingly less inclined to attend any form of meeting about land matters. One of the Buffelshoek respondents, Paulina a 40-year-old unemployed mother of four complained:

> We don't have time to go and sit in meetings because we are too busy … who will feed the kids, cook, and clean the house if we sit in meetings all day?

Perspectives like these, as raised by the beneficiaries, thus highlights the need for a continued interrogation of the extent to which the MCPA could be 'voicing' the interests of a communal Moletele community.

Finally, despite efforts by MABEDI (now Vumelana) to capacitate these community representatives sitting on the MCPA structure, the reality is that 'community' members join commercial partners at a boardroom table, and are expected to make sure that their *de jure* (legal) rights are protected and translated into 'effective rights' in a power-differentiated context using a discourse and a setting they are not familiar with. Both the MCPA representatives and the strategic partners I interviewed thus conceded that these meetings were fairly frustrating encounters. The strategic partners complained that they felt as if they were required to 'help community members catch up', while community representatives felt as if they were only there to 'rubber stamp' decisions already made. It is thus clear that the discourse used to articulate and enforce rights, and the lack of business acumen amongst the community representatives in this predominantly agri-business arena, is likely to sway the *cumulative outcomes* from these encounters (i.e. struggles) in favour of the agribusiness partners leaving the community fairly 'voiceless' to a certain extent.

Discussion

It is clear that the continued introduction of partnership models to settle rural restitution claims would have far-reaching implications for the South African agrarian structure. The perceived ease with which these CPP models (management contract arrangements) can be negotiated could also contribute to an increase in the number of settled rural restitution cases. This would definitely effect a change in the racial profile of ownership of commercial farmland in South Africa. Hall (2004) refers to this process as the 'blackening of the landownership structure'. At the same time, however, the model signals a distinct move away from actual involvement in the farming activities by the restitution communities. By implication, restitution communities could be reduced to becoming very remote and fairly marginalised landlords or rent collectors with very little control over activities or production on their own land, while agri-business interests are allowed to 'hop in' and accumulate from their land without constraining attachments or obligations – that is, a variation of Li's (2009) 'detached accumulation'. Land claimants might therefore be able to call themselves landowners who have been 'incorporated' into value chains, but they might end up with no decision-making or orientation power, based on the business model being used. The level of congruence between 'state', agribusiness, and community interests achieved by these models is therefore fairly questionable.

Furthermore, from the interviews with respondents it is clear that the 'voices' of subgroupings *within* communities is also being drowned out, especially in instances where these subgroupings might be calling for access to land for non-commercial farming purposes. Expectations articulated beyond the scope of commercial farming production have been left unfulfilled for the most part, and the interviews revealed that beneficiaries wanted different things depending on their positionality and the nature of their social relations. In some instances, some sub-groupings in fact did not even want to be absorbed into capitalist production circuits, thus demonstrating the need for restitution policymakers to acknowledge that the land question is broader than the agrarian question.

Conclusion

The theoretic 'inclusion' of a restitution community into the global value chain via inclusive business model arrangements, particularly in the case of the Moletele community, seems to have resulted in (what can only be labelled as) ambiguous outcomes. The MCPA seems to be committed to ensure continued production on the land, but, until they come up with viable strategies of distributing benefits from the production and other value chain related activities to the communities, their efforts only seem to be promoting corporate interest, rather than community interests. From the Moletele case it is thus clear, after more than 20 years of democracy, that the need to introduce innovative and community responsive partnership arrangements in the restitution context can no longer be ignored. For more than twenty years we have been grappling with the legacies of apartheid. Yet, at the same time we have been reproducing institutions that continue to meet only the interests of capital. I would thus like to end by saying that we need the type of innovative models that acknowledge and respond to the diverse nature of restitution beneficiaries with their divergent needs and aspirations. Models that allow people access to land and the opportunity to have their 'voices' heard.

To conclude, in reflecting on some of the limitations of my research, I felt that my vantage point as an outsider/researcher presented me with a distinct challenge. I also feel a sense of urgency about acknowledging my own internal struggle with questions regarding the 'authenticity' or truthfulness of the responses that were given to me during my process of inquiry. As the fieldwork progressed, I realised that my presence (and of cause misconceptions about my presence) within the community, was causing a tremendous stir. Some respondents thought I was representing government or that I could influence decision making by government regarding the claim. Many of these respondents asked me to please go and 'speak' to government officials on their behalf. Even before interviews commenced, I therefore tried to explain at great length the purpose of the interview, who I was, and what will be happening to the responses they provide. Despite my lengthy introductions, I still feared that my inquiry into expectations about the settlement of the claim and interviewees knowledgeability about the partnerships could in fact be influencing the very expectations I was trying to gauge. Thus, congruent with the realist perspective, I have to acknowledge that my understanding of events is probably still incomplete and fallible on account of my positionality as an outsider/researcher, which could also have compromised the very reality I was trying to capture.

References

Akram-Lodhi, A.H., & Kay, C. (2010). Surveying the agrarian question (Part 1: unearthing foundations, exploring diversity). *The Journal of Peasant Studies*, *37*(1), 177–202.

Barrientos, S., & Visser, M. (2012). South African horticulture: opportunities and challenges for economic and social upgrading in value chains. *Capturing the Gains, economic and social upgrading in global production networks,* (Working Paper), 12 September 2012.

Bolwig, S., Ponte, S., Du Toit, S., Riisgaard, L. and Halberg, N. (2010). Integrating Poverty and Environmental Concerns into Value-Chain Analysis: A Conceptual Framework. *Development Policy Review*, 2010, 28 (2): , 173–194.

Davis, N.C. (2014). *Inclusive business models in South Africa's land reform: great expectations and ambiguous outcomes in the Moletele land restitution claim, Limpopo.* (Unpublished PhD Thesis). University of the Western Cape (PLAAS).

Derman, B., Lahiff, E., & Sjaastad, E. (2006). *Strategic Questions about Strategic Partners: Challenges and Pitfalls in South Africa's New Model of Land Restitution.* Paper prepared for Conference on Land, Memory, Reconstruction and Justice: Perspectives on land restitution in South Africa, 13–15 September 2006.

DLA (Department of Land Affairs). (2008). *Strategic sourcing and partnership framework.* Government Printers: Pretoria.

Franco, J., & Borras, J. (2010). Towards a broader view of the Politics and Global Land Grab: Rethinking Land issues, Reframing Resistance. May 2010. *ICAS Working Paper Series No. 001.* http://www.tni.org/work-area/agrarian-justice.

Harvey, D. (2003). *The New Imperialism.* Oxford: Oxford University Press.

Hall, R. (2004). A political economy of land reform in South Africa. *Review of African Political Economy*, *100*, 213–227.

Lahiff, E. (2007). *Business Models in Land Reform.* Research Report 27. Cape Town: Programme for Land and Agrarian Studies, University of Western Cape.

Lahiff, E. (2008). *Land reform in South Africa: A Status Report 2008*. Research Report 38. Cape Town: Programme for Land and Agrarian Studies, University of Western Cape.

Lahiff, E., Davis, N., & Manenzhe, T. (2012). *Joint ventures in agriculture: Lessons from land reform projects in South Africa.* London, Rome, Cape Town: IIED/IFAD/FAO/PLAAS.

Li, T.M. (2005). Beyond 'the state' and failed schemes. *American anthropologist*, *107*(3), 383–394.

Li, T.M. (2009). To Make Live or Let Die? Rural Dispossession and the Protection of Surplus Populations. *Antipode, 41*(S1 2009 ISSN 0066-4812), 66–93.

Moletele CPA. (2008). Moletele Bulletin. October 2008. Issue 2 Volume 1. Moletele Communal Property Association.

Moletele CPA. (2013) Unpublished Annual Report.

Oya, C. (2012). Contract farming in sub-Saharan Africa: a survey of approaches, debates and issues. *Journal of Agrarian Change*, 12(1), 1–33.

Spierenburg, M., Cousins, B., Bos, A., & Ntsholo, L. (2012). Connecting Communities and Business: Public Private Partnerships as the Panacea for Land Reform in Limpopo Province, South Africa. In M. De Bruijn & R. Van Dijk, *The Social Life of connectivity in Africa* (2012). New York: Palgrave Macmillion.

Vermeulen, S., & Cotula, L. (2010). Making the most of agricultural investment: A survey of business models that provide opportunities for smallholders. London, Rome, Bern: IIED/FAO/IFAD/SDC.

CHAPTER 9

'We Won't Have Zim-style Land Grabs'*: What Can South Africa Learn from Zimbabwe's Fast-track Land Reforms?

Grasian Mkodzongi

Introduction

> Zimbabwe has become an important framing device for reading land reform in South Africa; for some a haunting spectre of potential disaster, for others a hopeful sign of the possibility for radical change.
>
> ALLISON GOEBEL, 2005

In April 2014, South Africa celebrated 20 years of democracy after the end of apartheid. Although apartheid officially ended in 1994, the country's agrarian structure has stubbornly remained unchanged. A minority of white farmers continue to own most of the productive land, while the historically marginalised black population continue to wait for the 'promised land'. Across South Africa's countryside, landlessness and rural poverty is on the increase. The position of farm workers has become more precarious with increasing retrenchment, evictions, and casualization of labour (Lahiff, 2007; Hall, 2004). Land redistribution has been too slow to meet the high demand for land in both rural areas and the urban periphery. Many of those who lodged claims under the land restitution programme continue to wait for such claims to be processed. Others have simply died while waiting for their claims to be processed (News 24, 27 August 2014). Although the deadline for land claims under the land restitution programme have been extended to 2018, it is highly unlikely that a significant amount of land will be successfully reclaimed by that cut-off date. There is now a near universal agreement in academia and among policymakers that South Africa's market-based land reforms, comprising of land restitution, tenure reform, and land redistribution have largely failed to address the land question (Ntsebeza & Hall, 2007; Lahiff, 2008; Walker, 2008; Hall, 2004; Hendriks et al., 2013; & O'Laughlin et al., 2013).

---

* Statement by Gugile Nkwniti, South Africa's Rural Development and Land Reform Minister.

 | DOI 10.1163/9789004362550_010

Given the above, a major question to be asked is: are market-based land reforms the best mechanism to transfer land to the poor and landless given South Africa's experience so far, or is there now a need for a radical rethink of the land-reform policy in order to speed up the process of land redistribution?

This chapter is a provocative attempt to reflect on South Africa's unresolved land question. It utilises Zimbabwe's recent fast-track agrarian reforms to argue that South Africa must take lessons from Zimbabwe in order to 'fast-track' the transfer of land from white landowners to the landless poor. The chapter is largely based on the review of literature and some empirical data gathered in Zimbabwe.

In terms of structure, the chapter provides a very broad overview of the literature on the outcomes of South Africa's land reforms; this review is by no means exhaustive. The literature review is followed by a brief critique of Market Led Agrarian Reforms (MLAR) approaches, in terms of their failure to restructure agrarian relations in favour of the poor. This is followed by an analysis of Zimbabwe's fast-track land reforms and potential lessons for South Africa. The chapter concludes by suggesting that South Africa should take lessons from Zimbabwe's recent experience with land reform, which could potentially speed up the process of land reform and rural transformation.

South Africa's Land Reforms 20 Years After Democracy

In order to locate South Africa's land question in its historical context, it is important to provide a snapshot of the agrarian structure inherited by the African National Congress (ANC) government at the transitional moment of 1994. Due to centuries of colonial dispossession meticulously analysed by various scholars (Bundy, 1979; Legassik, 1974; Bernstein, 1996a), at the dawn of independence in 1994, 'white farms occupied 85.8 million hectares, 86 per cent of rural land ... about 15 million people, roughly half of the African population lived in the Bantustans on some 14 million hectares, one sixth of them are fenced by 60,000 white farms' (Bernstein 2013, p. 1). By 2010, sixteen years post-apartheid, an odd 4 million hectares of land (5 per cent) had been transferred under South Africa's three pronged land-reform programmes. By 2014, twenty years after democracy, those figures had hardly changed; this demonstrates a 'spectacular' (Hall, 2004) failure of South Africa's market-based land reforms.

Although the land issue was central to anti-apartheid struggles, at the dawn of independence in 1994, it did not feature prominently on the agenda of the African National Congress (ANC) political party (Levin & Weiner, 1996; Goebel, 2005). Various reasons can be cited for the above. Firstly, since the transition from apartheid was a 'negotiated' process, this had a bearing on future land-reform policies. Secondly, during negotiations to end apartheid, the ANC lacked a coherent land policy; this allowed white landowners a free reign to secure their property rights in anticipation of the end of apartheid. According to Goebel (2005, p. 350), the historic compromises made during the transitional moment resulted in a revolution 'far less complete than the proponents had envisioned'. More importantly, the white farming establishment took advantage of lack of policy coherence in the ANC by hedging their bets on 'life' after apartheid. This involved, inter alia, the deregulation of agrarian markets and privatisation of state-owned agricultural marketing boards (Bernstein, 2013) and the entrenchment of their property rights in the constitution.

Post-apartheid South Africa's land-reform policies have been largely based on the 'willing buyer, willing seller neoliberal-concept'. This essentially commits the government to a local variant of a market-based land-reform policy. Under this policy, it was anticipated that 30% (24.6 million hectares) of white owned land could be redistributed in a five-year period. According to Hall (2004, p. 214) 'World Bank advisors had proposed this target as feasible, noting that 6% of agricultural land is transacted each year'. Furthermore, it was anticipated that 24.6 million (30 per cent) hectares of white-owned land could be transferred to blacks by 1999. In hindsight, this proposition was rather ambitious, given the way events on the ground were to unfold. We now know that by that date, a paltry 1.2 per cent of land had been redistributed, far below the 30% target.

As a result, the 30% target continues to be shifted, from 2014 and now to 2025 (Lahiff 2007, p. 1581; O' Laughlin et al. 2013, p. 8). Moreover, the 30% figure was based on a problematic assumption that under 'perfect' market conditions, land could be quickly transferred from white landowners to the landless poor. Proponents of market-led agrarian reform, believe that the removal of distortions in the land market, poor programme design, and excessive cost of acquiring land under state-led agrarian reforms makes MLAR programmes a more efficient way of land redistribution. However, as highlighted above, these claims have been proven to be problematic. Under South Africa's market-based land reforms, very little land have been transferred to the poor during a 20-year period. More importantly, the dualistic agrarian structure, dominated by a minority of mostly white commercial farmers remains in place, while landlessness and rural poverty persist in former Bantustans.

Apart from the failure to transfer meaningful amounts of land to the poor, as originally envisaged under the Settlement/Land Acquisition Grant (SLAG) policy, the focus of the land reform gradually shifted to promoting so-called 'emerging' black capitalist farmers under the Land Redistribution for

Agricultural Development (LRAD) programme. However, empirical data gathered in the Northern Province (Rusenga 2015) shows that some of the emerging farmers funded under the LRAD programme have encountered a wide range of challenges in the aftermath of resettlement. These range from the absence of adequate post-settlement support and differential access to agricultural markets, which remain dominated by whites.

The shift towards supporting emerging black farmers rather than the 'poorest of the poor' demonstrates the prominence given by the ANC government to commercial agriculture rather than equity in its land-reform programmes (Alden & Anseeuw, 2009). This is further demonstrated by the failure of the government to remove apartheid-era legislation, which disallowed the subdivision of farms (Van Den Brink et al., 2007). This is despite such policies having negatively impacted on the land-reform programmes. For example, under the SLAG program, people were forced to apply for land as groups, since the R16,000 grant offered by the government was too small to acquire large farms, which were available on the market. This led to the more 'entrepreneurial beneficiaries putting large groups together with the sole purpose of reaching the required farm price' (Van den Brink et al. 2007, p. 179). In some places redistributing land to large groups led to conflicts over control of the land in the aftermath, which in turn undermined agricultural productivity and the sustainability of land-reform projects. This is despite the fact that the subdivision of farms into smaller entities had the potential to address distortions in the landownership structure and improve efficiency, as more people were likely to gain access to land. The allocation of land to groups rather than individuals under Community Property Associations (CPAs), and the associated bureaucratic processes involved, shows some of the shortcomings of the land-reform policies and their implementation. To quote from Bernstein (2011, p. 5):

> ...there has been a kind of double 'whammy' of projectisation and its strait jackets: first the project framework of land transfers that have taken place (and the problems of Communal Property Associations, CPAs) and second in many cases the project framework of subsequent land use models, typifying CPASs into PPPs (Public Private Partnerships), SPVs, (Special Purpose Vehicles), and the like, that is under tutelage (at best) and extortion (by at worst) agricultural business 'expertise', typically contracted from white farmers and consultancy outfits.

As highlighted above, the failure to subdivide farms to smaller entities left beneficiaries with limited choice over tenure as it was deemed easier to give title over land to CPAs than individuals. While there is nothing wrong with group-based tenure, this *de facto* policy overlooked the problems faced by members of CPAs, in particular conflicts over how to run these *de facto* cooperative farming projects. Simply put, potential beneficiaries had limited influence over the process of acquiring land and how to utilise such land, this is despite the fact that people were supposed to be active participants in a land market, and should decide which land to buy and what tenure they preferred, and who to work with and how to utilise the land. However, 'state high modernism' (Scott, 1998) ran supreme over the land-reform projects, due to over centralisation of the land-reform process (Van den Brink et al., 2007). Ideologically, the ANC government has been largely influenced by the presumed 'superiority' of large farms over smallholder production, however, though more productive than smaller farms, the efficiency of large farms has been challenged under the so called 'farm size productivity debate' (Toulmin & Quan, 2000; Van den Brink et al., 2007).

Another problem is the overreliance of the government on the technical expertise of 'white farmers', the very people who have resisted the land reform or in some places have sought to extort money from the government during the land transfer process. Some unscrupulous elements among this group have taken advantage of their status as 'experts' to engage in rent-seeking activities during the land-transfer process. This is especially the case for some white landowners who have 'volunteered' to sell their land to government at a premium, while hiding the fact that such farms were already facing viability challenges and potential bankruptcy (Mkodzongi & Rusenga, 2015). Others sold their land to the government at distorted prices but re-emerged as 'consultants' to the land beneficiaries, who are paid large fees for their new role. This meant that financial resources, which would have benefited land beneficiaries, ended up benefiting white landowners due to their ability to 'work the system' to their advantage, while beneficiaries faced poverty even after gaining access to land (Somerville, 2014).

So called 'organised agriculture', a euphemism for the white farmers lobby (AGRI SA), have exercised undue influence over the trajectory of the land-reform process by lobbying the ANC government to maintain the bi-modal agrarian structure inherited from apartheid. As a result, the land reform has been depicted as a threat to food security and Foreign Direct Investment (FDI). The ANC government's negative attitude towards smallholder agriculture and its reluctance to dismantle the large farms is influenced by this lobby. Additionally, the financialisation of South Africa's agrarian sector post-apartheid has transformed white commercial farmers into local proxies of global capital and agribusiness (Bernstein, 2013). This has led to the conceptualisation of agriculture as a business, which must not be interfered with (through land reform), as this will affect 'investor confidence'. Resistance to redistributive land reform is thus not only local but also global. Global capitalist interests in South African agriculture are now essentially holding the government at ransom with threats of food shortages and economic decline if the government were to expropriate land. A major outcome of the corporatisation of agriculture has been the shift in government land-reform policies from redistributing land to the poorest of the poor, to giving land to those with the ability to farm commercially under its LRAD programme. The major losers in this are the landless rural and urban dwellers, who stood to benefit from redistributive land reform. The situation is worsened by the fact that the poor and landless lack an effective lobby to influence government policy from below and to challenge the dominance of agribusiness in the agrarian sector.

The conceptualisation of South Africa's land and agrarian questions has also been problematic; a revisionist debate heavily influenced by the classical agrarian question theoretical framework has dominated scholarship. Henry Bernstein (1996b), who has provided most of the theoretical rigour to this debate, has concluded that South Africa's agrarian question was resolved under apartheid industrialisation. Under this process of primitive accumulation, peasants were forcibly uprooted from their ancestral lands and turned into wage labourers. He has concluded that there is no longer an agrarian question in South Africa (in classical sense) and that what remains is a labour question. While this kind of theorising rightly demonstrates the trajectory of the classic agrarian question and its effects on the South African peasantry, it is too narrowly focused on the development of capitalist relations in agriculture to the detriment of a broader understanding of South Africa's contemporary agrarian questions. For example, the fate of the large mass of a 'floating' semi-proletariat with neither jobs nor land remains unresolved. A major question to be asked is what should happen to people in this group? Since the crisis of globalisation post-apartheid has created a large number of unemployed people, does this not make it urgent for the land question to be resolved as a way of potentially addressing rampant urban and rural poverty? Yet the classical theorisation almost glorifies this social tragedy to a point of downplaying the need for land reform among the indigenous black population. It is claimed (Hendricks 2013, p. 49) that people in this group depend 'heavily on transfers from the state in the form of pensions and grants or on remittances from urban areas, and the youth in general prefer the urban areas', very thin evidence is provided to support these claims. The agrarian question is thus conceptualised in a narrow economic sense, the broader aspects of land including issues of identity and belonging are largely ignored due to a 'fetish' with the development of capitalist relations in agriculture and the proletarianisation of peasants. More importantly, there is an attempt to underestimate the links between the urban and the rural, yet the reality on the ground is that those waiting to gain access to land are not only rural but also urbanites living in shanty towns and on white-owned farms with dubious rights over the land (Batisai, this volume).

There is evidence to suggest that many migrant labourers from rural areas in former Bantustans continue to maintain a connection with their rural homesteads, where their kinsfolk continue to engage in peasant agriculture to supplement livelihoods (Chitonge & Ntsebeza, 2012). Furthermore, by privileging the labour question, this theorisation has also downplayed the potential for land reform to create rural employment and address rural poverty. Yet empirical data gathered across various provinces of South Africa shows that land reform has the potential to create rural employment and reverse rural poverty. Ncapayi's study (this volume) based in the Eastern Cape shows that land reform can improve rural livelihoods if beneficiaries are given adequate post-resettlement support.

Similarly, Mnqobi's study based in Kwazulu Natal (this volume) shows that beneficiaries of land reform conceptualise land as a multi-purpose resource beyond its utility for agricultural production. The benefits of land reform cannot thus be narrowed to agricultural production. This is further confirmed by Kamuti (this volume), whose study in Kwazulu Natal shows that indigenous people attach multiple meanings to land, which tend to be ignored in mainstream debates. Land reform restores a sense of belonging among people whose ancestral lands were lost to colonial era forced removals; the recovery of such lands restores a sense of belonging and identity, as people are reunited with certain places where the graves of their ancestors are located. This was denied under the apartheid era agrarian structure. These studies show the shortcomings of a classical conceptualisation of South Africa's agrarian question, with its narrow focus on the development of capitalist relations in agriculture. This tends to ignore the diverse meanings of land, which are important to the indigenous population.

There is now a large corpus of studies that has sought to analyse the outcomes of South Africa's land and agrarian reforms (Ntsebeza & Hall, 2007; Lahiff, 2008; Walker, 2008; Cousins & Walker, 2015). This scholarship has correctly highlighted some of the shortcomings of South Africa's land-reform policy and the attendant bureaucratic challenges that have bedevilled its implementation. For example, in her study of the political economy of South Africa's land reform, Hall (2004, p. 219) has argued that 'big policy and a shrinking state' has limited the scale and trajectory of land reform as it seeks to 'maintain the structure of the commercial farming sector'. Similarly, Lahiff (2007) has argued that South Africa's market-based land reform lacks 'coherence' and is subject to 'competing imperatives and contending political forces'. This has led to what he calls 'a messy compromise that has proven to be extremely slow and has failed to deliver its key policy objectives'. However, a major weakness of this scholarship is that it has overly focused on government failure to redistribute land, while paying limited attention to structural limitations, which have undermined the transfer of land to the landless under the market-based land reforms.

Additionally, criticisms of current land-reform policies are not accompanied by proposals for a radical rethink of South Africa's MLAR policies, which have largely failed. It is implicitly assumed that under the current neoliberal macro-economic climate, distortions and injustices in the agrarian structure could be resolved. For example, in her criticism of land restitution, Walker (2015, p. 248) claims that the land restitution programme has promoted 'misplaced popular expectations' among land claimants; she however fails to address the question of why land restitution discourses are popular among the poor. Additionally, her critique gives undue prominence to 'logistics' and 'bureaucracy' as the root cause of the slow delivery of land under land restitution; while this is partly true, she pays little attention to the structural limitations imposed on land reform by the neoliberal orthodoxy, which has so far dominated policymaking.

Similarly, Cousins (2015, p. 267), has sought to downplay the need for a fundamental restructuring of the current agrarian restructure by arguing that 'land acquisition must be spatially targeted' and that the 'target of redistributing 30 per cent of farmland must be replaced by one of 60–80 per cent over two or three decades, with the productive core of 20 per cent of commercial farmers left aside for now'. Given the current crisis of poverty and unemployment in rural areas, these proposals seem bizarre, as they are politically unrealistic. Who is the 'productive core of 20 per cent'? Is this not akin to pandering to the whims of large-scale commercial farmers who have deployed the productivity discourse to resist land reform? Cousins and his colleagues have sought to reduce South Africa's land question to a problem of agricultural production, while ignoring the political economy of this racialized agrarian structure. Prominence is thus given to the maintenance of agricultural productivity and food security under the current agrarian structure rather than its replacement by a more democratic tri-modal (Moyo, 2011a) structure which could allow diverse group of farmers to participate in productive agriculture beyond the minority of landowners who currently own most of the productive land. Cousins' proposals ignore the fact that 'a decisive transformation of land and agrarian relations is intimately bound up with the construction of a new democratic order' (Levin & Weiner, 1996). Yet much of the of scholarship on the outcomes of South Africa's land reforms (Cousins & Walker, 2015) have sought to decouple the agrarian question from the broader question of national liberation, which as highlighted earlier was compromised during the transition from apartheid. This has been a major stumbling block in efforts to restructure agrarian relations in favour of the poor. Below, I explore the problem with MLAR policies and their impact on land reform.

The Problem with Market-led Agrarian Reform (MLAR): Conceptual Debates

Although there is now a near universal agreement among scholars that South Africa's variant of MLAR has failed, there has been very little effort both in academia and among policymakers to look for alternative approaches beyond the market. This is despite the fact that contrary to claims made by proponents of MLAR policies, they do not lead to a speedy transfer of land from landowners to the landless poor. The history of MLAR policies in post-settler economies of Southern Africa is that they have tended to privilege 'vibrant markets' in the transfer of land rather than historical redress. This is problematic in a context where the indigenous black population expected to recover their ancestral lands lost during colonial-era land grabs.

The process of historical redress cannot be simply left to the markets, as it requires state intervention to address historical injustices embedded in colonial-era agrarian structure. Furthermore, MLAR policies reduce land to an 'economic resource' and assume that markets are 'institutions in which participants are equal' (Akram-Lodhi 2007, p. 1421). The reality on the ground is that landowners have more power than the landless; they often use this power to resist land transfers, as is the case under South Africa's land reforms. Additionally, MLAR policies 'requires that sources of distortions in agricultural land prices, such as subsidised input and output markets, be abolished completely, in order to bring the market value of land closer to its productive value' (Lahiff et al. 2007, p. 1423). In a country recovering from historical injustices such as South Africa, leaving the landless poor alone to participate in a land market heavily biased towards landowners is at best 'irresponsible'; it cannot be expected to induce equity and speed up the transfer of land. Again the South African experience simply shows that markets do not remove distortions by themselves; the government has often been forced to pay above-market prices for marginal lands as a result of market distortions, which favour landowners (Mkodzongi & Rusenga, 2015). More importantly, participants in the 'market' are never 'equal', since landownership reflects power relationships; landowners have more leverage over land markets; they are able to deploy their financial and political power to resist the transfer of land to the landless, as this threatens their power. For example, under South Africa's land restitution program, land claims take forever to conclude, largely due to the entrenchment of private property rights of the white landowners in the constitution, which gives them too much leverage over the land transfer process. They often deploy this power to resist the transfer of land (Albertus, 2015). This has made the land-reform process unnecessarily expensive and drawn out, as landowners utilise legal instruments to resist agrarian reform.

MLAR policies also favour landowners who often use their privileged and political connections to benefit economically from the land reform. For example, under South Africa's land restitution program, landowners have used their status as 'experts' to benefit from the land restitution process. Under this process, beneficiaries of land reform are often coerced by the government to enter into land management contracts with former white landowners. Such contracts favour landowners due to their contradictory role of having sold land to the government and their new status as 'experts' hired by the same government to advise land beneficiaries. These so called 'experts' end up engaging in rent-seeking activities in order to 'harvest' land-reform grants meant for land beneficiaries. They often leave after the expiry of their management contracts having benefited from government grants. Meanwhile, beneficiaries of land restitution are left with rundown farming projects, having hardly received any dividends under such management contracts (Summerville, 2014).

The above shows that the MLAR model gives landowners too much leverage over the land-transfer process. Moreover, beneficiaries of land reform are not 'active participants' in land markets as they lack the legal and technical skills to navigate the often complicated and bureaucratic land transfer process, for example under South Africa's land restitution programme. The case of South Africa shows that the landless face many hurdles to access land under the MLAR model. Landowners have ironically been the major beneficiaries of the land reform, as they have returned their landholdings with minimal transfer of land or sold marginal lands to the government at a premium, a process that has undermined the democratisation of agrarian structure in favour of the historically marginalised black population. It has been argued that for land reform to be truly redistributive, 'it must effect on a pre-existing agrarian structure a change in ownership of and/or control over land … from the landed to the landless and land poor classes or from rich land lords to poor peasants…' (Borras 2007, p. 22). Yet the opposite has been happening in South African land reform; the transfer of a limited amount of land to the landless poor means that white landowners have retained most of the land. Since land rights reflect power relationships, the failure to redistribute land (in this case power) is akin to the failure to address power inequity between the landless and the landlords.

In their critique of MLAR policies Lahiff and colleagues (2007, p. 1425) have argued that 'MLAR has failed to live up to the many claims made for it in the area of beneficiary selection and land acquisition. Firstly, the volume of land transferred has been extremely low relative to programme targets and alternative approaches'. Their study indicates that, across many countries where MLAR was implemented, very little land was transferred to land beneficiaries:

> In the Philippines less than 1000 hectares were transferred in four years under textbook MLAR experiment as compared to with seven million transferred under state led approach. In South Africa, less than 4% of agricultural land was transferred in the first 10 years of reform, against a government target of 30% over five years. A similar figure is reported for Guatemala, over eight years. In Brazil over 10 times the number of people have benefited from 'traditional' (expropriatory) reform than from the various market led approaches currently being implemented…

The above shows that MLAR policies often fail to address injustices in the landownership structure. According to Borras (2006, p. 99), 'pro-market land policies show that they do not significantly reform pre-existing agrarian structures in favour of the rural poor'. Across South Africa's border in Zimbabwe, two decades of MLAR programmes failed to meet land-reform targets. As a result, in 2000, landless peasants were forced to occupy white-owned commercial farms, which forced the government to support a fast-track land-reform programme leading to the transformation of a colonial-era agrarian structure inherited at independence in 1980 (Moyo & Yeros, 2005, 2007; Moyo, 2011b). Given the failure of MLAR projects in many countries, it is surprising that South Africa has not considered other options in its quest to address the land question, given the fact that 20 years of MLAR have failed to reform the agrarian structure. The above shows that there is now a need to rethink land-reform approaches in order to transcend the neoliberal orthodoxy that has so far dominated policymaking. More importantly, the scholarship on South Africa's land reform must go beyond the current fetish with 'logistics' and 'bureaucracy' as the main stumbling block to a more redistributive land-reform process (Lahiff, 2007; Hall, 2004; Ntsebeza & Hall, 2007; Walker, 2008; Cousins & Walker, 2015). As the Zimbabwean case study explored in this chapter demonstrates, a more redistributive state-led land-reform process has the potential to dismantle the colonial-era agrarian structure, which has persisted for 20 years after the end of apartheid.

Below I explore the way Zimbabwe's recent fast-track land reforms successfully restructured agrarian relations in favour of the poor and landless. I argue that despite its shortcomings, Zimbabwe's fast-track land reforms provide important lessons for South Africa, given the failure of its MLAR-based policies.

Transcending Market Dogmas: Lessons from Zimbabwe's Radical Land Reforms

Zimbabwe's recent land reforms, implemented in 2000, have inspired a wide variety of debates and opinions across Southern African society. In general, the countrywide forceful occupation of white-owned farms was widely condemned by South Africa's landowning classes and in the media. Although certain radical elements in the ANC government supported the radical reforms, at policy level, the ANC adopted a rather ambivalent attitude towards Zimbabwe's land reforms. Senior figures in the ANC including former president Thabo Mbeki agreed that 'the crisis in Zimbabwe was the result of a failure to redistribute land' (Lahiff & Cousins 2001, p. 655). Mbeki's comments did not translate into the ANC fully backing Zimbabwe's radical reforms. Instead, the South African official government position was to condemn the agrarian reforms, while at the same time acknowledging their need. For example, senior ANC officials such as Kgalema Mohlante described the farm invasions as 'protest action' against the failure of land reform' (*ibid*, p. 655). Similarly, South African foreign minister at the time Nkosazana Dlamini Zuma was quoted as saying 'Zimbabwe's correcting an historic injustice. We may not agree with the methods but we agree with the correction of injustice' (quoted from Goebel, 2005, p. 362). These contradictory statements demonstrated the difficult balancing act that the South African government had to play when dealing with the politically sensitive events in Zimbabwe, given their own unresolved land issue.

Although fears of copycat land occupations by South Africa's landless and marginalised black population were largely unfounded, Zimbabwe's fast-track land reforms have had a profound effect on debates about land reform in South Africa. Most importantly, the fast-track reforms had the effect of bringing the land question back to the agenda of the ANC government (Goebel, 2005).

A dominant narrative popularised in certain sections of South Africa's academia (Lahiff & Cousins, 2000; Goebel, 2005; Walker, 2008; Aliber, 2015) was the depiction of the fast-track reforms as a politically motivated land grab. The structural inequality inherent in the colonial-era agrarian structure inherited at independence in 1980 was largely ignored. Additionally, its redistributive aspect, which led to the radical change in agrarian structure in favour of diverse land beneficiaries, was largely downplayed. This is despite the fact that 'in countries with highly unequal distribution of land, the case for land reform-redistributing property rights from the rich to the poor' is a *sine qua non* for 'conflict prevention, equity, economic growth, jobs and poverty reduction' (Van de Brink et al. 2007, p. 154).

Among South Africa's predominantly white commercial farmers, Zimbabwe's land occupations were condemned not least because of television images of white farmers being physically assaulted by war veterans aligned to the Zimbabwe African National Union Patriotic Front (ZANU PF) political party. Since many of the Zimbabwean white farmers held both Zimbabwean and South African nationality, the forceful confiscation of their property without compensation alarmed their 'kith and kin' in South Africa. It is no surprise that the forceful confiscation of white-owned farms was viewed a threat to the neoliberal regime of property rights, which has been widely entrenched across former settler colonies of southern Africa. As a result, land occupations were simply depicted as a return to barbarism and the abuse of human rights by Mugabe's regime. Selected acts of violence during the land occupations were used to show how these occupations were not about land hunger, but a 'political gimmick' by Mugabe to entrench his dictatorial rule.

While claims of violence surrounding the implementation of the land reform cannot simply be dismissed, such claims failed to take into account the broader political dynamics that underpinned the land occupations, and the fact that the ZANU PF government did not necessarily initiate them (Moyo & Yeros, 2005, 2007; Sadomba, 2011). In the media-driven frenzy that followed, peasants who led the occupations were often depicted as environmental bandits who lacked the skills to farm. Google maps were used to show the dramatic ecological degradation that had taken place across Zimbabwe's former white-owned commercial farming areas as evidence of an environmental disaster triggered by the land reform (Richardson, 2005). The historical injustices in the landownership structure, which had persisted post Zimbabwe's independence, were simply ignored in favour of a dominant narrative that reduced the land reform to a political gimmick.

Furthermore, the forceful eviction of white farmers was seen as having undermined Zimbabwe's agrarian-based economy. Nostalgic claims of Zimbabwe having been a 'bread basket' of Southern Africa before the evictions of white landowners and a 'basket case' in the aftermath became popular in the media and in academic writing. White farmers were often depicted as having been the backbone of Zimbabwe's agricultural economy, without whose skills the country could not feed itself. Furthermore, they were also depicted as *de facto* environmental activists whose eviction had endangered wildlife.

The decline in agricultural productivity witnessed after the land reform was simply reduced to the eviction of white farmers, other contributory factors such as western imposed sanctions and severe weather patterns (which are a common occurrence in Zimbabwe and the wider sub-region) and the prevailing difficult economic climate, which undermined the ability of the ZANU PF government to support the new farmers, were largely ignored.

A major weakness of this simplistic discourse of chaos and agricultural decline was the lack of empirical evidence. Many of the claims made in the early stages of Zimbabwe's fast-track reforms have been proven to be largely misleading given new empirical evidence that has emerged post the fast-track reforms (Chaumba et al., 2003; Moyo et al., 2009; Scoones et al., 2010; Sadomba, 2010; Moyo, 2011a; Chambati, 2011; Matondi, 2012; Hanlon et al., 2012; Mkodzongi, 2013a). These studies have demonstrated that the outcomes of Zimbabwe's fast-track land reforms were broad, and that a nuanced analysis need to be undertaken before broad generalisations can be made.

More importantly, empirical data shows that, although the land reform was underpinned by class, gender, and ethno-regionalism, landless peasants were the major beneficiaries (Moyo et al., 2009; Scoones et al., 2010; Hanlon et al., 2013). These studies challenge earlier claims of chaos and cronyism (Hammar et al., 2003; Zamchiya, 2011).

Although some of the new farmers particularly in the A2 sector (commercial farms) have struggled to utilise the land, claims that the new farmers are 'weekend' or 'cellphone' farmers have been proven to be misleading. Empirical data from across various study sites shows that the new farmers, in particular the A1 sector (peasant farmers), have made relatively large investments on their newly acquired land despite a hostile socio-economic environment which obtained post the land reform (Moyo et al., 2009; Scoones et al., 2010; Hanlon, 2012; Mkodzongi, 2013b). Additionally, although the agrarian sector is yet to fully recover post the land reforms, empirical data shows that certain sectors have dramatically recovered and that some of the new farmers are already 'accumulating from below' (Scoones et al., 2010). This is especially the case with tobacco where, by 2013, over 91,278 farmers were registered tobacco growers. Data from the Tobacco Industry Marketing Board (TIMB) shows that 82 per cent of the registered growers are peasant farmers (based in both communal areas and A1 farms); this makes them the major supplier of the crop post the land reform. More importantly, by 2014, the total number of registered tobacco growers had risen to 106,456, an annual increase of almost 10% (TIMB, 2014).

The tobacco sector contributes 10 per cent of Zimbabwe's annual GDP, with the value chain employing more than 1.2 million people, with an estimated 5 million dependents (ibid.). The fact that this sector is now dominated by peasants shows how the land reform has enhanced rural livelihoods. While claims that the industry has led to land degradation and environmental destruction cannot be simply dismissed, the tobacco industry has been implementing corrective measures. These include, *inter alia*, the Sustainable Afforestation Programme which seeks to 'correct the deforestation effects' in tobacco growing areas (TIMB 2014, p. 6) by investing in more fuel-efficient barns.

This shows that despite the challenges that have emerged in the aftermath, the change in agrarian structure has largely benefited a diversified group of farmers, although these are socially differentiated. More importantly, landless peasants who were the major beneficiaries of the land reform now have access to better quality land and other natural resources. These natural resources have played an important role in the diversification of livelihoods post the land reform (Mkodzongi, 2013).

But what can South Africa learn from Zimbabwe's 'dissident' (Moyo, 2007) model of land reform? This is an important question given the current challenges facing South Africa's market-based land reforms. Key points relevant to the South African context can be noted. Firstly, redistributive land reform can dismantle the big farm model, which was inherited from colonialism. Although some of these large entities were retained in Zimbabwe (Moyo, 2011a), dismantling the large farms has expanded the number of smallholders, while deracializing and diversifying the commercial agricultural sector beyond the white minority producers who dominated the sector before the land reform. This has had the dual effect of freeing up excess land and bringing efficiency to the agricultural sector. Secondly, the state as the arbiter of land rights must play a more active role in facilitating redistributive land reform as landowners often resist the transfer of land rights to the poor. Third, state-led land and agrarian reforms can reverse distortions in the landownership structure by transforming power relations that historically favour landowners who control most of the productive land and other natural resources, which is a direct cause of poverty among the rural poor and landless. Fourth, the nationalisation of land and compulsory acquisition without compensation or part payment removes the burden of rent-seeking, which tends to distort land markets during the land transfer process. As was the case in Zimbabwe, the state opted to only pay for improvements on the land rather than the land itself; this can make the land reform affordable and quicker to deliver. It also saves time, as landlords can no longer use legal tactics to delay the land reform. For example before the onset of the fast-track land reforms in 2000, Zimbabwe spent over 20 years

(1980–1999), pursuing market-based land reforms like South Africa, however these reforms only managed to resettle an insignificant number of peasants as highlighted earlier on. Some of the problems faced by Zimbabwe in its earlier land reforms are being experienced in South Africa today (Goebel, 2005).

Post the land reform, Zimbabwe was confronted by a severe economic crisis characterised by sky-rocketing inflation. Global financial institutions such as the WB and International Monitory fund (IMF) withdrew financial support and encouraged other major donors to financially isolate the Zimbabwean government under the guise of democracy and human rights. This forced the country to adopt a 'look east' policy in search of alternative sources of capital. Zimbabwe's experience demonstrates the economic and political power that white landowners continue to wield as proxies of global capital in the former settler economies of Southern Africa.

Despite the economic and political hazards that can result from redistributive land reforms, evidence from Zimbabwe shows that a radical restructuring of the agrarian sector can address historical injustices in the landownership structure and address rural poverty. This can create improved mobility and new livelihood opportunities for the marginalised rural citizens (Van den Blink et al., 2007; Toulmin & Quan, 2000).

More importantly, the distortions (multiple farm ownership, etc.) that were retained during the land reform particularly in the A2 farming sector are now being addressed. Recent proposals by the GoZ to impose a land tax will likely discourage multiple farm ownership among political elites, who are believed to be hoarding potentially productive land. The formation of a Land Commission to deal with farm disputes and other wider agrarian issues such as security of tenure is likely to address the challenges facing commercial agriculture post the agrarian reforms. This process signals the deepening of the process of agrarian reform, which remains incomplete despite the change in agrarian structure. This is likely to stimulate agricultural productivity and bring equity to the sector in the long term. It is important to highlight here that Zimbabwe's fast-track land reforms were overshadowed by political violence and contested electoral outcomes due to ongoing allegations of rigging by the opposition Movement for Democratic Change (MDC) political party. This matter largely remains unresolved due to succession struggles in the ZANU PF political party and the resultant democratic deficits, which have attracted international criticism and sanctions.

As South Africa stands at the precipice of uncertain agrarian futures, Zimbabwe's recent experience with redistributive land reform provides important lessons. Firstly, despite its short-term economic pitfalls, the compulsory acquiring of land without compensation for the land but improvements on the land has proven to be a cheaper and faster way of transferring land to the landless. This factor was highlighted by Aliber (2015, p. 160) who argued that 'there are only two types of regimes which could conceivably succeed in confiscating a significant proportion of white owned farms, namely totalitarian power such as that imposed by the United States military over defeated Japan at the conclusion of the second world war, or a regime characterised by state-condoned chaos and violence, like Zimbabwe…' Similarly, a study by Albertus (2015) shows that 'democracy often prevents individuals' property rights from being violated – which is typically required for large-scale land redistribution' and that South Africa's democratic institutions are holding back serious land reform as landowners utilise their private property rights to frustrate the radical transfers of property rights to the poor. Given the above, Aliber's characterisation of Zimbabwe's fast-track land reform as 'state-condoned chaos and violence' shows a typical failure of South African scholarship to appreciate some of the progressive aspects of the Zimbabwean experience.

With the risk of sounding rather optimistic, the threat of capital flight and economic decline post the land reform is real but can be temporary in nature. Although Zimbabwe was confronted by a difficult socio-economic crisis, which remains unresolved, the country has witnessed a gradual return of foreign direct investment especially in the extractive sector and certain sections of the agricultural sector such as tobacco. This process has signalled the return of capital to Zimbabwe due to the normalisation of diplomatic relations between Zimbabwe and western countries. This suggests that disinvestment and capital flight during a radical transformation of an agrarian structure is temporary. The potential economic impact of forcefully acquiring land from white landowners for redistribution is thus exaggerated and largely based on scare mongering. Post-redistributive land reform economic challenges must thus be viewed as temporary phenomena to be overcome in the long-term.

Zimbabwe's recent experience demonstrates that the benefits of transforming a colonial-era agrarian structure are immense despite the socio-economic challenges that can be encountered in the aftermath. South Africa can potentially learn from Zimbabwe's experience before it considers going along a similar path. This can help it to avoid some of the challenges and mistakes made by Zimbabwe during the process such as better preparation for post-settlement support and capital flight, which is synonymous with radical agrarian reforms. Threats of economic decline, sanctions, and other punitive measures popularised by those with vested interests in the current unjust agrarian structure must not deter the country from exploring such alternatives. The potential political hazards for maintaining the agrarian structure inherited from apartheid are huge and are best avoided.

Land Reform from Below: Future Prospects for South Africa

An important lesson from Zimbabwe's recent land reforms is the instrumentality of social movements in pressuring the state from below to radically restructure agrarian relations in favour of the poor (Moyo, 2011b). In countries where major land and agrarian reforms have been successfully undertaken, peasant-led social movements have utilised the land occupation tactic to pressure the state to expropriate land from landowners for redistribution to the rural poor (Moyo & Yeros, 2005). In Zimbabwe, war veterans utilised the land occupation tactic to force the state to abandon its market friendly land-reform policies in favour of a more radical land-reform programme. Despite the economic challenges confronted in the aftermath, it was a progressive process, which undermined the logic of colonial-era agrarian relations that had persisted after the country's independence in 1980.

The deepening crisis of neoliberalism in South Africa, characterised by high levels of unemployment and deepening rural poverty, has led to the ongoing service delivery strikes especially in poor urban areas. Community-based organisations and non-governmental organisations such as Abahlali basemJondolo and Ses'kona People's Rights Movement are engaged in ongoing struggles against poverty and marginalisation. Furthermore, in isolated rural areas, farm workers are engaged in ongoing struggles against super exploitation by white commercial farmers. Many of the service delivery strikes and wage protests are sometimes violently suppressed by the state. However, the major weakness of these issue-based 'service delivery' strikes is that the organisations behind them lack the political clout to pressure the state from below.

A major weakness in South Africa is the absence of a coherent social movement similar to the war veteran movement in Zimbabwe. This owes to the fact that, unlike Zimbabwe, the many disparate groups engaged in struggles to access land in rural areas and the urban periphery lack cohesion and a popular political programme to pressure the state from below. In short 'they lack politics' (Amin, 2012). Although in some places these groups have adopted the land occupation tactic in their quest to gain access to land, particularly in the urban periphery, lack of coordination and solidarity among the many groups has undermined their effectiveness in influencing government policy.

There is a need for the struggles of the poor to be coordinated for them to be effective in influencing the future trajectory of land-reform policy. Experience from elsewhere shows that the 'state cannot simply be transformed from above, but needs to be changed through a combination of action from above and below'. There is thus a need for 'sustained popular organisation' (Levin & Weiner 1996, p. 96) to exert pressure from below in order to force the government to implement radical structural reforms.

The Zimbabwean experience shows that a social movement rooted in the struggles of the poor can play a key role in challenging neoliberal policies which deny them access to land and other livelihoods opportunities. The emergence of such a movement in South Africa has the potential to force the ANC government towards a more redistributive macro-economic policy framework, which might quicken the pace of land and agrarian reform.

The decrease in the ANC majority in parliament in favour of smaller parties such as the newly formed Economic Freedom Fighters (EFF) political party demonstrates the growing popularity of leftist politics among the ANC's traditional black supporters who have borne the brunt of rising rural and urban poverty. Many poor people are now questioning the ANC pro-business policies and lack of 'service delivery' among the rural and urban poor. The reopening of land-restitution claims and proposals to strengthen the rights of farm workers through the 'Strengthening The Relative Rights Of People Working The Land – popularly known as the 50/50 Policy Framework – by 2019; and, the Regulation of Landholdings Bill, which will introduce land ceilings and prohibit land ownership by foreign nationals' (South African Government, 8 May 2015) must be viewed as a response to the growing pressure to address poverty among the poor and landless. While these proposals do not signify a radical shift in policy and have been criticised by both white landowners and the landless poor, they indicate that debates about land reform are likely to be radicalised in the future, as the ANC responds to popular pressure from below. In fact this is already happening; as the ANC seeks to recover votes lost to the Democratic Alliance and the EFF during the last municipal elections, there is already talk of more radical land-reform policies in favour of historically marginalized groups. As the ANC undergoes leadership change towards the end of 2017, time will tell if the new leadership will break with the party's neoliberal past in favour of more redistributive land-reform policies.

A potential coalition of leftist political parties and trade union movements such as EFF, the Association of Mine Workers and Construction Union (AMCU), the National Union of Metal workers of South Africa (NUMSA), and the newly formed South African Federation of Trade Unions are likely to challenge the ANC's neoliberal macro-economic project, which has undermined agrarian transformation. However, there is not yet any unity and meaningful political dialogue among these various movements, which is a major source of their weakness, given their potential strength if they were to be united. Samir Amin (2012, p. 23) has argued that social movements have a tendency to be fragmented, 'what is needed is to move beyond fragmentation and beyond a defensive position into building a wide progressive alliance emboldened with the force of a positive alternative'. A major question to be asked is can such a progressive alliance emerge among South Africa's fragmented social and political movements? This is of course a million dollar question with no easy answer. What can be said with the risk of sounding rather apocalyptic is that the current agrarian structure cannot remain unchanged, as it is a potential source of political unrest in the near future as experience in Zimbabwe in 2000.

Conclusions

This chapter has demonstrated how 20 years of MLAR policies in South Africa have largely failed to transform a bi-modal agrarian structure inherited from apartheid in favour of the historically marginalised black citizens. Despite claims that market-based approaches are an efficient way to transfer land to the poor, this has not been the case in South Africa. Very little land has so far been transferred to the landless poor under the country's MLAR policies. Instead the land reform has benefited white landowners who have taken advantage of 'market' conditions to sell marginal lands to the government at a premium. Some of these white landowners have also benefited from the land-reform process as 'experts' or consultants who are hired by the government and paid large sums of money to provide 'advice' to land-reform beneficiaries. An important lesson from South Africa's MLAR experiment is that, under market conditions, land reforms are likely to benefit landowners due to their privileged access to information and financial resources. Such landowners can utilise their privileged financial position to either delay the transfer of land to the landless, or to take advantage of economic opportunities provided by the land-reform process. Moreover, under market conditions, the landless are reduced to passive beneficiaries of the land-reform processes with limited influence over what type of land they are given and how to utilise it. Lack of information and financial resources means the poor are often excluded from key decision making processes during the implementation of land-reform projects. This puts them at a disadvantage unlike landowners who tend to be in a better economic position to influence the land-reform process to their advantage.

The Zimbabwe case study explored in this chapter shows what can happen if the poor and landless are actively involved in the politics of land. They have the ability to push the state from below and influence the 'radicalization' of the state towards a more redistributive land-reform agenda. This chapter thus highlights the centrality of grassroots social movements in coordinating the struggles of the poor and influencing government policy from below. This is currently lacking in South Africa. In conclusion, the chapter contends that the rise of leftist political parties such as the EFF, and trade union movements such as AMCU and NUMSA, and the reconfiguration of political forces within the ruling ANC political party towards a radical political and economic agenda have the potential to influence future land-reform debates. Time will tell if political events that are currently unfolding in South Africa can influence the radicalisation of the land question towards a more redistributive land-reform agenda.

References

Akram-Lodhi, A.H. (2007). Land, markets and neoliberal enclosure: an agrarian political economy perspective. *Third World Quarterly, 28*(8), 1437–1456.

Albertus, M. (2015). *Autocracy and Redistribution: The Politics of Land Reform.* Cambridge: Cambridge Studies in Comparative Politics.

Alden, C., & Anseeuw, W. (2009). *Land, liberation and compromise in Southern Africa.* London: Palgrave Macmillan.

Aliber, M. (2015). The 'willing buyer/willing seller' approach to land reform: Opportunities and limitations. In B. Cousins & C. Walker, C. (Eds.), *Land divided, land restored: land reform in South Africa for the 21st century.* Jacana: Auckland Park.

Amin, S. (2012). Contemporary Imperialism and the Agrarian Question. *Agrarian South: Journal of Political Economy, 1*(1), 11–26.

Bernstein, H. (1996a). South Africa's Agrarian Question: Extreme and Exceptional? *Journal of Peasant Studies, 23*, 2–3 & 1–52.

Bernstein H. (1996b). South Africa's agrarian question: Extreme and exceptional? *Journal of Peasant Studies, 23*(2/3), 1–52.

Bernstein H. (2013). Commercial agriculture in South Africa since 1994: Natural, simply capitalism. *Journal of Agrarian Change, 13*(1), 23–46.

Borras Jr, M.S. (2006). The Underlying Assumptions, Theory, and Practice of Neoliberal Land Policies. In R. Patel & M. Courville (Eds.), *Promised Land, Competing Visions of Agrarian Reform.* Oakland: Food First.

Borras Jr, M.S. (2007). *Pro-poor Land Reform: a Critique.* Ottawa: University of Ottawa Press.

Bundy, C. (1979). *The rise and fall of the South African peasantry* (Vol. 28). Oakland: University of California Press.

Chambati, W. (2011). Restructuring of agrarian labour relations after Fast Track Land Reform in Zimbabwe. *Journal of Peasant Studies, 38*(5), 1047–1068.

Chaumba, J., Scoones, I., & Wolmer, W. (2003). From jambanja to planning: the reassertion of technocracy in land reform in southeastern Zimbabwe. *The Journal of Modern African Studies, 41*(4), 533–554.

Chitonge, H., & Ntsebeza, L. (2012) Land reform and rural livelihoods in South Africa: Does access to land matter? *Review of Agrarian Studies, 2*(1), 87–111.

Cousins, B., & Walker, C. (2015). *Land Divided Land Restored, land Reform in South Africa for the 21st Century*. Johannesburg: Jacana Media.

Goebel, A. (2005). Is Zimbabwe the future of South Africa? The implications for land reform in Southern Africa. *Journal of African Cultural Studies, 23*(3), 345–370.

Hall, R. (2004). A political economy of land reform in South Africa. *Review of African Political Economy, 31*(100), 213–227.

Hammar, A., Rapfopoulos, B., & Jensen, S. (Eds.) (2003). *Zimbabwe's Unfinished Business: Rethinking Land, State and Nation in the Context of Crisis*. Harare: Weaver Press.

Hanlon, J., Manjengwa, J., & Smart, T. (2012). *Zimbabwe takes back its land*. Boulder, CO: Kumarian Press.

Hendriks, F. (2013). Rhetoric and Reality in Restitution and Redistribution: Ongoing Land and Agrarian Questions in South Africa. In F.T. Hendricks, L. Ntsebeza, & K. Helliker (Eds), *The promise of land: Undoing a Century of Dispossession in South Africa*. Johannesburg: Jacana Media.

Hendricks, F.T., Ntsebeza, L., & Helliker, K. (2013). *The Promise of Land: Undoing a Century of Dispossession in South Africa*. Johannesburg: Jacana Media.

Lahiff, E. (2007). 'Willing buyer, willing seller': South Africa's failed experiment in market-led agrarian reform. *Third World Quarterly, 28*(8), 1577–1597.

Lahiff, E., (2008). *Land reform in South Africa: a status report 2008*. Programme for Land and Agrarian Studies. Cape Town: University of Western Cape.

Lahiff, E., & Cousins, B. (2001). The land crisis in Zimbabwe viewed from south of the Limpopo. *Journal of Agrarian Change, 1*(4), 652–666.

Lahiff, E., Borras Jr, S.M., & Kay, C. (2007). Market-led agrarian reform: policies, performance and prospects. *Third World Quarterly, 28*(8), 1417–1436.

Legassick, M. (1974). South Africa: capital accumulation and violence. *Economy and Society, 3*(3), 253–291.

Levin, R., & Weiner, D. (1996). The politics of land reform in South Africa after apartheid: perspectives, problems, prospects. *The Journal of Peasant Studies, 23*(2–3), 93–119.

Matondi, B. (2012). *Zimbabwe's Land Reform*. London: zed Books.

Mkodzongi, G. (2013a) *Fast Tracking Land Reform and Rural Livelihoods in Mashonaland West Province of Zimbabwe: Opportunities and Constraints 2000–2013*. (Unpublished PhD Thesis) Edinburgh: University of Edinburgh.

Mkodzongi, G. (2013b) New People, New Land, New Livelihoods: A Micro-Study of Zimbabwe's Fast Track land Reform: Agrarian South. *Journal of Political Economy*, 2, 3, 1–22.

Mkodzongi, G., & Rusenga, C. (2015). *Land and Agrarian Reform: Towards an Inclusive Poverty Alleviation Policy Agenda*. Cape Town: Institute for Justice and Reconciliation, Transformation Audit (2015).

Moyo, S. (2007). The Land question in Southern Africa, a comparative review. In Ntsebeza L & Hall R, (eds) *The land question in South Africa: The challenge of transformation and redistribution*. Cape Town: HSRC Press.

Moyo, Sam. (2011a). Changing agrarian relations after redistributive land reform in Zimbabwe. *Journal of Peasant Studies*, *38*(5), 907–934.

Moyo, Sam. (2011b). Land concentration and accumulation after redistributive reform in post settler Zimbabwe. *Review of African Political Economy*, *38*(128), 257–276.

Moyo, S., & Yeros, P. (2005). Land Occupations and Land Reform in Zimbabwe: Towards the National Democratic Revolution. In S. Moyo & P. Yeros (Eds.), *Reclaiming the Land: The Resurgence of Rural Movements in Africa, Asia and Latin America* (165–208). London: ZED Books.

Moyo, S., & P. Yeros (2007). The radicalised state: Zimbabwe's interrupted revolution. *Review of African Political Economy*, *111*, 103–121.

Moyo, S., Chambati, W., Murisa, T. Siziba, D., Dangwa, C., Mujeyi, K., & Nyoni, N. (2009). *Fast Track land Reform Baseline Survey in Zimbabwe: Trends and Tendencies 2005/06*. Harare: AIAS.

Ntsebeza, L., & Hall R. (2007) (Eds.). *The land question in South Africa: The challenge of transformation and redistribution*. Cape Town: HSRC Press.

O'Laughlin, B., Bernstein, H., Cousins, B., & Peters, P.E. (2013). Introduction: Agrarian change, rural poverty and land reform in South Africa since 1994. *Journal of Agrarian Change*, *13*(1), 1–15.

Richardson, C. (2005). The Loss of property rights and the collapse of Zimbabwe, *CATO Journal*, 25. Available from: http://www.cato.org/pubs/journal/cj25n3/cj25n3-12.pdf [Date accessed: April 2011].

Rusenga, C. (2015). *Land reform and market access: An investigation of the agribusiness model's effect on beneficiaries' incomes and job creation in Greater Tzaneen Municipality, Limpopo province*. (Unpublished draft PhD thesis). University of Cape Town.

Sadomba, Z.W. (2011). *War Veterans in Zimbabwe's revolution: Challenging neo-colonialism & settler & international capital*. Harare: Boydell & Brewer Ltd.

Scoones, I., Marongwe, N., Mavedzenge, B., Mahenene, J., Murimbarimba, F., & Sukume, C. (2010). *Zimbabwe's Land Reform: Myths and Realities*. London: James Currey.

Scott, J.C. (1998). *Seeing like a state: How certain schemes to improve the human condition have failed*. New Haven: Yale University Press.

Somerville, M. (2014). Financial investments in agriculture and their implications for land reform processes and agrarian transition in South Africa. Paper presented at the First Conference on Land Grabs in Africa, Midrand, 20–21 October.

Tobacco Industry Marketing Board (2014). Harare: Annual Statistical Report.

Toulmin, C., & Quan, J. (2000). *Evolving land rights, policy and tenure in Africa*. London: International Institute for Environment and Development.

Van den Brink, R., Thomas, G.S., & Binswanger, H. (2007). Agricultural land redistribution in South Africa: Towards accelerated implementation. In L. Ntsebeza & R. Hall

(Eds.), *The land question in South Africa: The challenge of transformation and redistribution*. Cape Town: HSRC Press.

Walker, C. (2008). *Landmarked: land claims and land restitution in South Africa*. Johannesburg: Jacana Media.

Zamchiya, P. (2011). A synopsis of land and agrarian change in Chipinge district, Zimbabwe. *Journal of Peasant Studies*, *38*(5).

Government Sources

Minister Gugile Nkwinti: Rural Development and Land Reform Dept Budget Vote 2015/16: http://www.gov.za/speeches/minister-gugile-nkwinti-rural-development-and-land-reform-dept-budget-vote-201516-8-may (Accessed on 7 August 2015)

Newspaper Articles

Pensioner dies while queuing to lodge land claim: https://m.news24.com/SouthAfrica/News/Pensioner-dies-while-queuing-to-lodge-land-claim-20140827/comments (accessed on 08 August 2015).

PART 4

Agency, Identity, and Belonging

CHAPTER 10

Khoisan Revivalism and Land Question in Post-Apartheid South Africa

Chizuko Sato

Introduction

In July 2014, the *Cape Times* (2/7/2014) reported the signing of the Restitution of Land Rights Amendment Act (2014) by President Zuma with the headline 'San, Khoi can now make land claims'. This was however misleading, as the purpose of the Act was to re-open the restitution claim lodgement process for five years until the end of June 2019 without changing the original cut-off date. This meant that descendants of Khoi and San could lodge land claims like any other South Africans as long as they had lost land after the Natives Land Act (1913), and not before. This is different from shifting the cut-off date to prior to 1913, which has been advocated by some Khoisan[1] activists. The signing of the Act by Zuma was a culmination of a policy process initiated in his State of the Nation address (SONA) in February 2013, the centenary year of the Natives Land Act (1913). In this SONA Zuma stated the plan to reopen restitution claim lodgements and to look into land claims by the descendants of Khoisan who had lost land prior to 1913, and thus had been excluded from the restitution programme (Zuma, 2013). When the Restitution of Land Rights Amendment Bill (2013) was announced in May, various stakeholders including academics, land NGOs, and existing claimants began heightened debates on the pros and cons of the reopening of restitution claims. At the same time, Zuma's announcement of revisiting the land restitution policy created misunderstanding of its content and increased the expectation among a wide range of parties (including media, politicians, and Khoisan activists) that the bill would enable Khoisan to lodge claims to land that they had lost before 1913.

1 The term Khoisan (Khoi-San) is nowadays commonly used in South Africa as a collective noun of Khoi (Khoikhoi) and San, even though these groups historically appear as separate entities. Some use Khoesan (Khoe-San) in accordance with the modern Nama orthography. The hyphenated notation is used to emphasise that the two are separate groups (Besten, 2009, p. 135). This chapter acknowledges this, but uses the term without a hyphen in order to keep it simple.

 | DOI 10.1163/9789004362550_011

However, reopening the restitution lodgement process and reconsidering the cut-off date of the restitution claim, even though they could be related to each other, are essentially two separate things. The widespread confusion partly emanated from the fact that in spite of the buzz and increased media attention in the matter, the nature and contents of Khoisan land claims and how they can be handled in twenty-first century South Africa are both not clear. Paucity of information and a somewhat opaque policy consultation process initiated by the Department of Rural Development and Land Reform (DRDLR) following the SONA with various Khoisan groups and activists also contributed to the general misunderstandings. Moreover, the lack of a representative voice among numerous Khoisan groups and activists, together with the fluidity of their organisations and the frequent alliances and conflicts among them, make it difficult for anyone to pin down who they are and what they are fighting for.

There are several roots of Khoisan revivalism movements in South Africa since the mid-1990s (Bredekemp, 2000; Lee, 2003; Waldman, 2007; Besten, 2009). Tracing the trajectories of various Khoisan groups and their engagements with the South African government is beyond the scope of this chapter. Rather, what this chapter attempts to do is to give a glimpse of Khoisan activists and groups who engaged in revival movements in Cape Town during the two years immediately after Zuma's announcements in 2013 SONA. As discussed by Comaroff and Comaroff (2009), land was an essential element for the formation of new groups based on ethnic identity in both the USA and in South Africa. In the latter context, two famous land restitution cases involving Khoisan groups in the Northern Cape, namely ≠Khomani San and Richtersveld land claims, are known to have contributed to bringing out their Khoisan identities. During the process of these claims, divisions within the claimant communities, which are prevalent in most restitution cases, took ethnic form and the authenticity of their identities came to be contested (Robins, 2008, Chapts. 2 & 3). Among urban Khoisan groups in the Western Cape, the situation is more complex and the competition over legitimacy could be tougher. The agency of Khoisan activists undoubtedly plays an important role in the policy formation process, but to what extent can they present themselves as a unified voice is a question to be investigated. Moreover, what are the intentions of the government to focus on Khoisan in the centenary year of the 1913 Land Act? Is there going to be a sustained engagement or is it just a brief effort to gain support for the ruling party in the year before the general elections? These are some of the issues and questions this chapter aims to address by discussing the Khoisan land demands articulated by Khoisan groups and activists in the Western Cape, and by examining their engagements with the government in the land policy formation process since early 2013.

This chapter is largely based on my interviews and more informal interactions with Khoisan leaders and activists in the Western Cape, and attending some of their meetings and public hearings of the Restitution Amendment Bill (2013), as well as on interpretation of policy documents and media reports. I was based in Cape Town as a research associate of the Institute for Poverty, Land and Agrarian Studies (PLAAS) at the University of the Western Cape from March 2013 to February 2015. It was during this period that the Restitution Amendment Bill (2013) was announced, and at two public hearings of the bill in Cape Town in June 2013 I met several Khoisan activists[2] who wore kaross or fake fur, claimed to be Khoisan chiefs, and pleaded to the DRDLR officials to listen to their demands. Since this unexpected encounter, I began to seek ways to meet different Khoisan groups and activists. Through these gatherings I began comprehending their arguments by listening to their life history, organisational plans, and their opinions on the contemporary politics of the country and its land policy. I also became a regular attendant in free Khoisan language classes offered by a Khoisan activist in Cape Town in 2014, and learned some greetings and sang songs in a Khoisan language.

State of Khoisan Revivalism Movements in Cape Town in the Western Cape in 2013 and 2014

Historians and anthropologists have long argued that Khoi and San no longer existed as distinct groups in the 20th century in South Africa (Elphick 1985, p. xviii; Barnard 1992, p. 27–28). However, after 1994, there emerged a group of people who claimed to be Khoi, San or Khoisan as aboriginal (indigenous) people of South Africa among those who had been classified as coloured during the apartheid era. They denied the view that Khoisan had been absorbed into the coloured society throughout history, rejected the designation of coloured, and began to claim Khoisan identity (Lee, 2003; Besten, 2006, 2009). There are two aspects in this invocation of Khoisan identity. On the one hand, accepting

2 I cannot say how many Khoisan activists or Khoisan people attended these hearings, but there were several people who dressed in kaross (Fieldnotes, 4/6/2013; 12/6/2013). As this was my first encounter with them, at that time I had no knowledge of who they were or who was active in the Khoisan revivalism movements in Cape Town. Only after these encounters, did I begin reading relevant literature on coloured identity and Khoisan revival and come to know who they were. Some of the Khoisan chiefs and activists I met there agreed to meet with me later for interviews, and they were the ones who introduced me to their Khoisan activist circles.

and claiming a Khoisan identity is something very personal. It is a personal journey to seek and discover one's 'real' or 'true' identity, history and self-affirmation. This journey was made possible by the end of apartheid, which had imposed a fixed racial classification on every South African. On the other hand, this phenomenon is not limited to an individual, personal level, and has manifested itself as Khoisan revivalism movements that submit their demands to, and engage in negotiations with the government.

One of the focal areas where Khoisan revivalism has taken roots is the Western Cape, where people classified as coloured consist of close to the half of the total population. Here the main proponents of Khoisan revivalism are those who live in former coloured townships in the urban areas, not least in Cape Town. Their urbanised lifestyle is not different from their non-Khoisan neighbours. They seem to wear 'traditional' attire such as kaross and/or headbands only when they have their own gatherings and/or they have meetings with the government, and not in everyday life. Therefore one cannot say whether someone is Khoisan or not by just looking at their appearance. With the implementation of such policies that put emphasis on race and ethnicity as the Employment Equity Act (1998), the Black Economic Empowerment Act (2003) and the Traditional Leadership Framework Act (2003), more and more people began identifying as Khoisan and Khoisan revivalism has expanded in the twenty-first century (Besten, 2009). Nevertheless, specifying their number is impossible, and it is also difficult to obtain an overall picture of Khoisan revivalism movements. While Khoisan activists often claim that all coloured people are Khoisan, not all coloured people are willing to be called as such. Moreover, while some groups, most notably the Griqua National Conference, seem to have records of leadership for an extended period of time and organisational structure, others appear to consist of just a few or a dozen individuals or members of family. Some organisations have a website, but it is rarely updated. The announcements of meetings or events, sharing information, and discussion tend to take place on social network sites such as Facebook and chat programmes like WhatsApp. Yet, there are certain individuals, activists and organisations that claim to represent Khoisan with whom different levels of government engage in policy consultations.

My initial attempt to canvass an overall picture of different Khoisan groups and organisations in the Western Cape or just in Cape Town turned out to be difficult, partly because there are too many such groups, as one of my interviewees (a Khoisan chief) told me that 'nowadays, there is at least one Khoisan group in every coloured township' (Interview, 1/11/2013). Also, while there are certain individuals and groups that are keen to talk to an obvious outsider like me (perhaps in order to obtain my sympathy for their understanding of the current situation of South African politics and especially their predicament of not being officially recognised in the Constitution), there are also others who didn't like my presence in the meetings. In order to stay informed of the upcoming meetings and events concerning Khoisan groups and their engagements with the government, I had to rely on certain activists who were willing to help or tolerate my presence in such occasions, and I think a relationship was thus established between myself and certain individuals. This was seen as me siding with certain people and/or groups. As I discuss later, rivalry and suspicions among different activists and groups are intense, and opening a door to one group can result in closing a door to another. Nonetheless, I dare attempt to classify Khoisan groups and organisations that were active in Cape Town in 2013 and 2014 into the following three categories.

The first category refers to groups that consist of people who claim to be chief or king of a Khoisan group or sub-group and their associates. Some explanation is required here. Since the late 1990s, the South African government has engaged in consultations with certain Khoisan representatives in order to give recognition to Khoisan communities and their leaders. This consultation has not been finalized yet after many years, and therefore at the moment Khoisan is not legally recognised as a distinct group with cultural attributes in South Africa. In other words, people who call themselves Khoisan are doing so merely as self-identification, which is not officially recognised. However, as part of this consultation process, the government commissioned a research report in late 1990s, which identified five main Khoisan groupings in South Africa, namely Griqua, Korana, Nama, Cape Khoi, and San (DTA, 2011). One Khoisan activist in Cape Town recalled the genealogical research conducted by researchers and remembered being asked such questions like who his father was, where his family came from, and so on. However, he was not sure if the report was completed, as he thinks that it was never made public (Interview, 28/10/2013). Another Khoisan activist told me that he had seen the report, implying that the report was completed, but he no longer had a copy (personal communication, 26/09/2014). My attempt to get a copy or information on the report from the Department of Traditional Affairs (DTA) was not successful.

At any rate most of those who claim to be chief of a Khoisan group or sub-group, and set up a quasi-traditional structure, either adopt one of these five groups identified by the governmental research, or sub-groups of Khoisan such as Cochoqua and Hessequa, whose encounter with Dutch settlers in the 17th century was discussed by the historian Richard Elphick in *Khoikhoi and the Founding of White South Africa*, published in 1975. It is believed that some chiefs may be able to prove by documents and/or oral tradition that they belong to historically prominent ancestry, but most of them seem to be self-appointed leaders who do not have any historical foundation. Among Khoisan leaders, it seems that they accept that there are both bloodline chiefs and appointed or elected chiefs.[3] They address each other as chief or king. Some of them wear kaross and headbands in order to show their status when they attend meetings with the government. Although the tendency of Khoisan activists to assert their leadership by claiming to be a chief of 'the original Khoi clans encountered by Jan van Riebeeck' (Lee 2003, p. 101) has existed since the late 1990s, there has certainly been a proliferation of Khoisan chiefs after the mid-2000s. This would probably have something to do with the Traditional Leadership Framework Act (2003) and the subsequent policy developments, which increased the benefits to be gained if one is recognised by the government as a traditional leader. Not all chiefs are men; there are also female chiefs.

One of the Khoisan activists whom I met in Cape Town introduced himself as a Korana chief. He was about 70 years old, and always wore a fake leopard fur coat and headband with several quills whenever I saw him in the meetings with other Khoisan activists or with the government. I also learned from Internet search that he often appeared in media as a chief of Xoraxoukhoe (or Gorachouqua[4]) house. He was an eloquent person, speaking up to the DRDLR officials at a public hearing of the Restitution Amendment Bill (2013), and seemed to be respected by other Khoisan activists, partly because of his seniority (age). He is a retired civil servant who used to work for the City of Cape Town and was active in trade union movements during the apartheid period. He was originally from Namaqualand in the Northern Cape, but lived in one of the coloured townships in Cape Town for his adult life. He said that he recognised his Khoi identity when he was young, but during apartheid, the fighting was focused on getting rid of racial oppression and they didn't need to question their identity or culture. In the 1990s, there was a revival of culture and recovery of history became more important. He claims that in 2009 President Motlanthe said that Khoi would have recognition by the end of the year, but it didn't happen (Interview, 30/7/2013). He seems to be one of those local leaders in the coloured communities, who had been active earlier as leaders of community organisations, religious organisations, and/or trade unions, and took up the cause of the Khoisan revivalism after 1994.

---

3 However, whether and to what extent ordinary people, who identify themselves as Khoisan and attend various events organised by Khoisan groups such as meetings, marches, and language classes, and who do not claim to be in a position of leadership, accept having their leaders as a chief is a different question.

4 Spelling is not consistent on the various Internet sources.

The second category is activist organisations that advocate the recognition of indigenous status for Khoisan in South Africa, their rights as indigenous people including the aboriginal land rights, and the restoration of indigenous culture. One such organisation is the Institute for the Restoration of the Aborigines of South Africa (IRASA).[5] Its leader featured prominently in newspaper articles when people led by her went to occupy flats allocated to the restitution claimants of District Six, claiming that it is the land of their Khoisan ancestors (*Cape Times*, 18/6/2013). Other organisations such as the Khoe and San Awareness Group (KSAAG)[6] and Khoisan Kingdom[7] seem to be more culturally oriented, focusing on restoration, protection, and promotion of Khoisan languages, heritage, and/or rituals. The founding leader of KSAAG has been focusing on the revival of khoekhoegowab (one of the Khoisan languages), which he learned in Namibia. According to him, khoekhoegowab is a standardized version of the Nama language, which is still widely spoken in mainly the southern part of Namibia (Interview, 20/8/2013). Since late 2013, he has offered free khoekhoegowab lessons to anyone who is interested in learning it in Cape Town. Although IRASA and KSAAG are very different organisations, not only in terms of the people involved but also in terms of what they are fighting for, I argue that language revival activities of KSAAG and awareness activities by IRASA and other similar organisations among coloured communities through road-shows, workshops, and meetings also contributed to the growth of Khoisan revivalism.

The third category is Rastafarians with their distinguishing dreadlock hairstyle. Rastafarians are by no means a homogeneous group and not all of them are involved in Khoisan revivalism. Nonetheless, at least in the Western Cape, they show their presence at various Khoisan gatherings. A number of regular attendants at the khoekhoegowab free lessons offered by the leader of KSAAG were Rastafarians, although this could be because of him being a Rastafarian as well. Some of them even claim that Khoisan came from Ethiopia, the motherland for Rastafarians (Interview, 5/10/2013). One of the reasons why some Rastafarians took up Khoisan identity is probably because they find affinity (or similarity) between the oppressed history of Khoisan and their daily experiences of being treated as misfits in the present South African society (Tolsi, 2011). In addition, they seem to share their longing for an idealized lifestyle of Khoisan who rely on herbal medicine and find great value in harmony

5 http://aboriginalkhoisan.org/ (Accessed on 28 July 2014).
6 http://ksaag.wordpress.com (Accessed on 28 July 2014).
7 http://www.khoisan.net/ (Accessed on 28 July 2014).

with nature. However, some Khoisan activists do not agree that a Rastafarian can also be a Khoisan simultaneously (Interview, 1/11/2013), while others are critical of habitual use of dagga (marijuana), illegal in South Africa, by many Rastafarians. I should also add that Rastafarians are not the only ones among Khoisan people or activists who strongly believe in nature. One of the female Khoisan activists who worked together with Khoisan chiefs, and whom I interacted with many times, told me about the use of buchu (a kind of herb) water to relax at night and cleanse the internal body.

The above three categories of Khoisan groups in the Western Cape have different focuses. While groups led by chiefs and IRASA, which occupied District Six, often expressed their demands in terms of land and recognition of their indigenous status,[8] KSAAG and Rastafarians seemed to have aligned themselves more with the lifestyle and linguistic revival aspects. These different groups are not necessarily antagonistic to each other. There are repeated attempts by different groups to form an umbrella body or to collaborate with each other. Daily communications by email or WhatsApp, and networking among prominent leaders and activists who are particularly eloquent at meetings and in the negotiations with the governments, are also strong. However, there are also power struggles among different leaders and activists, who fight over who is suitable and legitimate as a Khoisan leader or chief. Moreover, various organisations and groups compete with each other over legitimacy and representativeness, over who should be invited to the governmental meetings, and over who has the right to negotiate with the government on behalf of Khoisan. Splitting of groups or organisations also happens. During the course of my fieldwork, I met several Khoisan activists and leaders who called for unity in the movements, but they were also the same people who were quick to criticise existing leaders for lack of consultation, transparency, legitimacy, or tangible progress.[9] Thus the number of Khoisan people has increased, but the movements have fragmented. The Khoisan revivalism movements I encountered in Cape Town in 2013 and 2014 lacked unity or any unified voice.

The Land Demands of Khoisan Revivalism

Next, let us look at the land demands of Khoisan revivalism and their rationales. In both public meetings on the Restitution Amendment Bill (2013) in

8 However, as far as I understand, IRASA does not advocate for recognition of Khoisan chiefs.

9 One of the most vocal voices in this regard is a Khoisan activist who writes a blog called 'People of South'.

Cape Town,[10] and my private conversations with Khoisan activists and leaders, an argument that Khoisan have a right to the whole of South Africa or even beyond its borders has been repeatedly expressed. This seemingly abstractive assertion of the right to the whole of South Africa, rather than a restitution claim on a specific piece of land, has been well expressed by a Khoisan activist in Cape Town.

> Whoever came here, from wherever, found us [Khoisan] here. We are the original inhabitants of this land. We want our land back and our languages recognised. If we can have land, we can end this cultural slavery. We were a sovereign people before the Europeans came here.
>
> BASIL COETZEE, quoted in Besten, 2009, p. 147

Yet, the Khoisan people are not demanding the full restoration of their historical land, the construction of a Khoisan homeland or a Khoisan state. He continues that 'we're not saying that all immigrants should leave the country. There's enough land for all of us' (Besten 2009, p. 147). This notion that South Africa belongs to Khoisan is not only often expressed in public forums and private conversations but also some Khoisan activists have gone on to lodge land claims before the previous deadline of the end of 1998. One such example is land claims known by some Khoisan activists in Cape Town by the reference numbers of K452, K453, and K454, which had been lodged by a Khoisan king in the Northern Cape. He claimed 'the Northern Cape, Western Cape and Eastern Cape (All Cape Lands)', based on aboriginal rights to the land, but all his claims were dismissed as they were beyond the scope of the Land Restitution Act (1994).[11]

What does it mean that South Africa belongs to Khoisan in practice? Pressed on this question, another Khoisan activist (chief) in Cape Town gave me an example of the Royal Bafokeng Nation in North West, which is often referred to as the richest chieftaincy group in the country, thanks to mineral wealth on their land. He passionately talked about the prospect of getting royalties from business activities, including commercial farming on Khoisan people's land, that is, the whole of South Africa, ignoring my comment that it might mean that people would be taxed twice (Interview, 30/7/2013). This illustrates that the Khoisan people's demand to land is not only symbolic but they also see land as an economic resource, and one can say that, ultimately, they are

10 I attended four such meetings on 4/6/2013, 12/6/2013, and 28–29/1/2014.

11 Email correspondences with the regional land claims commission in the Northern Cape, October-December, 2013.

demanding their share of the wealth generated in the new South Africa. However, as Comaroff and Comaroff (2009, Chapt. 5) discuss on the Royal Bafokeng Nation, being the richest chieftaincy group doesn't necessarily mean that everyone who is part of that group is wealthy or even has a comfortable life.

The view that the whole of South Africa belongs to Khoisan is closely related to their demand for the constitutional accommodation of Khoisan as the indigenous people in South Africa. This claim is based on their presence here before Bantu Africans came, and their demand includes the right of representation at all levels of the government (Le Fleur, 2001). There is no doubt that Khoi and San had lived in the land defined by the boundary of current South Africa before the coming of Bantu Africans. This has been endorsed by works of historians and archaeologists, and by rock art that is widespread in the country. Yet, if people who call themselves Khoisan claim to be descendants of Khoi and San who appear in South African history books, and claim the right to participate in decision-making in politics and the right to have a share in the economic wealth, one might wonder on what basis they are making such claims. In particular, the lifestyle of Khoisan activists, whom I met in Cape Town in 2013 and 2014, and who lived in urban areas, was largely no different from their coloured neighbours who lived in the same townships. Moreover, most Khoisan groups in South Africa retain no cultural institutions such as languages, rituals, and so forth.

The disappearance of cultural institutions among contemporary Khoisan groups in South Africa is partly due to the historical complexity of the coloured identity. Due to the fact that the apartheid regime stipulated the availability of privileges depending on one's racial classification, it has been argued that a coloured person longed to become a white person or become closer to white (Adhikari, 2005). This seems to have caused many of them to have an inferiority complex about their appearance and has encouraged them to have a distorted sense of beauty. It was beautiful to have fair or light skin. Having darker skin or frizzy hair, associated with 'Bushman' and 'Hottentot', was the subject of ridicule and discrimination. Many coloured women have gone to extraordinary lengths to straighten their hair by combing or applying hair creams (Erasmus, 2001; Interview, 30/9/2013). While the connection with white ancestors was emphasized and their photos decorated at home, the presence of other ancestors was ignored (Adhikari 2005, p. 11–16, 27–29). In a significant sense, Khoisan revivalism, especially in its emphasis on restoration, protection, and promotion of Khoisan languages, heritage, and culture, has contributed to giving due recognition to their Khoisan ancestors, who had been subjected to ridicule in the coloured communities in the past, and to see their Khoisan heritage in a positive light.

In arguing for indigenous status, Khoisan activists often refer to ILO Convention 169, known as the Indigenous and Tribal Peoples Convention (1989), which South Africa has not ratified as of yet. However, their reference to ILO 169 puzzles me, as it doesn't seem to me to give Khoisan exclusive indigenous status in South Africa. Specifically, it defines indigenous people as those 'who [descended] from the populations which inhabited the country … at the time of conquest or colonisation or the establishment of present state boundaries and who … retain some or all of their own social, economic, cultural, and political institutions' (ILO, 1989). Since the time reference point of ILO 169 is the time of conquest or colonisation, not only Khoisan but also black Africans are considered to be indigenous in South Africa under this convention. Realising this, some long-standing Khoisan activists have refined their argument and begun advocating 'first indigenous' status, distinct from mere 'indigenous' status in South Africa (Interview, 29/11/2013).

Khoisan activists in Cape Town tend to express their land demands on the whole of South Africa, the former Cape Colony, or a large part of Cape Town (Verbuyst, 2015), instead of on specific pieces of land with which they have some tangible historical connection. However, with the growth of debates on the Restitution Amendment Bill (2013), some Khoisan groups in Cape Town began to claim 'ancestral' ownership to such lands as District Six and Oude Molen near Pineland, and went on to occupy them (*Cape Times*, 18/6/2013; idem, 2/6/2014). District Six occupies a unique position in the local history of Cape Town, especially for the 60,000 non-white residents, who had lived there until the 1960s, when they were forcibly relocated to townships on Cape Flats after it was declared a white area by the Group Areas Act (1950), and their descendants. It became a symbol of the brutality of apartheid regime, as well as a local focal point to fight against it (Jeppe & Soudien, 1990). After 1994, many former residents submitted their restitution claims, but the restitution programme at District Six has only progressed at a snail's pace due to various reasons (Beyers, 2010).[12] Occupation of these lands by Khoisan activists didn't last long, but did create serious conflicts with both the government and the District Six land claimants. Some Khoisan activists have also distanced themselves from these occupying people by voicing criticisms against it (*Cape Times*, 25/6/2013).

12 According to the latest figure released by the DRDLR, a total of 2670 restitution claims on District Six were submitted to the government by the end of 1998. Of these, 1439 claimants opted for financial compensation and 1126 claimants chose to return to the area. Moreover, since the reopening of the restitution claim lodgement in July 2014, 1300 new claims were submitted by December 2015 (DRDLR, 2016).

Khoisan Land Policy Formation and Consultation Process

So far, this chapter has discussed the Khoisan revivalism and its land demands. In this final section, I shall turn to what the government is prepared to offer them by looking at the current proposals.

1997 White Paper on Land Policy and Rationale for the 1913 Cut-off Date

Firstly, let us revisit the rationales for the 1913 cut-off date enshrined in the South African Constitution (South Africa, 1996). Since most Khoisan lost their rights to land long before 1913, this is considered as the principal obstacle to the Khoisan land claims and some people argue that this is arbitrary (Cavanagh 2013, p. 104–109). However, there were at least three reasons for the 1913 cut-off date.

If we remember the discussions around land reform in the early 1990s when the National Party government and the African National Congress (ANC) were negotiating future political settlements, there were three options for the possible cut-off dates: (1) 1652 when the Dutch East India Company led by Jan van Riebeeck came to settle down in Cape Town, (2) 1913 when the Natives Land Act was introduced, and (3) 1948 when the National Party came into power. Out of these three, 1913 was chosen, as 1948 was considered too soon and therefore the scale of redressing past injustice would be too small. If 1652 was chosen, the scale of redressing past land dispossession and colonialism would have been very substantial. But it was also thought that verifying historical details on dispossessions and possible claimants would be more difficult.[13] So, 1913 was a convenient middle ground, and this was just another example of compromises reached in negotiated settlements.

The current scope of land restitution was not only determined by the compromise of political negotiations. When discussions over future land reform began in the early 1990s, consensus existed among different stakeholders that land reform was necessary. But there was no consensus on what kind of land reform. In this situation, there existed emergeant and vocal groups of people who had owned land before 1913, but who were dispossessed or threatened

13 Interview with Derek Hanekom, head of the agricultural desk: Dept of Economic Planning (ANC) (February 1993), *Barometer on Negotiation*, 5(1), p. 15. Hanekom became the Minister of Land Affairs under the Mandela government. It may be worth noting that the National Land Committee, which was the national representative voice of land NGOs from late 1980s to 1990s, argued at that time that the cut-off date for land restitution claim should be 1652 when white settlers came to South Africa (NLC, 1994).

with dispossession since then. Labelled 'black spots' by the apartheid government, as they were pieces of land owned by black people in white South Africa, residents and former residents of these 'black spots' not only demanded the moratorium of their removals but also requested restitution of dispossessed land.[14] These rural-based groups or communities were supported by urban-based land NGOs under the umbrella body of the National Land Committee. Through petitions, memorandums, marches, and direct negotiations with President de Klerk, they were putting direct influence on the formation of future land-reform policy (Sato, 2010; Weideman 2004, p. 227–229).

It is also important to stress that the land restitution programme never intended to determine who the most legitimate owner of land was in South Africa. Doing so would not only be impossible practically, the 1997 White Paper argued, but it also could end up 'awaken[ing] and/or prolong[ing] destructive ethnic and racial politics', because '[l]arge parts of South Africa could be subject to overlapping and competing claims where pieces of land have been occupied in succession by, for example, the San, Khoi, Xhosa, Mfengu, Trekkers and British' (DLA 1997, p. 77–78). Nor was it meant to accommodate 'ancestral land claims' based on aboriginal rights to the land. If we were to consider such claims, how and on what basis should we identify the legitimate descendants? To many, it was like 'opening a Pandora's box' (Leggasick, 2013).

Nonetheless, the possibility of redressing land dispossession before 1913 was not completely excluded, as the 1997 White Paper states that '[h]istorical claims arising from dispossession prior to 1913 should be accommodated within the discretion of the Minister. Preferential status could be granted to such claims in land redistribution and development programmes' (DLA 1997, p. 78). The government was prepared to deal with pre-1913 land dispossession on a case-by-case basis. Yet, it seems that this Ministerial discretion has never been utilised for this purpose until today, for unknown reasons.[15]

National Khoisan Dialogues and Land-reform Proposals

From the 1997 White Paper to President Zuma's address in early 2013, there was no particular move by the DRDLR to consider Khoisan land demands. However, soon after Zuma's address, the DRDLR held the first national policy consultative conference for representatives of the Khoisan groups in Kimberley in April

14 One of the leading communities that demanded the restitution of their 'ancestral land' in the early 1990s was Roosboom in northern KwaZulu-Natal. See Sato (2010) for history of its land struggles and how the dynamics of community politics unfolded in Roosboom during the post-1994 land reform process.

15 I am grateful to Rafael Verbuyst for confirming this point with an official of the DRDLR.

2013 in order to explore 'the exceptions to the 19 June 1913 cut-off date ... to accommodate land claims of the descendants of the Khoi and San' (DRDLR, 2013a). At the conference, Minister Nkwinti stated that '[i]t became clear to the President and the government that national cohesion would be superficial if the Khoi and San communities continued to occupy the periphery, while the rest of their fellow South Africans occupied the centre-stage in nation building and national reconciliation' (DRDLR, 2013b). Thus, Minister Nkwinti specifically acknowledged that Khoisan have been marginalised even after 1994, and his Department was going to address that.

At the same time, it was apparent that the government wasn't going to look at Khoisan land issues from the perspective of aboriginal rights to the land. At the Kimberley conference, Advocate Ntsewa, speaking on behalf of the DTA about its consultation process of recognising Khoisan communities and leaders, made it clear:

> I'd from the beginning state that I am not dealing with the so-called indigenous communities or first nations, because so far, this has not been established that there can be any community in South Africa that can claim to be more indigenous than the other African communities.
>
> NTSEWA, 2013

Some participants were not willing to accept this view, and the claim that Khoisan should be recognised as aboriginal (indigenous) was expressed in several commissions that were part of the conference. At any rate, the Kimberley conference kick-started the process. In the following month of May, Khoisan leaders gathered again in each province and elected five provincial representatives. They formed the National Khoe and San Reference Group (NAREG), which was tasked to assist DRDLR to formulate policy proposals. John Witbooi, a Nama leader from the Western Cape, was elected as chairperson.

Not much is known about the consultation process between DRDLR and NAREG. The latter received constant criticisms especially from Khoisan groups and activists in the Western Cape, who alleged that NAREG never reported back to the people who elected them in the first place (*Eerste Nasie Nuus 5*, November 2013, p. 4). An older Khoisan body called the National Khoisan Council (NKC/NKSC), set up in 1999 by then Department of Provincial and Local Government (DPLG), tried to take over the process by telling Minister Nkwinti that '[a]ny organisation purporting to represent the Khoi & San people shall come via the NKSC in their deliberations, discussions and consultation with all organs of the State' (*Eerste Nasie Nuus 4*, October 2013, p. 12). It seems that NKC saw NAREG as a rival to its own status as an official, representative voice of Khoisan communities, and didn't like the fact that DRDLR had set up an alternative body.

Nevertheless, exactly one year after the Kimberley conference, the DRDLR convened another one in April 2014 titled 'National Khoe-San Dialogue 2' (also referred to as Kimberley II) where two policy proposals were presented to about 500 Khoisan representatives. The first proposal stated that it would amend land redistribution legislation in order to allow the DRDLR to acquire land for the descendants of Khoisan who had been dispossessed before 1913. This means that DRDLR proposed to deal with the Khoisan land claims not through a restitution programme, which requires rigorous historical research to establish the validity of a claim, but through a redistribution programme. This would not require changing the Constitution. The second proposal stated that it would amend heritage legislation in order to allow people to acquire the ownership of heritage sites and historical landmarks such as graves and burial grounds. It was explained that the latter proposal was not exclusively for Khoisan but for all South Africans, and it would be implemented by proclaiming and redistributing sites as heritage sites and landmarks (DRDLR, 2014).

Political Background of Proposals and Evaluation

Given that Khoisan were hardly mentioned at all in the debates over land reform up until very recently, one cannot help but question why the government all of a sudden began paying attention to Khoisan in 2013. Technically speaking, it is possible to deal with pre-1913 land claims through ministerial discretion without amending a law or introducing a new policy. One of the reasons may have been the expansion of Khoisan revivalism since the mid-2000s, as it has made their presence more visible. In addition, at least three reasons can be pointed out. Firstly, the policy consultation process between the government and Khoisan leaders over the bill (the Traditional Affairs Bill[16]), which will give legal recognition to Khoisan communities and their leaders, is at last reaching the final stage. The bill published by DTA for public comment in September 2013 proposes to establish Khoi-San councils and include Khoisan leaders in the proposed new structure of the National House of Traditional and Khoi-San Leaders (DTA, 2013). The bill has been criticised by some academics and civil

16 The name of this bill has now been changed to the Traditional and Khoi-San Leadership Bill (2015), and public hearings on the bill were held in the Parliament's Portfolio and Select Committees on Co-operative Governance and Traditional Affairs in February 2016. According to the committee chairperson, this 'public hearing was only the beginning of a long process that would include country-wide public consultations' (Mokoena, 2016). Thus it seems that it will take more time before the bill becomes an act.

society organisations as bringing back apartheid-era Bantustan legislation in the sense that it would entrench tribal boundaries and leadership structures (Merten, 2015). Among Khoisan leaders, opinions on the bill differ. For some, this has been the only tangible result over the recognition of their status. NKC, which has negotiated the bill for more than ten years, has repeatedly urged the government to pass it into law (CoGTA, 2012; *The Herald*, 21/1/2014). On the other hand, *Eerste Nasie Nuus* (First Nation News), a monthly community newspaper launched by two Khoisan activists in Cape Town in July 2013, conveys numerous dissatisfactions with the bill by several Khoisan activists. One of the issues raised by them is that the bill does not give Khoisan first nation status. Another is that the bill does not give Khoisan leaders a separate house from traditional leaders, and thus they will be perpetual minority in the same house (*Eerste Nasie Nuus 4*, October 2013; idem, *5*, November 2013).

Secondly, the government needed to introduce a new land policy in order to highlight the centenary year of the 1913 Land Act in 2013, when more than usual interest and resources were directed at the land issue. New land policy for Khoisan and the reopening of restitution claims were two chosen policies in this context. In fact, the origin of these two policies dates back not to Zuma's SONA but to the resolutions of the 53rd National Conference of the ANC in 2012 that proposed these two policies as part of the Natives Land Act centenary (ANC 2012, p. 26). Given that the electoral support for the ANC is weakest in the Western Cape, one of the focal areas of Khoisan revivalism, one may be compelled to suspect a political calculation by the ANC to increase votes in the general elections in the following year (2014) by proposing a new land policy for Khoisan. During my interactions with Khoisan activists and leaders in 2013 and 2014, there were often discussions about the merits and demerits of the Western Cape and Cape Town being ruled by the Democratic Alliance (DA). They also talked about being approached by different political parties including the ANC, the Economic Freedom Fighters (EFF), and the Minority Front (MF) before the general elections. Some people believed that Khoisan could be a kingmaker in the elections in the Western Cape (Interview, 2/8/2013).

Thirdly, I should add Zuma's own policy preference, real or perceived. Zuma gave an opening address as a deputy president at the first national conference for Khoisan in South Africa, known as the National Khoisan Consultative Conference, held in Oudtshoorn in the Western Cape in 2001 (Zuma, 2001). This conference was a highlight of the earlier Khoisan revivalism that emerged in the late 1990s, and thus Zuma had personal interactions with emergeant and eloquent Khoisan activists and leaders. Some of the latter expectantly saw Zuma as someone who valued culture and tradition. In addition, Zuma might have considered introducing new land policies as part of his own legacy projects, as otherwise his presidency might be remembered only through negative incidents like the enormous public spending for upgrading his residence in Nkandla. According to Minister Nkwinti, when he was appointed to the post of Minister of Rural Development and Land Reform, he was given two challenges by Zuma. These were to come up with plans to give opportunities to those who missed the 1998 restitution claim deadline and to those who were excluded from the restitution programme.[17] If this was the case, Zuma had these policies in mind since the very beginning of his presidency in 2009.

Now, if one considers whether the proposals presented at Kimberley II will satisfy the demands of Khoisan revivalism, one has to admit that they will not. It is true that not all Khoisan groups express their demands in terms of land. Some are more interested in cultural or linguistic revivals. However, 'restitution of Khoisan land rights and economic empowerment' has been identified as one of the outstanding issues and concerns surrounding the Khoisan people and organisations since 2001 (NKCC, 2001). Several Khoisan groups and activists in Cape Town argue that the whole of the Cape colony or South Africa should belong to Khoisan, rather than claiming a stake in specific pieces of land. At a public hearing of the Restitution Amendment Bill (2013) in January 2014 organised by the parliamentary portfolio committee in Gugulethu township, a group of men dressed in some traditional attire and introducing themselves as Khoisan held up a map and asserted that 'Khoisan owned the country, the whole of South Africa'.[18] Both at Kimberley II and afterwards, some Khoisan activists seemed confused or disappointed with the proposals. For one thing, the proposals were presented as they were, and there was practically no room for discussion at Kimberley II. Several frustrated participants from the Western Cape went on to ridicule the programme director, Witbooi, who was the

17 From my fieldnotes on the address by Minister Nkwinti at the Nama festival in Wellington, Western Cape, 1 December 2013. The festival was organised annually by Captain Witbooi and his associates, and this was the second or third occasion. In this particular one, a group of Nama people from southern Namibia also participated. They sang and danced in traditional Nama clothes in front of Minister Nkwinti and some members of NAREG. The festival was open to the public and advertised in a few local and community papers, but, as far as I can make out, most participants were from coloured communities in the Western Cape.

18 My own observation at the public hearing on 28 January 2014 and the quotation is from my fieldnotes. A member of the parliamentary committee responded: 'The Section 25 of the Constitution determines that pre-1913 claims are unconstitutional. President Zuma spoke about alternative policy development process. Please concentrate on that process'.

chairperson of the NAREG that prepared the proposals with the DRDLR.[19] For another, the general confusion between two policies, namely restitution reopening and Khoisan land policy, persisted and therefore most Khoisan participants at Kimberley II were expecting to hear that their land demands would be addressed through land restitution. However, in my view, using land redistribution rather than restitution to cater for Khoisan land demands makes sense and in fact would favour them, as it doesn't require deep historical and genealogical research to establish the legitimacy of historical landownership of some particular land by a particular people who also have to be proven to be descendants of the historical owners. This is an undoubtedly onerous task, especially if you have to look for ancestors over the past 350 years or so. It is also less likely to increase the overlapping claims and associated conflicts, as seen in the occupation of District Six by some Khoisan groups discussed above. Moreover, it is important to stress that, to date, DRDLR has framed the Khoisan land policy as an exception to the 1913 cut-off date. Khoisan are not the only people who lost land before 1913. If the government allows Khoisan to lodge restitution claims to land that had been dispossessed before 1913, it would also need to allow other groups to do so. In fact it was reported that Zuma encouraged traditional leaders to get a good lawyer to prepare their land claims at the opening of the National House of Traditional Leaders in early 2014. The Zulu king and chiefs also declared their intentions of launching land claims in KwaZulu-Natal (Claassen, 2014).

Conclusion

This chapter discussed the land demands of Khoisan revivalism that became animated since President Zuma's SONA in early 2013 and the subsequent engagements of Khoisan activists with the government in the Khoisan land policy formation and consultation process. The purpose and mobilisation points of Khoisan revivalism, which has gained momentum since the mid-2000s, were multiple, and land was just one of the numerous demands they had expressed to the government. This situation changed somewhat dramatically and a new policy consultation platform created by the DRDLR became a rallying point for Khoisan activists to articulate their land demands. This chapter has thus confirmed the importance of land issues for existing social movements based on ethnicity and identity in South Africa.

19 I got an opportunity to observe Kimberley II first-hand thanks to a Khoisan group from the Western Cape who organised their own transport from Cape Town and gave me a lift.

The Khoisan land policy formation and consultation process turned out to be difficult and not as straightforward as anticipated. On the one hand, Khoisan revivalism did not have a unified voice, and a new platform to engage with the government ended up intensifying existing power struggles among the Khoisan activists in search of leadership legitimacy. On the other, it became clear that the Khoisan land demands cannot be entertained within the current scope of the land restitution programme. The DRDLR presented proposals, which do not recognise aboriginal rights to land. Nor do they shift the 1913 cut-off date further back into the past. The government is careful not to generalise pre-1913 land claims, which could bring about the nation-wide rewriting of landownership. In this sense Zuma's announcements in SONA 2013 were careless statements, which invoked expectations that could not be met. This chapter has described the most exuberant period of formulating the Khoisan land policy in South Africa to date. It began in the centenary year of the Natives Land Act (1913), when more than the usual amount of interest and resources were directed at land issues. It remains to be seen if this momentum to formulate the Khoisan land policy will continue and bring tangible results.

References

Adhikari, Mohamed (2005). *Not White Enough, Not Black Enough: Racial Identity in the South African Coloured Community*. Athens: Ohio University Press.

ANC (African National Congress) (2012). 53rd National Conference Resolutions, http://www.anc.org.za/docs/res/2013/resolutions53r.pdf (Accessed on 6 December 2014).

Barnard, Alan (1992). *Hunters and Herders of Southern Africa: A Comparative Ethnography of the Khoisan Peoples*. Cambridge: Cambridge University Press.

Besten, Michael (2006). 'Transformation and Reconstitution of Khoe-San Identities: AAS Le Fleur I, Griqua Identities and Post-Apartheid Khoe-San Revivalism (1894–2004)'. PhD Dissertation, University of Leiden.

Besten, M. (2009). 'We are the Original Inhabitants of This Land': Khoe-San Identity in Post-Apartheid South Africa. In Mohamed Adhikari (Ed.), *Burdened by Race: Coloured Identities in Southern Africa* (p. 134–155). Cape Town: UCT Press.

Bredekamp, Henry C. Jatti (2000). Defining Khoisan Identities in Contemporary SA: A Question of Self-Identity? Department of History and Institute for Historical Research of the University of the Western Cape Contemporary History Seminar, 9 May, No. 116.

Cavanagh, Edward (2013). *Settler Colonialism and Land Rights in South Africa: Possession and Dispossession on the Orange River*. Basingstoke: Palgrave Macmillan.

Claassen, Aninka (2014). Land Claims Could Blow Up in Zuma's Face. Mail and Guardian Online, 8 August, http://mg.co.za/article/2014-08-07-land-claims-could-blow-up-in-zumas-face (Final access on 16 January 2018).

CoGTA (Ministry of Cooperative Governance and Traditional Affairs) (2012). Joint Press Statement by Minister for Cooperative Governance and Traditional Affairs (CoGTA), Mr Baloyi and the National Khoi-San Council (NKC), June.

Comaroff, John L., & Comaroff, Jean (2009). *Ethnicity, Inc.* Scottsville: University of KwaZulu-Natal Press.

DLA (Department of Land Affairs) (1997). *White Paper on Land Policy*. Pretoria: DLA.

DRDLR (Department of Rural Development and Land Reform), (2013a). Concept Note: Khoi and San National Consultative Workshop, http://www.ruraldevelopment.gov.za/services/270-documents-for-branches/400-national-khoi-san-dialogue-15-16-april-2013 (Final access on 8 January 2014).

DRDLR (Department of Rural Development and Land Reform), (2013b). Speech by the Minister of Rural Development and Land Reform, Mr G. Nkwinti, http://www.ruraldevelopment.gov.za/services/270-documents-for-branches/400-national-khoi-san-dialogue-15-16-april-2013 (Final access on 8 January 2014).

DRDLR (Department of Rural Development and Land Reform), (2014). The Codification of Exceptions to the 1913 Natives Land Act Cut-off Date, Presented by Deputy Land Commissioner at the National Khoe-San Dialogue 2, Kimberley, 10 April.

DRDLR (Department of Rural Development and Land Reform), (2016). Media Release: Commemorating 50 Years of Struggle for District Six, 12 February, http://www.ruraldevelopment.gov.za/news-room/media-statements/file/4210 (Accessed on 2 March 2016).

DTA (Department of Traditional Affairs), (2011). Background Information on the National Khoisan Council, Department of Traditional Affairs website www.dta.gov.za (Accessed on 29 July 2013).

DTA (Department of Traditional Affairs), (2013). Traditional Affairs Bill, *Government Gazette*, No.36856, 20 September.

Elphick, Richard (1985). *Khoikhoi and the Founding of White South Africa*, Second Edition. Johannesburg: Ravan Press.

Erasmus, Zimitri (2001). Introduction: Re-imagining Coloured Identities in Post-Apartheid South Africa. In Zimitri Erasmus (Ed.), *Coloured by History Shaped by Place: New Perspectives on Coloured Identities in Cape Town*. Cape Town: Kwela Books and SA History Online.

ILO (International Labour Organisation) (1989). Indigenous and Tribal Peoples Convention, 1989 (No.169).

Jeppie, Shamil, & Soudien, Crain (Eds.) (1990). *The Struggle for District Six: Past and Present* (A Project of the Heads Off District Six Committee). Cape Town: Buchu Books.

Lee, Richard B. (2003). Indigenous Rights and the Politics of Identity in Post-Apartheid Southern Africa. In Bartholomew Dean & Jerome M. Levi (Eds.), *At the Risk of Being Heard: Identity, Indigenous Rights, and Postcolonial States* (p. 80–111). Ann Arbor: University of Michigan Press.

Le Fleur, Anthony (2001). Khoisan Grondwetlike Akkommodasie. In NKCC, 2001, *Proceedings of National Khoisan Consultative Conference, 29 March to 1 April 2001, Oudtshoorn*. Cape Town: UWC Institute for Historical Research.

Leggasick, Martin (2013). Racially Motivated Land Dispossession in Gordonia, Memorial Lecture on the 1913 Natives Land Act, Kimberley, 15 April, http://www.ruraldevelopment.gov.za/services/270-documents-for-branches/400-national-khoi-san-dialogue-15-16-april-2013 (Final access on 8 January 2014).

Merten, Marianne (2015). Khoisan Bill a 'Continuation of Apartheid', *Cape Argus*, 2 October, http://www.iol.co.za/news/politics/khoisan-bill-a-continuation-of-apartheid-1924469 (Accessed on 27 February 2016).

Mokoena, Sakhile (2016). South Africa: Mixed Views Heard at Traditional Leadership Bill Public Hearings. *AllAfrica*, 3 February, http://allafrica.com/stories/201602040778.html (Accessed on 27 February 2016).

NKCC (National Khoisan Consultative Conference) (2001). *Proceedings of National Khoisan Consultative Conference, 29 March to 1 April 2001, Outshoorn*. Cape Town: UWC Institute for Historical Research.

NLC (National Land Committee) (1994). *Report of the Community Land Conference, 12 and 13 February 1994*. Johannesburg: NLC.

Ntsewa, Tommy (2013). Talk by Adv Tommy Ntsewa on Work Done by the DTA on Khoi-San during the Khoi-San Dialogue 'Reversing the Legacy of the 1913 Natives' Land Act: Kimberley', 15 April, http://www.ruraldevelopment.gov.za/phocadownload/branch/presentations/2013/KhoiSan_15_160413/cogta_presentation_150413.pdf (Final access on 8 January 2014).

Robins, Steven (2008). *From Revolution to Rights in South Africa: Social Movements, NGOs and Popular Politics after Apartheid*. Suffolk: James Currey.

Sato, Chizuko (2010). Land Restitution and Community Politics: The Case of Roosboom in KwaZulu-Natal. In Cherryl Walker, Anna Bohlin, Ruth Hall, & Thembela Kepe (Eds.), *Land, Memory, Reconstruction, and Justice: Perspectives on Land Claims in South Africa* (p. 215–231). Athens: Ohio University Press.

South Africa, (1996). *Constitution of the Republic of South Africa, 1996*. No. 108 of 1996. Cape Town: *Government Gazette*, No. 17678, Government Printer.

Tolsi, Niren (2011). The Rise and Rise of the Rastafali. *Mail and Guardian Online*, 14 October, http://mg.co.za/article/2011-10-14-the-rise-and-of-rastafari (Accessed on 15 October 2014).

Verbuyst, Rafael (2015). Claiming Cape Town: Ethnographic Interpretations of Khoisan Activism and Land Claims. (Master's thesis). Leiden University.

Waldman, Linda (2007). *The Griqua Conundrum: Political and Socio-Cultural Identity in the Northern Cape, South Africa*. Bern: Peter Lang.

Weideman, Marinda (2004). Who Shaped South Africa's Land Reform Policy. *Politikon*, *31*(2), 219–238.

Zuma, Jacob (2001). Address by Deputy President Zuma to the Opening Ceremony of the National Khoisan Consultative Conference. Issued by Office of the Presidency, 29 March.

Zuma, Jacob (2013). State of the Nation Address by His Excellency Jacob G Zuma, http://www.thepresidency.gov.za/speeches/state-nation-address-his-excellency-jacob-g-zuma%2C-president-republic-south-africa-0 (Final access on 16 January 2018).

CHAPTER 11

The Land-reform Programme and Its Contribution to the Livelihoods of Poor People

Fani Ncapayi

Introduction

This chapter discusses the contribution of land to the livelihoods of beneficiaries of the South African land-reform programme. Specifically, the chapter focuses on group-based projects, where both landownership and production are collectively held and controlled. The chapter specifically challenges scholars and researchers who are critical of the prospects of group-based projects' contribution towards the improvement of the livelihoods of the beneficiaries. They argue that group-based land-reform projects, where land is held and production is organised on a collective basis are, on the whole, unsuccessful. For this reason, these scholars and researchers propose that large farms should be subdivided and land allocated on an individual/family basis, where small-scale farming will be the order of the day.

Using a case study, Delindlala, this chapter shows that under given conditions, in this case academic research and social facilitation, large groups can contribute to the improvement of not only the lives of their beneficiaries but also those of the wider societies they come from (see Ncapayi, 2013).

This chapter is structured as follows. First, I locate the debates within the broader context of tracing the current debates to historical Marxist discussions in Europe. This is followed by discussion of the contemporary debates in South Africa, showing links between the contemporary debates and the historical Marxist debates. Finally, empirical evidence is provided to show a group-based land-reform project, which provides insights about the possibilities of group projects contributing to the improvement of the livelihoods of the beneficiaries of the land-reform programme.

Broader Context of the Debates about Land Reform

The contemporary debates in South Africa follow on historical debates between liberal scholars, on the one hand, and radical scholars or Marxist as well

 | DOI 10.1163/9789004362550_012

as social historians, on the other. They follow on Marxist debates whose origins are in Europe (Byres, 1986; Levin & Neocosmos, 1987; Bernstein & Byres, 2001), as Marxists sought to explain the transition of agrarian societies to capitalist ones (Byres, 1986). Some Marxists believe that the development of capitalism involves the flow of rural people to urban areas as the rural subsistence economies collapse, leading to the undermining of social relations[1] in these rural societies (Ntsebeza, 2012). However, other scholars challenged this deterministic view by showing that this route was specific to English experiences (Brenner, 1976; Aston & Philpin, 1985). Brenner (1976) has argued that feudalism in England transformed into capitalist agriculture as landlords expropriated land and maximised profits through the use of wage labour. However, the transition took a different route in India (Chibber, 1998).

In South Africa, the debates have broadly followed similar lines and have zoomed into the influence of land in changing social relations among rural people. While there has been broad consensus among scholars that land played an important role in defining social relations in land-based African societies at the time of colonial contact (Bundy, 1979; Maylam, 1986; Hammond-Tooke, 1993), disagreements have developed regarding the role of land in changing social relations from the period of mineral discovery and the development of capitalism up to the 1960s. Liberal scholars saw no association between racism and the country's capitalist development. To them, the implementation of racism hindered the development of capitalism (SAHO).[2] They have argued that, from the 1930s, land had ceased to be important in the lives of Africans because of, among other reasons, the collapse of agriculture in rural areas due to the use of primitive agricultural methods by Africans (Macmillan, 1919; Henderson, 1927; De Kiewiet, 1936; Houghton, 1955; Marais, 1967). Henderson (1927) highlighted a decline of 46 per cent in financial returns from agricultural production in the reserves, and that by 1925 rural households spent 63 per cent of their wage income on foodstuffs. The *Report of the Native Economic Commission* of 1932 also confirmed the deteriorating conditions in the native reserves

1 Social relations refer to the manner class, race, gender, and social position influence how people relate to each other. Social relations also include situations of dominance and subordination based on social inequalities, e.g. 'ruler-ruled, rich-poor, white-black …' (Borgatta & Borgatta, 1992, p. 1852), as well as unequal distribution of resources and rewards (Johnson, 2000, p. 285), such as land, which contributed to the emergence of the group of peasants and African farmers in South Africa in the nineteenth century (Bundy, 1979).

2 See article entitled 'Theoretical debates and methodological controversies' in South African History Online (SAHO) (Accessed on 13 January 2016).

(Houghton & Dagut, 1973).[3] Interestingly, despite government interventions through policies such as the Natives Land Act of 1913, with negative effects, the deterioration of conditions in the reserves is still blamed on Africans, allegedly for using primitive agricultural methods (De Kiewiet, 1936; Houghton, 1955; Marais, 1967). Essentially, the scholars conclude that there was no production in the reserves. Thus, land had become less important.

In response to the liberal view, radical scholars such as Wolpe (1972; see also Legassick & Wolpe, 1976) have shown that the development of capitalism and its penetration into African societies in South Africa led to the deterioration of the subsistence economy and, consequently, the conversion of the majority of land-based African people into wage workers. During the period of capitalist development, 'the African redistributive economies' existed side-by-side with 'labour tenancy and crop-sharing on White farms' (Wolpe 1972, p. 431). As in other parts of the world, the development of capitalism went hand-in-hand with the destruction of non-capitalist relations in those countries. For instance, mining and industrial development demanded abundant cheap labour, hence the emergence of the migrant labour system in South Africa.

However, unlike in Europe, where the workers totally lost access to land, in South Africa some migrant workers retained access to limited land in the reserves. This contradictory co-existence of two modes of production in rural areas was untenable, and one of them – the redistributive economic system – had to give way (ibid., p. 432). Consequently, as the African subsistence economies faded by the 1920s, the majority of rural Africans became landless (i.e., they were 'freed from productive resources'). Thus, production 'of a marketable surplus became increasingly rare, finally disappearing altogether' in the reserves (1972, p. 433).[4] Wolpe concludes that land became a 'less important element in subsistence' for the majority of rural people (1972, p. 437–438). Wolpe explains how this happened, 'by not later than 1920 the overwhelming economic and political power of the capitalist sector had succeeded, whether through unequal terms of trade or otherwise, in under-developing the African economy so that it no longer presented any significant competitive threat to White farmers' (1972, p. 433). Bundy (1979) concurs with this line of thinking, arguing that:

3 See also G68 ED (AGRI) S. Department of Agriculture and Forestry. Annual Report of the Secretary for Agriculture and Forestry for 1935. See p. 493–495. UCT Library.

4 Various versions of Wolpe's major work on the proletarianisation of rural dwellers were republished at various times, including the article used in this study, which was republished in 1995.

> ... the transition of a majority of her people – the rural African population – from their precolonial existence as pastoralist-cultivators to their contemporary status: that of sub-subsistence rural dwellers, manifestly unable to support themselves by agriculture and dependent for survival upon wages earned in the 'white' industrial areas or upon 'white' farms (1979, p. 1).

According to him, the transition was due to the 'diminution of Africans' lands by conquest and annexation, the creation of the "Reserves", the deterioration of these into eroded, overstocked and overcrowded rural ghettoes that function as the supply source of migratory labour' (ibid., p. 1).

Thus, though both scholars come to the same conclusion that, by the 1930s, land was no longer an important factor in the livelihoods of rural people, they advance difference reasons why land lost its importance. Wolpe cites diminished production as the reason land became less important to Africans, whereas Bundy identifies the shortage of land as the reason.

Even Beinart (1995) who initially disagrees with Wolpe that rural people became objects in the process of their conversion from independent producers to wage workers, later concedes that, by the 1950s, the majority of rural people had become wage workers (ibid., p. 177). Hendricks (1990) has taken issue with both the revisionists and social historians that continued access to land by Africans in the reserves meant that the process of proletarianisation was impeded or the peasantry persisted. For him, the continued access to land by rural dwellers concealed the extent to which rural people had been proletarianised. He concludes that, by the 1960s, the former reserves had become home to a group of 'displaced proletarians' (ibid., p. 3). Thus, land had become irrelevant in the lives of rural people by the 1960s, according to scholars of the proletarianisation thesis.

Similarly, the de-agrarianisation thesis – a variant of the proletarianisation thesis – argues that, from the 1960s, rural people had become less interested in land-based livelihoods. According to the thesis, instead of committing to land-based lifestyles, rural residents engaged in non-agricultural activities (Brycesson, 1997; Bank, 1997; Manona, 1999). This means rural people had less inclination towards agriculture, which implies land had become less important in their livelihoods. Importantly, the period of the 1960s is characterised by less state spending and involvement in the provision of public and social services. As the states withdraw, market forces replace the state in the provision of public goods (McMichael, 2007).

As will be seen in the next section, these international development trends have a bearing on the South African context.

Contemporary Debates Regarding the Role of Land Reform to Livelihoods of Rural People

Much similar to the de-agrarianisation thesis, proponents of the view questioning the relevance of land reform justify their position by pointing out that rural people lack interest in agricultural land. The alleged lack of interest in agricultural land by black people, but interest in jobs and land for housing, is cited as one of the reasons for failure of the land-reform projects (Bernstein, 2005; Makhanya, 2012). Bernstein argues that because South Africa is urbanising, the pressing need is land for housing in urban areas, not in rural areas. Thus, there is no need for land reform for agricultural purposes (2005, p. 13). Similarly, Makhanya, who has become one of the avid critics of the land-reform programme, argues that:

> … our country is wasting time, money and energy trying to get an urban-inclined population to love the land. Just observe the hundreds of thousands of hectares of fertile land that lie fallow. So why would you want to interfere with commercial farming in order to satisfy a mythical desire for agricultural land?

On the other hand, while not doubting the relevance of land reform, Hall (2009) questions the contribution of group-based land-reform projects to the livelihoods of rural people. She identifies two types of land-reform projects in South Africa: 'group-based ownership and production', where production 'involves not only joint ownership of the land but also the pooling of assets and labour', as well as 'group-based ownership with household production' (2009, p. 26). The latter is different from the former form of land-reform projects in that it is only the land that is managed jointly in the latter. Hall attributes the failure of land-reform projects to improve the livelihoods of beneficiaries to the first form of group-based farming. According to her, the structure of the LRAD grant forces beneficiaries to acquire land as groups, hence the dominance of group-based farming. She argues, group-based ownership and production has produced 'similar outcomes to those it was intended to remedy' (ibid., p. 27), when the LRAD replaced the SLAG in 2001. Furthermore, plans to 'engage jointly in production have sometimes failed to get off the ground', and 'non-realisation of project plans' fuels conflicts and 'competition over resources' (ibid.). Hall's conclusion is that land 'underutilisation is widely reported, and there is substantial evidence that livelihood benefits have been very limited' in group-based projects (ibid., p. 55).

Similarly, Lahiff also believes that 'group access to land for large-scale agriculture' has failed (2007a, p. 6). According to him (ibid.), the failure of the projects is due to unequal commitment of labour and resources by members. His solution is the ...

> ... subdivision of land (even informal subdivision) and individualisation of agricultural production (to the household level) has the potential to be a more inclusive model, that is appropriate to the skills and resources of community members and delivers more immediate and tangible benefits (2007a, p. 8).

Umhlaba, Agricultural and Rural Development Research Institute (AARDRI) and Phuhlisani Solutions (2010, p. ix) also associate the failure of a number of the projects with 'internal conflicts among beneficiaries and beneficiary defection, based on a study of six land-reform projects in the Western Cape, Northern Cape, KwaZulu-Natal, and Mpumalanga.

The failure to manage interpersonal relations within the groups, which escalate into internal conflicts, is also blamed as the cause of the problems. Similarly, Anseeuw and Mathebula (2008, p. ix) highlight the existence of inequalities and internal conflicts in the groups. The blame for failure of the projects is also put on lack of or poor targeting and recruitment of beneficiaries. Aliber and colleagues argue that, because the LRAD targets well-resourced people as beneficiaries, it fails poor people as 'communal area dwellers and communal area farmers are almost systematically neglected by land redistribution', and are only drawn into redistribution 'as recruits to help populate SLAG applications that had no real reference to their situation or their interests' (2011, p. 245). The writers add that, because of its grant structure, LRAD also marginalises farm workers. This is despite the government's rhetoric that farm workers and farm-dwellers are the 'key target group' (ibid.). The commentators' observations are very similar to the position taken by some scholars who earlier on criticised the LRAD for targeting well-resourced beneficiaries at the expense of poor people (see Ntsebeza & Hendricks, 2000; Greenberg, 2003; Hendricks & Ntsebeza, 2004). The overall conclusion from the various views, though, is that group-based projects have failed to improve the livelihoods of beneficiaries.

The above seems applicable to projects led by government officials. Farmers who want to sell their land adopt a different approach. In collaboration with estate agents, who also act as consultants, the farmer recruits his workers, and, where the farm workers cannot meet the price of the farm, other people from surrounding communities are also recruited (Aliber et al. 2011, p. 58).

For example, in the case of Makhamotse, a land-reform project in Limpopo, the consultant responsible for formation of the group persuaded the farm workers to recruit villagers in the neighbourhood (ibid.). Consequently, the project was plagued by internal fights and the ultimate withdrawal of members. Thus, targeting and recruitment is viewed as a contributor to the failure of the projects.

The vexed issue of support for land-reform beneficiaries is also often cited. While some complain about the lack of support, others identify the manner in which the support is provided as contributing to the problems of the projects. Hall and Cliffe (2009, p. 2) aptly capture the dilemma of support. They argue that:

> … [u]nderutilisation of redistributed land is widespread and has been attributed primarily to three factors: an enforced structure of group farming; the imposition through business planning processes of commercial and capital-intensive production models inappropriate to the needs and capabilities of beneficiaries; and a chronic problem of insufficient (or absent) support, extension services and market access (2009, p. 2).

Umhlaba Rural Services, AARDRI and Phuhlani Solutions cast more light on the nature of the support the government often provides:

> The shaping and planning of land-reform projects in South Africa has been characterized by the over-reliance on external agency, particularly during the early years. Business plans, which were usually prepared by consultants, were not adequately internalized by the land-reform beneficiaries and in some instances completely unrealistic (2010, p. 27).

Thus, the imposition of ideas on beneficiaries is the main problem regarding support. This view is further confirmed by Minister Nkwinti's address to the National Assembly on 7 June 2011, in which he noted that his department …

> … had not been successful in ensuring all 2.9 million hectares of land given to beneficiaries remained productive. The department had therefore been forced to introduce its recapitalisation programme.[5]

Therefore, the department was looking for consultants to serve as mentors 'to help turn around 852 land-reform projects at risk of collapse' and make them

5 Nkwinti: Govt. needs help with land reform (2011/06/08). See http://www.fin24.com/Economy/Nkwinti-Govt-needs-help-with-land-reform-20110708 (Accessed on 26 September 2014).

'commercially viable and productive'.[6] As can be seen, failure is equated to perceived inability or lack of capacity, on the part of the beneficiaries, to use the land commercially. As Ngubane's (Chapter 12) chapter also shows, the success or failure of the land-reform projects is judged on the basis of whether they farm commercially or not. In questioning the conception, he warns that land reform should not be viewed as about economics only or about promoting the emergence of a class of black farmers.

Lahiff, on the other hand, points out that the land-reform projects struggle to access support services such as 'credit, training, extension advice, transport and ploughing services, veterinary services, and access to input and produce markets' (2007b, p. 31). This lack of support is in relation to the general withdrawal of support for farmers by the state. However, commercial agriculture continues to get support from various other sources, such as commercial and co-operative providers; land-reform projects and small-scale farmers, however, struggle to get the support (ibid.). The support provided by the provincial department of agriculture and non-governmental organisations (NGOs) seems inadequate, as only few projects access it. Jacobs et al. have made similar comments earlier that:

> ... (c)urrently, no specific institution has responsibility for driving and coordinating the provision of post-transfer support to redistribution beneficiaries, and little has been forthcoming in the area of financial resources to fund such assistance (2003, p. 19).

These critics further indicate that, in most cases, the support is provided only after the land is transferred.

Clearly, the discussion above identifies the issue of support as problematic in that it is often absent, and, where it is provided, it is not in line with what the beneficiaries want. Thus the issue of support needs to be viewed critically.

Anseeuw and Mathebula (2008) point to three land-reform projects in Limpopo that they consider to be success stories, one of which is worth closer examination. This is a restitution project that involves 427 beneficiaries on 7 148 hectares of land. The project started operating in 2004 and has been getting support from Nkuzi – a non-governmental organisation (NGO) – and the Legal Resources Centre (LRC). Nkuzi helped members of the project to draft their constitution and continued to monitor and support the project (ibid., p. 41–42). Members of the project have confirmed that the constitution

6 Ibid.

'reflects their concerns and desires' (ibid., p. 42), indicating that members have both internalised and own the constitution.

Importantly, a lesson from the example of Nkuzi is that support for the projects does not have to come from the government, NGO support is also critical. What also makes the NGO support crucial is the fact that it is not once-off support, but continuous, as shown here.

Land also makes a difference in the livelihoods of beneficiaries in projects where production is carried out at an individual household level (Hall, 2008). Hall shows that, from their land, the beneficiaries provide for themselves and gain income from the sale of the produce (ibid., p. 28). Sharing experience about land reform in Namibia, Ndala concurs with Hall and shows that '[s]ome beneficiaries have managed to produce food for their own consumption and some have produced surplus for the market' (2009 p. 67).

Additionally, Dlamini (2008) shows that non-monetary benefits accrue in having access to land. He argues:

> Providing poor people with access to land and improving their ability to make effective use of the land that they occupy are central to reducing poverty and empowering them and their communities (2008, p. 24).

Besides showing the non-monetary benefits of land, this also shows that land reform contributes to the livelihoods of rural people. Davenport (2008, p. 35) also shows that land reform contributes to improvement of the livelihoods of residents in Grahamstown, Bathurst, and Fort Beaufort. These are residents that have used the land-reform programme to access municipal commonage land and use it for collection of firewood, medicinal plants, and livestock rearing (ibid.). Cousins and Scoones (2010) make a similar point about the contribution of land to the livelihoods of rural people. They show that:

> In rural economies land is seen as a basic livelihood asset ... from which people produce food and earn a living, and comprises cropland, grazing land and common lands from which a range of natural resources can be harvested (2010, p. 42).

Importantly, Cousins and Scoones stress that beneficiaries do not use land for crop production only but also to collect natural resources. This is a point Ngubane (Chapter 12) also makes. Additionally, preliminary findings of a study of land-reform projects in the Chris Hani District Municipality (CHDM) between 2009 and 2010 paint an optimistic view. The findings show that most beneficiary households have more livestock and better access to food than non-beneficiaries (Chitonge & Ntsebeza 2012, p. 19–20). Findings of the study show vast improvements in the livelihoods of beneficiaries not only economically but also in non-monetary ways. According to Chitonge and Ntsebeza:

> [t]he role of land is not restricted to quantifiable monetary or material improvements, but is conceived broadly to include non- material aspects such as enhanced sense of justice, self-esteem, security, dignity and self-respect (2012, p. 2).

Significantly, land-reform beneficiaries are also less dependent on government social grants, compared to non-beneficiaries (ibid., p. 16).

While this section has cited literature that shows the failure of land-reform projects, particularly group-based land-reform projects, other literature has also been presented that makes a clear case for the positive contribution land reform makes in the livelihoods of the beneficiaries. The next section comprises the case study of Delindlala Communal Property Association, a group-based land-reform project where both landownership and production are collective.

Implementation of Land Reform in Luphaphasi and Its Impact

The case study of Delindlala[7] shows that under specific conditions (academic research and social facilitation in this case) group-based land-reform projects can improve the livelihoods not only of the beneficiaries but also of the communities where the beneficiaries come from. Academic research, which helped to identify the target group and the nature of support needed – as well as providing constant support in the form of social facilitation before and after land acquisition – has enabled this group-based land-reform project to continue operating, thus contributing to the livelihoods of beneficiaries of the land-reform programme and communities of origin for the beneficiaries.

In 2001, fourty people from Luphaphasi acquired the 2029-hectare Thornhill Farm from Mr Etienne Cloete at Indwe through a R1.3 million LRAD grant. The group's members consist of families of descendants of the progressive African farmers and peasants that Bundy refers to in his book – *The rise and fall of the South African peasantry* – and the landless former farm workers or *amalose* (Ncapayi, 2013). These are people who have always maintained their links with land-based livelihoods, even though the majority of them had at some stage

7 Delindlala means to defy hunger, in reference to the main objective of the project, which is about using the land to fight poverty in households.

been migrant workers. Some even invested their wage incomes on agricultural implements (Ncapayi, 2005). Former farm workers have always been linked to land-based livelihoods as labour tenants of the African landholders in the village. Therefore, the beneficiaries are a differentiated group, consisting of livestock (sheep and cattle) owners (mainly men), some with arable land, others with none; livestock owners with only residential sites; and residents with residential sites with no livestock.

While the Cala University Students Association (CALUSA)[8] – a local NGO – assisted the group in planning before taking over the farm, the group itself decided on those issues that were relevant for our purposes. Firstly, they decided not to relocate to the farm; instead, teams of 10 members would commute weekly from the village. After a week on the farm, this team would be replaced by another; each team was assisted in developing a weekly plan, taking into account the tasks performed by the previous team. Each team evaluated its plan at the end of the week (CALUSA 2002, p. 19). Thus, although the members had become land-reform beneficiaries, they did not relinquish their rights to land and membership to Luphaphasi. Secondly, to manage livestock numbers, the group also resolved that each member could keep a maximum of ten cattle and 50 sheep on the farm, while building the livestock of the collective. Thirdly, the group also resolved on group-based (i.e. collective) production on the farm (Ncapayi, 2013). Lastly, and linked to the first and third points, the group decided not to subdivide the farm. Their argument was that subdividing it would lead to development of a village on the farm, something the DLA officials warned the group against.[9]

The relevance of the last resolution is the fact that, because of commitment to collective group farming, the beneficiaries decided against subdividing the land. Yet, as will be shown later, this group-based land-reform project on an unsubdivided large-scale farm has not collapsed as the other group-based land-reform projects mentioned earlier.

The period between 2002 and mid-2003 at Delindlala confirms the problems Lahiff (2007a, 2007b) and Hall (2009) highlight regarding group-based production projects, such as, reluctance of some members to commit their labour to the project, lack of capital, and cases of poor discipline among members

8 CALUSA, established in Cala in 1983, is one of the two organisations that have been working with communities in Xhalanga since the 1980s. The other NGO was Health Care Trust (HCT). The organisations have had an influence in the turn of events in Xhalanga, where Luphaphasi is located (Ntsebeza, 2006).

9 See CALUSA Annual Report of 2001.

(including misuse of the project's assets).[10] The project also lacked start-up capital to implement its plans.[11]

At the same time, individually owned livestock production succeeded from the outset. Men were mostly the culprits, as they tended to focus on their individual livestock and other income-generating activities – such as rural transportation – while ignoring the activities of the collective. Women remained concerned with crop production for the group. Thus, women were the ones concerned about food security in their households, as it were. This also means that the activities on the farm were divided along gender lines.

Sustained social facilitation from CALUSA helped the project to develop strategies of dealing with the problems and to pursue collective crop production (CALUSA, 2002, 2003, 2004).[12] Already before the acquisition of land, CALUSA field staff organised workshops for communities, including Luphaphasi, to understand the land-reform programme (CALUSA, 2001; Ncapayi, 2013). Exposure visits to other land-reform groups were also organised and discussions about lessons from the visits were also held. Research helped in identifying the land-reform projects to be visited. After land acquisition, the field staff encouraged and ensured that project members would hold weekly planning meetings (CALUSA, 2001). Thus the support ensured that Delindlala members were focused and pursued the project's objectives.[13]

Consequently, by mid-2003 most of the problems had been overcome and the project's collective crop production showed improvements. For instance, in April 2003 Delindlala produced 165 bags of potatoes compared to 100 bags in 2002. Fifty-four of the bags were shared among members, while the other 111 bags were sold to villagers in Luphaphasi. The project also produced cabbages, spinach, pumpkins, and maize. Some of the produce was sold in the village, whilst members consumed some (CALUSA 2003, p. 19). And, although erratic, from the beginning of 2003, extension officers also started visiting Delindlala to provide advice and support. For example, at the end of January 2003, Mr Mnguni – the extension officer – introduced the group to Mr Tokwe of Umthonyama, a training organisation, to discuss the training of Delindlala members in poultry farming and farm management.[14]

10 Minutes of the general meeting at Delindlala on 1/3/2002. Delindlala minute book.

11 Minutes of Delindlala Management Committee meeting on 14/09/2002.

12 Minutes of Delindlala's Management Committee meeting on 23/05/2002.

13 See Minutes of a meeting at Delindlala on 22/10/2002.

14 Minutes of a meeting of Delindlala and the Department of Agriculture (undated–possibly in late January 2003).

The livestock owners were not immune from problems. They encountered severe stock losses through diseases and theft. To assist in combatting the stock losses, CALUSA contracted Luthando Ndondo, an independent local farmer-trainer in Cala, to provide stock management training and to support the livestock owners in the project (CALUSA 2003, p. 20). Additionally, Dr Thembela Kepe of the Programme for Land and Agrarian Studies (PLAAS), who visited the project in 2004, organised funds to purchase medication for the livestock and exerted pressure on the veterinary services of the then Department of Agriculture, now Department of Rural Development and Agrarian Reform (DRDAR), to support the livestock owners. Consequently, stock losses were curbed by 2004 (CALUSA, 2004). To combat stock theft, the project members decided on meetings with the nearby community of Machubeni. Indeed, with the co-operation of the headman of Machubeni, members of the Management Committee of Delindlala attended some community meetings in the village to address the residents (CALUSA 2003, p. 20). Eventually, a community police forum (CPF), which involved representatives from the various villages, the police, and Delindlala, was established.[15]

Despite the above challenges, the livestock owners were very content with the development of their livestock on the farm. The response of Mr Sunduza Nkomana to the extension officers in a meeting on 2 May 2003 indicates this: 'There is a big difference in our livestock now. The number of cattle has increased and the quality of wool of our sheep has also improved'.[16] Mr Nkomana's views were further confirmed by Mr Chophiso.[17] They attributed the improvements to the quality of grazing land on the farm.

While originally, it had problems, like other group-based farming projects, unlike them, Delindlala did not collapse, as it had the constant support from CALUSA, before and after land acquisition, initially, and from the DRDAR, later.

The Move to Greater Collective Production in Delindlala

Earlier problems aside, the period from mid-2003 to 2005 saw growth in interest among members towards collective crop and livestock production. The turning point in this development occurred when women took over leadership of the project towards the end of 2003 and injected energy into the group.

15 Minutes of meetings of Delindlala and CALUSA on 13/03/2003 and 7/5/2003. Ibid.

16 Minutes of a meeting of Delindlala with extension officers on the farm on 2/5/2003. Delindlala minute book.

17 Ibid.

The leadership of Nosamnkele Eleni, Nozolile Qayi, and Zithulele Ntshwenca (the farm manager) was at the centre of the processes taking place in Delindlala, with CALUSA more in the background now as the leadership had developed confidence to run its affairs.

Subsequently, the women-dominated leadership orchestrated an internal discussion that culminated in the enforcement of a resolution the group took during the planning phase for each household to donate sheep to the collective.[18] Although the households initially failed to make their donations, some members eventually made their donations between May and July 2003.[19] Remarking about the donations, Zwelinzima Dyantyi stressed that 'everybody should donate their sheep and stop making excuses, because without the donations, members will have no claim in Delindlala (*wonke umntu makakhuphe igusha zikaDelindlala, singabe sisenza amabali, ngoba ukuba asizikhuphi asinalifa kuDelindlala*)'.[20] The pressure resulted in some households eventually making the donations.[21] Livestock production thus became also collective in Delindlala, showing the commitment of members to collective ownership and production.

From the beginning of 2004, Nozolile Qayi – as the deputy chairperson of the group – started showing her power by calling for a resolution on the lack of commitment of some members to the activities of Delindlala. In a Management Committee meeting in early-January 2004, she argued that, because of this unresolved issue, only six members were involved in the planting of cabbages that month. Consequently, members agreed to revive sub-committees, to encourage the participation of members in project activities.[22] Indeed, the following sub-committees were re-established: assets management, the management of fields, livestock management, and farmhouse care. Nozolile Qayi reiterated her point in the general meeting that 'members who fail to commit their labour to activities of the group should be called to order immediately (*umntu ongafuni kwenzanto eyenziwa ngabantu simxoxise ngelo xesha*)'.[23] Clearly, Qayi was beginning to stamp her authority on the group.

The discussions in the meeting also drifted towards what should be planted, with members agreeing on cabbages, potatoes, and beans.[24] By this time, more

18 Telephone communication with Nozolile Qayi, 28/6/2012.

19 Minutes of the Management Committee meeting of Delindlala on 14/5/2003. Ibid.

20 Minutes of a general meeting of Delindlala on 17/7/2003. Ibid.

21 Minutes of a general meeting of Delindlala on 16/6/2003. Ibid.

22 Minutes of the Management Committee meeting of Delindlala on 5/1/2004. Delindlala minute book, Delindlala office.

23 Minutes of the general meeting of Delindlala on 5/1/2004. Ibid.

24 Ibid.

than twenty hectares of land were collectively cultivated. The project used seven hectares to plant potatoes and also planted 6000 cabbages, as well as hay for the livestock of the collective (CALUSA 2004, p. 10).

However, individual members were not deterred in growing the numbers of their own livestock. By 2004, individuals had 612 cattle and 980 sheep on the farm (CALUSA, 2010). Talking about their stock, MamQwathi Mrhawuli indicated: 'Because livestock is well fed due to the improved grazing land on the farm, the cows mate while they still have calves'.[25] Mistake Chophiso also shared these sentiments.[26] This meant a faster increase in the rate of livestock of numbers in Delindlala than in Luphaphasi.

By the end of 2004, group dynamics between men and women played themselves out on the farm. Women openly challenged men in their steamrolling of decisions on the farm. For example, in the group's meeting on 6 October 2004, an argument emerged between members, mostly men, who unilaterally planted lucerne for their individual livestock, and women, who wanted to plant maize for household consumption. The women eventually won the debate, and maize was planted for the benefit of all households, instead of the lucerne that would only benefit livestock owners. Central to the argument was that the decision to plant lucerne had not been taken in a proper meeting but by some men within the group.[27] This example illustrates the growth in confidence of women and the changes in power relations within Delindlala. It also illustrates the critical role women played in driving collective crop production on the farm.

The growth in confidence of the women was further illustrated by their taking over the project's leadership in 2005. The development also boosted the project's efforts to pursue collective crop production. Their consistent involvement in activities of the project put them in a stronger position to be in control.[28] Significant changes such as greater involvement of the children of beneficiaries in activities of the farm, regular weekly planning meetings of the Management Committee, working teams on the farm, as well as the recognition and payment of the labour of members who committed more time on the farm, were introduced during the era of the women's leadership in the project. For instance, in recognition of her commitment and contribution to the project, Nozolile Qayi received a monthly wage of R1300, which is also given to seven

25 MamQwathi Mrhawuli interviewed by the author at Delindlala, 21 May 2005.

26 Mistake Chophiso interviewed by the author at Delindlala, 6 May 2005.

27 Minutes of the general meeting of Delindlala on 6/10/2004.

28 Minutes of a meeting at Delindlala on 31/10/2002.

other members of the project for committing their labour to its activities.[29] The income and the fact that she also has livestock on the farm have improved her financial position. She explains:

> There are many benefits in being part of the farm. I have cattle and sheep, even though not much ... When schools opened this year, we sold a cow in preparation for our child who studies at the University of the Western Cape. These are the reasons I say there is benefit in having a farm.[30]

As can be seen from the extract, a combination of the monthly wage and sale of stock provide income to her.

Nolikhaya Makatesi, a widow with no other income except what she gets from the farm, confirms Qayi's claims:

> I was able to purchase household items such as a fridge from income I get from the farm. My children are also at school. Yet other residents who have not benefited from the land-reform programme are unable to do what we do as the land-reform beneficiaries.[31]

Additionally, Nobuntu Khutshwa, another widow, also demonstrates economic independence because of Delindlala. Although her husband's death occurred at a time when their son was about to go to the initiation school, she still managed to send him and to organise *umgidi* afterwards.[32] Support from other project members, as well as the monthly income she gets from the farm, assisted her. The members of Delindlala contributed in various ways towards the success of her son's *umgidi*. The members also encouraged and gave her moral support when she wanted to withdraw from the project.[33] Thus, Delindlala also has a social role as members provide social support to each other.

From 2005, Delindlala received more attention and support from DRDAR than previously. The department provided agricultural infrastructure support. Nozolile Qayi explains:

> We got support from CASP (Comprehensive Agricultural Support Programme) to renew the farm's boundary fence, the camps, and the arable

29 Nozolile Qayi interviewed by the author at Delindlala, 3/02/2011.

30 Ibid.

31 Nolikhaya Makatesi interviewed by the author at Delindlala, 3/02/2011.

32 *Umgidi* is a ceremony organised to mark a son's return from the initiation school.

33 Conversation with Nobuntu Khutshwa at Delindlala, 17/06/2008.

> lands. The department also installed an irrigation system to fifteen hectares of the fields. The total costs for this work was R300,000.[34]

Mr Martins from the DRDAR concurs: 'They wanted assistance to make improvements on their farm. For instance, they applied for fencing material, which was supplied by the Department of Agriculture'.[35] In January 2005, two contractors began installing the irrigation system[36] and completed it in August.[37]

The decision to revive the fields illustrates the determination to pursue collective crop production. Indeed, collective crop production increased to 700 bags of potatoes and 317 bags of maize by June 2005. The increase in crop production was largely due to the commitment of women who pushed members to go to the fields.[38] Thus, unlike the projects Lahiff (2007a, 2007b) and Hall (2009) refer to, collective production succeeded in Delindlala. The leadership continued to invest in skills development for members. In June 2006, the project's leadership entered into an agreement with the Department of Labour for the training of members in animal husbandry, poultry, and farm management.[39] The training led to collective poultry production on the farm, which started with 250 chickens (CALUSA 2006, p. 18). The poultry project has since been scaled up by the installation of structures that accommodate 600 chickens.[40]

At the same time, there was tremendous increase in the livestock of individuals on the farm in 2006. Importantly, stockowners constituted 52.5 per cent (21 out of 40 members) of the beneficiaries. Sheep had increased from 345 in 2001 to 969 in 2006. Additionally, the cattle of individuals increased from 154 to 262 over the same period. The increase in livestock occurred despite the stock losses due to diseases and theft, as well as sales by some stockowners (CALUSA, 2006).

From 2007, collective crop production picked up due to financial support from the National Development Agency (NDA), which assisted in the purchase

34 Nozolile Qayi interviewed by the author at Delindlala, 3/02/2011.

35 Mr Martins interviewed by the author of in Dordrecht, 21/11/2006.

36 Minutes of the meeting between Delindlala and extension officers (undated).

37 See also minutes of the meeting between Delindlala and the contractors on 25/8/2005. In the meeting the extension officers wanted to find out if Delindlala members were happy about the irrigation system.

38 Minutes of the general meeting of Delindlala on 27/6/2005 and undated between Delindlala and CALUSA.

39 Minutes of the meeting of the Management Committee of Delindlala on 19/6/2006.

40 Conversations with Nozolile Qayi and Thando Bengo, December 2014.

of another tractor for the project (CALUSA 2006, p. 17). There was a marked increase in land under production as well as an increase in both the amount of produce and the crop varieties produced on the farm compared to the situation in 2003. For example, in 2003, the group utilised less than a hectare of its thirty-five hectares of arable land to produce maize and vegetables, while more than 20ha of land was used to produce a variety of products such as vegetables, maize and animal feed in 2008. There was also demonstrable growth in the volume of produce on the farm from 1000 cabbages in 2004 to 20,000 in 2008. This meant that collective crop production was succeeding on the farm – a fact that was publicly acknowledged as the project started winning prizes in farmer competitions both in the district and in the province from 2008.[41]

Between 2010 and 2011, there was a further increase in food production from 40,000 cabbage to 60,000, respectively. The project also harvested 30 bags of potatoes, most of which were sold at R30 per bag: a sign of a shift of the project towards production for the markets. Extension officers successfully negotiated with Boxer Stores and KwikSpar in Lady Frere, Dordrecht, Cala, and East London for Delindlala to sell its produce.[42] The availability of new markets also influenced the increase in production.[43] The project also sold some of its produce in Luphaphasi and the surrounding villages, meaning that it did not only focus on formal markets but also informal markets. Thus, the project directly contributed to poverty alleviation in communities.

Furthermore, the project also achieved recognition as it was chosen as the best land-reform project in CHDM and won R45,000 in 2011. This followed an assessment by provincial agricultural officials from Bisho and a journalist from the *Farmers Weekly*. The assessors also visited Delindlala and took photos to verify the production.[44] This is further public confirmation of the success of Delindlala's crop production.

Between 2006 and 2009, there was a decline in livestock numbers on the farm, as shown in Table 11.1 on next page.

Stock sales, stock theft, and implementation of the resolution to restrict livestock of individuals on the farm account for the decline. For example, the Chophiso family sold ten sheep and six cattle in 2009. According to No-andile Chophiso, her family 'reduced [their] livestock by selling it so that it

41 Nozolile Qayi interviewed by the author at Delindlala, 3/02/2011.

42 Ibid. See also Minutes of the Management Committee meeting between Delindlala and representatives of RuLIV, 21/8/2009. Delindlala minute book.

43 Nozolile Qayi interviewed by the authored at Delindlala, 3/02/2011.

44 Nozolile Qayi interviewed by the author at Delindlala, 03/02/2011.

TABLE 11.1 *Livestock of individuals in Delindlala.*

Years	Sheep	Cattle
2006	969	262
2009	800	329

Table adapted from CALUSA Annual Report, 2010.

is manageable'.[45] Sigqibo Dyantyi confirms the stock sales: 'We sell livestock for our livelihoods (*sitya imfuyo*)'.[46]

Between 2009 and 2010, the leadership of Delindlala unsuccessfully tried to resuscitate the group's discussion about phasing out the livestock of individuals on the farm, which had been put in abeyance since 2001. The leaders wanted enforcement of restrictions on the livestock numbers of individuals. However, livestock owners hedged and sought postponement of the discussion (CALUSA 2009, p. 13). Importantly, sharp class differences between some livestock owners, who selfishly wanted to keep their own stock, and members with an interest in the development of livestock for the collective emerged during the discussions. According to Nozolile Qayi, '[A]lthough the livestock of some members was above the limit on the farm, when we started to enforce the resolution, there was reluctance in some members to reduce their livestock when told to do so. The members preferred to take their livestock back to the village.[47] For example, Sindiswa Nkomana, Zwelinzima Dyantyi, Sigqibo Dyantyi, Mistake Chophiso, Ndoyisile Eleni, and Zalusile Eleni reduced their livestock on the farm from 2010.[48] This contributed to the decline in livestock numbers of individuals on the farm. Figure 11.1 below clearly shows the tremendous increase in the livestock of individuals on the farm until 2010 and the sharp decline in 2011.

Some members sold their stock to purchase vehicles, for example Zithulele Ntshwenca, Sigqibo Dyantyi, Zwelinzima Dyantyi, and Titshala Dyantyi.[49] Some of them were also involved in rural transportation as an extra non-agricultural activity. The investment in rural transportation illustrates the diversification of the sources of income by some livestock owners. Additionally, the ability

45 No-andile Chophiso interviewed by the author at Delindlala, 03/12/2010.

46 Sigqibo Dyantyi interviewed by the author in Luphaphasi, 24/10/2009.

47 Nozolile interviewed by the author at Delindlala, 10/02/2009.

48 Thembelani Dyantyi interviewed by the author at Delindlala, 11/7/2012.

49 Ibid.

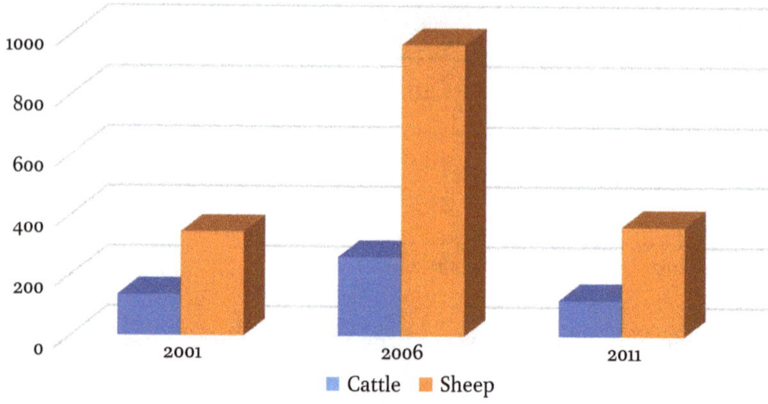

FIGURE 11.1 *Livestock of individuals on the farm.*
GRAPH DESIGNED BY THE AUTHOR.

of some livestock owners to purchase vehicles shows the contribution of land reform to livelihoods of beneficiaries. Nevertheless, the resolution of the issue ensured that livestock accumulation by individuals did not disadvantage other members.

Delindlala's experience is not unique, though. Funokuhle Agricultural Project is another example of a land-reform project where land acquisition and increased livestock improved the financial position of the household. In addition to purchasing a vehicle, and despite getting very limited government support, David Kiyane, educated his grandson to become a qualified agronomist at the end of 2012. To achieve this, Kiyane sold his livestock and produce. Like the study by Chitonge and Ntsebeza (2012), these examples demonstrate that livestock ownership is critical in the livelihoods of beneficiaries of the land-reform programme.

Land acquisition also contributes to food security in the households of members. Members spend less money on food, since they obtain some from the farm. According to Nozolile Qayi, 'members also get a portion of the produce as their share during the harvest'.[50] This is in addition to the standard share from produce each member is entitled to, irrespective of whether the member has worked or not.

Thus, the evidence presented in this section questions the blanket argument that group-based land-reform projects fail to improve the livelihoods of beneficiaries (Lahiff, 2007b; Hall, 2009; Hall & Cliffe, 2009). The evidence shows that proper identification of beneficiaries through research, sustained support not only after land acquisition but also before, as well as the existence

50 Nozolile Qayi interviewed by the author at Delindlala, 10/02/2009.

of determined and focused leadership were some of the key factors for the success of Delindlala. The project has had an immeasurably positive impact on the livelihoods of the beneficiaries. As shown above, Delindlala is not the only successful project. The project supported by Nkuzi in Limpopo is another one.

Conclusion

This chapter set out to show that under certain conditions group-based land-reform projects can improve the livelihoods of the beneficiaries. The chapter focused on a group-based project, where both landownership and production were collectively held and controlled. The chapter engaged with scholars and researchers who are critical of the prospects of group-based projects' contribution towards the improvement of the livelihoods of the beneficiaries. The scholars argue that group-based land-reform projects where land and production are collectively organised are, on the whole, unsuccessful. For this reason, these scholars and researchers propose that large farms should be subdivided and land allocated on an individual/family basis where small-scale farming will be the order of the day.

The chapter presented a case study of Delindlala – a group-based land-reform project in the Emalahleni Local Municipality, under the Chris Hani District Municipality. Before taking over the farm, members of the project decided not to subdivide the farm into plots for individual members. The decision made and still makes sense, as subdividing the farm would defeat the group's principle of working collectively on the farm. Secondly, the decision was informed by a realisation that subdividing the farm would lead to the development of a village on the farm: something the members were determined to avoid. Nonetheless, the group has continued to operate collectively on the farm.

The case study of Delindlala has illustrated that research and social facilitation before and after land acquisition are critical factors in ensuring that group-based land-reform projects contribute to the livelihoods of the beneficiaries. Research helped in determination of the nature of land need, and the identification of people with passion for land-based livelihoods. It also helped with information during implementation of the project.

By the same token, social facilitation also enabled the members to deal with their problems associated with internal group dynamics. Social facilitation, which included assisting in planning and implementation of the plans, also helped in resolving differences among members, maintaining unity among members, keeping the group focused on its objectives, as well as linking the group with other institutions for further support. Importantly, social facilitation was instrumental in the development and emergence of women's leadership in the project.

The chapter has also shown that Delindlala is one among other group-based land-reform projects that show the contribution of land in the livelihoods of landless people in the former reserves. As pointed out, there have been other cases of operating group-based land-reform projects such as the Nkuzi-supported project in Limpopo. Thus, the sceptical view about group-based land-reform projects overlooks specific cases such as Delindlala, which illustrate the immense contribution such projects make in the lives of the beneficiaries.

References

Aliber, M., Maluleke, T, Manenzhe, T., Paradza, G., & Cousins, B. (2011). *Livelihoods after land reform: Trajectories of change in Limpopo Province, South Africa*. Bellville: Institute for Poverty, Land and Agrarian Studies.

Anseeuw, W., & Mathebula, N. (2008). Evaluating land reform's contribution to South Africa's pro-poor growth pattern. *TIPS Annual Forum: South Africa's economic miracle has the emperor lost his clothes?*

Aston, T.H., & Philpin, C.H.E. (1985). *The Brenner debate. Agrarian class structure and economic development in pre-industrial Europe*. Cambridge: Cambridge University.

Bank, L. (1997). Of livestock and deadstock: Entrepreneurship and tradition on the South African Highveld. In D.F. Brycesson & V. Jamal (Eds.), *Farewell to farms: De-agrarianisation and employment in Africa* (p. 185–202). Hampshire: Ashgate Publishing Ltd.

Beinart, W. (1995). Chieftaincy and the concept of articulation: South Africa circa 1900–50. In Beinart, W. and Dubow, S. (eds.). *Segregation and apartheid in twentieth-century South Africa.* (p. 176–188). New York: Routledge.

Bernstein, A. (2005). *Land Reform in South Africa. A 21st century perspective. Abridged. CDE Research. Policy in the making 14*. Johannesburg: Centre for Enterprise Development.

Borgatta, E., & Borgatta, L. (1992). *Encyclopaedia of sociology* (Volume 4). New York: Macmillan.

Brenner, R. (1976). Agrarian class structure and economic development in pre-industrial Europe. In Aston, T. H. and C.H.E. Philpin. The Brenner debate: Agrarian class structure and economic development in pre-industrial Europe. Cambridge: Cambridge University Press.

Bryceson, D.F. (1997). De-agrarianisation in Sub-Saharan Africa: Acknowledging the inevitable. In D.F. Bryceson & V. Jamal (Eds.) *Farewell to farms: De-agrarianisation and employment in Africa* (p. 1–38). Hampshire: Ashgate Publishing Ltd.

Bundy, C. (1979). *The rise and fall of the South African peasantry*. Cape Town: David Phillip.

Byres, T. (1986). The Agrarian Question, Forms of Capitalist Agrarian Transition and the State: An Essay with Reference to Asia. *Social Scientist* (Nov.–Dec., 1986), *14*(11/12), 3–67.

Byres, T., & Bernstein, H. (2001). From peasant studies to agrarian change. *Journal of Agrarian Change*, (*1*)1, 1–56.

CALUSA Annual Reports (2001, 2002, 2003, 2004, 2006, 2009, 2010).

Chibber, V. (1998). Breaching the Nadu: Lordship and Economic Development in Pre-colonial South India. *Journal of Peasant Studies*, (*26*) 1, 1–42.

Chitonge, H., & Ntsebeza, L. (2012). Land Reform and Rural Livelihood in South Africa: Does access to land matter? *Review of Agrarian Studies* (RAS), (2)1, 87–111.

Cousins, B., & Scoones, I. (2010). Contested paradigms of 'viability' in redistributive land reform: perspectives from southern Africa. *Journal of Peasant Studies*, (*37*)1, 31–66.

Davenport, N. (2008). *The contribution of municipal commonage to local people's livelihoods in small South African towns*. Unpublished Masters Degree Thesis. Grahamstown: Rhodes University

De Kiewiet, C.W. (1936). Social and Economic Developments in Native Tribal Life. Cambridge History of the British Empire. Cambridge: Cambridge University Press.

Dlamini, S. (2008). Taking land reform seriously: From willing seller-willing buyer to expropriation. (Unpublished Master's of Law Degree thesis). University of Cape Town. http://www.publiclaw.uct.ac.za/usr/public_law/LLMPapers/dlamini.pdf. (Accessed on 3/6/2012).

Greenberg S. (2003). Redistribution and access in a market-driven economy. *Development Update*, (*4*)2.

Hall, R. (2008). Land Reform in South Africa: Constructive Aims and Positive Outcomes – Reflecting on Experiences on the Way to 2014. Paper presented in seminar on 26–27 August 2008. Roode Vallei Country Lodge, Pretoria. South Africa.

Hall, R. (2009). Land reform for what? Land use, production and livelihoods. In R. Hall (Ed.). *Another countryside? Policy options for land and agrarian reform in South* Africa (23–62). Bellville: Institute for Poverty, Land and Agrarian Studies.

Hall, R., & Cliffe, L. (2009). *Introduction*. In R. Hall & L. Cliffe (Eds.), *Another countryside? Policy options for land and agrarian reform in South Africa* (1–22). Bellville: Institute for Poverty, Land and Agrarian Studies.

Hammond-Tooke, D. (1993). The roots of black South Africa. Johannesburg: Jonathan Ball Publishers.

Henderson, J. (1927). The Economic Condition of the Native People. *South African Outlook*, (*57*)674, July, 75–77.

Hendricks, F. (1990). *The Pillars of Apartheid. Land tenure, rural planning and the chieftaincy*. Stockholm: UPPSALA, Almqvist and Wiksell International.

Hendricks, F., & Ntsebeza, L. (2004). *Report on the People's Land Tribunal, organised by the Trust for Community Outreach and Education in Port Elizabeth*, December 2003. (Unpublished).

Houghton, H.D. (1955). The place of the Native Reserves in South Africa's changing economy. In H.L. Samuels, H. Houghton, & F.C. Fourie (Eds.), *South Africa's changing* economy (19–35). Johannesburg: South African Institute of Race Relations.

Houghton, D.H., & Dagut, J. (1973). *Source Material on the South African Economy, 1860–1970*. Cape Town: Oxford Paperbacks from South Africa, Vol. 3.

Jacobs, P., Lahiff, E., and Hall, R., (2003). *Land redistribution*. PLAAS. Bellville: An occasional paper series, No. 4.

Johnson, A.G. (2000). *The Blackwell Dictionary of Sociology. A User's Guide to Sociological Language* (2nd edition). Oxford: Blackwell Publishing.

Lahiff, E. (2007a). *Business Models in Land Reform*. University of the Western Cape. Institute for Poverty, Land and Agrarian Studies. Research Report 27.

Lahiff, E. (2007b). *Another Countryside? Policy Options for Land and Agrarian Reform in South Africa*. Conference on 24–25 October 2007, Lord Charles Hotel, Somerset West.

Legassick, M., & Wolpe, H. (1976). The Bantustans and Capital Accumulation in South Africa. *Review of African Political Economy*, (7).

Levin, R., & Neocosmos, M. (1987). Agrarian Struggle in South Africa. Special Edition. *African Perspective: New Series*, (1)5 & 6.

Macmillan, W.M. (1919). *Poverty in South Africa. The South African Agrarian Problem and Its Historical Development* (42–55). Witwatersrand: Central News Agency for the Council of Education.

Makhanya, M. (2012). Apartheid denialism drives a knife into belly of black SA. http://www.timeslive.co.za/opinion/columnists/2012/02/19/apartheid-denialism-drives-a-knife-into-belly-of-black-sa (Accessed on 3/6/2012).

Manona, C. (1999). *De-agrarianisation and the urbanisation of a rural economy: Agrarian patterns in Melani village in the Eastern Cape*. Paper presented in a conference on 'Between town and country: Livelihoods, settlement and identity formation in Sub-Saharan Africa', 27–30 June 1999. East London: Rhodes University Campus.

Maylam, P. (1986). A history of the African people of South Africa: from the Early Iron Age to the 1970s. David Philip: Cape Town.

McMichael, P. (2007). Contesting development. Critical struggles for social change. New York: Routledge.

Ncapayi, F. (2005). *Land Demand and Rural Struggles in Xhalanga, Eastern Cape: Who wants land and for what?* (Unpublished Master's Thesis). Bellville: University of the Western Cape.

Ncapayi, F. (2013). *Land and Changing Social Relations in South Africa's Former Reserves: The case of Luphaphasi in Sakhisizwe Local Municipality, Eastern Cape*. (Unpublished PhD thesis). Department of Sociology, University of Cape Town.

Ndala, L.E. (2009). *The effects of the market-based reform on the agrarian structure: A study of post-independent land reform in Namibia.* Unpublished Masters Degree Thesis. The Hague: International Institute of Social Studies

Nkwinti, G. (2011). Govt needs help with land reform. http://www.fin24.com/Economy/Nkwinti-Govt-needs-help-with-land-reform-20110708 (Accessed on 28/3/2014).

Ntsebeza, L. (2012). *Land and livelihoods in rural South Africa: What prospects for agricultural activities?* Paper presented to the International Conference on 'Dynamics of Rural Transformation in Emerging Economies' held at NASC Complex at Pusa, New Delhi, India, April 14–16.

Ntsebeza, L., & Hendricks, F. (2000). *The paradox of South Africa's Land Reform Policy.* Harare: SARIPS Annual Colloquium.

Umhlaba Rural Services, Agricultural and Rural Development Research Institute and Phuhlisani Solutions. (2010). A review of experiences of establishing emerging farmers in South Africa. Case lessons and implications for farmer support within land reform programmes. http://www.fao.org/docrep/012/i1385e/i1385e.pdf. Accessed 19/1/2018.

Von Mises, L. *Liberalism in the Classical Tradition.* New York: The Foundation for Economic Education.

Wolpe, H. (1972). Capitalism and cheap labour-power in South Africa: from segregation to apartheid. *Economy and Society*, 1(4): 425-456.

CHAPTER 12

'Disrupting Spatial Legacies': Dismantled Game Farms as Success Stories of Land Reform?

Mnqobi Ngubane

Introduction

> Imfuyo [livestock] is life my child. The game reserve must make way for livestock because the game reserve is not beneficial. Recently we erected a fence, but people have cut it severely, because they do not want the game reserve. I want livestock and an end to this [the game reserve], and we should build our homesteads inside the game reserve. We should not be living like this! This place is like a township. My chickens compete with the neighbour's for food, and this might lead to tensions between my neighbour and myself. In the past, when we were living inside the game reserve, we were separated by a considerable distance ... People were forcibly removed from the game reserve and dumped amongst other people to make way for the game reserve. What was invisible will now be visible and what was hidden will be revealed because people have been oppressed, some were dumped along the road [the R33], and their cattle are knocked down by passing-by vehicles.[1]
>
> Ngome Community Member, June 2010

This chapter explores conceptions of success in South Africa's land reform through the lens of dismantled private game farms in the KwaZulu-Natal (KZN) Midlands, against the backdrop of contradictory notions of success in South Africa's land reform since 1994. Dismantled game farms as a result of land reform are an undocumented aspect of land reform in protected areas.[2] The literature in this area of land reform appears focused on land claims

1 The opening quote of this chapter is from an interview with a disgruntled land beneficiary who explicitly expressed that livestock is the preferred land use option instead of Ngome Community Game Reserve.

2 Protected areas are understood here as nature reserves, game parks, game farms, conservancies, etc.

 | DOI 10.1163/9789004362550_013

on protected areas that have given rise to various community-based natural resource management initiatives for the perpetuity of 'nature conservation' as a viable land use. In particular this literature illuminates unequal land rights characterizing community nature conservation land (Ramutsindela, 2002, 2003; Magome & Murombedzi, 2003; Kepe et al., 2003; Kepe, 2004, 2008, 2010; AFRA, 2004; Spierenburg et al., 2008; Walker, 2008; Robins & Van der Walt, 2008, 2010; Ngubane, 2012; Ngubane & Brooks, 2013). Both state and privately owned protected areas are affected by land claims. However, a clear distinction has to be made between land claims on state-protected areas and those on private game farms/nature reserves. These differ significantly on the ground. This chapter is about outcomes of land reform on private game farms in the KZN Midlands, where some private game farms have become community game farms through land reform (Ngubane, 2012; Ngubane & Brooks, 2013). The chapter illuminates that running parallel to the emergence of community game farms in the KZN Midlands has been dismantled game farms, a specter haunting the private wildlife industry. So far, there are only a few cases of dismantled private game farms in the KZN Midlands as a result of land reform. On the other hand, state-protected areas subject to land claims in that province and elsewhere have remained intact after the transfer of land to claimant communities as enforced by the Memorandum of Land Claims on Protected Areas (Ramutsindela, 2002; AFRA, 2004; Meer, 2010).

The chapter suggests that in analysing these outcomes after 23 years of democracy in South Africa, scholars need to take account of deeper meanings of land restitution (Walker, 2008) and to think beyond conventional verdicts of 'failure' and 'success' in land reform. This chapter posits that land reform is not only about economics or an emerging class of black farmers but also about land justice and a sense of landownership for land beneficiaries beyond materialist ideals. That is the main argument of this chapter. Against the backdrop of the perpetuity of community nature conservation as an ideal in settling land claims on nature conservation land, this ideal of 'nature conservation in perpetuity' is inseparable from the current large-scale agriculture model promoted in land reform (Aliber & Cousins, 2013, Lahiff, 2009). Both are part of a very powerful discourse focused on 'rural development' for 'rural employment' creation as touted by current land and agricultural ministries and supported by the private sector, as well as foistered on the rural landscape by the local rural ruling elite (Ngubane, 2012; Ngubane & Brooks, 2013).

These outcomes are analysed here in the context of the history that occurred: the racialised forced removals of blacks in many parts of the country during past undemocratic regimes (Carruthers, 2008; Ramutsindela, 2002;

Platsky & Walker, 1985). For the KZN Midlands, where the fieldwork was conducted, forced removals for private game farming was mainly orchestrated by white farmers, especially on labour-tenant farms converted from mainly cattle farms to game farming from the 1960s (Brooks et al., 2008, 2011). Through land reform, some of these private game farms have become community game farms, but it appears that land beneficiaries have no sense of landownership in these community game farms. Community trustees (the rural ruling elite) and the private wildlife industry appear to be the main beneficiaries of community game farms and not land beneficiaries themselves (Ngubane, 2012; Ngubane & Brooks, 2013). This chapter therefore provides a perspective on those situations where community game farms have been dismantled for the benefit of the rightful beneficiaries, who would have otherwise been rendered landless should the land have remained 'nature conservation land', under the rhetoric of 'community-based natural resource management' (Magome & Murombedzi 2003, p. 116).

The chapter shows that land beneficiaries have gained access to land for 'communal grazing' (Cousins, 1999) and other natural resources such as streams, firewood, etc., and more importantly access to land for settlement. In contrast, these land rights are prohibited in other community nature conservation areas such as Dwesa-Cwebe and Mkambati Nature Reserve in the Eastern Cape (Ntshona et al., 2010; Fay, 2007; Kepe, 2004), and for the Makuleke community that 'owns' a portion of Kruger National Park (Reid, 2001; Ramutsindela, 2002; Spierenburg et al., 2008).

Land beneficiaries of dismantled game farms in the KZN Midlands of South Africa see these outcomes as clear successes in terms of land restitution and land justice, but the elite in these communities hold contrasting views, as they have internalised the ideals of 'modernism', 'rural development', and 'employment creation',[3] romanticising the idea of community nature conservation in perpetuity. The specter of dismantled game farms in the KZN Midlands counters these dominant discourses, which are part and parcel of powerful discourses in the wider South African land-reform debate about what constitutes success in land reform. At least for the land beneficiaries studied here, these outcomes are much closer to their ideals as people living in rural areas: having enough land for settlement, communal grazing, and access to natural resources.

3 These are some of the concepts used by community trustees and community nature conservation advocates legitimising and bolstering the perpetuity of an imposed and fixed idea of community nature conservation for claimants of nature conservation land.

Furthermore, I observe that these outcomes have led to significant increases in livestock (cattle, goats, sheep, chickens, ducks) for the occupants since the game farms were dismantled. These findings seem to suggest that certain levels of disruption should be allowed in South Africa's land reform for land justice, which may inevitably lead to other just outcomes such as access to land to accumulate livestock for land beneficiaries, which would have been impossible if the land had remained a community game farm as shown by other cases elsewhere in the country. Overall, the chapter charts a path for further research into the lives of people living on dismantled game farms, as more private game farms are dismantled as a result of land reform in the KZN Midlands. For example, 6 private game farms had been dismantled in the KZN Midlands within a 50km radius at the time of writing this chapter. So far research has been conducted on only 2 of these dismantled game farms. More research is needed in all dismantled game farms to show how livelihoods have changed since these community game farms were dismantled, against the backdrop of what constitutes success in land reform.

Background

The main reason there are land claims on nature conservation land in South Africa today is the fact that there were racially based forced removals of black people from land 'earmarked' (Ramutsindela, 2003) as nature conservation land, beginning in the colonial era (Carruthers, 2008) and intensified during apartheid (particularly from the 1960s on) and reached a peak point in the 1990s (Cousins, Sadler, & Evans, 2008; Hofmeyr, 2002). As stated in the introduction, land claims have been lodged on both state and private protected areas, illuminating a history of forced removals for nature conservation countrywide, and in many parts of the world (Ramutsindela, 2003; Kepe, 2008). My concern in this chapter is with regard to people forcibly removed from private livestock farms on the eve of conversion to private game farming. As stated above, since the 1960s an increasing number of livestock private farms were converted to wildlife enterprises in many parts of the country (Carruthers, 2008). These conversions had adverse implications for labour tenants (or farm dwellers) living on these farms, often in the form of forced relocation (Brooks et al., 2011; Cousins, Sadler, & Evans, 2008; Brooks et al., 2008; Hofmeyr, 2002). Much the same can be said about the studied victims of forced removals for the creation of Bhambatha's Kraal game farm in 1972 (which became Ngome Community Game Reserve in 1997) and Khobotho game reserve in 1982 (Ngubane, 2012; Ngubane & Brooks, 2013). This chapter is based on research conducted on these two neighbouring community game farms in the KZN Midlands, which were acquired through land reform and dismantled on two separate instances.

Ngome Community Game Reserve was acquired in 1997 and dismantled in 2013. The neighbouring Khobotho game reserve was acquired in 2007 and dismantled in the same year, shortly after it was acquired through a labour tenant claim (Ngubane, 2012; Ngubane & Brooks, 2013). Both land beneficiary communities are the so-called Zondi community of Ngome associated with the legendary Zondi chief, Bhambatha Ka Mancinza Zondi, who engaged colonial authorities in the so-called Bhambatha Rebellion of 1906 (Guy, 2005). Initial research was conducted on Ngome Community Game Reserve in 2010 for my Master of Arts in Geography dissertation (Ngubane, 2012), which found a neighbouring dismantled Khobotho game reserve coincidentally. This changed the research towards thinking about the implications of dismantled game farms at their interface with professional 'nature conservation discourses' and 'dominant land-reform models' in South Africa. I then continued fieldwork on the dismantled Khobotho Game Reserve in 2012. These were occasional fieldwork trips until the neighbouring Ngome Community Game Reserve was dismantled in 2013 by its own beneficiaries, with their bare hands, out of anger at the lack of benefits from a community game farm that was acquired in 1997. I went to witness this myself, and took photographs of the dismantled infrastructure and what was left of a community game farm that was. Since then I have embarked on comparative research (which I admit requires a longitudinal study of over, say, 10 years, a point to which I return below) between the dismantled Ngome Community Game Reserve and Khobotho game reserve. The former had not been resettled by the time of writing this chapter, a point to which I return to below in relation to access to communal grazing. The latter had 14 households at the time of writing this chapter, 9 of whom were returnee former labour tenant households who were forcibly removed for the creation of Khobotho game reserve in 1982;[4] the other 2 households were landless people who sought access to land for settlement via the Zondi traditional authority.[5]

Subsequently both dismantled game farms function as communal grazing land for livestock (cattle, goats, and sheep) and also offer access to other common natural resources such as water, firewood, and thatch grass. The evidence presented in this chapter shows that livestock numbers of people living in that part of Ngome increased quite substantially after the two game farms were

4 Only 3 households remained in Khobotho game reserve for their labour.

5 The Zondi traditional authority has been instrumental in claiming land in that part of KZN Midlands and subsequent 'rural development' thereafter (see Ngubane, 2012).

dismantled.[6] However, perhaps such evidence is insufficient to make claims about 'accumulation from below' (Mamdani, 1987; Cousins, 2013) – perhaps only a longitudinal study over (say 5–10 years) may substantiate such claims. But, in my view, processes of accumulation from below are evident; at least in the context of obtaining income from selling livestock in the informal market after increases in both goat and cattle herds, after the community game farms were dismantled.

Land Restitution Outcomes on Nature Conservation Land in South Africa

The following quote illuminates forced removals of people for nature conservation on a world scale, and the particular racialised discrimination this process entailed in South Africa, and how legal land restitution attempts are underway in that relatively young democracy.

> It must be pointed out that the Restitution Act does not specify the type of land or areas that could be subjected to land claims. The Act is concerned with all victims of racially motivated removals in both urban and rural areas, these include people who were removed from areas earmarked for national parks and nature reserves. Such removals are not unique to South Africa – they form a strand in the history of nature conservation in many parts of the world.
>
> RAMUTSINDELA, 2003, p. 43

In South Africa, forced removals for 'nature conservation' were not only orchestrated by state-controlled nature conservation authorities but also by private game farmers on private farms converted to game farming (Ngubane & Brooks, 2013; Cousins, Sadler, & Evans, 2008; Carruthers, 2008; Hofmeyr, 2002). However, much of the literature on land claims on nature conservation areas focuses on state protected areas, and seldom on private game farms. Nonetheless institutional dynamics and politics in the settlement of such land claims are similar: land rights are contested in both accounts, often prohibiting settlement and agricultural land uses for land beneficiaries (Lahiff, 2009; Walker, 2008; AFRA, 2004; Ramutsindela, 2002). Some scholars and land

6 See Ngubane (2012) for land beneficiaries' complaints about barred grazing rights in Ngome Community Game Reserve before it was dismantled.

rights NGOs have been questioning the manner in which land claims on nature conservation land are settled, often citing the marginalisation of land beneficiaries as a major contradiction to the unfolding of the land restitution processes on nature conservation land (Ramutsindela, 2002; Kepe, 2004, 2008, 2010; Magome & Murombedzi, 2003; AFRA, 2004; Walker, 2008; Spierenburg et al., 2008; Lahiff, 2009). The Association for Rural Advancement (AFRA) has been a very useful reference to these issues, particularly for their action research in KwaZulu-Natal.

According to Walker (2008, p. 215) 'a substantial proportion of land that has been restituted in KwaZulu-Natal and the Northern Province (Limpopo) in particular, is [nature] conservation land, which in terms of current restitution policy is to remain designated as protected areas, hence not legally available for use by claimants for residential or agricultural purposes'. Lahiff (2009, p. 98) draws similar conclusions: 'much of the land transferred (or 'delivered', to use the official term) under the restitution programme has been transferred in nominal ownership only, as it remains incorporated into nature reserves and state forests and, in terms of restitution agreements, it is not accessible for direct use by restored owners'.

Furthermore Maano Ramutsindela's analysis of land claims on nature conservation land also illuminates the marginalization of land beneficiaries' land rights in the settlement of land claims on nature conservation land. Ramutsindela's work on the Makuleke, who claimed part of Kruger National Park, is one of many examples throughout the country where land beneficiaries have limited land rights on nature conservation land. Ramutsindela in particular draws our attention to this irony in relation to the Makuleke community who claimed part of the Kruger National Park: 'The compromise reached between the South African National Parks (including state departments) and the Makuleke in 1998 was that the Makuleke could claim restoration of land rights in the Pafuri on condition that they use the area for ecotourism (conservation in general) … To a large extent, the settlement of the Makuleke land claim … does not effectively address racial landownership patterns' (Ramutsindela 2002, p. 22). Similar conclusions were reached by Magome and Murombedzi (2003) in their analysis of the same Makuleke land claim on a portion of Kruger National Park. They observe that 'local people are expected to trade off their short term livelihood needs against long term survival of wildlife, to tolerate their conflict with wildlife, and, in the extreme form, to endorse Western conservation ideals' (Magome & Murombedzi 2003, p. 116). The chapter suggests that this could remain the case as long as the beneficiaries of nature conservation land do not have a sense of ownership on community nature conservation land they supposedly own, and as long as their land remains in the hands of nature conservation authorities and the local ruling elite. Land justice could remain meaningless to them.

During the Land Divided[7] conference held at the University of Cape Town in March 2013, this irony was illuminated in one of the plenary sessions where a land activist for land rights of people claiming Dwesa Cwebe Nature Reserve (located in the Eastern Cape province of South Africa) spoke strongly against the 'myth of community nature conservation' against the backdrop of land rights.[8] As the Makuleke, and other claimants of nature conservation land elsewhere in the country, the claimants of Dwesa Cwebe do not have settlement and other land rights such as agriculture (Ntshona et al., 2010; Fay, 2007). Similarly, and based on work on Mkambathi nature reserve, Kepe et al. (2003, p. 14) confirm that 'while they may have won their land rights on paper, in practice local communities are often at the mercy of conservation agencies who tend to pursue conservation goals and the prevention of consumptive use of natural resources at all costs'. Such denial of land rights and marginalisation of land beneficiaries was central to the sentiments of the land activist that spoke at the Land Divided conference, and in vignettes of disgruntled beneficiaries of Ngome Community Game Reserve presented in this chapter.

In the wildlife industry, nature conservationists, game farmers, professional and leisure hunters, hunting associations, and their (stalwart) supporting agencies and followers[9] have been unsurprisingly challenged by land claims on nature conservation land in terms of land claims on high-value agricultural land. For many, this reality, brought about by a wave of democracy, has put their livelihoods at stake, and of course their histories and identities, which took decades (if not centuries) to construct, imprint, and foister onto the rural landscape, creating spatial legacies with the support of previous undemocratic regimes. Of course they had to do something about land claims in defense of their legacies, otherwise all that they stand for would be eroded by a wave of democracy. Strategic decisions of political expediency have been taken in closed circles consisting of mainly officials (the black elite in particular), and there has been very little community engagement beyond rhetoric (Hart, 2002,

7 The 2013 Land Divided conference marked a 100-year anniversary of the passing of the notorious Land Act of 1913 – a piece of legislation instrumental in the land dispossession of blacks in South Africa.

8 See Fay, 2007; Kepe, 2008; Ntshona et al., 2010 for detailed accounts of the political intricacies of the Dwesa-Cwebe land claim.

9 This refers to those elites that wield most power in rural areas – the dominant classes in agrarian structures.

2014). Nonetheless, in the context of land claims on nature conservation land, it seems these closed circles discuss very little beyond referring to existing models of community-based natural resource management templates as fixed land-use models imposed on beneficiaries of nature conservation land (Ngubane, 2012). Blueprint success in these cases is simply the perpetuity of nature conservation as a viable land-use as imprinted in policy documents of settling land claims on state protected nature conservation land in South Africa (Ramutsindela, 2002; Magome & Murombedzi, 2003; Kepe, 2004). Uniform definition of success has been applied in settling land claims on private game reserves throughout the country.

Very often community management structures are created between community trustees (or community representatives) and nature conservation officials to manage nature conservation land after a successful land claim (Reid, 2001; Ramutsindela, 2002; Magome & Murombedzi, 2003; Kepe, 2004, 2008; Walker, 2008; Robins & Van der Waldt, 2008, 2011; Ngubane & Brooks, 2013). As Kepe (2008, p. 312) notes: 'Following the settlement of almost all land claims on South Africa's protected areas, co-management arrangements have been created between the relevant conservation authorities and the successful land claimants. It is important to note that even though some officials involved in the management of protected areas that are affected by land claims prefer to use concepts such as joint-management and claimant participation, rather than co-management; in policy and in practice there is no difference among these' (Kepe 2008, p. 312).

Indeed, co-management arrangements on nature conservation land affected by land claims take many forms and are associated with skills transfer and mentorship programmes for land beneficiaries, for a set period, after which land beneficiaries are expected to operate their community nature conservation areas on their own. Administratively 'this policy aims to combine formal claimant ownership of protected areas with the continued conservation status of their land, by means of partnerships between claimant entities and national or provincial conservation agencies' (Walker 2008, p. 110). Furthermore, co-management partnerships also include private hunting associations that partner with beneficiary communities for skills transfer (Ngubane & Brooks, 2013), and appear to have drawn some inspiration from strategic partnerships or joint ventures in land-reform cases involving high-value agricultural land (Lahiff, 2009). However, as Walker states, 'whether ownership without rights of settlement will be felt to constitute redress is another question' (Walker 2008, p. 221). These questions arise against the backdrop of no sign of land justice for land claimants in the settlement of land claims on nature conservation land (Ramutsindela, 2002; Magome & Murombedzi, 2003; AFRA, 2004; Kepe, 2004, 2008; Ngubane & Brooks, 2013). In reporting about the KZN Midlands,

Ngubane and Brooks (2013) document the lack of benefits for beneficiaries of community game farms.

Similar conclusions were drawn by Meer (2010) in her analysis of land invasions on a community game reserve, Ndumo in northern KZN. Furthermore, Ngubane and Brooks note that it is rather unrealistic to expect small private game farms, previously used as leisure homes for the benefit of the owner and his family, to benefit a community of 500 land beneficiaries. It is clear that communities are not benefiting from community nature conservation regardless of the size of the nature conservation enterprises from which they are supposed to derive some form of benefit or income. For example, one would imagine that the Makulekes are deriving major benefits from Kruger National Park given its size; however, that may not be the case (Ramutsindela, 2002; Magome & Murombedzi, 2003). For land claimants, land rights and land justice cannot be simply reduced to pecuniary terms; land justice is far more important than financial compensation for land. Land is also about identity and dignity (Kepe, 2004; Walker, 2008) not just about deriving income through the sale of agricultural commodities or tourism experiences.

The literature on land claims on nature conservation areas has been critical of forced removals of blacks for nature conservation in the first place (Platsky & Walker, 1985), and also exposed the marginalisation of land rights of claimant communities in the settlement of land claims on nature conservation land (Lahiff, 2009; Walker, 2008; AFRA, 2004; Ramutsindela, 2002). In response, this chapter provides evidence that counters dominant models of settling claims on nature conservation land. The next section illuminates what it has meant for land beneficiaries to dismantle a game farm. In this instance, beneficiaires were well aware of the dynamics of community nature conservation, since they had experienced it and had witnessed what happened to their neighbours (the example of the people of Ngome in KZN Midlands, who dismantled two community game farms, Ngome Community Game Reserve and Khobotho game reserve, two adjacent private game farms they had received through land reform, respectively).

'Disrupting Spatial Legacies': Dismantled Game Farms as Successful Stories of Land Reform

The disruption of the spatial legacies[10] of pre-colonial Africa has arguably been finalised by colonial and post-colonial spatial legacies from above (see

10 The notion of 'disrupting spatial legacies' was adapted from a conversation I had with Maano Ramutsindela in preparation for the South African Geographical Society conference

for example Beinart, 2001). Forced removals for the creation of state owned and private game farms have disrupted black communities and their historical legacies. Reversing this history will thus require some level of disruption, hence the question: are dismantled game farms successful stories of land reform? This question probes the notion of success in land-reform narratives against the backdrop of the 'failure rhetoric' characterising the South African land-reform process. Success, it seems, is more associated with the perpetuity of land use, fixed, as it was under the previous owner, the willing seller. Anything other than that is deemed a failure within the dominant large-scale commercial farming model (Aliber & Cousins, 2013; Hebinck, Fay, & Kondlo, 2011). Seemingly the ideal of continuation with land use in the case of high value commercial agricultural land has been a useful framework in settling land claims on nature conservation land for its proponents (Ngubane & Brooks, 2013; Ngubane, 2012, 2009; Lahiff, 2009).

This chapter tells a story of dismantled game farms, a counter-narrative to the perpetuity of game farming/nature conservation often propagated in land-reform circles. Unlike elsewhere (Ramutsindela, 2002; Magome & Murombedzi, 2003; Robins & Van der Waldt, 2008, 2011; Kepe, 2008, 2010), the land beneficiaries under study dismantled their community game farms. In the case of Khobotho game reserve, this transpired after the ministry of land failed to pay for the wildlife on the property, which led to the culling of most of the wildlife (best described as a heartless shooting spree[11]), conducted by the previous owner himself (Ngubane, 2012). The unintended benefit of this deliberate shooting spree was that it allowed land-reform beneficiaries to choose which form of land use would appear preferrable in terms of benefitting the land beneficiaries themselves (Ngubane & Brooks, 2013).

However, it is noteworthy that, when it became clear that Khobotho game reserve was to be dismantled, the ministry of land and agriculture advised cattle ranching as a viable socio-economic activity on the land and promised to establish livestock auction markets in the area to facilitate market access. However, none of these promises had materialised at the time of writing this chapter. Erstwhile land beneficiaries have been settling back and establishing themselves on their own, without any form of support from the state. Those who have accumulated significant numbers of livestock over the years have

---

at the University of Fort Hare in June 2014. Spatial legacies are understood here as those geographical imprints on the landscape illuminating manifestations of power and identity in particular moments of historical formation (see Ekers, M.; Hart, G.; Kipfer, S.; & Loftus, A. (2013) *Gramsci: Space, Nature and Politics*).

11 It is ironic and contradictory that Ezemvelo KZN Wildlife, a provincial nature conservation authority, would grant such 'a shooting spree permit' in light of animal rights.

done so purely on their own, along with the assistance of other livestock owners in the area with regard to everyday issues such as dipping and fencing. Furthermore, land beneficiaries have recently resorted to contributing personal funds towards the purchasing of fencing to control their livestock – a point which I return to below (see Case 1). Since 2009, 14 households have settled back onto the dismantled Khobotho, their ancestral land.[12] Furthermore, there were 6 clearly marked sites for returning households who had not yet settled there, at the time of writing this chapter. However, not many households keep livestock, as some people are engaged in off-farm employment elsewhere, whilst some are farm workers in nearby timber plantations. Nonetheless, livestock keeping and access to land are the major reasons to settle back on the land for many, including new entrants, some of whom were landless people who negotiated access to land through the traditional council. In order to draw the reader into some detail of the lives of the returning households and what it has meant for them to return, I draw on two vignettes: a relatively well-established household that returned in 2009 and a relatively new household that returned in 2013. Case 1 presents the first vignette, which is about a household head from one of the returnee households who is currently unemployed, but has seen some improvement since settling back on the land. The second vignette, Case 2, is about another household head who has more recently settled back onto the dismantled Khobotho. He is also very keen on livestock keeping as a socio-economic activity in light of unemployment.

> **Case 1: Returnee Household on the Dismantled Khobotho Game Farm**
> Since his return in 2009, Mr X has seen major changes in his homestead; he has accumulated livestock (cattle, nguni sheep, goats, ducks, and free-range chickens) over the past 5 years. His situation is much better than previously, when he worked as a farm worker under labour tenant settings, since eviction in 1982 from the cattle farm that became Khobotho Game Reserve, where he grew up in a labour tenant household. He views livestock as an important source of income and has dedicated his time on a daily, full-time basis to this activity. He therefore has the most number of livestock in the community and has been instrumental in fence erection, which he and other men that live on the dismantled game farm have jointly purchased to revamp camps on their farm for cattle ranching. As

12 These families have a history of labour tenancy in the KZN Midlands, which became one of very few options available to access land by the Zondi clan, after Bhambatha was conquered in 1906 (Guy, 2005).

noted in this chapter, land beneficiaries have resorted to erecting the fence on their own after unmet promises from the land and agricultural ministries to assist occupants in venturing into so-called cattle ranching.

Case 2: Returnee Household on the Dismantled Khobotho Game Reserve

Unlike Mr X, referred to above, Mr Y's household has recently returned (in 2013) after decades of labour tenancy in KZN Midlands (Kranskop farming area). This particular household was amongst many that was forcibly removed for the creation of Khobotho Game Reserve in 1982 and found refuge on a labour tenant farm, which they left in 2013 to settle on the dismantled Khobotho game farm. At the time of writing this chapter, Mr Y was planning to go and collect his cattle from the labour tenant farm on which he had been residing for the past 31 years. He hopes that by returning to his ancestral land, his livestock herd will accumulate and supplement his wife's income, a farm worker in timber plantations, and the only breadwinner in the family. For Mr Y, the land restitution process has certainly raised hopes for a new life, better than what he had previously as a labour tenant whose livestock accumulation was restricted to specific herd numbers, living on a labour tenant farm. As other (unemployed) men residing on the dismantled Khobotho, he is very keen on livestock keeping as a livelihood option.

These outcomes have been quite different to other land restitution outcomes where private game farms have been transferred to land beneficiaries, in KZN Midlands and elsewhere, and even more so in state-protected areas subject to land claims (Ramutsindela, 2002; Kepe, 2008).

Furthermore, in illustration, I will draw on a controversial story of Ngome Community Game Reserve (a neighbour of the dismantled Khobotho Game Reserve, separated by a fence), which had contentiously operated as a community game farm since 1997 (Ngubane & Brooks, 2013; Ngubane, 2012; Umhlaba Wethu, 2012), and was therefore unsurprisingly dismantled in 2013. On 6 June 2012, an agricultural industry magazine entitled *Farmers Weekly* quoted myself as predicting a possible land invasion of Ngome Community Game Reserve by its own beneficiaries.[13]

Of course my commentary followed at least 5 years of attentive observation of the debate and research on land claims on nature conservation land; hence

13 http://www.farmersweekly.co.za/news.aspx?id=23396&h=Beneficiaries-invade-own-land-on-land-reform-game-farms.

I concluded elsewhere (Ngubane 2012, p. 186) that 'somewhat unnoticed, land invasions and unrest on nature conservation land have been taking place in the country, for example, at Dwesa Cwebe Nature Reserve (Ntshona et al., 2010) and Mkambati Nature Reserve in the Eastern Cape (Kepe, 2004); Dukuduku forest (Sundnes, 2011) and more recently in Ndumo Game Reserve (Meer, 2010) in northern KZN and Mapungubwe in Limpopo (Maano Ramutsindela, personal communication, 22 August 2011)'. Furthermore such commentary followed a detailed study conducted by myself (Ngubane, 2012), documenting strong community resentment and resistance towards Ngome Community Game Reserve in KZN Midlands due to the lack of benefits from the community game farm, fueled by everyday struggles over new fencing, which encroached onto 'communal rangeland' (Cousins, 1999) and other natural resource commons such as water and firewood, infringing on the land rights of land beneficiaries. The following quote is from an interview in Ngome to illuminate the lack of benefits emanating from Ngome Community Game Reserve, resulting in strong community resentment. The quoted land beneficiary insisted that his full name[14] be used for this research, illuminating a strong sense of resentment towards the community game farm to the point of readiness for confrontation:

> Write this down, I [anonymous] am not benefiting from the game reserve and have given up of ever receiving any benefits. It has been here for years and years, I'm turning grey now. Previously it benefited Abelungu (the white previous owners); that is before the land was transferred to black people. Back then, the previous owners benefited from hunters and so did the staff, depending on what was offered to them by the hunters. At the end of the hunting season the previous owners would slaughter a cow for them, and in some cases make some offerings of any form. But they did not say it was revenue from the game reserve that made such offerings possible. This was so when the game reserve was still under white control. But since its transfer to black ownership, I do not see anything positive. You will see the lodge that remains unutilised – it was built by funding for Ngome community. We have not seen any benefits! I have not seen any benefits, for example there is no structure such as a clinic that was constructed through funding that came from the game reserve. Nor there is a school, nor preschool built in courtesy of the game reserve. It is a community game reserve by name ... But nobody can say: *'Look my son, here are the trousers I purchased with money I*

14 Nonetheless, for ethical reasons the author chose to record the interview as anonymous.

> *received from the game reserve, here is the house built in courtesy of the game reserve and look at what I have done for my child, with the help of the game reserve'.* The game reserve has not helped me in anyway; it has not purchased a sack of maize meal for my household. The game reserve is in operation, hunters come and go, but we do not know what happens to the money.
>
> Ngome Community Member, June 2010, cited in Umhlaba Wethu 14. 2012

The lack of benefits from Ngome Community Game Reserve and further marginalisation of land beneficiaries evoked wrath on the part of community members (see Ngubane & Brooks, 2013; Ngubane, 2012) to the point of resorting to utilizing 'weapons of the weak' (Scott, 1986), manifest in the cutting of the community game reserve fence since 2010 (Ngubane, 2012). The new fencing and extension of the community game farm (which begun in 2010) was seen as a threat to communal rangeland and other natural resources such as water and firewood. This may have been exacerbated by the fact that land beneficiaries of Ngome Community Game Reserve were not allowed to settle on the community game farm in the first place, as well as being further aggravated by evictions from the same community game reserve that were orchestrated by the community trust against land beneficiaries in 2003 (see Ngubane, 2012). Such anger has subsequently led to further disintegration of Ngome Community Game Reserve, characterised by manifestations of anger to the point of, what the state police and the 'formal legal system' would narrowly deem, vandalism of infrastructure. The lodge, chalets, and other luxuries have all been hammered and smashed since 2013, invoking images of what happened in the neighbouring Khobotho soon after it was dismantled in 2007, and a clear message to authorities or the rural elite.

The crux of Ngome Community Game Reserve controversy was a fierce battle between community representatives (the community trust in particular) and the land beneficiaries. The latter felt that the traditional authority was imposing itself on the land issue (Ngubane & Brooks, 2013; Ngubane, 2012; Umhlaba Wethu, 2012). This conflict lies at the heart of the debate about the role of traditional authorities in land reform (Ntsebeza, 2005; Oomen, 2005; Mathis, 2007). In Ngome, the traditional authority and the community trust are inseparable, and have been instrumental in infiltrating neoliberal community nature conservation ideals (Magome & Murombedzi, 2003) as viable land-uses in the context of land reform for 'rural development' (Brooks & Ngubane, 2013; Ngubane, 2012). However, on the ground, this role of chiefs in rural development has been fiercely challenged and has met with strong community resistance over the years since Ngome Community Game Reserve was created in

1997 (ibid.), which culminated in what is left of the remnants of a community game farm that was.

Whilst the land beneficiaries of the dismantled Ngome Community Game Reserve decide what to do with the dismantled community game farm, goats and cattle roam freely. The roaming of livestock in a dismantled game farm invoked a seminar about the same community game farm, Ngome Community Game Reserve, hosted by the Institute for Poverty, Land and Agrarian Studies (PLAAS) at the University of the Western Cape on 31 May 2012. There, Benjamin Cousins, an expert of agrarian studies and common resources in particular, who knows the Ngome area quite well, expressed that the geography, landscape, and ecology of the study area is more suitable for livestock, and goats in particular. In his comments, he seemed unsurprised by land beneficiaries' resentment towards the encroachment of the community game farm onto communal grazing land and other natural resources such as water and firewood (see Cousins, 1999). In responding to his comments, I expressed that indeed goats and cattle are important for land beneficiaries in the study area, and pointed out that in fact some informants referred to the importance of livestock and natural resources on their livelihoods. It is therefore perhaps indisputable that livestock herds (goats and cattle in particular) will increase since both neighbouring game farms were dismantled. Evidence from both Ngome cases sustains this view.

In another PLAAS seminar (23 August 2012) entitled *'Dismantled game farms in the KZN Midlands'*, Maano Ramutsindela, an expert on land claims in nature conservation areas, cautioned that it might be too early to judge this a successful case and recommended a longitudinal study to sustain my claims. Consequently, in following Maano Ramutsindela's advice, my claims were confirmed by recent fieldwork in 2013 and 2014 respectively, which confirms that the emerging trend of dismantled game farms in KZN Midlands is indeed a success story of land reform for reasons outlined in this chapter.[15]

Some land beneficiaries expressed that the restoration of land-use rights in the dismantled game farms is tantamount to the pre-colonial era by virtue of accessing enough land for livestock keeping, human settlement, and crop cultivation. Such reference to the pre-colonial era invokes a particular localized history of the study area. Take for example the previous name of Ngome Community Game Reserve, Bhambatha's Kraal. In relation to this, Ngubane (2012, p. 82) remarks that 'it is perhaps ironic that the game farm was named Bhambatha's Kraal – referring to the legacy of the legendary Zondi chief

15 But I do admit that a longitudinal study, over ten years for example, is necessary, as stated in the background section of this chapter.

who opposed British authority in the so-called Bhambatha Rebellion of 1906 (see Guy, 2005), – while at the same time developing an exclusive private game preserve which no longer had a place for Bhambatha's people'. Ngubane explains that 'possibly the idea of developing a cultural tourism attraction played a role in the choice of name (increasingly, battlefields tourism has been a money-spinner in KwaZulu-Natal province)' (Ngubane 2012, p. 82). The spirit of Bhambatha was also invoked in marketing for Ngome Community Game Reserve, for example, in referring to phase one of the construction of a new lodge, *The Witness* reported[16] that 'visitors to the lodge will get a tourism experience linked closely with the famous Bhambatha Rebellion – in which Bhambatha kaMancinza [Zondi] led an uprising against the poll tax in 1906'.

Nonetheless, the specter of dismantled game farms in Ngome draws our attention to deeper meanings of land restitution (Walker, 2008) for land justice, against the backdrop of Bhambatha's legacy, a rebel hero who led a rebellion against the marginalisation of black people on their land. His reward then was a brutal murder by British colonialists (Guy, 2005). That was 1906; since then, Bhambatha's people, the Zondi clan have experienced exacerbated marginalisation, which can be best described as an 'arch of dispossession' (Hart & Hunter, 2004), which culminated in forced removals of labour tenants for private wildlife ranching in the 1970s and 1980s. This was followed by the incorporation of successive 'modern' Zondi chiefs into 'neoliberal community nature conservation' ideals (Magome & Murombedzi, 2003) imposed on Bhambatha's people after 1994,[17] and then forced removals of Bhambatha's people from Ngome community Game Reserve, orchestrated by the Zondi chief and other community game farming proponents (the local ruling elite in particular) in 2003 (see Ngubane, 2012), and finally the resistance of Bhambatha'a people against these injustices manifest in the cutting of the community game reserve fence since 2010 (ibid.) and final disintegration of Ngome Community Game Reserve in 2013. One would be forgiven imagining a depressed game farmer wondering whether the specter of dismantled game farms that haunted the private wildlife industry in the context of Ngome and Bhambatha's people was not the spirit of Bhambatha himself, an ancestral militant chief who rebelled against colonial state authority (Guy, 2005).

The disruption of spatial legacies referred to in the title of this chapter illuminates deeper sentiments of land restitution for land justice beyond

16 http://www.news24.com/Archives/Witness/Community-to-develop-lodge-20150430.

17 This may have been influenced by the role of iNkosi Mangosuthu Buthelezi as a 'champion' of nature conservation in many parts of Zululand under his 'controversial' reign as Prime Minister (see Draper, 1998; Ngubane, 2010).

conventional verdicts of what constitutes success in land reform. Clearly the disruption of so-called community game farms in Ngome is arguably tantamount to the restoration of the lost pre-colonial spatial legacies (see Guy, 2005; Beinart, 2001) of land in abundance, obtainable through access to land for settlement, crop cultivation, and livestock keeping, a simple rural life complemented by trade and labour in various markets, beyond unrealistic models of community game farming imposed on land beneficiaries by authorities.

The Myth of 'Nature Conservation' in Private Game Farming: Implications for Farm Dwellers

It is important for the reader to note that the dismantled private game farms under study were mere hunting operations and were thus implicitly not about nature conservation but about the pleasure of the male hunter with his rifle, and of course the accumulation of capital. Nonetheless nature conservation narratives are often evoked to serve particular strategic needs, mainly associated with profit-making in these hunting operations. To illustrate, I draw from an interview with a professional hunter and proponent of community game farming or 'community conservation areas' on private game farms subject to land claims, who has this to say:

> We – until now, we were essentially a hunting association, but we call ourselves KZN Hunting and Conservation. The conservation up till now was isolated activities. Our approach is new now. We say the concept of conservation per se is outdated. We need to manage biodiversity. What does conservation mean? I think it's a term that has reached the end of its time. We have to look at the total environmental systems and we have to manage that. It is essential that we hunt here, because it is a fenced area and it's an isolated animal population, so there will be growth beyond the carrying capacity. It is expensive to relocate, to catch and relocate and release somewhere else. So we have to manage the excess numbers. The best way to manage and to generate funds is via the hunting tool. But hunting is not the first and foremost thing we want to do. For us to be able to harvest the impala – it must have land to live on, it must have food, it must have water, it must have shelter. All those systems to make this a viable entity must be managed. We must look at the earth in its totality. We can't look at individual elements. That is what we want to teach the people. That is the message we want to get across.
>
> KZNHCA Official, July 2010, cited in Ngubane 2012, p. 147

The above quote is somewhat convincing, but it is also important to consider the fact that most of the species that were contained in the private game farms studied were imported from elsewhere, and even from abroad – these were not endangered indigenous species that had to be saved from extinction. Furthermore, it is important to consider the fact that the farms that were converted to private game farms, at least in the KZN Midlands, perhaps could not even qualify to be protected in the context of critical nature conservation, since many of them were labour tenant farms located in the 'thornveld' regions of the KZN Midlands, and most importantly they were inhabited by people. Soon before or after the farms were converted to game farming, (new) private owners swiftly moved-in to forcibly remove farm dwellers, making way for imported wildlife species, transported in by 'game-in-transition trucks' to serve the dream of game farmers, their farm managers, and a trigger-happy male clientele. Some game farms are unprofitable beyond the hunting season, leading to managers thinking on their feet and switching to eco-tourism rhetoric in summer and hiding their rifles. One of the previous managers of the former Bhambatha's kraal game farm admitted to this, further exposing the myth of 'nature conservation' in private game farming.

Overall, and more importantly, black communities should not suffer at the expense of serving unrealistic nature conservation myths and pipe dreams. Their resistance to this will obviously remain and erupt until (land) justice is served. Land beneficiaries of the dismantled Khobotho were fortunate that the private game farm they claimed was dismantled by coincidence due to financial constraints on the part of the Ministry of Land. On the other hand, Ngome Community Game Reserve was dismantled by land beneficiaries themselves, with their bare hands, who revolted against the community game reserve due to the lack of benefits emanating from it, and for other political reasons, as this chapter has shown.

Conclusion

A clear message illuminated by this research is that prescribed land-uses in land reform are not always the best or preferred options for land beneficiaries. The government and its advisors are there to guide the land-reform process and not to prescribe or impose unrealistic land-uses on land beneficiaries. As alluded to elsewhere (Ngubane, 2012), it is rather absurd to expect a community of land beneficiaries in their hundreds to draw equitable benefits from a small unprofitable community game farm that used to be a leisure home for its previous owner and family. The story of dismantled private game farms in the KZN Midlands challenges dominant notions of success in South Africa's land reform. It also challenges the 'failure rhetoric' characterising South Africa's land reform that has become wrongfully stereotypical of land beneficiaries. Such 'failure rhetoric' appears to be a racial construct and political tactic by 'conservative white farming groups, who are trying to slow down processes of land reform and restitution' (Bank & Minkley 2005, p. 7). Reversing the history of forced removals should be radical and disruptive in order to bring about redress, land restitution, and land justice, instead of continuity with fixed land-uses as enforced by the Memorandum of Land Claims on Protected Areas in the context of land claims on nature conservation land (Ramutsindela, 2002). Nonetheless, such disruption is nothing compared to the historical disruption experienced by victims of forced removals (see Platsky & Walker, 1985).

Therefore, for political reasons, certain levels of disruption should be allowed in order to bring about social justice or land justice. At a scholarly level, scholars need to accept that this could happen and perhaps requires nothing more than a change of mindset beyond dominant models of land reform imported from elsewhere; in practical terms beneficiaries of nature conservation land should have more land-use rights, such as agriculture on their land, even in cases where the notorious memorandum is effectively implemented. Should this not happen, then perhaps the inevitable will happen, as it happened in Ngome Community Game Reserve, which is more beneficial now for land beneficiaries, as communal rangeland for livestock, than it was as a community game reserve operating as an unprofitable hunting operation and tourism attraction. Much the same can be said about the current land use of the dismantled Khobotho game reserve as illuminated by anecdotal evidence presented in this chapter showing land beneficiaries accessing land and accumulating livestock in a former private game reserve. Overall, this research will lead to more work on other dismantled game farms in the KZN Midlands, and will particularly compare beneficiaries of dismantled game farms in relation to beneficiaries of operational community game farms without land-use rights, such as settlement and agriculture in that part of the country. The South African land-reform process is yet to be radical for the benefit and materialization of justice for marginalized land beneficiaries and landless people.

References

Aliber, M., & Cousins, B. (2013). Livelihoods after Land Reform in South Africa. *Journal of Agrarian Change*, *13*(1), 140–165.

Association for Rural Advancement (2004). Communities, Conservation, Eco-tourism and Tenure Security Workshop Report (online) http://www.afra.co.za/upload/files/AP19.pdf (Accessed on 12 November 2010).

Bank, L., & Minkley, G. (2005). Going Nowhere Slowly? Land, Livelihoods and Rural Development in the Eastern Cape. *Social Dynamics: A journal of African studies, 31*(1), 1–38.

Beinart, W. (2001). *Twentieth-Century South Africa.* Oxford: Oxford University Press.

Brooks, S., Brandt, F., Lukhozi, K., Ntsebeza, L., Snijders, D., Spierenburg, M., & Wels, H. (2008). Exploring New Social Geographies of Private Wildlife Production: Farm Owners and Farm Dwellers in KwaZulu-Natal and the Eastern Cape, Position paper to Conservation and Capitalism Symposium, University of Manchester, Manchester, UK, 9–10 September 2008.

Brooks, S., Spierenburg, M., Van Brakel, L., Kolk, A., & Lukhozi, K.B. (2011). Creating a commodified wilderness: Tourism, private game farming, and 'third nature' landscapes in KwaZulu-Natal. *Tijdschrift voor Ekonomische en Sociale Geografie, 102*(3), 260–274.

Carruthers, J. (2008). 'Wilding the farm or farming the wild'? The evolution of scientific game ranching in South Africa from the 1960s to the present. *Transactions of the Royal Society of South Africa, 63*(2), 160–181.

Cousins, B. (1999). Invisible capital: the contribution of communal rangelands to rural livelihoods in South Africa. *Development Southern Africa, 16*, 299–318.

Cousins, B. (2013). Smallholder Irrigation Schemes, Agrarian Reform and 'Accumulation from Above and from Below' in South Africa. *Journal of Agrarian Change, 13*(1), 116–139.

Cousins, J.A., Sadler, J.P., & Evans, J. (2008). Exploring the Role of Private Wildlife Ranching as a Conservation Tool in South Africa: Stakeholder Perspectives. *Ecology and Society, 13*(2), 43–60.

Draper, M. (1998). Zen and the Art of Garden Province Maintenance: The Soft Intimacy of Hard Men in the Wilderness of KwaZulu-Natal, South Africa, 1952–1997. *Journal of Southern African Studies*, 24(4): 801–828.

Ekers, M., Hart, G., Kipfer, S., & Loftus, A. (2013). *Gramsci: Space, Nature and Politics.* Oxford: Wiley-Blackwell.

Fay, D. (2007). Mutual Gains and Distributive Ideologies in South Africa: Theorizing Negotiations between Communities and Protected Areas. *Human Ecology, 35*(1), 81–95.

Guy, J. (2005). *The Maphumulo Uprising: War, Law and Ritual in the Zulu Rebellion.* Durban: University of KwaZulu-Natal Press.

Hart, G. (2002). *Disabling Globalisation: Places of Power in Post-Apartheid South Africa.* Pietermaritzburg: University of Natal Press.

Hart, G. (2014). *Rethinking the South African Crisis: Nationalism, Populism, Hegemony.* Pietermaritzburg: UKZN Press.

Hart, G., & Hunter, M. (2004). Special Issue: Writing in Transition in South Africa: Fiction, History, Biography. *Journal of Southern African Studies, 30*(4), 915–917.

Hebinck, P., Fay, D., & Kondlo, K. (2011). Land and Agrarian Reform in South Africa's Eastern Cape Province: Caught by Continuities. *Journal of Agrarian Change, 11*(2), 220–240.

Hofmeyr, M. (2002). South African National Parks as providers of game animals. *Proceedings of a Symposium on Game Ranching Planning and Management, Onderstepoort, 1–2 November 2002.* Onderstepoort: Wildlife Group of the South African Veterinary Association.

Kepe, T. (2004). Land Restitution and Biodiversity Conservation in South Africa: The Case of Mkambati , Eastern Cape Province. *Canadian Journal of African Studies, 38*(3), 688–704.

Kepe, T. (2008). Land Claims and Comanagement of Protected Areas in South Africa: Exploring the Challenges. *Environmental Management, 41*, 311–332.

Kepe, T. (2010). Land Claims and Comanagement of Protected Areas in South Africa: Exploring the Challenges. In C. Walker, A. Bohlin, R. Hall, & Thembela Kepe (Eds.). *Land, Memory, Reconstruction and Justice: Perspectives on Land Claims in South Africa.* Athens: Ohio University Press.

Kepe, T., Wynberg, R., & Ellis, W. (2003). Land reform and biodiversity conservation in South Africa: Complementary or in conflict? *An occasional paper series No. 25.* Cape Town: Programme for Land and Agrarian Studies, School of Governance, University of the Western Cape.

Lahiff, E. (2009). With what land rights? Tenure arrangements and support. In R. Hall. (Ed.), *Another Countryside? Policy Options for Land and Agrarian Reform in South Africa.* Cape Town: Institute for Poverty, Land and Agrarian Studies, School of Government, University of the Western Cape.

Magome, H., & J. Murombedzi, J. (2003). Sharing South African National Parks: Community Land and Conservation in a Democratic South Africa. In W.M. Adams & M. Mulligan (Eds.), *Decolonizing Nature. Strategies for Conservation in a Post-Colonial Era.* London: Earthscan.

Mamdani, M. (1987). Extreme But Not Exceptional: Towards an Analysis of the Agrarian Question in Uganda. *Journal of Peasant Studies, 14*(2), 199–225.

Mathis, S.M. (2007). The Politics of Land Reform: Tenure and Political Authority in Rural KwaZulu-Natal. *Journal of Agrarian Change, 7*(1), 99–120.

Meer, T. (2010). *Finding the Community in Community-Based Natural Resource Management: The Case of Ndumo Game Reserve, South Africa.* (Unpublished MA thesis). Halifax: Dalhousie University.

Ngubane, M. (2009). *Game farming in the context of land beneficiaries: A viable land restitution option?* (Unpublished BA (Honours) thesis). Bloemfontein: University of the Free State.

Ngubane, M. (2012). *Land Beneficiaries as Game Farmers in the 'New' South Africa: Land Reform in Relation to Conservation, the Hunting Industry and Chiefly Authority in KwaZulu-Natal.* (Unpublished MA thesis). Bloemfontein: University of the Free State.

Ngubane, M., & Brooks, S. (2013). Land beneficiaries as game farmers: conservation, land reform and the invention of the 'community game farm' in KwaZulu-Natal. *Journal of Contemporary African Studies, 31*(3), 399–420.

Ntsebeza, L. (2005). *Democracy Compromised, chiefs and politics of land in South Africa.* Cape Town: HSRC Press.

Ntshona, Z., Kraai, M., Kepe, T., & Salilwa, P. (2010). From land rights to environmental entitlements: Community discontent in the 'successful' Dwesa-Cwebe land claim in South Africa. *Development Southern Africa, 27*(3), 353–361.

Oomen, B. (2005). *Chiefs in South Africa: Law, Power and Culture in the Post-Apartheid Era.* Durban: University KwaZulu-Natal Press.

Platsky, L., & Walker, C. (1985). *The Surplus People, Forced Removals in South Africa.* Johannesburg: Ravan Press.

Ramutsindela, M.F. (2002). The perfect way to ending a painful past? Makuleke land deal in South Africa. *Geoforum, 33*, 15–24.

Ramutsindela, M.F. (2003). Land reform in South Africa's national parks: a catalyst for the human-nature nexus. *Land Use Policy, 20*, 41–49.

Reid, H. (2001). Contractual National Parks and the Makuleke Community. *Human Ecology, 29*(2), 134–155.

Robins, S., & Van der Waal, K. (2008). 'Model Tribes' and Iconic Conservationists? The Makuleke Restitution Case in Kruger National Park. *Development and Change*, 39(1), 53–72.

Robins, S., & Van der Waal, K. (2010). 'Model Tribes' and Iconic Conservationists? Tracking the Makuleke Restitution Case in Kruger National Park. In C. Walker, A. Bohlin, R. Hall, & Thembela Kepe (Eds.), *Land, Memory, Reconstruction and Justice: Perspectives on Land Claims in South Africa.* Athens: Ohio University Press.

Scott, J.C. (1986). Everyday forms of Peasant Resistance. In James C. Scott & Benedict J. Tria Kerkvliet (Eds.), *Everyday forms of Peasant Resistance in South-east Asia.* London: Frank Cass and Company Ltd.

Sundnes, F. (2011). Scrubs and squatters: Exploring the environmental history of an indigenous forest: The Dukuduku Forest in KwaZulu-Natal, 1850s–1990s. *Paper for the 23rd Biennial Conference – Southern African Historical Society, 27–29 June 2011.* Durban: University of KwaZulu-Natal.

Umhlaba Wethu 15. *Is land reform still necessary?* Cape Town: Plaas. http://www.plaas.org.za/plaas-publication/uw-15 (Accessed on 1 July 2014).

Walker, C. (2008). *Landmarked: Land Claims and Land Restitution in South Africa.* Johannesburg: Jacana.

PART 5

Conclusion

CHAPTER 13

Agency and State Planning in South Africa's Land-reform Process

Femke Brandt and Grasian Mkodzongi

In this book emerging scholars presented their findings and ideas about South Africa's land-reform dynamics based on new empirical research findings generated across different places in the country. They focused on the lived experiences of land beneficiaries, farm workers, mine workers, elderly women, and other actors engaged in South Africa's land-reform process. The fact that the voices and stories of people directly affected by land reform are central to the analysis is a key factor that sets this volume apart from other contributions aiming to understand land reform under post-apartheid democracy. The chapters consist of detailed descriptions of the ongoing contestations over meanings and realities related to land. Land-related struggles and demands appear in rural and urban settings and unfold in many different ways, ranging from 'unruly' land beneficiaries resisting imposed land uses by the government's market approach, to the revival of Khoi San activists engaging the ANC government to reclaim their ancestral lands linked to issues of belonging and power in post-apartheid society.

In this concluding chapter we provide a discussion of the book chapters that focuses on issues of agency and state-planning to further reflect on the state of land reform and democracy in post-apartheid South Africa. Firstly, we contrast land-reform plans and realities to illustrate the actual workings of the ANC's neoliberal policy framework and its claim to promote transformation. Despite the inherent problems with market-based land-reform policies that disempower beneficiaries, we draw attention in the second section to the ways beneficiaries make land redistribution and restitution work for them nevertheless. In the third section we highlight the significance of land issues for different constituencies in the country and the ways in which they raise issues of gender, ethnicity, and democracy. In the final discussion we present a debate around the role of the state and state intervention in land reform and social change.

Land-reform Plans and Land-reform Realities

South Africa's post-apartheid land reform has been largely shaped by the governments' adoption of a neoliberal macro-economic framework. Added to the

 | DOI 10.1163/9789004362550_014

above were the compromises made by the ANC government during the transition from apartheid, which has compromised prospects for a radical transformation of socio-economic relations in favour of the historically marginalised groups. The case studies in this book highlight the shortcomings of South Africa's land-reform policies after twenty years of ANC rule. The constitutional protection of private property, the government's alliances with the private sector in land-reform projects, and the willing-buyer willing-seller model, have undermined the government's attempt to address historical injustices in the agrarian structure through its land reforms (comprising of land redistribution, restitution, and tenure reform).

This is not simply a 'mismatch' between government policy and people's needs; subsequent ANC governments have pursued neoliberal macro-economic policies, which tend to favour large-scale commercial farming rather than the dismantling and redistribution of such farms to the landless poor. Across various levels of government, there seems to be a bias towards wildlife conservation projects such as the Gongolo Wildlife Reserve owned by a group of wealthy landowners instead of allowing land claimants to engage in small-scale farming on land given to them through restitution claims (Kamuti, Chapter 7). For example, the adoption of the Game Theft Act of 1991 has helped to bolster the economic position of the white landowners (who dominate the sector) by transferring property rights of wildlife from the state to private landowners. This further promotes the perpetuation of an unjust system of landownership, which encloses the country's land and natural resources and excludes the majority of the people from access and use of these resources and places. Brandt's chapter (Chapter 4) presenting farm workers' experiences in the semi-arid Karoo in Eastern Cape shows how 'dangerous game' involving private game farms has undermined the transformation of social relations. The South African land-reform policies have been influenced by productivity discourses, which put agricultural production at the centre of the land-reform process (Mkodzongi & Rusenga, 2015). The government believes that land reform must be intertwined with agricultural productivity as a way of safeguarding food security and economic development. This is reflected in the way the government formulates, and understands, people's participation in land reform and farming, notably the focus on productivity and food security. The land-reform policies have been heavily influenced by the productivity discourse, which is promoted by AGRI-SA, an influential white farmers lobby with close ties to government.

Underlying the productivity discourse are policy assumptions about the lack of capabilities and skills of land beneficiaries to farm productively. There is a persistent notion by government that emerging farmers ('emerging' is telling) or land claimants require technical training in order for them to farm productively. Ironically, such training is expected to be delivered by white farmers, the very people resisting transformation of the agrarian sector and, given their vested interests in maintaining the status quo, how are they going to provide such training? At the same time, white farmers who are heavily indebted or those who left farming altogether are not labelled as failed or incompetent farmers but are viewed as victims of global competition in agrarian markets. There has been a persistent paternalistic tone and practice in the way farming models are imposed on the beneficiaries of land reform.

This book provides several examples of the government's technocratic and centralised approach to land reform. The government's paternalistic attitude towards land-reform beneficiaries is demonstrated by what an official of the Regional Land Claims Court (RLCC) said during an interview with Kamuti (Chapter 7): he claimed that communities in Kwa-Zulu Natal do not understand rational business proposals and that one has to 'come down to their level' to engage meaningfully. This institutionalized paternalistic attitude by government officials is reflected in Kaur's chapter (Chapter 6) as well. Kaur observes how particular sports development discourses in Western Cape government departments negate structural inequalities and political contestations over the agrarian structure. The experiences of research informants across case studies in this book indicate that government policies have failed to meet ordinary people's expectations. This disparity between land-reform implementation and people's expectations is prominent in Davis' chapter (Chapter 8), which shows how land beneficiaries are coerced by the government to enter into joint ventures with private business where they gain 'access without ownership' to land and remain unable to make their own decisions in terms of utilising the land offered to them by the government.

How Beneficiaries Make Land-reform Work

Given the above, land beneficiaries have been forced to deviate from land use plans imposed by the government. Ngubane's work in Kwa-zulu Natal (Chapter 12) shows how land beneficiaries dismantled game farms offered to them through land restitution and converted them into grazing land for their livestock. This demonstrates the agency of land beneficiaries who do not necessarily reject government policies but utilise 'weapons of the weak' by adjusting imposed land use plans to suit their own needs. This modest or covert form of resistance is not directly challenging the existing agrarian relations and structure but is nevertheless important to highlight (Scott, 1984). One could argue that despite the flaws in land-reform projects and their implementation, people have the agency to make some things work in their own way even if this does to comply with the government imposed land-use plans. This shows that success in land-reform projects is relative and depends on our understanding of what people are doing on the ground in order to get a better picture of the outcomes of land-reform projects.

For example, Ncapayi's contribution (Chapter 11) shows that the often-critiqued group dynamics in land-reform projects ('rent a crowd') do not always lead to failure of land-reform projects. Based on data gathered in Luphaphasi in the Eastern Cape, Ncapayi demonstrates that people who were offered land in groups were able to improve their livelihoods due to continued support by an NGO. In addition, his work also brings out the importance of involving women in leadership positions in land-reform projects and demonstrates that land reform has the potential to transform women's economic position if they are allowed access to land. Thus, under specific conditions people make state interventions work even though they might look like they are in conflict with their expectations. In doing so, land beneficiaries, farm workers, informal settlement dwellers, and activists challenge dominant notions of success and failure as defined by planners and technical experts.

Many chapters in this book show how white commercial farmers have resisted and opposed the state's attempts to transform agrarian relations in favour of the poor (Tariro, Brandt, & Mkodzongi). The establishment of game farms and wildlife reserves has been another tactic utilised by white landowners to resist land restitution and transformation of rural agrarian relations. However, as mentioned earlier, the white farmers have used their lobby to convince the state that game farming is a viable and profitable land-use activity critical for economic development. As noted by Ngubane in the case of Kwazulu Natal, state-protected areas and private game farms have been exempted from land restitution on the pretext that they create local employment and contribute to the economy through tourism.

The scholarship on South Africa's land question does not transcend the current dominant neoliberal macro-economic context, which has underpinned agrarian policymaking. Very few scholars have questioned the structural limitations imposed on land reform by this neoliberal context. Attempts have been made to explain the policy 'mismatch' or lack of political will to explain the failed land reforms, however, there has not been a call for a radical re-interpretation of land reform to challenge the current neoliberal order, which has protected the economic interests of landowners in the guise of democracy and property rights. For example, Cousins has promoted the idea of a smallholder-farming model, while at the same time arguing that in a capitalist economy some degree of reconcentration of landownership is inevitable (2015, p. 268). This ignores the fact that across continents (Latin America and Southern Africa), the neoliberal conceptualisation of land reform has been contested. Land-based social movements have forced states to overcome neoliberal orthodoxy in land-reform processes in favour of redistributive land reform (as Mkodzongi argues in his chapter). This shows that there is a need for epistemological pluralism, in the way success and failure in land-reform processes are conceptualised. This requires deploying different concepts and lenses such as food sovereignty, which have yet to enter the mainstream debates on land and agrarian questions.

Power and Belonging in the New Democracy

As mentioned earlier, land encompasses more than the site of a production unit or a commodity. Land also represents and relates to concepts like citizenship, identity, justice, and belonging. Therefore, the land question transcends the agrarian question. Access to land is crucial in maintaining connections with ancestors and the fulfilment of spiritual needs. For example, the land claimants in Davis' chapter (Chapter 8) pointed out that they wished to move back to their ancestral land in order to connect with their ancestors. Moreover, people did not see why land could not be used both for commercial fruit farming and for other purposes such as spiritual rituals and livestock grazing. The claimants expressed that they wanted more options to decide how to use the land beyond agricultural purposes. Several chapters in this book alluded to the importance of land for notions of citizenship and belonging in a democratic South Africa. Therefore, land struggles are at the core of the diverse ways South Africans feel about their working and living conditions, their treatment as citizens of a democratic South Africa, their sense of belonging, and the power configurations shaping their everyday realities.

Batisai's chapter (Chapter 5) highlights voices of elderly black women on Gauteng's East Rand and addresses the gender gap in debates on land in South Africa. The women's' narratives are about struggles for residential land in urban areas. The women, who all came to Johannesburg around 1994 in search of opportunities during the transition to democracy, are disillusioned with post-apartheid promises. They question the meanings of freedom and citizenship in South Africa, whilst they have to survive in poorly serviced townships and informal settlements. Batisai illustrates how the current and continued service delivery protests, notably driven by women activists, are linked to urban land questions. These poor women's land demands are silenced in policy and scholarly debates focusing on the racial make-up of the agrarian structure.

A group that has started to become visible in land policy formation are Khoisan revivalist movements. Sato's chapter (Chapter 10) highlights the salience of these movements in post-apartheid state-making processes. For example, people identifying as indigenous Khoisan are mobilizing and seeking ways to engage government in order to recover their ancestral lands lost during colonial occupation. Their land claims reflect the wider politics of belonging and an upsurge of ethnicity questions emerging in post-apartheid South Africa. Bruchhausen and Naicker (Chapter 2) elucidate that South Africa's land and agrarian questions are linked to broader struggles for justice, dignity, and humanity that require structural socio-economic and political change, in line with how 'ordinary' people practice politics. Their chapter articulates a particular point about organization and democracy under post-apartheid conditions, namely that the Marikana protesters practice a form of direct democracy. This practice exists concurrent with, or in opposition to, traditional labour unions or customary rule. A crucial contribution of their work is its evidence that ordinary people are actively 'thinking' and participating in politics. Furthermore, they show that ordinary people (farm workers, mine workers, land claimants), who are often assumed to be oppressed by unjust policies, have the ability to resist, organise, and reconfigure the balance of power in everyday and persistent ways.

What do these projects tell us about the relations between the state and the people? In various chapters we highlight how power relations have shaped the trajectory of state-led land reform. We show how the government's land-reform policies have been heavily influenced by white landowners, while it has adopted a paternalistic approach towards land beneficiaries, granting them only a limited influence on the policymaking process. In the Western Cape, for example, the state allocates resources aimed at getting farm workers into mainstream sports instead of supporting their existing networks and practices (Kaur, Chapter 6). The book also presents evidence of subaltern struggles against state-imposed land tenure; this is especially the case with the ways in which people are disregarding land use plans dictated by the government. These struggles are the result of a state-led land-reform programme that is biased towards the interests of large capitalist farmers. In joint ventures consisting of land beneficiaries and private partners, the state remains a main actor as the funder and facilitator of such partnerships. This means that the state plays an active role in market transactions and relations.

Drawing on Scott (1998) land reform can be seen as a tool in South Africa's state-making process, which allows the state to control access to land and to legitimise imposed land uses. A large-scale commercial farming economy is easier to tax, monitor, regulate, and register. A small-scale farming economy and the kind of social relations that it is made up of, look chaotic and illegible to state officials. A result of state high modernism is that, in order to have a legible economy and society, the state promotes and supports farming and land-use models that are not necessarily the most efficient and preferred ones for the well-being of its citizens.

The Role of the State in Land Reform?

Debates about the role of the state in agrarian transformation processes remain highly contested. Lack of state intervention, especially in land reforms, is viewed by some as problematic. This is based on the fact that markets alone have been proven to fail in transferring land from landowners to the landless poor (Akram-Lodhi, 2007; Lahiff, 2007; Borras, 2007). Some scholars view the lack of pressure 'from below' as a direct cause of the failure to transform agrarian relations in favour of the poor (Mkodzongi, Chapter 9; Albertus, 2015). Such scholars argue for the need for more state intervention to address the slow pace of land reform (Mkodzongi & Rusenga, 2015). Others have argued that state intervention in land reforms distorts land markets, and that land reforms must be left to market forces under the so-called 'willing seller and willing buyer' concept. However, such approaches have been proven to fail in many countries, including South Africa, which is the focus of this book. In this final section we discuss different views on the role of the state in land reform and agrarian transformation processes based on the findings of this book and existing agrarian scholarship.

Based on experiences from Zimbabwe, Mkodzongi (Chapter 9) argues that unresolved land questions have the potential of being a source of socio-political instability in the near future. Under the current neoliberal crisis, unresolved land and agrarian questions should be urgently addressed. Mkodzongi holds the view that to transform land and agrarian relations inherited from a colonial past, a coercive state is needed. In the Zimbabwean context the widespread land occupations of white-owned farms radicalised the state, which then opened up access to land outside of market-driven reform processes. Mkodzongi holds the view that, in South Africa, the landless lack the political power to influence government policy, and he looks towards the radicalisation of the land question from below to potentially generate a new politics of land. The unsustainability of leaving the land structure intact will intensify the fragmented struggles caused by growing urban and rural poverty, service delivery strikes, and land occupations. Mkodzongi argues that there are limits to state repression of grassroots struggles, and whether the limit has been reached in South Africa will become clear in the near future.

According to Brandt (Chapter 4) state coercion is not desirable to transform social relations. She questions the nature of the state as an appropriate form of organization to improve people's lives. Drawing on Scott (1998) she argues that historically the state, whether ideologically socialist, liberal, or neoliberal, tends to be authoritarian and willing to utilise its monopoly on violence (Scott, 1998) to enforce state-sponsored projects. State-led land reform allows the state to control and order society into categories of people and groups that can be managed on the government's terms, that is, Khoisan, land beneficiaries, and farm workers. State-making processes in themselves and the forms of resistance to them are shaping trajectories of change and raise questions about the suitability of states to manage transformation processes. Moreover, Brandt holds the view that there is no absence of a politics of land or pressure from below in South Africa. Land politics are made up of everyday contestations on commercial farms, as evidenced throughout this volume, in land-reform projects, on soccer fields, and in conference centres where people engage the state in their demands for land, recognition, and democracy.

In existing debates, agrarian scholars from the Southern African region like Moyo et al. (2013), Hendricks et al. (2013), and Cousins and Walker (2015) debate the question of where transformation or revolution in postcolonial societies would come from: states, social movements, civil society, peasants, and/or landless people? Change from above or below? Hendricks et al. (2013) argue that key to a democratic future in South Africa is dismantling the former Bantustans through radical land redistribution (ibid., p. 348). The authors propose a civil society-led campaign around expropriation of land, especially targetting under-utilised farms and farms that are in debt (ibid., p. 349). Unemployed people should be 'drawn into pursuing land-based activities through joining producer co-operatives (ibid., p. 350). How would the state 'draw in' people? How would the state persuade and force people to cooperate in their schemes intended to improve people's lives? Experiences from compulsory villagization and collectivization plans in other parts of the world have taught us that such schemes lead to force and oppression, even when large-scale social engineering was planned and implemented by a 'relatively benign and weak state' (Scott, 1998; Chapter 7, p. 223).

On the question of how different policies will be achieved Hendricks et al. (2013, p. 351) state that these proposals should not be driven from above. At the heart of land, housing, and governance struggles should be the people directly affected, in other words there should be pressure and mobilization from below. Although they acknowledge the recent upsurge in rural struggle by farm workers in the Western Cape, Hendricks and colleagues (ibid., p. 357) point out that massive rural mobilisation is required in order to bring about meaningful social change as well as a radicalised state. According to them, both don't currently exist in South Africa. However, Paret and Runciman (2016) view the wave of protests by workers and communities since 2009 as having a major impact on South African politics, especially in the formation of political parties, organized labour movements, and social movement organizations (2016, p. 302). They cite the 2012 protests in the Western Cape farming sector as an example of a significant shift in collective action beyond existing institutional frameworks like unions and a departure from the traditional ANC alliance (ibid., p. 306–307). Importantly though, these protests have resulted in cases of severe repression and even the killing of protesters and strikers, instead of radicalizing the state in favour of the poor.

Cousins (2015, p. 266–269) proposes a land-reform model (which is agrarian reform mostly) focusing on smallholder farmers. He argues that 20% of the white farmers' businesses should be left for food production, while the other 80% should make way for the 200,000 to 250,000 black smallholder farmers who would be targeted for land transfer. He suggests that 'a highly interventionist role for the state is critically important if policies are to radically reconfigure agrarian structure' (ibid., p. 268). The proposal is ambiguous: on the one hand, he argues that the key constraint to land reform and agrarian development since 1994 has been state capacity, while, on the other, he proposes more state intervention to implement this model. What kind of state is likely to implement his proposed model given the fact that the democratic state has largely failed to address the land question?

The above highlights an important aspect that has received limited attention in the literature, which is the interconnectedness of the agrarian question to the national question (Moyo et al. 2013). Yet both Hendricks et al. (2013) and Cousins (2015) do not explicitly discuss South Africa's national question: the nature of the state that is going to implement their land-reform redistribution proposals. The role of the state in the land-reform process thus remains largely problematic in terms of its own ideology and its attempts to play a hegemonic role in the countryside, post-apartheid. This is an important lacuna to be addressed in future research. The issue of state capacity raised by Cousins (2015) raises other questions that are important both methodologically and conceptually in terms of future research. How can a state that was compromised during the transition from apartheid be expected to deliver land to the landless given its bias towards the protection of private property? How can we expect the agrarian question to be resolved when the broader national question remains unresolved? How realistic is it to expect that a successful land-reform process can take place under such a state? How do we engage these questions without taking into account positions such as those of Albertus (2015), who has argued that redistributive land reforms seldom takes place under a democratic state? These are important questions emerging here and crucial for future research.

The focus on agency and state high modernism in South Africa's land-reform process has been a useful lens to reflect on people's experiences in different places and processes twenty years after the transition to democracy. The disparity between government plans in relation to land reform and what people actually end up doing provides insights into contemporary struggles over land, power relations, critiques of democracy, and questions of identity and belonging.

References

Akram-Lodhi, A.H. (2007). Land, markets and neoliberal enclosure: an agrarian political economy perspective. *Third World Quarterly*, *28*(8), 1437–1456.

Albertus, M. (2015). *Autocracy and Redistribution: The Politics of Land Reform.* Cambridge: Cambridge Studies in Comparative Politics.

Borras Jr, M.S. (2007). *Pro-poor Land Reform: a Critique.* Ottawa: University of Ottawa Press.

Cousins, B. (2015). "Through a glass darkly": Towards agrarian reform in South Africa. In Cousins, B., & Walker, C. (Eds.). *Land Divided Land Restored, land Reform in South Africa for the 21st Century.* (p. 250–269). Johannesburg: Jacana.

Cousins, B., & Walker, C. (Eds.) (2015). *Land Divided Land Restored: Land Reform in South Africa for the 21st Century.* Johannesburg: Jacana.

Hendricks, F., Ntsebeza, L., & Helliker, K. (Eds.) (2013). *The Promise of Land: Undoing a Century of Dispossession in South Africa.* Johannesburg: Jacana.

Lahiff, E. (2007). 'Willing buyer, willing seller': South Africa's failed experiment in market-led agrarian reform. *Third World Quarterly* *28*(8), 1577–1597.

Mkodzongi, G., & Rusenga, C. (2015). *Land and Agrarian Reform: Towards an Inclusive Poverty Alleviation Agenda.* Cape Town: Institute of Justice and Reconciliation.

Moyo, S., Jha, P., & Yeros, P. (2013). The Classical Agrarian Question: Myth, Reality and Relevance Today. *Agrarian South: Journal of Political Economy*, 2(1), 93–119.

Paret, M., & C. Runciman (2016). The 2009+ South African protest wave. *Working USA: The Journal of Labour and Society*, *19*, 301–319.

Scott, J.C. (1984). *Weapons of the Weak: Everyday Forms of Peasant Resistance.* New Haven: Yale University Press.

Scott, J.C. (1998). *Seeing like a state: How certain schemes to improve the human condition have failed.* New Haven: Yale University Press.

Index

www.ingramcontent.com/pod-product-compliance
Lightning Source LLC
Chambersburg PA
CBHW071429230926
51846CB00001B/165
* 9 7 8 9 0 0 4 3 6 2 1 0 9 *